MW00851139

ABRAHAM KUYPER

Collected Works in Public Theology

GENERAL EDITORS

JORDAN J. BALLOR

MELVIN FLIKKEMA

AbrahamKuyper.com

ON EDUCATION

ABRAHAM

KUYPER

Edited by
Wendy Naylor and Harry Van Dyke

LEXHAM PRESS

ACTON INSTITUTE
FOR THE STUDY OF RELIGION AND LIBERTY

On Education

Abraham Kuyper Collected Works in Public Theology

Lexham Press, 1313 Commercial St., Bellingham, WA 98225
LexhamPress.com

Print ISBN 9781577996774
Digital ISBN 9781683591160

Lexham Editorial: Claire Brubaker, Sarah Awa, Justin Marr
Cover Design: Christine Gerhart
Typesetting: ProjectLuz.com

CONTENTS

GENERAL EDITORS' INTRODUCTION

In times of great upheaval and uncertainty, it is necessary to look to the past for resources to help us recognize and address our own contemporary challenges. While Scripture is foremost among these foundations, the thoughts and reflections of Christians throughout history also provide us with important guidance. Because of his unique gifts, experiences, and writings, Abraham Kuyper is an exemplary guide in these endeavors.

Kuyper (1837–1920) is a significant figure both in the history of the Netherlands and modern Protestant theology. A prolific intellectual, Kuyper founded a political party and a university, led the formation of a Reformed denomination and the movement to create Reformed elementary schools, and served as the prime minister of the Netherlands from 1901 to 1905. In connection with his work as a builder of institutions, Kuyper was also a prolific author. He wrote theological treatises, biblical and confessional studies, historical works, social and political commentary, and devotional materials.

Believing that Kuyper's work is a significant and underappreciated resource for Christian public witness, in 2011 a group of scholars interested in Kuyper's life and work formed the Abraham Kuyper Translation Society. The shared conviction of the society, along with the Acton Institute, Kuyper College, and other Abraham Kuyper scholars, is that Kuyper's works hold great potential to build intellectual capacity within the church in North

America, Europe, and around the world. It is our hope that translation of his works into English will make his insights accessible to those seeking to grow and revitalize communities in the developed world as well as to those in the global south and east who are facing unique challenges and opportunities.

The church today—both locally and globally—needs the tools to construct a compelling and responsible public theology. The aim of this translation project is to provide those tools—we believe that Kuyper's unique insights can catalyze the development of a winsome and constructive Christian social witness and cultural engagement the world over.

In consultation and collaboration with these institutions and individual scholars, the Abraham Kuyper Translation Society developed this 12-volume translation project, the *Collected Works in Public Theology*. This multivolume series collects in English translation Kuyper's writings and speeches from a variety of genres and contexts in his work as a theologian and statesman. In almost all cases, this set contains original works that have never before been translated into English. The series contains multivolume works as well as other volumes, including thematic anthologies.

The series includes a translation of Kuyper's *Our Program* (*Ons Program*), which sets forth Kuyper's attempt to frame a Christian political vision distinguished from the programs of the nineteenth-century Modernists who took their cues from the French Revolution. It was this document that launched Kuyper's career as a pastor, theologian, and educator. As James Bratt writes, "This comprehensive Program, which Kuyper crafted in the process of forming the Netherlands' first mass political party, brought the theology, the political theory, and the organization vision together brilliantly in a coherent set of policies that spoke directly to the needs of his day. For us it sets out the challenge of envisioning what might be an equivalent witness in our own day."

Also included is Kuyper's seminal three-volume work *De gemeene gratie*, or *Common Grace*, which presents a constructive public theology of cultural engagement rooted in the humanity Christians share with the rest of the world. Kuyper's presentation of common grace addresses a gap he recognized in the development of Reformed teaching on divine grace. After addressing particular grace and covenant grace in other writings, Kuyper here develops his articulation of a Reformed understanding of God's gifts that are common to all people after the fall into sin.

The series also contains Kuyper's three-volume work on the lordship of Christ, *Pro Rege*. These three volumes apply Kuyper's principles in *Common*

Grace, providing guidance for how to live in a fallen world under Christ the King. Here the focus is on developing cultural institutions in a way that is consistent with the ordinances of creation that have been maintained and preserved, even if imperfectly so, through common grace.

The remaining volumes are thematic anthologies of Kuyper's writings and speeches gathered from the course of his long career.

The anthology *On Charity and Justice* includes a fresh and complete translation of Kuyper's "The Problem of Poverty," the landmark speech Kuyper gave at the opening of the First Christian-Social Congress in Amsterdam in 1891. This important work was first translated into English in 1950 by Dirk Jellema; in 1991, a new edition by James Skillen was issued. This volume also contains other writings and speeches on subjects including charity, justice, wealth, and poverty.

The anthology *On Islam* contains English translations of significant pieces that Abraham Kuyper wrote about Islam, gathered from his reflections on a lengthy tour of the Mediterranean world. Kuyper's insights illustrate an instructive model for observing another faith and its cultural ramifications from an informed Christian perspective.

The anthology *On the Church* includes selections from Kuyper's doctrinal dissertation on the theologies of Reformation theologians John Calvin and John a Lasco. It also includes various treatises and sermons, such as "Rooted and Grounded," "Twofold Fatherland," and "Address on Missions."

The anthology *On Business and Economics* contains various meditations Kuyper wrote about the evils of the love of money as well as pieces that provide Kuyper's thoughts on stewardship, human trafficking, free trade, tariffs, child labor, work on the Sabbath, and business.

Finally, the anthology *On Education* includes Kuyper's important essay "Bound to the Word," which discusses what it means to be ruled by the word of God in the entire world of human thought. Numerous other pieces are also included, resulting in a substantial English volume of Kuyper's thoughts on Christian education.

Collectively, this 12-volume series will, as Richard Mouw puts it, "give us a much-needed opportunity to absorb the insights of Abraham Kuyper about God's marvelous designs for human cultural life."

The Abraham Kuyper Translation Society along with the Acton Institute and Kuyper College gratefully acknowledge the Andreas Center for Reformed Scholarship and Service at Dordt College; Calvin College; Calvin Theological Seminary; Fuller Theological Seminary; Mid-America

Reformed Seminary; Redeemer University College; Princeton Theological Seminary; and Southeastern Baptist Theological Seminary. Their financial support and partnership made these translations possible. The society is also grateful for the generous financial support of the J. C. Huizenga family and Dr. Rimmer and Ruth DeVries, which has enabled the translation and publication of these volumes.

This series is dedicated to Dr. Rimmer DeVries in recognition of his life's pursuits and enduring legacy as a cultural leader, economist, visionary, and faithful follower of Christ who reflects well the Kuyperian vision of Christ's lordship over all spheres of society.

Jordan J. Ballor
Melvin Flikkema

Grand Rapids, MI
August 2015

EDITOR'S INTRODUCTION

God has so ordained that at the present time our four million fellow-citizens are divided into three almost equal parts: Rationalists, Calvinists, and Roman Catholics. We accept this fact. And we maintain that in a people comprised of such a mixture, the state may not use its supremacy to favor one part of the nation over another. All spiritual compulsion by the state is an affront to the honor of the spiritual life and, as an offense to civil liberty, is hateful and abominable.

—Abraham Kuyper, *Niet de Vrijheidsboom maar het kruis*

Abraham Kuyper accomplished much over the course of his lifetime, but perhaps his most lasting contribution to Dutch society was a radical restructuring of the Dutch school system according to the principle of religious liberty.[1] Over a span of almost fifty years (1869–1917), he and

1. This essay includes and adapts some material that previously appeared as Wendy Naylor, "Religious Liberty and Educational Pluralism: Abraham Kuyper's Principled Advocacy of School Choice," in *The Wiley Handbook of Christianity and Education*, ed. William Jeynes (Hoboken, NJ: Wiley-Blackwell, 2018), 325–53.

his Antirevolutionary Party[2] worked diligently to establish the right of all parents to provide their children with a quality education in accordance with their deepest convictions and values. In 1917, as a culmination of these efforts, the Dutch constitution was amended to guarantee this right, and in 1920, the year Kuyper died, a new education bill was passed which put that amendment into practice.

One hundred years later, the Dutch school system continues to grant complete funding (per child) to all elementary and high schools, whether they be religiously oriented (and privately managed) or not. If a school that reflects a specific belief system does not exist in a geographic area, like-minded parents are encouraged to form a nonprofit association to be governed by an elected board according to bylaws which clearly articulate their worldview. There are government regulations concerning the minimum number of students required, the setting of teacher salaries, and the minimum standards of academic achievement to be demonstrated, to name just a few. But these regulations are forbidden by the constitution from touching on the particular belief system which underlies the curriculum and culture of the school.

In 1920, when this amendment was first put into practice, three different kinds of publicly funded schools emerged: Catholic, Calvinist, and "neutralist" (so called because they believed that knowledge and education could and should be value neutral). Over the course of many decades that list has expanded to include Islamic, Orthodox Jewish, Liberal Jewish, Hindu, Pietistic Calvinist, "Liberated" Calvinist, evangelical, generally Protestant, and generally Christian schools as well as schools inspired by particular pedagogues such as Montessori and Rudolph Steiner. The important exceptions to this panoply of worldviews include those worldviews which advocate violence or which find their identity in class, race, language, political ideology, or gender. Schools are forbidden to advocate violent jihad, for instance, or to espouse white supremacy. There are no elementary schools to which only the wealthy have access. All schools teach exclusively in the

2. The ARP was established in 1879 with a political platform that sought to implement justice and liberty in every sphere of society. While eschewing any ecclesiastical overreach, it argued for a more thorough implementation of the constitutional liberty of freedom of conscience. Believing that human society consisted of specific "spheres" which operated according to intrinsic principles, the ARP sought to encourage human flourishing by recognizing that all human authority is limited in scope and to a particular sphere of society.

Dutch language.[3] And there are no schools oriented exclusively to those of Turkish, Moroccan, Dutch, or any other descent. In effect, the Dutch constitution has been interpreted to mean that religious or philosophical *beliefs* about the nature of the world, of humanity, and of the existence of God constitute the core of human experience and community, rather than other aspects of human life such as class, gender, ethnicity, and race. This insight may rightly be considered the fruit of Kuyper's social thought and political work.

In later decades of the twentieth century a system of funding was developed which granted more government resources for the education of immigrant children and children from lower socioeconomic levels who face significant linguistic and cultural challenges. The principle remains to provide sufficiently for the educational needs of all children according to the religious, philosophical, or pedagogical preferences of their parents.

A program of educational liberty was first articulated by Kuyper in a series of newspaper articles published in the newspaper *The Standard* during the 1870s. Kuyper himself also presented this principle and program in his first speech in Parliament in 1874. He drew an analogy with the Netherlands' system of canals and dikes, which were federally funded but locally managed according to the specific needs of each locality. In the same way, he argued, Protestants, Catholics, and neutralists should each be able to design and manage their own schools with an equal share of state support. His speech was vehemently opposed by both government and school leadership. What possible reason was there for separate, "sectarian" schools when neutral state schools were increasingly available for no charge? Why should we interrupt our progress toward a national and rational system of schooling, which wisely kept all religion outside of the schools' purview? Why should we fan the flames of religious dissension by actually allowing fanatics to have separate schools? They were unable to see religious schooling as anything other than backward and dangerous. They sought to preserve national unity in the only way they understood at the time, which was to insist that all Dutch children attend state-run elementary schools, which offered nonsectarian neutral education.

Kuyper, having expected this rejection, was not discouraged by it. His eyes were not closed to the political reality; most Christians (both Catholic and Calvinist) were not wealthy and therefore lacked suffrage. What was

3. With the exception of schools designed for the expatriate community.

needed was a radical change of public opinion, and that would take time. Kuyper urged his constituency to put their hope in the sovereign God, to whom their cause was dear and for whom nothing was impossible. He also urged them to appeal to the nation's conscience. Was the Netherlands, which for centuries had been a haven for persecuted religious minorities, now going to crush the hope of Christian minorities? Was the Netherlands, which proudly stood for equal treatment under the law, now going to accept a system in which only the wealthy could provide their children with a Christian education?

The primary purpose of this introduction is to present a summary of Kuyper's multifaceted rationale for his educational program, a rationale rooted in a commitment to religious liberty and developed over the course of many decades. It is hoped that this presentation of the thought and faith behind Kuyper's work will help the reader to better understand the documents included herein. But first, a short history of the Dutch educational system is in order.

HISTORICAL BACKGROUND

For centuries after the Reformation, the Netherlands was known for the intensity with which its citizens held to their religious beliefs, as well as for their acceptance of religious minorities (as long as they also accepted a religiously plural society). Shortly after the Reformation, Spain (which governed the Netherlands) cracked down harshly on the open proclamation and practice of Protestant beliefs. In submission to Prince William the Silent, Dutch Protestants rose up in resistance to this persecution; thus began the Eighty Years' War (1568–1648), which eventually resulted in the political independence of the Netherlands with a Calvinist church as the state church. While there were, of course, privileges and status that went with membership in the Dutch Reformed Church, Catholics, Independent Protestants, and Jews did not fear for their lives, and enjoyed the freedom to practice their faith freely, if not always publicly. By the nineteenth century, however, many Calvinist leaders had lost the life and joy of the gospel, and were therefore ill-equipped to discern and reject the influence of the French Revolution, which swept through the leadership of much of Dutch society even before Napoleon's invasion in 1795. The school leaders were busy creating a centralized school system (based on the French model) with the goal of civilizing and unifying the Dutch citizenry. As part of this effort, certain churches and schools began to teach a new interpretation of

Christianity summed up in the phrase "Christianity above doctrine." Many Protestants were impressed; the emphasis on God's love for all humankind instead of on arid doctrine must have felt like a breath of fresh air. Catholics, however, were not so impressed. Whether doctrinal or not, the schools were still under Protestant leadership, and it was still illegal to establish independent schools. Seeing no way forward, many of them joined the movement to secede and in 1830 succeeded in breaking away from the Netherlands to form Belgium.

It was not until a pietistic revival known as the Réveil swept through much of northern Europe, including the Netherlands, that many Protestants reembraced their orthodox Calvinist roots and began to resist the increasing influence of deistic rationalism in public institutions. A conflict developed between the Dutch Reformed leadership and a growing portion of its laypeople, who saw the new "Christianity above doctrine" as a new title for deism. Eventually, in 1834, a group of orthodox believers seceded from the national church and sought the right to also establish their own schools. That this attempt was repeatedly denied led Groen van Prinsterer (1801–76), a member of Parliament and the historian for the Royal House of Orange, to proclaim in 1840:

> Parents, who with or without sufficient grounds, are sincerely convinced that the direction of the existing schools is unchristian, must not be prevented, either legally or indirectly [i.e., from lack of funds], from providing their children such an education as they consider God to require of them. The coercion, I will say it plainly, is unbearable and must come to an end.[4]

Eventually the constitutional revision of 1848 did grant parents the legal right to establish and maintain schools independent of both church and the state. Unfortunately, this new legal liberty came at a time when the Netherlands suffered an economic depression so severe that the liberty which was now legally granted was not substantively available to more than the wealthy. In 1857 the constitution was again revised; it called on all state schools to nurture children "into all Christian and civic virtues." However, lest anyone think that these new neutral schools were Christian,

---

4. T. M. Gilhuis, *Memorietafel van het Christelijk Onderwijs: De Geschiedenis van de Schoolstrijd* (Kampen: Kok, 1974), 87.

Prime Minister Justinus van der Brugghen (1804–63) assured Parliament that under his new school law:

> All doctrinal and dogmatic components, everything, in a word, that belongs to the concept of Christianity, that belongs to its truths, facts, its history, must remain removed from the public school. ... Everyone, Protestant, Roman Catholics, and Israelites, can be assured that nothing will be shared with their children that is offensive, that is in conflict with their "religious convictions."[5]

With such plain talk, the new deism no longer fooled either orthodox Calvinists or Catholics who were offended by the state's disregard for their deepest interests. And so the school struggle intensified. Some Catholics moved to Belgium, where there were Catholic schools. Some Calvinists immigrated to North America, where there was property to own at affordable prices and complete freedom to establish their own schools. Those who could not move either kept their children home from schools or started their own schools at tremendous sacrifice. The offense to their conscience by the state continued to be deeply felt.

By the second half of the nineteenth century the Netherlands encompassed three major subgroups of people with distinct and intensely held convictions: Calvinists, Catholics, and what Kuyper called Rationalists (what we might call secular, but which included Jews and those Christians who accepted deistic theology). Not surprisingly, this made the formation of a unified national school system a challenge, and in that attempt, there were two primary strategies.

On the one side were people who had embraced deistic rationalism; they sought to open the eyes and minds of children and parents to a worldview in which religious faith was irrelevant to learning and nurture. Many leaders throughout society held to this view primarily because they had been educated in universities which for over half a century had thoroughly advocated deism. Some saw it as a temporary way to placate the masses. Others were well intentioned, believing that this was the only way to promote the modernization and unity of the nation. In either case, they were determined to brook no argument. Any opposition to their views was deemed ignorant, dangerous, and evidence of why such a system was so urgently needed.

---

5. Gilhuis, *Memorietafel van het Christelijk Onderwijs*, 109–10.

On the other side was the political platform of the Antirevolutionary Party, published first in 1879, which proclaimed in its twelfth article that the Antirevolutionary Party

> desires that the state (unless compelled by lack of vitality among the citizens) abandon the premise that government is called upon to provide education; that it prevent government schools, if need be, from being misused for propaganda for religious or antireligious ideas; and so extend to all citizens, irrespective of their religious or pedagogical views, equal rights also in the matter of education.[6]

Supporters of the Antirevolutionary Party educational agenda simply wanted the substantive right to educate their children according to their deepest convictions and were prepared to grant everyone else that right as well. Although they consisted of roughly two-thirds of the nation's citizens, they formed a very small part of Parliament. Most Orthodox Calvinists and Catholics were among the "little people" who lacked suffrage, higher education, and the rhetorical skill to voice their views in public contexts. Many of them were wage laborers whose days were full with providing a very basic living, but they believed that the state schools would do their children harm and were ready to resist. For that enterprise they needed a leader, and it fell to Abraham Kuyper to be that for them.

It is certainly true that Abraham Kuyper was only one of the key leaders in what came to be called the school struggle. But just as Martin Luther King Jr. is known as the voice and inspiration of the civil rights movement, so also was Kuyper recognized as the inspiration and leading proponent of educational liberty in the Netherlands. Through his many articles, speeches, and editorials, he sought to awaken Christians to the fact that their core belief in the sovereignty of God was diametrically opposed by the deism taught in state schools. He called Christians across the land to exit state schools and set up their own schools at tremendous sacrifice. He helped to formulate a thoroughly pluralistic national educational policy which granted orthodox Christians the same rights as their deistic neighbors. He urged parents to pray that laws would be changed. He appealed to the moral conscience of his opponents and taught his constituency to do the same. When faced with new threats to the survival of free schools (including school improvement

6. *OP*, 188.

laws with unfunded mandates), he insisted that justice would eventually triumph over such immoral laws. Together with Herman Schaepman (1844–1903), leader of the Catholic party, he organized a national petition to the king in 1878, which, in simple but powerful language, pled their case for the right and ability to educate their children in the way their conscience required. It was carefully monitored and signed by 469,869 parents, far surpassing the number of actual voters in the Netherlands, which totaled 127,000. The king refused.

Against all odds, they endured. Kuyper's ability to respectfully and rationally communicate with those who opposed him began to have effect, and many in the conservative party began to understand that remove the key principle at stake was religious liberty. Finally, in 1889, an education bill was passed, which provided a small amount of financial aid to religious schools. Although Kuyper had advocated that government aid be granted to parents on the basis of need, he nevertheless rejoiced that the principle of educational liberty was recognized for the first time. In the years to come, Kuyper worked hard to see that amount of support increased. As a journalist, as a party leader, as a university professor, and eventually as prime minister, Kuyper worked hard for a pluralistic school system rooted in the highest law of the land; eventually he saw the day that educational liberty was guaranteed by a constitutional amendment.

My purpose in the rest of this introduction is to present an overview of Kuyper's multifaceted rationale for a pluralistic educational program.

FREEDOM OF CONSCIENCE

Kuyper argued that the Dutch school struggle was first and foremost about extending the freedom of conscience heralded in the Dutch constitution to parents who desired an education for their children in keeping with their religion. Very early on, he realized that no one type of schooling could ever meet the needs of parents from a variety of educational beliefs. He insisted that the state was neither called nor equipped to discern, much less enforce, religious truth. As such, the only way to guarantee liberty of conscience to all parents was to allow for a variety of schools, each with an equal claim (per child) on the resources of the state. As the economy of the Netherlands changed and took fathers away from the home during the day, schools ended up taking on a greater degree of children's nurture and upbringing. It thus became more and more urgent that the strong arm of the state not be used to impose on children a worldview which violated the conscience of their parents.

> And nothing was so grievous as when the state in our land for a long time claimed the right to set up the school for *all* children, and to force the parents to send their children to a school whose spirit and direction opposed the spirit of their family and were in open battle with their convictions.[7]

He was met with powerful resistance at first, largely because the concept of schools which were independent of both church and state was new, and many thought he was proposing a return to church-led schools.[8] He continued to argue his case as clearly and as carefully as he could so that the nature of what his party proposed could be clearly understood before it was debated. When he met with continued and increased opposition to a pluriform educational program, he began to think that either his opponents could not recognize the subjectivity of their own religious commitments, or they refused to do so in the quest to hold on to power. As Kuyper understood it, there were only two principled ways to resolve the school struggle: either through force or through liberty. Either the state would insist on granting parents of only one worldview all public educational resources, or it would grant parents of all major worldview perspectives an equal proportion of those resources. To do the first was to infringe on the conscience of a majority of the population. To do the second was to protect the rights of parents to an education for their children in accordance with their deepest values. Although Kuyper was accused of wanting to establish a theocracy, the reality was that the Antirevolutionary Party insisted that no worldview receive a monopoly on state resources. As their platform clearly stated, it sought to prevent a situation in which the government could use schools to propagandize either for or against any religion:

> To that end we ask only for one thing: that *freedom of conscience*, both direct and indirect, be completely restored. … We do not want the government to hand over unbelief handcuffed and chained as though for a spiritual execution. We prefer that

7. Abraham Kuyper, *De Gemeene Gratie* (Amsterdam: Höveker & Wormser, 1904), 3:396 (my translation).
8. See Abraham Kuyper, *De Schoolkwestie I. Naar Aanleiding Van Het Onderwijs-Debat in De Kamer* (Amsterdam: J. H. Kruyt, 1875).

> the power of the gospel overcome that demon in free combat with comparable weapons. Only *this* we do not want: that the government arm unbelief to force us, half-armed and handicapped by an assortment of laws, into an unequal struggle with so powerful an enemy. Yet that *has* happened and is happening *still*. It happens in all areas of popular education, on the higher as well as the lower levels, by means of the power of money, forced examinations, and official hierarchy.[9]

THE ROLE OF CORE BELIEFS IN HUMAN EXPERIENCE AND KNOWLEDGE

Kuyper argued that it was impossible to teach and learn outside a worldview which tied facts together into meaning. Human beings are creatures who naturally seek not isolated facts but the meaning which explains those facts. Instead of believing that reason was and should be the foundation for belief, Kuyper believed that subjective core belief was the root of experience and reason. Different worldviews were exactly that: different ways of interpreting the facts of our life according to the core beliefs by which we live. Two worldviews could be equally logical and consider all the available data and still arrive at different understandings. Kuyper himself was in university when he first began to formulate this understanding. A professor of his had drastically changed his argument, not on the basis of any new data, nor because of any flaw in his previous research, but solely because he had experienced a change of worldview and interpreted matters differently.[10]

This started Kuyper on a journey of thought which eventually led to his development of a theory of knowledge which was far ahead of his time. His claim that deep-seated belief (which all humans have) informs and guides the intellectual process was a surprisingly postmodern understanding of the nature of knowledge, with one significant difference. Many postmodernists claim that no objective truth exists, that all knowledge is humanly constructed, and that all we have are conflicting narratives in a power struggle for official status. Kuyper, on the other hand, believed that there was objective truth, and while human knowledge is always imperfect, he believed that the Calvinist worldview offered a much better understanding

9. Abraham Kuyper, "Maranatha," in *AKCR*, 224–25.

10. R. D. Henderson, "How Abraham Kuyper Became a Kuyperian," *Christian Scholar's Review* 22, no. 1 (1992): 22–35.

of the nature of reality than others. Of course, he understood that rationalists, Catholics, and those of the Jewish or Islamic faith felt the same way about their own worldview. There simply was no autonomous temporal power qualified to determine which worldview was, in fact, the closest to reality.[11] Not wanting to leave the matter of religion in schools to the vicissitudes of a political maneuvering, he argued that the only equitable solution was for the state to support schools operating from a variety of worldviews.

TAKING EDUCATION OUT OF POLITICS

On December 7, 1874, Kuyper gave his first speech in Parliament, in which he argued that "It should have been possible to provide our nation, too, with a school system that was not subject to partisan politics. Education in my opinion is not first of all a political issue but a social issue."[12] No political party (that represented people of similar worldviews) should have the power to decide the manner in which all the nation's children would be educated. Kuyper developed a social theory called "sphere sovereignty," in which he argued that each sphere of society had its own roots in the nature of humankind, and as such could only develop freely when it was free from intrusive control from another sphere.[13] While the spheres of the home, arts, state, schools, business, church, and science were certainly interdependent, they also needed to develop from their own root and according to their own insights and authority in order for society to flourish to its maximum capacity. Thus, says Kuyper,

> In a Calvinistic sense we understand hereby, that the family, the business, science, art and so forth are all social spheres which do not owe their existence to the state and which do not derive the law of their life from the state, but obey a high authority within their own bosom; an authority which rules, by the grace of God, just as the sovereignty of the state does. … These different developments of social life have nothing above themselves but God, and the State cannot intrude here and has

11. See Del Ratzsch, "Abraham Kuyper's Philosophy of Science," *Calvin Theological Journal* 27, no. 2 (1992): 277–303.
12. Abraham Kuyper, "Ideas for a National Education System," Speeches as a Member of Parliament, Dec. 7 and 8, 1874.
13. See Abraham Kuyper, "Sphere Sovereignty," in *AKCR*, 461–90.

> nothing to command in their domain. As you feel at once, this is the deeply interesting question of our civil liberties.[14]

While the state, of course, had the important role of protecting individuals from abuses within each sphere, it must never take on itself the task of deciding which core beliefs would pervade the school, nor ever dictate the content, style, and pedagogy of schools. Those were matters best left to those whose life and calling were entwined in the life of schools:

> Education is a distinct public interest. Education touches on one of the most complicated and intricate questions, one that involves every issue, including the deepest issues that invite humanity's search for knowledge—issues of anthropology and psychology, religion and sociology, pedagogy and morality, in short, issues that encroach upon every branch of social life. Now it seems to me that such an element of cultural life has the right in every respect to an absolutely independent organization; always in the sense that education should function in the spirit of what the British call *a body corporate*.[15]

There must be laws which granted all worldviews the right to develop their own parent-governed schools, with minimum state standards, to be sure, but independent of politics. The way in which schools operate, and especially the beliefs which informed their perspectives and curriculum, should not depend on which party had the most power at any one time. Under the current constitution, he argued, one party or perspective "can devote the entire, immense power of the state's authority in order to indoctrinate the nation with its principles by means of the school. That is not fair."[16] People with minority worldviews must be assured that "such an unbearable tyranny will never happen." Therefore, "the power of the majority with the bonds of justice."[17]

In arguing that the school no longer be controlled by the state, he was well aware that in the past, it had been the Dutch Reformed Church which

---

14. Abraham Kuyper, *Lectures on Calvinism* (Grand Rapids: Eerdmans, 1994), 90–91.
15. Abraham Kuyper, "Ideas for a National Education System," Speeches as a Member of Parliament, Dec. 7 and 8, 1874.
16. Kuyper, "Ideas for a National Education System."
17. Kuyper, "Ideas for a National Education System."

had intruded on the school and made it into a force for teaching true religion to the nation's children. He believed that the Netherlands was now at a historical point in which the guardianship of church and state was no longer needed and had, in fact, become harmful to the wholesome development of schooling and of young people:

> The nurturing of children is born by three factors: first by domestic nurture, secondly by ecclesiastical teaching, and thirdly, by the influence of society. The first factor belongs to the family, the second to the domain of the church, and only the last stands in the soil of society. … That the school is a phenomenon in the life of society was not understood in earlier times. … Only when the normal elementary school grows from her own root can she flourish in freedom and become what she must be.[18]

THE UNITY OF THE CHILD

Kuyper argued that the child is an organic unity whose healthy development requires that the nurture he receives in home, school, and church spring from the same core beliefs. Only in this way could the child develop strength of character. Later in life, of course, children were free to change their religious views, and the strength of character they had developed in the service of one religion could be used to serve in another. Kuyper himself had been converted from a very general form of Protestantism to Calvinism as a minister in his first parish.[19] But to teach and nurture children with conflicting norms, beliefs, and authority was to foster a debilitating skepticism and eventual malaise which undermined the development of conviction, character, and responsibility:

> Life itself requires that both the personal formation and the academic learning happen at the same time. Both are so interconnected; and thus not only the family, but also the school is called to help complete the general formation of the child *as a unity*. The child is not divided into compartments; an intellectual compartment, a moral compartment, a religious

---

18. Abraham Kuyper, *Parlementaire Redevoeringen* (Amsterdam: Van Holkema & Warendorf, 1908–12), 3:174–75.
19. See Abraham Kuyper, "Confidentially," in *AKCR*, 46–61.

> compartment, a compartment of character, and a compartment for practical skills. The child is one, and must be formed in this unity. Otherwise the left will tear down what the right has built up and there develops in the child the hopeless and unnerving confusion which prevents the development of all firmness of character.
>
> From this comes the requirement that there be agreement between the nurture in the school and the nurture in the home, and that they fit together. The school must not only build on the foundations that have been laid in the home, but also stay connected with the nurture that continues to happen in the home.[20]

Kuyper argued that an educational system which either ignored religion or imposed a particular religion on children contrary to their experience at home violated not only the conscience of the parents, but also a fundamental pedagogical norm. In Kuyper's view, the public school

> has attempted to establish next to, and eventually in opposition to the domestic nurturing of the baptized child, another nurture and in this she sinned against the pedagogical principle that all nurture will go wrong if it lacks a unity of root principle, and in such a way fails to clarify and enlighten the consciousness of the child, but confuses and troubles it.[21]

Kuyper was so convinced of this norm that he could speak of the rights of a child being violated when he was denied a unified upbringing:

> It is not only the right of the parents, but also the right of the child that is injured here. The child was helpless. It could not defend itself. His nurture and education was controlled by a power that he could not withstand. ... The child has a moral right to be raised in a consistent manner, in one direction, according to firm principles, because otherwise it will not be strengthened but weakened, not enlightened but brought into confusion, and morally undermined.[22]

---

20. Kuyper, *De Gemeene Gratie*, 3:393 (my translation).
21. Kuyper, *De Gemeene Gratie*, 3:393–94 (my translation).
22. Kuyper, *De Gemeene Gratie*, 3:394 (my translation).

SOUND PEDAGOGY

Kuyper knew that childhood is a time in which children learn how to learn. He believed that early childhood is the best time for natural habits of inquiry, questioning, exploration, evaluation, and synthesis. The doctrine of common grace was essential to Kuyper's thought and political action, and a full development of it is far beyond the scope of this chapter. Suffice it to say that he believed that God granted his common grace to all humankind so that sin was leashed in and development of human life continued. Although he believed that God granted his special grace (salvation from sin) only to Christians, he took seriously the sayings of Jesus that God causes his sun to rise on the righteous as well as the unrighteous (Matt 5:45). By this he in no way believed that only Christians were moral and good people. Quite the contrary, he knew that sometimes it was those who lacked the Christian faith who far exceeded Christians as outstanding examples of courage and love. This he explained as God's common grace.

Kuyper also taught that each sphere of society needed to learn the ways in which God's common grace maintained and developed life within that sphere. In the realm of learning and education, he believed that God had granted humankind a natural curiosity about life and the ability to observe, question, experience, and discover new aspects of the way this world operates. While the knowledge which bore fruit within a secular (or other) worldview often needed to be reinterpreted in order to more accurately reflect the nature of God's world, it was still valuable knowledge and essential to the development of humankind. He believed that schools should foster a child's natural curiosity and instincts to explore, consider, and learn. He fervently opposed the method currently used in many state schools of imposing abstractions which had little if any connection to the child's realm of experience.

The connection between his pedagogical views and his pluralist educational views was as follows. Kuyper believed that children experience core beliefs and natural curiosity in a unified remove and inseparable way. To identify these types of learning as separate was possible for adults but not for children. Therefore, in order for children to develop their common-grace instincts of learning, they needed to be in schools which fostered and extended the core beliefs which they experienced at home. While separate religious schools certainly did not guarantee a pedagogy which fostered curiosity, a "neutral" school which wanted to appeal to a child's primary experience (as in the thought of John Dewey) was hindered by the fact that each child was immersed in a different kind of primary experience (which reflected the faith the child experienced at home). Kuyper believed that primary experience was intertwined with and embedded in the root of communal core belief: "Learning is our glory, provided it is not detached from the instinctive foundation of our existence, thus to degenerate into abstraction."[23]

Likewise it was the attempted divorce of core beliefs from a child's innate inclinations which was artificial. One simply could not respect and foster a child's innate and natural inclinations to learn outside a shared and communal worldview. Because many of the state schools were designed to teach that reason was autonomous and independent of religion to children whose basic experience was decidedly religious, they tended to resort to abstractions which suppressed a child's appeal to his own experience. In this way, the state schools were a corrosive force which worked not only against the child's unified development but against all reliance on experience as in any way revelatory.

Identifying this perspective historically, Kuyper writes,

> But the French Revolution ... ignores the importance of the human heart and bypasses it. It neglects moral liberty and concentrates only on the head, for the civilized people, and for the uneducated people, the violence of the hand. Their spiritual fathers are not moral characters but philosophers. They have attempted to establish their power in sinful intellectualism through education and academic knowledge, not in the moral ideal.[24]

And on the pervasiveness of this perspective in modern society, he observes,

> Proponents of government schools are often called *intellectualists*. With what right is obvious. There is a general complaint that throughout our school system ... familiarity with factoids has replaced genuine knowledge and mature wisdom for life. ... Almost every teacher complains, and every informed observer admits, that superficial polymaths are steadily increasing

23. Abraham Kuyper, "Our Instinctive Life," in *AKCR*, 261.
24. Abraham Kuyper, *Niet de Vrijheidsboom maar het kruis* (Amsterdam: J. A. Wormser, 1889), 12.

> among the boys, but among the men "in robes and togas" spinelessness and dullness are rampant.[25]

Kuyper called the state schools the "sectarian schools of the Modernists"[26] and claimed that the advancement of the so-called neutral schools coincided with the increase in rampant intellectual corruption in the schools. They often hired teachers whose primary recommendation was their mastery of revolutionary ideology. Many teachers were ill-equipped to really connect with children's hearts and so proceeded to fill their students' heads with abstractions. They ended up teaching a little bit about everything instead of dealing with anything in great depth. Thus his referral to young "polymaths" filled with pseudo-knowledge and lacking humility:

> The result has been that the teachers without pedagogical talent have created a void in the schools that is now simply being filled by mechanical drill and rote learning. Talented teachers, on the other hand, have tended to concentrate on those subjects that are less restricted by the straitjacket of neutrality. Superintendents, inspectors, members of parliament, and ministers keep raising their demands for expanding the school curriculum. In this way, along a threefold path, as the bitter fruit of a false principle, a cancer has insinuated itself into our educational system that we have branded with the not too strong label of intellectualism.[27]

PARENTAL RIGHTS

During the early and middle part of the nineteenth century, the view that children belonged first and foremost to the state was spreading among many school leaders at both the national and municipal level. Children were considered to be individuals who stood in direct relation to the state without the mediation of the family. Of course, the family took care of children's physical care, but the mind of the child must be formed by the state. It can be quite difficult to imagine the power of this doctrine and the fierce opposition it encountered among poor and religious families. Many

25. *OP*, 205–6.
26. *OP*, §156, p. 192.
27. *OP*, 206.

parents felt an instinctive horror at the prospect of sending their children to a school where a powerful state would teach them how to think and believe. It is no wonder that some parents kept their children at home rather than submit to what they believed to be indoctrination.

By way of contrast, Kuyper and the Antirevolutionary Party believed that children belong first and foremost to their parents, whose duty and right it is to nurture and educate them in accordance with their own deepest beliefs. While the state has an interest in the education of its citizenry, it does not have the responsibility to manage or direct that education:

> The father is the only lawful person, called by nature and called to this task, to determine the choice of school for his child. To this we must hold fast. This is the prime truth in the whole schools issue. If there is any axiom in the area of education, this is it.[28]
>
> ... The parental rights must be seen as a sovereign right in this sense, that it is not delegated by any other authority, that it is inherent in fatherhood and motherhood, and that it is given directly from God to the father and mother.[29]

Kuyper also argued that the healthy upbringing of a child reckoned with what was already within the child, which could be more clearly discerned by parents than by anyone else. The spirit of the parents was, he argued, usually also the spirit of the child. By this he meant that the "direction" of a child's heart (his own core beliefs, whether understood yet or not) was usually in harmony with that of his parents. There was an intergenerational harmony which was important to acknowledge and respect for the best kind of learning to occur. A secular school was simply incapable of educating baptized children in harmony with the root of their being:

> The moral and religious nurture of the child can only succeed when we begin by seeking out the inclinations and tendencies within the child and bring those to consciousness. And this we can only measure according to what is in us. Just as a mother nurses her infant at her breast, so also with this nurture, our own consciousness must teach us what consciousness is in our

28. *OP*, 203.
29. Kuyper, *Parlementaire Redevoeringen*, 1:493.

> child. ... It must be our own awareness and life that we give as food to our children. This concerns the principled continuity of the generations. That which you find strange, you cannot give to your child. ... The provision of this need can only be given when the treasure of moral and religious life that is in the heart of the father, is transferred to the heart of the child.[30]

Last, Kuyper argued for parental rights in education because he understood the state insistence on controlling the direction of the schools to be an unjustifiable use of state force in an effort to shore up its positions of power. That was the heart of the entrenched resistance to freedom of education, he insisted. If parents were allowed to establish their own schools and enabled to send their children to them, then liberals stood to lose control, not only of schooling, but also in Parliament, in the universities, in the media, and even in the churches. Four years before the culmination of the school struggle with passage of the constitutional amendment, Kuyper continued to communicate what he understood the heart of the struggle had been. The radicalized liberals, he says,

> were not content to raise their own children as full-blooded liberals, so long as the children of their neighbor (who exceeded the number of their own children by ten percent) were raised in an opposite manner. And therefore, their state-school had to reach over the entire land, and they required that their school have far more power. Only [... by means of] the liberal state-school in which they set the tone and inspired all the people with that tone, was their position in our land safe. ... How must the child be nurtured? The answer to that question determines the lot of all of our people in the future. Now we say that you must ask God that question and that he says in his Word that the parents are the first ones responsible for the children. ... But the new-modern culture workers don't want to hear anything of this parental right. They are directed by a heathen wisdom as with Plato. The child is the responsibility of the state, he believes, and not of the parents. You must entrust the nurture of your child

30. Kuyper, *De Gemeene Gratie*, 3:377–78 (my translation).

> to the teachers that they choose. ... They are as afraid of true freedom as they are of death. ... Therefore, as the old saying goes: "Stay away from our children!"[31]

Interestingly, Kuyper also claimed that the parental rights were also limited by the nature of schooling. On November 30, 1896, Kuyper wrote an interesting article in which he emphasized that the antirevolutionary motto "The school belongs to the parents," should not be understood as granting parents the right to sovereignty *within* the school. The school was an independent sphere in which educators exercised their calling under God and in submission to the worldview mandated by the board. Parents had the fundamental right to establish schools according to their worldview and to freely choose among these schools, but in most cases it was not their calling to determine the specifics of curriculum. The curriculum needed to be designed by those who had spent years developing discernment for how best to teach from the life of their shared, communal core beliefs. There were issues of pedagogy which were crucial to a quality education, as I have mentioned above. In most cases, those people were the teachers, not the parents. Thus, although he believed schools should be set up by parents according to the rules for nonprofit foundations, he did not consider the schools to be subject to parents in all matters. Educators were accountable to parents for the worldview they taught but not for the way in which they did that. The school was a separate sphere that was directly accountable to God. He expressed his disappointment that in some free schools parents considered the teachers to be appointed underlings and refused to grant them the respect and authority that befit their calling.[32]

CHURCH RIGHTS

Humanly speaking, the continuance of the church of Christ universal (the communion of all those in every country and in every time who have placed their trust in Christ alone) requires that each new generation imbibe the spiritual, moral, and intellectual lifeblood of Christianity. It was each church's right, therefore, to require all parents to raise their children as Christians in thought, word, and deed. In Catholic and Calvinist churches,

---

31. Abraham Kuyper, *De Meiboom in De Kap* (Kampen: Kok, 1913), 16.
32. Abraham Kuyper, "De principiëele bezwaren tagen het UNIE-Rapport (VI)," *De Standaard*, November 30, 1896, no. 7589, p. 1.

this responsibility is expressed in the sacrament of infant baptism. Calvinist doctrine taught that the baptism of infants was the public recognition that this child of the covenant was set apart to glorify God as a member of his church. Before an infant was baptized in the Reformed churches, parents were visited by the minister or elder in order to ascertain whether they were serious about raising their children in the faith. In the baptism ceremony the parents made a binding vow to raise their children in the fear and admonition of the Lord, a vow considered as holy as the marriage vow. Kuyper argued that the fulfillment of those vows necessitated that parents provide their children with a distinctly Christian education.

> Because the children have received the holy baptism, the church has the duty to make sure that the educational requirements for baptism be fulfilled and to make sure that the child's education is not one-sided by teaching only in common grace, but also does justice to the ties of the child to particular grace.[33]
>
> *Baptism and school belong together for by far the larger portion of our people,* and you have heard what an anti-Christian and anti-national stamp countless of unbelieving and socialist teachers try to press upon the heart of the child. That may, that must not so remain.[34]

In this respect Kuyper also argued that the church had a valid right to correct and discipline parents who neglected their duty to raise their children in a Christian worldview. He was also quick to acknowledge that such authority was limited to the parents' continued submission to the church themselves:

> The church obligates the father by means of very positive, clearly defined promises, made in the presence of witnesses, that he will raise the child, to her satisfaction, in her doctrine, thus in her whole approach to life and the world. We must certainly concede, to ease the conscience, that such promises are binding only for as long as the father remains a member of that church.[35]

33. Kuyper, *De Gemeene Gratie*, 3:404 (my translation).
34. Abraham Kuyper, *Voor Den Slag* (Utrecht: G. J. A. Ruys, 1909), 8.
35. *OP*, 199–200.

PREPARATION FOR FUTURE SERVICE TO SOCIETY

Kuyper believed that schools which recognized and articulated their core beliefs would better prepare young people for the task of influencing society for the common good. He argued that all Christians were called to be salt and light (Matt 5:13–16) in society, people who influenced the nation toward high standards of morality, the preservation of their constitutional liberties, the development of enterprise, the arts, and scholarship, as well as influencing their neighbors through their love. He was grieved that there were so few Christian schools, but he was equally grieved when Christian schools neglected the wisdom of common grace and focused exclusively on religious training, leaving their students ill-equipped for influential participation in society.

> Voters, do not forget, that this great evil still survives, that the masses, especially in the large cities, still attend a school without God or prayer, while it is precisely in the large cities where the strongest influence goes out over all the land, and in which, through the press, the power of money and concentration of intellect, the fate of our land is decided.[36]

> If only these Christians had clearly seen that the treasures of common grace come also from God, they would never have fallen into the false idea that they could ignore the formation in common grace in order to focus exclusively on formation in special grace. Precisely in this way (that they lost sight of the value of common grace), they themselves are to blame for falling so far behind the general development of unbelievers and, even worse, that the leadership in this general development was taken away from them and is now very one-sidedly dominated by unbelievers.[37]

Kuyper lamented that in response to the disrespect and mockery Christians had faced from those who resisted educational liberty, many Christians had receded into their own circles and neglected to pray or think in terms of common grace or the common good. He called on Christians

---

36. Abraham Kuyper, *Heilige Orde: Rede in Den Bond Van Antirevolutionaire Kiesvereenigingen Te Amsterdam Gehouden Op 30 Mei 1913* (Kampen: Kok, 1913), 23.
37. Kuyper, *De Gemeene Gratie*, 3:403 (my translation).

to have thicker skins and to design schools which prepared children to be servants of God in every facet of society and at every level of society, schools in which

> our children, from their youth up, learn to reverence God's wonderful common grace at work in the gradual development of the various levels of society, and feel themselves called to participate in this wonderful work of God each in their own way. Then thanksgiving, rather than pride, comes into the heart, a sense of calling instead of self-exaltation, and the development of the nation can proceed well. Then that which is "Christian" will no longer be considered in opposition to "development" but the Christian circles will also realize that participating in the higher development of the nation is a calling from God, because only when that development has its root in the Christian religion can it lead to true civilization. Not only, "How do I help my children through the world?" but also the other question: "How can I help the world through my child?" shall then give direction and guidance to education.[38]

At the same time, he called on teachers to foster humble attitudes among their students, not only in their personal lives, but also in their attitudes toward those of other faiths. They needed to understand that by God's common grace, those in other faith communities had much to teach Christians. While young people needed to learn to embrace their own experience and perspective and learn to communicate it to others, they also needed to learn to respect and listen to those with other worldviews. Not only because humility was a quality which Christ modeled and commanded, but also people of other religions often have knowledge and insight which Christians lack, and which Christians need in order to grow as people and as disciples of Christ. Kuyper insisted that children not be allowed to be haughty and content to live in isolation from others. They must be spurred not only to communicate across faith traditions, but also to listen. In this way, differences in political or social views across religions would be less easily attributed to moral failings than to different starting points. This, too, was crucial to a well-functioning democracy.

38. Kuyper, *De Gemeene Gratie*, 3:401 (my translation).

FREE INITIATIVE AND CIVIL SOCIETY

Kuyper believed that a system of free schools would strengthen civil society and foster national development in a number of ways. First, it provided a training ground for parents in the exercise of free initiative and independence, thereby restoring habits and dispositions that had decreased over the past century. Because this was an area of life very dear to parents, it was an ideal first step toward regaining the sense of liberty and resilience that was so essential to a strong civil society.

> It is always and again the family that resists the uniformity [of modern society] with the rich blessing of an endlessly and richly nuanced life. We are not a line of poplars planted in a row, but form a luxurious park with endless variation and it is precisely the calling of the family and, within the family, of the bond between parents and children, to bring this rich differentiation to its right.[39]

Such differentiation and respect for the home was not only valuable in its own right, Kuyper argued, but was also essential to the ongoing development of the nation.

> The struggle for Christian education against the uniform elementary schools was also a struggle for the preservation of our national development. Without continual nurture, our national life will collapse, and it is not the neutral school, but only the school of a particular direction that can nurture in harmony with the nurture that occurs in the home.[40]

Second, he believed that by appealing to children's subjective experience, the curriculum and the pedagogy of free schools were more likely to foster character and resilience among young people. The artificial abstraction that was prominent in the state schools was destructive of a child's ability to think and act freely on the grounds of experience. Thus, so-called neutral schools, which sought to please all by separating instruction from a child's particular religious experience, had hindered thousands of children from developing the mindset, initiative, and skills needed to sustain a strong civil

---

39. Kuyper, *Heilige Orde*, 23.
40. Kuyper, *De Gemeene Gratie*, 3:396 (my translation).

society. A system of free schools, he claimed, was urgently needed in order to restrain the degeneration of civil society in the Netherlands:

> For many people, their upbringing has been a curse rather than a blessing. We can go even further and say that if the upbringing is not bad, but nevertheless leads down the wrong path, it can cause an entire nation to sink and degenerate. This danger has also existed in our country, and it is only due to the vigor of the free school that this evil has partially been arrested and can be resisted with hope and good results in the future.[41]

Kuyper also argued that a system of free schools strengthened civil society by relying heavily on private charity as well as parental sacrifice, thereby fostering the dispositions and habits of love and self-government rather than those of passivity and compulsion.[42] An exploration of Kuyper's views on exactly how government funding and regulation of free schools should be implemented is, unfortunately, outside the scope of this chapter. Suffice it to say that for forty years he stridently opposed a system in which the government would grant complete subsidy to all schools; he was convinced that such a system would gradually erode both the free initiative of parents and the distinctive identity of religious schools. Two principles, he argued, guided this issue, that of equality and that of liberty; and the best way to accommodate both principles was to limit state funding to a certain portion of all costs. Taxes should be decreased so that parents would be able to take initiative in how their children were educated.

By 1911, however, it became very clear that the state was not willing to decrease its support of state-managed schools. It became clear that while Parliament was more open to a system of free schools, it was not willing to consider a two-tiered system in which state schools were better supported than free schools. After all, the argument had been one of equal treatment under the law. Eventually Kuyper was willing to compromise, not in the least because he considered it unrealistic for families to financially support both their churches and their schools.[43]

41. *CG* 2.29.3, p. 252.
42. *OP*, §159.
43. Abraham Kuyper, "Subsidien," *De Heraut*, May 31, 1901.

JUSTICE FOR THE POOR

Kuyper was especially concerned for the poor, who suffered the most under the current system. Many were unable to afford even a meager portion of the tuition, and could only send their children to school when a scholarship made that possible. He urged Christians throughout the country to give toward such scholarships. And he pled their case before Parliament:

> One should not forget that many people are of the belief that when a child is raised apart from faith in Christ it suffers eternal harm. I do not ask whether all members of the Chamber think of it in this way, but it is the view of thousands upon thousands. To be forced to send one's child to a school where it will be nurtured in a spirit that is opposed to that of its parents is an evil that may no longer be perpetuated.[44]

Elsewhere he proclaimed:

> Some men ... want to work to expand freedom for the middle class but ... they leave unmet the need for freedom of conscience among the poor. ... But it seems to me, Mr. Chairman, that there is no nobler struggle than for the freedom of conscience, particularly for the poor. Government money is well spent for that.[45]

Kuyper also understood the school struggle as a struggle for social justice, not only for individuals but also for religious communities. In an interesting newspaper article dated April 12, 1878, Kuyper responded to the "brutal gas-argument" of the liberal press, which had confused even some of the free-school supporters.[46] The argument went as follows: the state provides for gas lighting on the streets in our cities and asks everyone to help pay for it, even those who choose not to walk outside at night and therefore have no personal profit from it. In the same way the state provides for the intellectual enlightenment of the nation's youth, and requires all citizens to help pay for it, whether or not their children profit from this provision.

---

44. Kuyper, *Parlementaire Redevoeringen*, 4:987.
45. Kuyper, *Parlementaire Redevoeringen*, 4:406.
46. Reprinted as "Het Gas-argument," in Abraham Kuyper, "*Ons Program*" (Amsterdam: J. H. Kruyt, 1879), 698–701.

The crucial mistake in this analogy, Kuyper argued, was that unlike street lighting, if a parent finds that the state education violates his conscience, he must set up another kind of school and that is very costly. Using the same analogy he described the current school system as like the government providing street lights for only certain neighborhoods, but requiring citizens in all neighborhoods to pay for them. The crucial point was that when the government now provided an education which *was suited for* only one part of the populace, it violated the conscience of all others: "Wherever we recognize a fundamental right for our citizens to provide their children with an alternative means of 'enlightenment,' then it becomes clear that requiring those citizens to pay for education twice, while others only have to pay once, is unjust."[47]

Kuyper expressed his sincere appreciation for all those fellow travelers who had joined their cause out of concern for social justice:

> We cannot deny that, especially since 1878, not a few have joined with us, who were only awakened by the injustice that was done to us in the School Question, whereas in many other aspects of politics they continued to disagree with us. They were not driven by their own interests and even less by our political principle. What drove them was the desire for justice. They saw before their eyes that we suffered injustice. ... They wanted to help stop the injustice. That it was not in the least their personal interest but rather an offended sense of justice which drove them to action, was nowhere made more convincing than in their generous offerings.[48]

> The school struggle brings a completely different matter to order, namely, the matter of justice. Two groups within our population, that possess equal rights with all people, were treated in such an offensive and shamefully unequal manner in an area of such tender feelings as that of their children's nurture, such that the one group received virtually everything for free while the other group had to pay for everything themselves—that clashed so grievously with the first demand of all sense of justice, that those who pressed for the cutting out of

47. Kuyper, *Ons Program*, 700.
48. Kuyper, *Parlementaire Redevoeringen*, 1:530.

> such a cancer within our midst could not be in the least seen as motivated by special interest.[49]

NATIONAL UNITY

National unity was a valid concern for many in national leadership as the schools issue became more pronounced. Many leaders were concerned that allowing for separate schools would result in reinforced subgroups which opposed each other, increasing the religious tension within the Netherlands. Kuyper argued the opposite: that a system of free schools which respected the right of each community of faith to preserve and express their identity would promote national unity:

> Unity of the nation is not brought into danger by having children attend different kinds of schools but by wounding the right and limiting the freedom so that our citizens are offended not in their material interests but in their deepest life convictions, which is all-determinative for the best of them. That sows bitterness in the hearts and that divides a nation. ... Instead of asking what the state school will receive and what the free school will receive, as sons of the same fatherland we should commit to raising the development of our entire nation. Then ... the feeling of unity will grow stronger and more inspired.[50]

As one of America's beloved poets, Robert Frost, has stated, "Good fences make good neighbors." It was by acknowledging the differences between our citizens and allowing for a clear demarcation between schools of different beliefs that religious tolerance and national unity are best fostered. Kuyper argued that it was the political game of "winner takes all" that fostered animosity between subgroups. When an elite clique is allowed to impose a worldview on all schools, is it any wonder that a deep animosity and anger results? Kuyper argued that the strongest kind of national unity was one which made room for a multiplicity of communities of faith. Pluriformity, not uniformity, must be the goal, the beauty of a natural forest

---

49. Kuyper, *Parlementaire Redevoeringen*, 1:529.
50. Kuyper, *Parlementaire Redevoeringen*, 4:408–9.

with all the variety of vegetation and species, rather than that of a garden in which poplar trees were uniformly planted in straight rows.[51]

DUTCH CULTURE AND HERITAGE

Last, Kuyper argued that religious liberty lay at the core of Dutch culture and identity. At the end of the Eighty Years' War, the Netherlands became known as a place of refuge for religious minorities who were oppressed in other lands. Although the Dutch Reformed Church was the national church, Catholics were at liberty to worship in their own churches. Jews fleeing the Inquisition in Spain and Portugal were also welcome in the Netherlands and built one of the most beautiful synagogues in the world. Kuyper argued that the concept and practice of religious liberty had come to its fullest expression in the Calvinist nations. Believing that God was absolutely sovereign, and that salvation was in the hands of God alone, these nations eventually understood that the spreading of "true religion" was not actually susceptible to the use of force, and therefore not a matter for the civil authorities.[52]

He therefore argued that a school system in which parents were free to choose their children's school was completely in harmony with the religious liberty at the roots of Dutch culture. In response to accusations that he wanted to set up a school system which was primarily sectarian, he insisted that the Antirevolutionary Party's educational policy was a *national* program, not sectarian, because it honored the rights of all parents to direct children's education.

In a significant speech given before an Association of Christian Teachers in 1869 titled "The Appeal to the National Conscience," Kuyper called on the supporters of free schools to show their countrymen how thoroughly Dutch a pluralist system of free schools was. He urged them to "appeal to the national conscience" by asking their countrymen five questions designed to awaken them to the customs, instincts, concepts, and values of religious liberty that slumbered in their national consciousness. Ask them, he declared,

- whether the moral calling of the Netherlands allowed us to remove religion from the national schools,

51. See Abraham Kuyper, "Uniformity: The Curse of Modern Life," in *AKCR*, 19–44.
52. See Abraham Kuyper, "Calvinism: Source and Stronghold of our Constitutional Liberties," in *AKCR*, 310.

- whether requiring teachers to teach historical facts devoid of interpretation was an acceptable methodology for schools,
- whether the Netherlands, known for the strength of its domestic life, should now exclude the family's identity from the school,
- whether a free and self-governed nation like the Netherlands could tolerate the complete state control of how children were educated,
- whether the Dutch people could, in good conscience, deny the lower classes the freedom of conscience that the upper classes enjoyed?[53]

These questions were designed to remind the Dutch people that they did indeed cherish religious freedom, intellectual freedom, parental rights in education, self-government, and equal treatment under the law for poor and rich alike, values which Kuyper argued were under attack by the current educational system. The questions were also designed to expose the current school system, which worked from the top down, as entirely foreign to the Dutch way of doing things. This was one more reason, he argued, why educational liberty should no longer be considered a privilege to be bought, but a guarantee to be established by the highest law of the land.

SOME THOUGHTS ON EDUCATIONAL LIBERTY IN AMERICA

Recent national events have brought to the fore a deep division between the ways different segments of our population think and see the world. This split has been portrayed as being between the college educated and those with less formal education, or between rural and urban populations. It has also been portrayed as a split between those who cherish democracy and those who do not. Still others portray it as a split between conservatives and liberals, or between traditional values and progressive values.

What I would like to propose, however, is that for *many* Catholics and evangelical Protestants, a situation similar to the Dutch school struggle

53. Abraham Kuyper, *"Het beroep op het volksgewetern": rede ter opening van de Algemeene vergadering der "vereeniging voor Christelijk Nationaal-Schoolonderwijs"* (Amsterdam: B. H. Blankenberg, 1869), 11–13. See also in this volume, "The Appeal to the Nation's Conscience."

has existed for decades. Increasingly evangelical Protestant and Catholic parents have withdrawn their children from public schools, largely because of what they perceive as the blatantly secular beliefs which underlie the curriculum and culture of those schools. And so they exit.

While Catholics have long accepted their need to set up alternative schools, tuition has risen in recent decades as archdioceses have been less able to supplement the schools with personnel and financial aid. Evangelicals have also accepted their need to set up independent schools, but what is starting to irritate and anger people is the continued claim that public schools are entirely appropriate for all American children. In a word, many are fed up with what they perceive as the unstated assumption that liberal elites have a monopoly on insight and morality.

The problem is not that people think differently; the problem is when people believe that those who think differently are not worth listening to. Nowhere is this more keenly felt than by the poor who desire a distinctly Christian education for their children and simply cannot afford it. Quite aside from the abysmal education that is offered in many of our inner-city public schools, there is the matter of how the United States of America can justify forcing parents of limited means to send their children to a school which so violates their beliefs. I worked in a Christian school on the south side of Chicago in which some of the students regularly arrived in the morning extremely hungry. After some discussion, our staff eventually realized that apparently their parents had made a very difficult choice. They had decided that the benefits of a Christian education outweighed the benefits of breakfast for their family. We began setting out apples in every classroom after that. But the question we need to ask is whether any American should have to choose between feeding their children and having them educated in a school which does justice to their own deepest convictions. We ought to listen carefully to parents who sacrifice so greatly in order to protect their children from what they clearly perceive to be harmful indoctrination in our public schools.

Wendy Naylor

VOLUME INTRODUCTION

KUYPER AND FREE SCHOOLS, THEN AND NOW

During the seven-decade political struggle in the Netherlands to allow parents to select schools corresponding to their religious convictions, Abraham Kuyper articulated a concept of "sphere sovereignty" that translates, in policy terms, into principled structural pluralism. That Dutch experience, and its eventual resolution in the "Pacification" of 1917, is highly relevant for the present situation in the United States: popular revulsion against the condescension and intolerance of a liberal elite toward the values and interests of many of their fellow citizens, leading to deep political and social as well as cultural divides. Kuyper referred to such division, in a 1904 address to teachers from Christian schools, as "the contest between the two forces that contend for the soul of the nation."[1]

1. This volume, page 360.

A primary locus of this conflict, in nineteenth-century Netherlands and elsewhere in Europe, was public schooling, the sphere in which, more than any other, government reaches into the lives and confronts the intimate convictions of parents. While claims of state sovereignty over all aspects of society had been made at least since Jean Bodin (1530–96), the development of a central government role in promoting popular schooling was essentially a nineteenth-century phenomenon, though with earlier anticipations in Prussia and other German states.[2]

While town support for schooling as early as the late Middle Ages had been motivated by economic motives, such as the advantages of literacy and numeracy in commercial enterprises, the more recent adoption of central-government measures was almost always intended to promote among the common people a shared loyalty to a national project, to turn "peasants into Frenchmen."[3] Thus it was as Prussia absorbed territories in other parts of Central Europe that Prussian leaders made popular schooling a matter of state policy, an example followed with more or less success by centralizing governments in France, Spain, Italy, and other countries a century later. In the Netherlands, this was part of the agenda of the Batavian Republic during the Napoleonic period, influenced by contemporary Jacobin efforts to remake the French people.[4]

Insistence on the uniquely civic role of government-managed public schools and on the dangers represented by schools not under direct government control, especially if they had a religious character, developed in elite circles over the course of the nineteenth century. Increasingly assertive national states grew unwilling to continue to allow religious organizations not under government control to play a role in shaping the loyalties and mores of the rising generations.

Schooling as an instrument by which the state forms its citizens to a unique pattern of loyalties seeks to create, as Robert Nisbet writes, "a political order free of all ties or relationships save those which proceed directly

2. Ludwig Fertig, *Zeitgeist und Erziehungskunst: Eine Einführing in die Kulturgeschichte der Erziehung in Deutschland von 1600 bis 1900* (Darmstadt: Wissenschaftliche Buchgesellschaft, 1984); Charles L. Glenn, *Contrasting Models of State and School* (New York: Continuum, 2011).
3. Eugen Weber, *Peasants into Frenchmen* (Stanford, CA: Stanford University Press, 1976).
4. Charles L. Glenn, *The Myth of the Common School* (Amherst: University of Massachusetts Press, 1988); Mona Ozouf, *L'école de la France: Essais sur la Révolution, l'utopie et l'enseignement* (Paris: Gallimard, 1984).

from the state, itself based upon the sovereign General Will, and empty of all rights and liberties of individuals—whose renunciation or 'alienation' of these is the condition of entry into the redemptive state."[5]

Kuyper, whose political movement defined itself precisely by opposition to the French Revolution, saw this claim of the state to a monopoly on the schooling of youth as a fundamental threat. "What we combat, on principle and without compromise," he wrote in laying out the program of his political movement in 1879, "is the attempt to totally change how a person thinks and how he lives, to change his head and his heart, his home and his country—to create a state of affairs the very opposite of what has always been believed, cherished, and confessed, and so to lead us to a complete emancipation from the sovereign claims of Almighty God."[6]

Repeatedly throughout his public career, as reflected in the writing and speeches that follow, he rejected the claim of the state to use schooling in this manner. Recalling, as prime minister in 1905, the *schoolstrijd* thirty years before, he accused Liberal leader Kappeyne van de Coppello (1822–95) of holding "to a religion that is best described as the deification of the state. ... The state was for him the Moloch to which children could be sacrificed if need be. Thus with the best of intentions he became the father of the tyrannical [school] law of 1878."[7] Kuyper had earlier warned, as a member of the States General in 1874, that the lack of protection for educational freedom meant that a political group in power "can devote the entire, immense power of the state's authority in order to indoctrinate the nation with its principles by means of the school."[8]

The political and cultural struggle over schooling boiled up in 1878, when a new generation of Dutch Liberals came to power, committed to government intervention in popular schooling and explicitly hostile to confessional schools.[9] "Religion, they insisted, especially religious education among young children, bred ignorance, superstition, and backwardness. It stunted the full development of the individual and of the nation."[10] They enacted legislation providing that the state would pay 30 percent of

5. Robert Nisbet, *History of the Idea of Progress* (New York: Basic Books, 1980), 245.
6. *OP*, 2.
7. This volume, page 289.
8. This volume, page 151.
9. D. Langedijk, *De Schoolstrijd* (The Hague: Van Haeringen, 1935), 140.
10. James D. Bratt, *Abraham Kuyper: Modern Calvinist, Christian Democrat* (Grand Rapids: Eerdmans, 2013), 115.

the cost of local public schools, and under some circumstances even more. Other provisions of this law increased significantly the costs of all schools, whether government-supported or not. The legislation was opposed by supporters of unsubsidized confessional education, since it would make their schools much more expensive to operate.

Confessional schools would remain free, Kuyper noted, "yes, free to hurry on crutches after the neutral [school] train that storms along the rails of the law, drawn by the golden locomotive of the State."[11]

The Liberals had overreached. This threat against the schools that many of the orthodox common people had labored and sacrificed to establish aroused and created a movement that, in a decade, reversed the political fortunes of the Liberals and brought state support for confessional schools. A massive petition drive collected, in five days, 305,102 signatures from Protestants and 164,000 from Catholics asking the king to refuse to sign the new legislation.

When that failed, a national organization, "The Union 'A School with the Bible,'" created a permanent mechanism for the mobilization of orthodox Protestants.[12] Together with the orthodox Protestant Antirevolutionary Party, the Catholic party gained a majority in Parliament by 1888, as a result not only of mobilization around the schools but also of a revision of the election law the previous year, which greatly extended the franchise among the (male) population, thus bringing the religiously conservative common people of the countryside and small towns into political participation for the first time. As a historian of Dutch liberalism has pointed out, the effort to smother the last flickering flame of orthodox religion only succeeded in fanning it into vigorous life, and "no one has done as much harm to liberalism as Kappeyne."[13]

Emancipation of the "little people" (*kleine luyden*), for whom their Catholic or orthodox Protestant beliefs were central, required intensive organization; their emergence into public life brought their convictions with them. The passions and the habits of cooperation developed during

11. T. M. Gilhuis, *Memorietafel van het Christelijk Onderwijs: De Geschiedenis van de Schoolstrijd*, 2nd ed. (Kampen: Kok, 1975), 152; Langedijk, *De Schoolstrijd*, 148–49.

12. C. Rijnsdorp, "'Met vreugd naar school' (Herinnering en tijdbeeld)," in *In het honderdste jaar: Gedenkboek Stichting Unie 'School en Evangelie' 1879–1979* (Kampen: Kok, 1979).

13. Harm van Riel, *Geschiedenis van het Nederlandse Liberalisme in de 19e Eeuw* (Assen: Van Gorcum, 1982), 108, 111, 128–29. "Kappeyne" refers to Liberal prime minister Kappeyne van de Coppello.

the long struggle for confessional schooling and then found expression across the whole range of social life. A Dutch political scientist notes of the phenomenon known as *pillarization* that "*verzuiling* is inexplicable apart from the 'school struggle.'"[14]

In the country that today has the most highly evolved system of educational freedom, under which schools reflecting a variety of worldviews and pedagogical approaches enjoy equal public funding and protection of their distinctiveness, these arrangements did not simply drop from the sky but were achieved through bitter struggle and mobilization of elements of the population who had been seen as the voiceless target of educational policy.

It was the overreach of a liberal and secularized elite that brought to naught what had seemed the inevitable progress of their agenda. In place of the unlimited intervention of the state to shape minds and hearts, loyalties and dispositions, through popular schooling, the resistance of the Protestant and Catholic "little people" led to a great flourishing of grassroots organizations and institutions to meet a wide variety of needs.

It is not that Kuyper denied the state a significant role in promoting schooling and ensuring its quality. In the same 1874 parliamentary speech cited above, he stressed that the state had the right to stipulate the level of educational performance of all schools, including private schools, to inspect them and to certify their results. Associated with this right, however, was a duty: to make it possible for all parents to afford schooling for their children, consistent with their freedom of conscience.[15]

As a result of the decades-long political struggle on the part of Kuyper's Antirevolutionary Party and its Catholic counterpart, the Dutch state's role in schooling became one of coordination, of support, of intervention only when local efforts failed. Since the Second World War, as in other countries, this role has become increasingly prescriptive in countless ways, but the fundamental principles of equal public support for all schools meeting academic standards and of respect for the distinctive character and

---

14. J. P. Kruijt and Walter Goddijn, "Verzuiling en Ontzuiling als sociologisch proces," in *Drift en Koers: Een halve eeuw sociale verandering in Nerderland*, ed. A. N. J. Hollander et al. (Assen: Van Gorcum, 1962), 232; P. W. C. Akkermans, *Onderwijs als constitutioneel probleem* (Alphen aan den Rijn: Samson, 1980), 159.
15. This volume, pages 139–163.

religious worldview—the *richting*—of each have remained in place and largely uncontested.[16]

THE DEEPER STRUGGLE OVER EDUCATION AND CULTURE

Kuyper's concern was not, however, limited to ensuring the freedom of parents, without financial penalty, to choose for their children schools that corresponded to their own convictions. He also saw education as a sphere where the dominance of secular modernism should be challenged. "The state," he told his fellow-legislators in 1874, "cannot teach morality because morality involves principles of anthropology and psychology of which the state is incompetent to judge. That is why Mr. Groen van Prinsterer fought tooth and nail against the education bill of 1857 because it would of necessity lead to the state's teaching its own religion and so create a kind of state church disguised as the public school."[17]

Kuyper insisted that the "neutrality" of the public school was an illusion; "How can a teacher nurture and form character," he asked, "and at the same time be neutral?"[18] After all, "there is no neutral education that is not governed by a spirit of its own. And precisely that spirit of the religiously neutral school militates against every positive faith."[19] Indeed, he had made the same point thirty-five years earlier, criticizing the supposedly Christian character of public schools:

> We must ask for a Dutch answer to the question whether that minimum of Christianity is really the Christianity of our forefathers, the Christianity that made our nation great and for which the blood of our people was shed. Given our diverse population, the state school must either weaken or pass over in silence the chief factor of our national history, lest anyone be offended. Accordingly, the very serious question must be put to

16. *Onderwijsraad, Artikel 23 Grondwet in maatschappelijk perspectief. Nieuwe richtingen aan de vrijheid van onderwijs* (Den Haag, 2012); see also Paul J. J. Zoontjens and Charles L. Glenn, "The Netherlands," in *Balancing Freedom, Autonomy, and Accountability in Education*, vol. 2 (Nijmegen: Wolf Legal Publishing, 2012).
17. This volume, page 163.
18. This volume, page 285.
19. This volume, page 290.

> the same judge of the national conscience, whether mutilating our history does not violate our national life.[20]

Before the national mobilization of Protestant and Catholic "little people" in the 1870s, most parents accepted this moralistic school-religion without sin or redemption as adequate to the religious nurture of their children. Kuyper insisted, in 1869, that this was a sham, that

> our people have been cast into the arms of materialism. ... For a long time the state school was a veiled image for our people—its essence hidden, its true visage invisible. It just stood there, covered by a garment in which the misleading terms of "toleration" and "Christian virtues" were woven with shiny gold thread. Misled by appearances, our people did not believe what some trustworthy individuals told them about the heinous form that would become apparent as soon as the veil fell off and the garment was removed. In the meantime, they had grown to love the school and become accustomed to it as an integral part of our national life. And now, it is finally clear that everything said about the school understates the appalling truth now revealed. The mask is finally thrown off and the school is displayed in all its naked barrenness. The dissembling about faith is gone and has been replaced with active efforts to "Silence God," and "eternal life." Yet they still dare to call out to our people [on behalf of the state school]: "You must send your children to me, you will entrust to me your baptized sons and daughters, although the name of Christ may not be heard within our walls and no talk about God and immortality will be permitted." And the Dutch nation is silent while thousands and tens of thousands send their children. There is still present an unholy desire to fight for the state school as one does for one's idol.[21]

Kuyper set himself, especially through the pages of his newspaper, to disabuse his readers of this illusion and remind them of the perennial "conflict between faith and unbelief."

---

20. This volume, page 318.
21. This volume, page 28.

The 1874 legislation reflected a growing antireligious sentiment in some elite circles. Liberal prime minister Kappeyne van de Coppello warned that making concessions to the advocates of public subsidies for confessional schools would have the result that "the struggle for liberty would have been useless, ... destroyed through the wrangles of factions. Dominance by priests and churchly intolerance would then be prevalent in our country."[22] While to an earlier generation of Liberals the role of the state was to provide support for schooling but without becoming involved in the content and goals of education, for "Kappeyne it was nearly the opposite: the State, the State, and again the State; everything must derive from it, in the spirit of 'the modern worldview,' which must penetrate the entire state apparatus, in a principled struggle with churchly authority, which was on its last legs." In an important parliamentary speech in 1874, Kappeyne insisted that "the State cannot leave to chance, to arbitrariness, to the care of any association whatsoever, what belongs to it in the first place: education."[23]

It was in opposition to this claim on the part of the state to shape the minds and hearts of youth, to be sovereign over the most intimate aspects of family and individual conscience, that Kuyper and his allies, as he wrote, "focused all our fight on the school struggle. For there the sovereignty of conscience, and of the family, and of pedagogy, and of the spiritual circle were all equally threatened."[24]

Kuyper was insistent, however, that it was not the intention of his Antirevolutionary Party to seek to impose its own approach to schooling in place of the secular and materialistic education that, he contended, had been promoted by the Liberals. To the contrary, he advocated a principled pluralism that would respect the consciences of all. As prime minister, in 1903, he pointed out that Dutch policymakers

> have to do with two basic worldviews that sharply oppose each other. That being so, the power of the state must not be used in favor of one of them. The contest between the worldviews must be decided in a free grappling of the spirits—provided

22. J. A. A. van Doorn, "Meer weerstand dan waardering: De Revolutie-ideeën en de Nederlandse politieke traditie," in *Van Bastille tot Binnenhof: De Franse Revolutie en haar invloed op de Nederlandse politieke partijen*, ed. R. A. Koole (Houten: Fibula, 1989), 161.
23. Van Riel, *Geschiedenis van het Nederlandse Liberalisme*, 111, 225.
24. Abraham Kuyper, "Sphere Sovereignty," in *AKCR*, 472.

> the conditions of the tournament are equal—so that at last both sides clear the air and make it possible to reach a compromise, a certain modus vivendi that satisfies both sides. I believe we have begun to arrive at such a happy modus vivendi in the area of primary education and will eventually be able to complete it. The more we work in this direction the more we will attain peace in every area of our national life and the more we will promote the interest of education in all its branches.[25]

Two years later, he explained how this pluralism had been given concrete structural form:

> In 1848 all parties agreed that exclusively public education did not satisfy the nation's needs, so freedom of education was enshrined in the Constitution. In 1889 consensus was reached that the free, independent, private school, being part of primary education, could not adequately fulfill its task unless it received some financial aid from the public treasury. The central government ... would henceforth give financial aid *"in equal measure"* to both public and private schools.[26]

Kuyper's distinctive contribution was, in the name of God's sovereignty over all aspects of life, to give his confessional political party a strong agenda of social policies going well beyond explicitly "religious" concerns; "by associating Calvinism with social reform, Kuyper was able to bring broad, *klein burger,* sectors and even segments of the working class behind the Anti-Revolutionary movement," as Erik Hansen writes.[27] This was the first party program in Dutch history and, in the very year when the Liberals achieved their goal of enacting legislation to place new burdens on confessional schooling, their opponents achieved the nationwide organization that enabled them subsequently to reverse the Liberal program.[28]

Kuyper and other Dutch antirevolutionaries defined their political program in conscious opposition to the French Revolution, with its assertion

25. This volume, page 284.
26. This volume, page 304.
27. Erik Hansen, "Marxism, Socialism, and the Dutch Primary Schools," *History of Education Quarterly* 13, no. 4 (Winter 1973): 370.
28. E. H. Kossmann, *De lage landen 1780–1980: Deel 1 1780–1914* (Amsterdam: Olympus, 2001), 251.

of the unlimited sovereignty of the nation-state, as famously expressed by Abbé Sieyès (1748–1836): "The Nation exists before everything, it is the source of everything."[29] Or, more officially, in article 3 of the *Declaration of the Rights of Man and Citizen* (also 1789), "All sovereignty resides essentially in the Nation. No body, no individual can exercise authority which does not explicitly emanate from it."[30]

Kuyper insisted on an alternative understanding of the nature of sovereignty as ultimately belonging to God and attributed in only limited fashion to different spheres of the created order, including government. "Sphere sovereignty defending itself against State sovereignty," he wrote in 1880, "that is the course of world history. ... It lay in the order of creation, in the structure of human life; it was there before State sovereignty arose. But once arisen, State sovereignty recognized Sphere sovereignty as its permanent adversary."[31] As Jonathan Chaplin puts it,

> For Kuyper, the principle of sphere sovereignty (*souvereiniteit in eigen kring*) expresses the idea that there exist a variety of distinct types of social institutions, each endowed with a divinely ordained nature and purpose, and each possessing rights and responsibilities that must not be conflated with or absorbed by those of other types.[32]

Contrary to the common stereotype about religious leaders in politics,[33] Kuyper did not seek to dominate the society and culture of the Netherlands, but to make room for institutional pluralism:

> He struggled against uniformity, the curse of modern life; he wanted to see movement and contrasting colors in place of gray monotony. ... Thus the "antithesis," that originally [among orthodox Protestants] meant the unrelenting struggle against devilish modernity, with Kuyper imperceptibly [changed] to a teaching about diversity and about the independent,

29. Emmanuel Joseph Sieyès, *Qu'est-ce que le Tiers Etat?* (1789).
30. Liah Greenfield, *Nationalism: Five Roads to Modernity* (Cambridge, MA: Harvard University Press, 1992), 172.
31. Kuyper, "Sphere Sovereignty," 469.
32. Jonathan Chaplin, *Herman Dooyeweerd: Christian Philosopher of State and Civil Society* (Notre Dame, IN: University of Notre Dame Press, 2011), 139.
33. See George Yancey and David A. Williamson, *So Many Christians, So Few Lions: Is There Christianophobia in the United States?* (Lanham, MD: Rowman & Littlefield, 2015).

> to-be-honored power of differences. All that was not logical … but it was successful and contributed to giving Dutch society a very distinctive flavor. The origin of what would later be called "pillarization" [*verzuiling*], the system through which each religious group thanks to government subsidies can create its own social world that includes everything from nursery school to sports club or professional association, lies in Kuyper's conservative love for pluriformity.[34]

THE AMERICAN "SCHOOL STRUGGLE"

A persistent myth about American public education is that it has been the unique focal point of unification of a diverse population.[35] Supporters of Dutch *openbare scholen* had made this claim, but Kuyper told his fellow legislators that, in fact, the "common school has not contributed to greater tolerance; it has instead inflamed party passions."[36] This has been the case for two centuries in the United States as well. Recently, something similar to the nineteenth-century Dutch school struggle has once again been happening in American politics, as evident not only in the populist resentment leading to the 2016 election but also in the political shifts in many states, and—with respect to education—the growth of thousands of alternatives to the district public schools that, fifty years ago, seemed an immoveable and central institution of American life.

Already, nearly three million students attend public charter schools, and nearly four hundred thousand are taking advantage of programs making it possible for them to use public funds to attend private schools; these numbers are growing sharply each year.

What we have been hearing again and again from the supporters of Donald Trump—though it by no means began with them—is resistance to what they perceive as the overbearing power of the national government and of the liberal "coastal" elites who are thought to set the agenda of that government and to impose it on society in general. The conservative media have been full of examples of the overriding of local and parental concerns, of which the issue of transgender use of bathrooms and locker rooms is only the latest sensation. There can be no denying the political potency

---

34. Kossman, *De lage landen*, 250.
35. See Glenn, *Myth of the Common School*.
36. This volume, page 273.

of such grievances, however exaggerated they may sometimes be.[37] Nor is it very different from what Abraham Kuyper wrote in 1873, with similar exaggeration:

> Can it be denied that the centralizing State grows more and more into a gigantic monster against which every citizen is finally powerless? Have not all independent institutions, whose sovereignty in their own sphere made them a basis for resistance, yielded to the magic formula of a single, unitary state? Once there was autonomy in the regions and towns, autonomy for families and different social ranks, autonomy for the courts as well as for the universities, corporations, and guilds. And now? The State has annexed all these rights from the provinces, one after another. Then it tells the towns what to do, comes in your front door. Expropriates your property. Commandeers the law, makes trustees and professors its servants, and tolerates no corporation but its own dependent.[38]

But Kuyper, unlike today's populists in the United States and in Europe, offered a conceptual framework for thinking about and prescribing in a principled and measured way for this overinflation of central government authority. He was able to do so by drawing on the Calvinist tradition of focusing on the fundamental significance of God's sovereignty for every sphere of human life.[39] Without such conceptual clarity, it is doubtful whether a solution could have been reached in the Netherlands, or could be reached in the United States today.

By asserting the unique sovereignty of God, Kuyper relativized and limited all other sources of authority and thus provided a basis for a democratic pluralism protecting the freedom of faith communities as well as of individuals. Is it too much to hope that we Americans can abandon the winner-take-all mindset that embitters our political discussions, and accept instead the principled pluralism that served as the basis of a lasting "Pacification" in the Netherlands? To do so would require "neither that we

37. David Goodhart, *The Road to Somewhere: The Populist Revolt and the Future of Politics* (London: Hurst, 2017).

38. In Bratt, *Abraham Kuyper*, 281–82.

39. Peter S. Heslam, *Creating a Christian Worldview: Abraham Kuyper's Lectures on Calvinism* (Grand Rapids: Eerdmans, 1998), 114.

agree completely with each other about our deepest beliefs (we don't) nor that we stop trying to convince each other about what we think is best (we shouldn't). Instead, principled pluralism simply asks us to agree to respect each other's convictions not only in private life but also in public life."[40]

Philosopher Nicholas Wolterstorff points out that "our contemporary proponents of the liberal position ... are still looking for a politics ... of a community with shared perspective. ... The liberal is not willing to live with a politics of multiple communities."[41] The consequence is that, unless prepared to maintain a radical separation like the Amish or Hasidic Jews, individuals with deeply held religious convictions, beliefs, and loyalties that "go all the way down" are forced in many respects to conform to the norms of the surrounding culture, and that culture in turn grows increasingly superficial because it is not allowed to evoke the deep motivations of life.

Such "comprehensive liberalism" is fundamentally partisan and intolerant, and political scientist William Galston stresses the threat that its ascendancy poses to traditional communities, since "liberalism is not equally hospitable to all ways of life or to all subcommunities. Ways of life that require self-restraint, hierarchy, or cultural integrity are likely to find themselves on the defensive, threatened with the loss of both cohesion and authority." As a result, Galston points out, "the more one examines putatively neutral liberal principles and public discourse, the more impressed one is likely to become by their decidedly nonneutral impact on different parts of diverse societies. Liberalism is not and cannot be the universal response, equally acceptable to all, to the challenge of social diversity. It is ultimately a partisan stance."[42] No wonder that religious organizations and individuals who take their beliefs seriously sometimes feel under attack in this allegedly tolerant society.

There is even more at stake than the right of individuals and groups to live out their religious convictions in the decisions they make about the education of their children. A "growing body of evidence suggests that in a

---

40. Stephen V. Monsma and Stanley W. Carlson-Thies, *Free to Serve: Protecting the Religious Freedom of Faith-Based Organizations* (Grand Rapids: Brazos, 2015), 97.

41. Nicholas Wolterstorff, "The Role of Religion in Decision and Discussion of Political Issues," in *Religion in the Public Square: The Place of Religious Convictions in Political Debate*, ed. Robert Audi and Nicholas Wolterstorff (Lanham, MD: Rowman & Littlefield, 1997), 109.

42. William A. Galston, *Liberal Purposes: Goods, Virtues, and Diversity in the Liberal State* (Cambridge: Cambridge University Press, 1991), 293, 297.

liberal society, the family is the critical arena in which independence and a host of other virtues must be engendered. The weakening of families is thus fraught with danger for liberal societies," Galston writes.[43] A healthy society requires citizens with the character, the "settled disposition," to act in accordance with the common good rather than with selfish interests at critical junctures, and there is a real danger that such citizens will not be available in a society whose prevailing culture has placed individual autonomy as the highest good, a culture in which the "secular, Enlightenment rhetoric of autonomy is bound up with a celebration of 'self' as the final arbiter, the trump to all moral claim," as Elizabeth Mensch and Alan Freeman write.[44]

In this welter of moral confusion, as Yuval Levin observes, "the ultimate soul-forming institutions in a free society are frequently religious institutions. Traditional religion offers a direct challenge to the ethic of the age of fracture. Religious commitments command us to a mixture of responsibility, sympathy, lawfulness, and righteousness that align our wants with our duties. They help form us to be free."[45]

This is of course exactly the opposite of the belief promoted in progressive circles today, that religious institutions are the epitome of unfreedom, subjecting children, in particular, to a numbing indoctrination, with "moral exhortations" which "effectively prevent many children from freely expressing themselves physically, exploring their sexuality, or even giving affection to others."[46]

Many see religious institutions in American society as under relentless attack, especially around issues of sexuality such as gay marriage and transgenderism. "The cultural left—which is to say, increasingly the American mainstream—has no intention of living in postwar peace. It is pressing forward with a harsh, relentless occupation," warns a recent book which has attracted wide attention.[47] The requirement that faith-based schools, for example, comply with legal requirements for curriculum content or

43. Galston, *Liberal Purposes*, 222.
44. Elizabeth Mensch and Alan Freeman, *The Politics of Virtue* (Durham, NC: Duke University Press, 1993), 130.
45. Yuvak Levin, *The Fractured Republic: Renewing America's Social Contract in the Age of Individualism* (New York: Basic Books, 2016), 204.
46. James G. Dwyer, *Religious Schools v. Children's Rights* (Ithaca, NY: Cornell University Press, 1998), 159.
47. Rod Dreher, *The Benedict Option: A Strategy for Christians in a Post-Christian World* (New York: Sentinel/Random House, 2017), 3.

protections for staff behaviors that are contrary to basic teachings of their religious traditions is a fundamental challenge to their mission.

In order to function effectively as educative communities, it is essential that schools—like families and churches—enjoy real independence to hold and to express distinctive worldviews, Levin writes:

> Being valued and protected is what these mediating institutions all require from the larger society. And in return, they help to form us as free citizens who can live together—not by agreeing with one another about everything (as different institutions and communities can inculcate quite different ethics), but by living out the genuine potential, and recognizing the real limits, of human liberty in practice. ... it is our attachments to these very institutions that have been most degraded in modern America. The progress of the ethic of diffusion and liberalization has meant growing estrangement from precisely these prerequisites for human flourishing.[48]

Democratic pluralism insists that no healthy society can be based exclusively on individual possessors of rights and an overarching state that guarantees those rights and possesses "the only legitimate authority."[49] To the contrary, says Galston, "our social life comprises multiple sources of authority and sovereignty—individuals, parents, associations, churches, and state institutions, among others—no one of which is dominant for all purposes and on all occasions. Nonstate authority does not exist simply as a concession or gift of the state. A well-ordered state recognizes, but does not create, other sources of authority."[50] Democratic pluralism calls instead for deliberate and even-handed support of the social, political, and economic arrangements that allow communities drawn together around shared convictions about the nature of a flourishing life to live side by side and cooperate in common tasks and respond to common challenges, drawing on the qualities of character and loyalty that cannot be developed in the "naked public square."

As Richard John Neuhas writes, a healthy

---

48. Levin, *Fractured Republic*, 205.

49. Levin, *Fractured Republic*, 206.

50. William A. Galston, *Liberal Pluralism: The Implications of Value Pluralism for Political Theory and Practice* (Cambridge: Cambridge University Press, 2002), 36.

> society has ... communities of memory and mutual aid, of character and moral discipline, of transcendent truth and higher loyalty. ... American society is best conceived as a community of communities. Citizens move in and out of communities, crossing lines and languages in often confusing ways—confusing to themselves and to others. The resulting dissonance is called democracy. The national community, to the extent it can be called a community, is a very "thin" community. The myriad communities that constitute civil society are where we find the "thick" communities that bear heavier burdens of loyalty.[51]

Ironically, "Today's ongoing attempts to drive believers out of the national conversation is not only inegalitarian. It thoroughly contradicts progressivism's claim to value social and intellectual diversity," says Mary Eberstadt.[52] Nevertheless, despite George Marsden's argument that "mainstream secular culture of the past half-century, despite its concerns for justice regarding other sorts of diversity (such as racial, ethnic, or sexual diversity), has not yet effectively addressed the difficult question of religious diversity,"[53] it seems clear, according to R. R. Reno, that

> present-day liberals are very unlikely to convert to principled pluralism. Doing so would require them to admit that theirs is a worldview on a par with those of devout Catholics, ardent Protestants, and observant Jews. That's a galling proposition for consensus liberals. ... The consensus of consensus liberalism is the consensus of the powerful, and so it's essential that liberalism should rule. That's why it so loudly announces itself as the arbiter and manager of pluralism without ever allowing itself to be a constituent.[54]

51. Richard John Neuhaus, *America against Itself: Moral Vision and the Public Order* (Notre Dame, IN: University of Notre Dame Press, 1992), 185.
52. Mary Eberstadt, *It's Dangerous to Believe: Religious Freedom and Its Enemies* (New York: Harper, 2016), 17.
53. George M. Marsden, *The Twilight of the American Enlightenment: The Crisis of Liberal Belief* (New York: Basic Books, 2014), 151.
54. R. R. Reno, "The Public Square," *First Things*, April 2014, 7.

This has led the Orthodox Christian author of one widely noted book to assert that "we've lost on every front. … Hostile secular nihilism has won the day in our nation's government, and the culture has turned powerfully against traditional Christians. We tell ourselves that these developments have been imposed by a liberal elite, because we find the truth intolerable: The American people, either actively or passively, approve."[55]

Once again, though, the example of Abraham Kuyper should remind us not to be discouraged by the apparent fact that those who give priority to God's sovereignty—or to other compelling sources of normative authority other than the state or personal preference—represent a minority of the American people. Kuyper's 1879 election manifesto *Ons Program* "recognized that Calvinists were in fact a permanent minority, fated to perpetual co-belligerencies with whoever was most congenial to their position on the issue at hand."[56] Kuyper's "neo-Calvinist" supporters "comprised no more than 9 percent of the Dutch population and never got more than 16 percent of the vote. Nevertheless, between 1900 and 1950, on six occasions, one of their own was prime minister of the Netherlands, with Kuyper being the first."[57] It was through tactical alliances on particular issues (notably with Catholics but also with organized Labor and other groups) and through persistence in building alternative institutions that the Dutch model of structural pluralism came into existence over several decades before its educational dimension was confirmed in 1917–20.

In the contemporary American scene, despite the cultural hegemony of an intolerant secularism, the social elements for constructing vigorous alternative institutions and communities are by no means lacking; indeed, they have been stimulated by the collapse of the postwar Judeo-Christian cultural dominance.[58] The willingness of many state legislatures to adopt voucher, tax credit, and other policies that support family choice of faith-based schools is a reaction to the focused demand of religious minorities for educational alternatives. And the unanimous decision of the United

55. Dreher, *Benedict Option*, 9.
56. Bratt, *Abraham Kuyper*, 138.
57. Harry A. Van Belle, "Vision and Revision: Neo-Calvinism in The Netherlands and Canada," in *Rethinking Secularization: Reformed Reactions to Modernity*, ed. Gerard Dekker, Donald A. Luidens, and Rodger R. Rice (Lanham, MD: University Press of America, 1997), 85.
58. David A. Hollinger, *After Cloven Tongues of Fire: Protestant Liberalism in Modern American History* (Princeton, NJ: Princeton University Press, 2013).

States Supreme Court in *Hosanna-Tabor Evangelical Lutheran Church and School v. Equal Employment Opportunity Commission* offers reassurance that the federal "Constitution's free exercise guarantee and no-establishment rule work together—not, as is sometimes thought, at cross-purposes—to protect religious groups' freedom by limiting the power of governments over the relationship between religious communities and their teachers, leaders, and ministers," writes Richard Garnett.[59]

Government-managed systems of popular schooling are always a tempting instrument of anonymous, impersonal, and inhuman power, which profoundly falsifies the nature of true education. Education in its authentic form occurs in the relationship over time between children or youth and trusted adults, in the first instance their own families and then other adults to whom their families entrust them. It occurs, of course, not only in schools but also in other expressions of the life of civil society, including formal and informal settings under the sponsorship of religious institutions, but by no means limited to these. After all, "children must be initiated into a particular home, a particular language, a particular culture, a particular set of beliefs before they can begin to expand their horizons beyond the present and the particular," says Elmer John Thiessen.[60]

By contrast, the mandatory and monopolistic "common school" so much praised since the days of Horace Mann as the crucible of democratic citizenship can no longer function as it did when it was the expression of a coherent local community but is instead a shopping mall of competing messages with no moral core, where the overriding virtue of tolerance "precludes schools' celebrating more focused notions of education or of character. 'Community' has come to mean differences peacefully coexisting rather than people working together toward some serious end."[61] The predictable effect of such moral chaos on young citizens is that, as Thiessen writes, "exposing them to plurality and a Babel of beliefs and values too soon will in fact prevent the development of abilities which are a key to

59. Richard W. Garnett, "Things Not Caesar's," *First Things*, March 2012, 19.

60. Elmer John Thiessen, *Teaching for Commitment: Liberal Education, Indoctrination, and Christian Nurture* (Montreal: McGill-Queen's University Press, 1993), 222.

61. Arthur G. Powell, Eleanor Farrar, and David K. Cohen, *The Shopping Mall High School* (Boston: Houghton Mifflin, 1985), 3.

later functioning in a complex and pluralistic environment."[62] Real and effective education is provided in a school that

> will be stabilized by its commitments and respond to the needs of a group of students and parents to whom it is committed rather than to the politically bargained preferences of society as a whole. ... Social trust and community feeling are higher when schools are distinctive and families have choices. In an ongoing study, the author has found that students in schools based on a clear set of common premises are more likely than students in less well-defined schools to engage in vigorous discussion of values and social policy. In schools that throw together students from different races and social classes without creating a common intellectual and values framework, students are likely to resegregate socially and academically along racial and class lines.[63]

Public policies supporting structural pluralism in schooling are thus capable not only, as in the Netherlands, of reducing significantly the political and cultural conflict so evident today, but also of permitting schools to be more effective in the development of character and citizenship. The resulting enhanced level of trust, based on the voluntary choice of families for a particular school, and of teachers who share a commitment to that school's explicit mission, can also have a measurable effect on academic outcomes. In Chicago, for example, "schools reporting strong positive trust levels in 1994 were three times more likely to be categorized eventually as improving in reading and mathematics than those with very weak trust reports."[64]

---

62. Elmer John Thiessen, *In Defense of Religious Schools and Colleges* (Montreal: McGill-Queen's University Press, 2001), 41.
63. Paul Hill, "The Supply-Side of School Choice," in *School Choice and Social Controversy*, ed. Stephen D. Sugarman and Frank E. Kemerer (Washington, DC: Brookings Institution, 1999), 151.
64. Anthony S. Bryk and Barbara Schneider, *Trust in Schools: A Core Resource for Improvement* (New York: Russell Sage Foundation, 2002), 111; see also Francis Fukuyama, "Trust: The Social Virtues and the Creation of Prosperity," in *The Essential Civil Society Reader: The Classic Essays*, ed. Don E. Eberly (Lanham, MD: Rowman & Littlefield, 2000), 257–66.

Opponents of allowing publicly funded schools to be autonomous and, in some cases, to have a religious character often argue that the effect of such policies will be to further divide society. Kuyper had an answer for that, too, exhorting his fellow legislators,

> *The unity of the nation!* There is unity and unity. As you want. Is it the unity of the house painter who covers everything with the same color, or that higher unity in the harmony of colors which the artist pursues with a rich diversity of shades and gradations? The first kind is the unity that the honorable member wants by casting everybody in the same mold; the unity that I aim at is the unity of the flowerbed whereby each flower retains its peculiar form and color from which is born that higher harmony.[65]

Opponents of educational pluralism have been warning of national disunity for nearly two hundred years, only to be proved wrong again and again by actual experience. Most other nations with advanced levels of universal schooling support such pluralism,[66] with no evident harm to their social fabric and with considerably less conflict over schooling than occurs in the United States. Surely the time has come for a similar American "pacification," through adoption of principled pluralism as the fundamental structure of our education system. As in so much else, Abraham Kuyper continues to be relevant for educational policy.

Charles L. Glenn

---

65. This volume, page 163.
66. See Charles L. Glenn and Jan De Groof, eds., *Balancing Freedom, Autonomy, and Accountability in Education*, 4 vols. (Nijmegen, The Netherlands: Wolf Legal Publishing, 2012).

ABBREVIATIONS

GENERAL AND BIBLIOGRAPHIC

AKCR	*Abraham Kuyper: A Centennial Reader*. Edited by James D. Bratt. Grand Rapids: Eerdmans, 1998.
CG	Kuyper, Abraham. *Common Grace*. Translated by Nelson D. Kloosterman and Ed M. van der Maas. Edited by Jordan J. Ballor and Stephen J. Grabill/J. Daryl Charles. 3 vols. Bellingham, WA: Lexham Press, 2016–.
ESV	English Standard Version
KJV	King James Version
OP	Kuyper, Abraham. *Our Program*. Edited and translated by Harry Van Dyke. Bellingham, WA: Lexham Press, 2015.

OLD TESTAMENT

Gen	Genesis	1–2 Kgs	1–2 Kings
Exod	Exodus	1–2 Chr	1–2 Chronicles
Lev	Leviticus	Ezra	Ezra
Num	Numbers	Neh	Nehemiah
Deut	Deuteronomy	Esth	Esther
Josh	Joshua	Job	Job
Judg	Judges	Ps (Pss)	Psalm(s)
Ruth	Ruth	Prov	Proverbs
1–2 Sam	1–2 Samuel	Eccl	Ecclesiastes

Song	Song of Songs	Obad	Obadiah
Isa	Isaiah	Jonah	Jonah
Jer	Jeremiah	Mic	Micah
Lam	Lamentations	Nah	Nahum
Ezek	Ezekiel	Hab	Habakkuk
Dan	Daniel	Zeph	Zephaniah
Hos	Hosea	Hag	Haggai
Joel	Joel	Zech	Zechariah
Amos	Amos	Mal	Malachi

NEW TESTAMENT

Matt	Matthew	1–2 Thess	1–2 Thessalonians
Mark	Mark	1–2 Tim	1–2 Timothy
Luke	Luke	Titus	Titus
John	John	Phlm	Philemon
Acts	Acts	Heb	Hebrews
Rom	Romans	Jas	James
1–2 Cor	1–2 Corinthians	1–2 Pet	1–2 Peter
Gal	Galatians	1–3 John	1–3 John
Eph	Ephesians	Jude	Jude
Phil	Philippians	Rev	Revelation
Col	Colossians		

PART ONE

ENTERING THE SCHOOL STRUGGLE

THE SOCIETY "FOR THE COMMON GOOD"

TEXT INTRODUCTION

On January 25, 1869, in the midst of an intense ecclesiastical struggle in the Dutch Reformed Church of Utrecht, to which he had been called in the summer of 1867, Abraham Kuyper traveled to Amsterdam and addressed a promotional rally for Christian education. His topic: "The 'Common Good' Movement" (*"De 'Nuts'-Beweging"*). An expanded version of the address came out a month later in an eighty-three-page pamphlet that significantly stoked the fires of the school struggle about the role of religion in Dutch public schools.

The target of Kuyper's polemic was *De Maatschappij "Tot Nut van 't Algemeen"* (that is, the Society "for the Common Good"). This was the primary nongovernment organization devoted to the improvement of education for Dutch children. Established in 1784 with the goal of bringing people of all religions together for the improvement of the "rational, moral and social conditions of the people, especially by exerting influence in the area of nurture and education," the society established chapters throughout the Netherlands and became an important player in the development of a national school system. By the time Kuyper delivered his address in 1869, the society had also become more aggressive in its promotion of a kind of secular neutrality in Dutch public education; the religious neutrality, prescribed by law, was being used to create room for an antireligious spirit.

Kuyper's polemic against the society was occasioned by a manifesto recently issued by its board of directors that described the movement for free, private elementary schools as a threat to the progressive well-being of the Dutch nation. Kuyper opens his critique with a lengthy citation from the manifesto.

This was not Kuyper's first encounter with the society. Only two years earlier, it looked more positive. As a minister in the Reformed Church of Beesd, Kuyper had been elected to serve on the board of a local chapter of the society for promoting community banking. But he had soon resigned, for reasons that are not entirely clear.

In the summary that follows, the dominant voice is Kuyper's own, although mostly paraphrased. A minimum of actual excerpts from the pamphlet are reproduced, for which page references are provided in parentheses. The result powerfully captures, at times with biting sarcasm, Kuyper's argument against the Society's advocacy of *education without religion* as a "common good" for the Dutch people.

Source: Kuyper, Abraham. *De "Nuts"-Beweging*. Amsterdam: H. Höveker, 1869. Translated, abridged, summarized, and annotated by John Bolt. Edited by Harry Van Dyke.

THE SOCIETY "FOR THE COMMON GOOD"

On November 8, 1868, the board of directors of the Society for the Common Good issued a manifesto to its local chapters about what it perceived as a threat to the public good in the arena of public education.[1] After reminding its members that improving Dutch public schools was one of the prime objectives of the society's founding, it observes that significant progress has been achieved, notably in religious tolerance. The Dutch nation, the manifesto notes, is a "free nation, which from of old has been a refuge for all those who were persecuted for their beliefs and convictions" (2). And now the schools, in large measure thanks to the dedicated work of the society, have arrived at the point where the present generation is being educated and formed so that all can live together in brotherly love. In spite of ecclesiastical and doctrinal differences, the nation has come to understand that "the law of mutual love is the first and highest law there is" (2).

But now there is a perceived threat to this progressive ambition. There are disturbers who "from many sides [are] trying to undo the beneficial fruit [that has been achieved] in the past" (2). The manifesto expresses deep concern that an "ecclesiastical movement" has revealed itself as opposed to

1. The contents of the paragraphs that immediately follow are paraphrased from the society's manifesto.

the religious neutrality of the public school. This is an effort to take back the gains that our nation, more than others, has enjoyed for more than sixty years.[2] In spite of the fact that the rights of our schools are constitutionally protected, that their beneficial fruits for a growing number are demonstrable, and that school authorities are always ready to listen to concerns about one-sided instruction, nevertheless, "seeds of resentment and discontent have been sown precisely in those places where sympathy and gratitude should prevail" (2). As these voices grow louder and louder, enlightened Netherlanders stand in danger of being robbed of that which is essential for the well-being of our children and the future of our nation. While their ability to attack is weak, their battle cry is loud and noisy.

We, the Board of Governors, regard this as a matter of grave concern and urge our members to be "vigilant" and to "keep a watchful eye on the forces which, however at odds they may be with one another, are nevertheless for the time being arrayed against the existence and flourishing of our present order, an order that is correctly seen as an essential condition for a united and independent Netherlands" (3). No upright Dutchman can look on this and remain indifferent; we in the society have struggled too long and too hard to bring about this order, and our efforts have garnered the sympathy of the nation and earned the tribute of all Europe.

We therefore call on our members to be awake and alert and to stand fast against those who would reverse the progress we have made in the elevation of all classes. If the thousands of our members remain firm, we can achieve an even greater harvest along with other enlightened [lit. "awakened"] people in our civilized world today. Let us strive to make our nation's schools even better and closer to the ideal we set for them. For eighty years our society has fought for our nation's welfare and culture, for civilizing our people; we remain committed to our conviction that a properly oriented school is essential for our nation's greatness. We call on our members and chapters to make our manifesto known, to zealously fight to preserve the gains we have achieved, and to resist those who would undermine them.[3]

---

2. Reference to the Education Act of 1806.
3. What now follows is Kuyper's response to the manifesto.

The subject of this manifesto is the neutral public school for which the society takes credit. Notice that this school is credited for making the Netherlands a free and tolerant nation, one in which ecclesiastical differences have been set aside by love. However, the manifesto claims at the same time that our nation has "from of old been a refuge for all those who were persecuted for their beliefs and convictions." On what basis, pray tell, can the society claim credit for what has been our nation's patrimony "from of old" (4–5)?

The society violates the very principle it celebrates when it speaks of our opposition to the direction of the public school as "ecclesiastical." It is of course more than that, but granting the premise for the moment, we run up against article 3 of the Elementary Education Act of 1857 that forbids taking sides in the struggle between church and state.[4] It is simply not true that we are trying to diminish the availability of schooling for all Dutch children. On the contrary, we seek to make it possible for more children to receive the religious education desired by their parents. We are told that we are fools who refuse to bring our grievances to the authorities who are always more than willing to listen to legitimate complaints. This simply misses the point. For us the issue was never about instances when the law was infringed[5] but about the law itself, because its demand of neutrality so grievously violates the conscience of many (5–7). The use of the term "ecclesiastical" reflects the problem that the society has with our movement. They cannot acknowledge that our movement is national because it would put the lie to their claim that support for a neutral school is generally accepted by Dutch citizens and therefore truly national. If they ignore us, the risk is that our movement grows; if they pay us too much attention, their premise that they represent the national will is not warranted. Therefore we get dismissed as "ecclesiastical" and as "fools."

---

4. Kuyper refers to article 3 of the Education Act later on (p. 11), where he observes that although the Society considers a "ban on participating in party strife" to be one of its chief dogmas, the manifesto is guilty of that very sin.
5. In certain regions of the country, authorities turned a blind eye if teachers made use of the Bible, in contravention of the spirit of the Education Act but for the purpose of placating parents, who then might conclude that the common public school was "Christian enough."

But even worse, those of us who object to the law are not only fools but said to be evil people. While the society sowed seeds of tolerance and love in the field of national education, we protesters are the enemy who sow bad seed among the good with the intention of destroying the harvest of good will and national progress. We are judged to be sinners sowing resentment and discontent in place of sympathy and gratitude and therefore not true, upright Netherlanders who love the Fatherland.

So much for the society's gospel of tolerance for all views. The lofty virtue of neutrality so important to its members flies out the window when it comes to those who oppose the neutrality of the schools. About such opposition one cannot be neutral, because such neutrality would be suicidal for the well-being of Dutch society.

It is a shame that humility is not one of the virtues that the Society wants taught in our national schools. Self-proclamations about earning "tribute from all Europe" strike us as a little too proud, not to mention instances of high-blown, empty rhetoric. To top it all off, the manifesto goes on to speak of "awakened" [enlightened] people who support neutral schools. Are they implying that those who do not are asleep (8–9)?

The members of the society are asked to mobilize against us under the banner "For the well-being of our people via civilizing work" by means of "supporting the neutral school with an energy that matches the energy we have seen in those who seek to undermine it" (10).

The above is sufficient to capture the rhetorical character of Kuyper's polemic against the Society "for the Common Good." As he goes on to provide further analysis, however, he does not continue solely in this vein but also introduces some appreciative notes. He praises them for their passion and for living out their convictions (9). He then reveals his own twofold intention in engaging the manifesto:

1. He wants to show how the manifesto has unmasked the myth of neutrality. The moment opposition arises, neutrality vanishes for those who are committed to neutrality and fiercely opposed to "party spirit"; instead, at that moment they become fiercely partisan. This is a welcome revelation.

2. Kuyper notes that an analysis such as he has given is necessary to enable people to see behind the curtain of politeness that hides the manifesto's true agenda (11). He wants to alert people who may have been longtime supporters of the society that it is no

> longer the organization it was in the past. The manifesto is a "declaration of war" against those who desire free schools (15).

Historically, however, Kuyper acknowledges the Christian consciousness that gave rise to the society in the late eighteenth century, a dark time in the Netherlands, a time of spiritual poverty in the midst of material plenty for a few. Kuyper praises the founders of the society for the genuine concern manifested toward the lower classes and the improvement of their lot through education. In spite of what the society has become, he does not hesitate to pronounce a blessing on its founding. In a key passage he describes the horrible condition of schools and compares it with what the society has achieved:

> For the first time education became education and since then there is a leading concern to connect with the life of the people. There is a growing conviction that the school exists for children and not children for the school. ... Musty hovels were replaced by brighter and larger spaces. ... Teachers' private family lives were now kept distinct from the classroom. ... A general educational method was developed. ... Improvement took place in teacher training and in textbooks. ... Drilling was replaced by more mature forms of discipline. ... Teachers came to be regarded as professionals. (25–27)

That is why the society enjoyed impressive growth and connected with the instinctive and national life of Netherlanders. Praiseworthy is its decentralized structure and the expectation from all members to participate sacrificially in its work. In all this one finds something authentically Dutch (29–36). At a time when the spirit of the nation was at a low ebb, the founding of the society helped lift it out of the moral doldrums. Also, its success points to the failure of the Dutch Reformed Church, a failure in the humiliating consequences of which one can see the hand of God's righteous judgment (37).

But was it Christian in its orientation or was it, as it is now, hostile to the Christian faith? We need to give different answers to that question, depending on the various periods of its history. Its founder, Mennonite pastor Jan Nieuwenhuyzen, clearly had a Christian heart but stood opposed to all forms of a Christian society and had no eye for the positive, renewing life-force of a Christianized culture. In Nieuwenhuyzen's day people still believed in revelation, in miracles, in the mystery of the atonement, but these convictions were taken for granted rather than passionately defended. The society tailored its religious dimension to the worst features of Dutch character—superficiality and moral indifference. In its initial phase, the society possessed a Christian tint but lacked the power of a thoroughly Christian vision for society.[6] The current that was hostile to Christianity soon turned into a colorless natural religion, with the essence of Christianity diminished to a simple Mosaic injunction, "Love God above all, and your neighbor as yourself," diluted in meaning to "universal love of man, plus love of the Supreme Being." The practice of virtue guarantees salvation; there is no sense of sin, nor of guilt (46). The society's ideal is a colorless religion that satisfies everyone and offends no one; an impossible general Christianity that transcends all particular religious divisions, a confession beyond all confessions (40–42).

The goal here is to eliminate particular confessions from public life, all in the name of tolerance. The tactics that once were used to suppress dissent in our nation's public schools are now proposed for our religious lives as well. Forbid alternative schools by law, and eventually there won't be any left. Discourage all expression of religious differences and so bolster unity and tolerance. In this way all thought will be suppressed, all conflict eliminated. Blow out the spark of life, and the struggle of life is eliminated. Then we will have tolerance all right, but a tolerance of indifference, of superficiality, of complete loss of principles. This tolerance spreads further and further, establishing its moving boundaries but becoming fanatic in its zealotry the moment a form of faith dares raise its head. "Over against the dogma of the society—'tolerance through giving up religious distinctions'—I do not hesitate to posit another proposition: 'respect for the convictions of others precisely by remaining firm in one's own convictions'" (43–45).[7]

But our critique cannot stop here.[8] No longer content to replace particular confessions with a generic Christianity that borrowed heavily from so-called natural religion, the society has in recent years undergone a complete metamorphosis and become aggressively modernist in its convictions.

---

6. On p. 57, Kuyper speaks of this first period of the Society (roughly 1784–1830) as "tinted by Christianity" (lit. Christianly colored).
7. On p. 57 Kuyper refers to this second period of the Society's history (1830–67) as "colorless."
8. Kuyper now starts to discuss the Society's final period (1867 to the present), which he calls "de-Christianized" or what we might call "secular."

This triumph of modernism (that is, theological liberalism) parallels that which took place in the Dutch Reformed Church. The result is that though the society claims to be neutral when it comes to conflicts in the church, writers in its annual Almanac advocate, "as with a single stroke of the pen," a view of history that "denies the possibility of miracles, repudiates the Bible and its portrayal of Israel's history, and destroys the church's faith in Christ and the things to come" (68). The final proof of the society's modernism can be found in its opposition to the free-school movement. Instead of religious neutrality, the society has publicly come out in favor of a modernist interpretation of Christianity:

> A brand-new difference has arisen. Indeed, every existing difference is cast into the shadow and reduced to nothing by the arrival of this powerful, dominating difference. On the one side are all the Christian confessions and, on the other side, a new school of thought that in a tone of fierce defiance throws down the gauntlet against everything that has up to now been regarded as Christian. ... Here we encounter a problem with the Education Act. It mandates a generic Christianity upon which all confessions can build. The society seeks a generic Christianity that will be opposed by every confession. (75–76)

This is nothing less than an attempt to annex the national school and turn it into a propaganda machine for modernism: "This is unjust! That is the reason for the vehement agitation about the nation's schools. The conscience of the nation properly rises up against this injustice!" (76). Kuyper ends his address:

> I conclude by calling, in the name of our Lord, on all who confess Christ: Men and Brethren! Go out from a society that has declared war against everything that your soul considers holy. And to the extent that God has gifted you or provided resources, do not lend pen or word or money to such a society!
>
> Whoever denies me before men, I shall ...
>
> But why call to mind what pulses through the heart and conscience of every professing Christian? I will have achieved my goal if this argument contributes even a small part to making intrinsic dishonesty and utter lack of principle more hated by friend and foe alike.

TEACHING IMMORTALITY IN THE PUBLIC SCHOOL

TEXT INTRODUCTION

This three-point tract on teaching the immortality of the soul in Dutch public schools was one of Kuyper's first public forays into the Dutch school struggle, which offered resistance to the secularization that was taking place in the latter half of the nineteenth century.

The Second Chamber of the Dutch Parliament became embroiled in a controversy about immortality on December 14 and 15, 1869, during the debate on the education budget. Dutch public schools were mandated by the Elementary Education Act of 1857 to inculcate nonsectarian "Christian virtues" in their pupils. But what did this mandate mean?

In defending the education bill twelve years earlier, Minister J. J. L. van der Brugghen (1804–63) had stated: "I believe the mixed [common] school can be good, can even be Christian in the true sense of the word, without specific doctrines. In fact, I must go on and add: without use of the Bible." He explained: "A nation such as ours, shaped by Christianity, harbors a common treasure, namely that of a (more or less intellectually developed) Christian conscience, the awareness of which lives in every heart, even with great differences in intellectual views or doctrines. ... This then is the area where the mixed school gives instruction in Christian virtues." The minister's opponent, G. Groen van Prinsterer (1801–76), impugned this "cut-flower morality" by arguing that one cannot have the fruit without the trunk and the root: Christian virtues must be taught on the basis of belief in Christ. To this the minister replied that the state, the government, is not competent to teach in a positive Christian spirit. With the passage of the bill Groen van Prinsterer saw himself obliged to abandon his ideal of a Christian public school (with a local option of separating into a Protestant and a Catholic school). Henceforth he became a national leader in the promotion of free, nonstate schools with a right to equitable public funding. This was the cause that Kuyper championed throughout his career.

In the meantime, voices in the radical, secular press were stirring the pot of controversy. Wherever school inspectors connived at the use of the Bible in certain regions of the country, the liberal press was eager to alert Catholic authorities to this evasion of the law. By 1869 liberal members of Parliament raised the issue of teaching the immortality of the soul and insisted that it was a religious dogma and therefore forbidden in the state schools. Furthermore, they said, if this simply has to be taught, it must be taught with complete neutrality because "no one has ever proved immortality; some believe in it, others do not." When the minister of internal affairs was pressed in the Chamber to repudiate this position, he concurred with it instead.

This official clarification by a government minister evoked a storm of protest from conservative and Roman Catholic sources. As the discussion continued in the daily press, Kuyper joined the fray, and his response appeared in *De Heraut* and was published in pamphlet form a few months later.

A striking feature of this piece is the lengthy second part, where Kuyper explicitly rejects the doctrine of the soul's immortality. Kuyper's real target here is rationalistic deism, a form of natural religion, associated with Edward Lord Herbert of Cherbury (1583–1648). Deism rejected the need for special revelation but continued to affirm—because it was reasonable—belief in God, in humanity's duty to worship him, in virtue as the chief means of worshiping God, in the obligation to repent of sin, and in a final judgment with rewards and punishments after death, hence in the immortality of the soul.

Also noteworthy is evidence of Kuyper's early political sensibilities. A full decade before the appearance of the Antirevolutionary Party platform he was thinking about building bridges and forming coalitions, in this case with some members of the conservative party. The young Kuyper appeared committed to carrying on the lifelong efforts of his old mentor Groen van Prinsterer to recruit the better conservative voices from among the "great Protestant party" and to persuade them that the only hope for stemming the progress of secular liberalism (here called "radicalism") lay in joining the voices of the antirevolutionary movement.

Source: Kuyper, Abraham. *De leer der onsterfelijkheid en de staatsschool.* Amsterdam: H. De Hoogh, 1870. Reprint from *De Heraut*, Dec. 24, 1869. Abridged, annotated, and translated by John Bolt. Edited by Harry Van Dyke.

TEACHING IMMORTALITY IN THE PUBLIC SCHOOL

The debate about the doctrine of immortality in connection with the state school demands our closest attention. Several of our radical newspapers have contended, and the minister for internal affairs has officially confirmed, that the doctrine of the soul's immortality is forbidden in our state school. With this in mind we shall demonstrate the following:

1. The minister and the radical press are undeniably correct in their claims.
2. The alarm raised against this explanation has been rung with the wrong bell.
3. This sensational incident displays in the sharpest relief the moral decline of our national life.

I

In the first place, the minister and the radical press are undeniably correct in their claims; they have the law on their side. This situation is not to our liking, not at all. It contradicts our Christian outlook on life and what is sacred to thousands. However, the School Law of 1857 is clear, and it alone sorts out what kind of cargo may be brought into the public school. This has had the curious result that even material [in the curriculum] that meets with general approval can be declared contraband. All that is required is a suspicion that those who think differently might be offended. Thus, only those topics may be admitted which offend absolutely no one.

This is what the law requires and must require. A state school that opens its doors to all must be colorless; it has to be strictly neutral. Here different faiths cannot be sacrificed to each other. The state has determined that schools built by everyone's money and designed for all children must be inoffensive to all.

Whether such a school is even conceivable is beside the point. It is required by the School Law, and state schools must obey the law. To answer the question about teaching the doctrine of immortality we simply have to ask whether all people in our nation without exception agree on the matter.

Sadly, such an investigation quickly reveals that the doctrine of immortality is openly attacked in the daily press and other writings. The School Law is clear: the doctrine of immortality must remain outside the walls of our state schools. The only possible wiggle room remaining depends on whether the exclusion rule is local only or nationwide. If local, people who are offended in a particular school could cause material to be excluded in that school only. If nationwide, the presence of any dissent anywhere in the nation would result in general exclusion of the offending material in all schools. In light of the accepted interpretation in favor of the latter, we see no grounds for invoking the School Law against the position of the minister and his henchmen.

An appeal to article 23 of the law is of no avail. True, this article requires that instruction in the public schools must be serviceable to the nurture of "Christian and civic virtues." But is belief in immortality a "virtue"? For the Christian, of course, there is no other virtue, no other work of God, than belief, than faith. But if immortality is a virtue in that sense, then there is no greater virtue than faith in Christ.

You can be sure that faith in Christ in this sense is not what the School Law had in mind. The School Law has been in place for twelve years, and government officials have been clear that article 23 does not permit schools to preach faith in Christ. It thus follows that the article does not open the possibility of teaching [the "lesser" virtue, namely belief in] immortality.

Another argument, namely that eliminating the doctrine of immortality knocks the bottom out of all morality, is not compelling. In our opinion one is on better grounds by contending that removing Christ cuts off the root of the plant on which alone all true morality can flourish. When this contention is countered by the response that the state school concerns itself only with the fruit of the tree and not with the tree itself, nor with its root, then it is self-evident that the doctrine of immortality cannot be tolerated just because many believe that its denial undermines all morality.

In conclusion, we need to add this: even if the doctrine of immortality were taught in the state school, this sensitive topic would not be safe in the hands of the state schoolteachers. Even those who acknowledge the existence of an invisible world entertain the most divergent views on a life beyond this life. To see how true this is already in the case of Christians, we need only mention terms such as "purgatory," "the coming judgment," "the return of Christ," "the resurrection of the body," and "universal salvation."

Now then, if it is not possible to speak about immortality without letting one's private feelings shine through, it becomes clear what an enormous gamble it would be to put this weighty doctrine in the hands of state school-teachers. It is thus inherent in the issue itself that even to condone the teaching of immortality might well lead to propaganda for a "state eschatology" or an official "state doctrine regarding immortality."

From this one senses that an honest interpretation of the law, in the interest of parents themselves, should sooner lead to banning the teaching of immortality than to permit its free dissemination in the state school.

II

Accordingly, in the second place, we believe that we are correct in explaining that the alarms raised against the minister's clarification are being sounded with the wrong bell. We have in mind the conservative and Catholic press. We read them with gratitude because every cry of indignation against such a cold indifference to robbing people of the hope of immortality makes us rejoice and stirs our hearts. Those are the times when we sense how much warmer is the heartbeat of the conservatives than that of the radicals. And, absent the existence of our own daily press,[1] the conservative press has been of inestimable worth in joining our protest.

1. Kuyper's daily *De Standaard* did not appear for another two years.

Nonetheless, at the same time it does not speak the language of our hearts. It lacks discernment and fails to draw consequences. Christians can expect very little from conservatives. First, if one judges that all morality has the bottom knocked out from under it by banning the teaching of immortality and then, second, that the School Law forbids this essential part of education, then only one conclusion follows: oppose the state school and tolerate it only as a corrective.[2]

Second, we note a failure of discernment and a lack of foresight. Had the tenor of the School Law been recognized, the minister's pronouncement would not have come as a surprise but been accepted as logically inescapable. This should then have led to joining us in our indignation and confessing: "It is true then, after all, what you have repeatedly claimed: in the state school there is 'no Christ, no immortality, no God.' From this hour on, your struggle against the state school is our struggle."

But that's not what happened. Notice was taken of the minister's pronouncement, but no opposition was raised against the state school itself. Merely raising alarm against the minister and the radicals fails to grasp that the flame which has flared up can only be extinguished by raising alarm against the School Law itself. The conservative attack on the radicals especially pains Christians. The conservatives had helped the radicals to remove Christ from the national public schools;[3] they concurred with the decision to silence all references to Christ's resurrection, on which all hope of immortality depends.

When we asserted that it was impossible to inculcate virtue as long as the Source of all virtue is barred, the conservatives took the side of the radicals against us and just stood by while everything that is holy to Christians, everything that distinguishes Christianity from what is not Christianity, was being removed from the state school. Keeping Christ out of the state school was just fine. But now, when the attack is directed not against Christianity but against the rationalistic triad of "God, virtue, and

2. "As a corrective," that is, as a government remedy when private initiative in establishing schools is wanting. In keeping with this conclusion, the Christian school movement before long adopted the slogan "The free school the rule, the government school the exception."
3. The Education Act of 1857 passed Parliament when conservative members voted in the majority for a bill that differed only slightly from what the liberals had long proposed.

immortality," now they are aroused, rush to the defense, and acknowledge that the moral character of the nation is at stake.

We need to take careful note of this. Ever since the conclusion of the previous century there have been two religious orientations in the national church. One proceeds from Christ and confesses the gospel anchored in Christ and expressed in twelve articles known as the Apostles' Creed. The other is not from Christ but from rationalistic philosophy with its Credo of three articles: "God, virtue, and immortality." The ultimate concern of the former is Christ and the gospel; of the latter, immortality.

The current public polemics against the minister are not on behalf of those who confess Christ and the gospel. This is no secret. What the protesters find especially offensive is that a doctrine is banned which is confessed also by Jews, Buddhists, Muslims, and modernist theologians. They are indignant because immortality has been believed throughout history by all people and is thus part of humanity's "natural religion." As long as the opposition was against "revealed religion" today's protesters were silent; but they have girded on their swords to defend natural religion. Can't they see why this makes us glad and sad at the same time?

We are glad because natural religion is better than no religion at all. We are sad because it is now crystal clear that the great Protestant party was willing to give up on revealed religion and even now, when it is apparent that it will also lose natural religion, is unwilling to turn back from the error of its ways. For us to identify the state school as a synonym for the "religionless school" can no longer be dismissed as hateful.[4]

Our protesters seem committed to fighting for immortality as the one crucial issue. But Christians should realize that it is the rationalists, not us, who are being deprived of the doctrine of immortality. For "immortality of the soul" is not an expression that is warranted by the gospel. The word immortality (in Greek, *athanasie*) is found in only two places in the Bible. In the one place (1 Cor 15:53) we are told that our body "must put on" immortality, and in the other place (1 Tim 6:16) that God alone has immortality. "Immortal" is that which cannot die, and the gospel teaches us that our souls are dead until renewed by the life of Christ. The Psalms do not speak of immortality (though some of our hymns do), and it is not confessed in the

4. The indictment of the religiously neutral public schools as "a-theistic" or "religionless" was first leveled by Groen van Prinsterer and taken over by Kuyper, who was angrily criticized for it by the "ethical-irenic" leaders in church and society.

Apostles' Creed. Though our confessions speak of "becoming immortal," they do not have in mind what is ordinarily understood by immortality. What rationalists call "immortality" Christians speak of as "eternal life." Eternal life! That is what Scripture teaches and to which our confessions testify; that is our joyful confession.[5]

Immortality of the soul is an unscriptural notion because it makes a false separation between body and soul, leading inevitably to a denial of the bodily resurrection at the last day and encouraging all those false ideas about life after death that are current today. It is unscriptural because it takes no account of the fact of sin, which results in spiritual death. So what is gained by teaching immortality in our schools without also teaching about the last judgment? And if one concedes that the idea of judgment is more important for morality than the idea of immortality, we then ask whether there is any benefit in teaching about a final judgment without reference to the atoning work of Christ. If the doctrine of the last judgment is separated from Christ's atoning work, it does not produce virtue but despair.

Christianity teaches that longing for God is the highest human good. The notion of immortality, by itself, leads humans to seek themselves as the highest good. We cannot remain silent when we see how thousands upon thousands kept silent when it was a question of depriving our nation's children of knowing the glorious Christ, who is eternal life in its fullness, and who then arm themselves to defend the barren, vapid notion of immortality. Eternal life, final judgment, resurrection of the body, and eternal misery are links that belong together on a single chain that cannot be broken.

But the chain was broken, link by link, and each link was removed from the state school, one by one. First the resurrection of the body, then eternal misery, then the last judgment, and finally eternal life—all turned away at the door of our schools. And now that loss is supposed to be made good by a cold, vague, lame idea of immortality.

We object to this and call on all who opposed the minister on behalf of natural religion to join us in our struggle to acknowledge the Christ. Join us as it becomes more and more apparent what Burke, Stahl, Guizot, and Groen have repeatedly told us, namely that there are only two life-principles:

5. See Belgic Confession, Arts. 19 and 37; see also Heidelberg Catechism, Q&A 57.

Christ, or the ideas of the French Revolution.[6] "Unbelief and revolution" are one.

From the hearts of the conservatives we regularly pick up tones that ring well in our ears. While the marble cold of the radicals chills us and makes us shiver, conservative voices exude a warmth that wishes us well. On occasion we read in their press and hear from their lips words that are (almost) ours. Why then do they not join our side? The radicals have one principle: the Revolution of 1789. We also have our principle: the Christ. But the conservatives have to live without a principle. Why not accept ours? Perhaps not all conservatives would be willing, but why do those men not join our side who regularly indicate that they want to do so? Surely this debate about immortality ought to have made it clear to conservatives that preserving their hegemony can only benefit rationalism, not Christianity. If rationalism wins out, the result will be a School Law that leaves room for "God, virtue, and immortality" but not for the Christ.

Therefore, though it is under protest, in this conflict we accept conservatives as allies, gladly acknowledging that our hearts are closer to theirs than they are to the radicals. At the same time we are also convinced that our shared goal of "maintaining faith in eternal life" will be better accomplished by facing the consequences of radicalism than by supporting rationalism.

The end result of radicalism will be to destroy the state school. Then, instead of including the tongue-in-cheek notion of immortality, with a wink to us Christians, Christian schools will be free to teach our nation's children the full gospel of eternal life, the last judgment, and the bodily resurrection. Upholding rationalism in order to battle radicalism leaves the state school invincible and after a long struggle would mean the death of our Christian schools. We do not understand how Roman Catholics could take the side of the conservatives. Even the Catholic Catechism does not set forth the notion of immortality that is under discussion.

III

In conclusion, our final observation: this sensational incident displays in the sharpest relief the moral decline of our national life. An esteemed pastor in our church said the other day: it is enough to make one weep that tens

6. Edmund Burke (1729–97), Julius Stahl (1802–61), François Guizot (1787–1874), and Groen van Prinsterer are often identified by Kuyper as being intellectual forebears and founders of the antirevolutionary movement.

of thousands of parents do not pull their children out of the state school in response to the minister.

And we add: It is more than enough to make one weep

- when a minister of the Crown, the moment he was able to see the immense implication of the School Law, did not immediately give his word that the School Law would not stay on the books any longer;
- when fifty representatives of the nation heard the minister's words, saw the frightful implication of the School Law and, in spite of this, continued to support it;
- when the powerful organs of the national press, those pages that govern the thoughts of our people, reported the minister's words with icy indifference as though their implications were nothing more than a tax law, acting instead as cheerleaders for a School Law which they extol, in spite of the bitter fruit it has produced, as the safeguard of our nation;
- when there still are people among our spiritual kin who confess the name of Christ yet continue to defend such a School Law and then reprimand you when you want to tear off the label "Christian" from the state school.[7]

No, we take nothing back from our earlier laments about the barrenness of the notion of immortality. But now that our nation has been dragged from the glorious heights of revealed religion down to the arid plains of natural religion and the thin atmosphere of rationalism, it is the trinity of "God, virtue, and immortality" that has automatically become the thermometer for measuring the temperature of our national life.

7. Kuyper may be thinking here of an incident the previous year when in the discussion following his address "The Appeal to the Nation's Conscience" (this volume, pp. 313), he said that the official interpretation of the phrase "Christian virtues" in the mandate of the state school was the product of a non-Christian concept of the state that was "satanic" and that the friends of Christian schools therefore proposed to stop the widespread false reliance on the phrase by having it scrapped from the Education Act. Thereupon his colleague in the church of Utrecht, the Rev. Dr. Nicolaas Beets (1814–1903), was horrified by what was being proposed and commented that there was something "demonic" about it.

And now even that natural religion has been canceled. However, that cancellation does not signal a climb upward, back to revealed religion, but on the contrary, a further and deeper sinking into the abyss of spiritual death. Now that even those elements still permitted by rationalism have been obliterated, our people have been cast into the arms of materialism. The burial of the notion of immortality is not accompanied by a joyful return of the rich doctrine of "eternal life" but by a dismissal of the entire unseen world and of everything that elevates the human heart.

That is what our people have witnessed. They have been told this to their face. Yet no cry, "To arms!" was heard throughout the land. For a long time the state school was a veiled image for our people—its essence hidden, its true visage invisible. It just stood there, covered by a garment in which the misleading terms of "toleration" and "Christian virtues" were woven with shiny gold thread. Misled by appearances, our people did not believe what some trustworthy individuals told them about the heinous form that would become apparent as soon as the veil fell off and the garment was removed. In the meantime, they had grown to love the state school and became accustomed to it as an integral part of our national life.

And now, it is finally clear at last that everything said about the school understates the appalling truth now revealed. The mask is finally thrown off, and the school is displayed in all its naked barrenness. The dissembling about faith is gone and has been replaced with active efforts to "Silence God," and "eternal life." Yet they still dare to call out to our people: "You must send your children to me, you will entrust to me your baptized sons and daughters, although the name of Christ may not be heard within our walls and no talk about God and immortality will be permitted." And the Dutch nation as a whole is silent while thousands and tens of thousands send their children. There is still present an unholy desire to fight for the state school as one does for one's idol.

Where are we headed ... ?

Do you not sense that going down this path will mean the end of your "immortality as a nation"?

PART TWO

CHRISTIAN EDUCATION AND ITS COUNTERFEITS

GOVERNMENT FUNDING OR CITIZEN INITIATIVE?

TEXT INTRODUCTION

Confusion continued to reign in the Netherlands well into the 1880s over the religiously neutral government schools. Were they useless for Christian parents, or were they "Christian enough"?

The Elementary Education Act of 1857 mandated the common public school to provide "instruction in Christian and civic virtues" but *without the Bible* or Christian doctrine, to avoid giving offense. When it passed Parliament after heated debates, it dashed the hopes of antirevolutionaries under the leadership of Groen van Prinsterer (1801–76) for a public education system separated out into Reformed and Roman Catholic schools in keeping with local conditions, each type of school to enjoy equal support from the public treasury. In the years following 1857, the idea of free, privately sponsored schools had taken hold and become the preferred solution for parents who had conscientious objections to using the common school and who wished to send their children instead to schools "with the Bible."

Now, in 1885, the antirevolutionary biweekly paper *De Banier* came with a proposal to divide the public school into a variety of state-funded schools that would reflect different religious persuasions.

Kuyper at this time was a staunch defender of free, nongovernment schools, the kind that more and more Christians had begun to establish after 1857, often at significant financial sacrifice. He realized that the proposal would be tempting to financially hard-pressed parents, but that it was a threat to the continuation of free Christian schools and to the self-help ethos that supported these private initiatives, including the first fledgling institutions at the secondary and tertiary levels of education. He combated the proposal strenuously in a series of three articles in *The Standard*.

Source: *De Standaard*, March 23, 27, and April 13, 1885. Translated, abridged, and annotated by Harry Van Dyke.

GOVERNMENT FUNDING OR CITIZEN INITIATIVE?

THE DEMISE OF THE FREE CHRISTIAN SCHOOL

The demise of free Christian schools, which have lately begun to flourish thanks to our tireless efforts, has become the stated aim, not just of the liberals, but also of fellow Christians.

Year after year we have warned that *De Banier* is entering on a path that someday must lead away from our party. That day seems to have arrived.

To be sure, *De Banier* appreciates Christian education. It does not support religious neutrality and respects the rights of parents. On all these points it sides with us.

However, after our party had held out for the parity system but consciously abandoned it in 1856,[1] replacing it with a system of free schools, *De Banier* now advises us to retrace our steps and again seek the public trough. The only difference with 1856 is that at that time parents would have had only two choices, whereas *De Banier* would like to see a great many options under a single public system. The various options available in any locality would be decided by a committee composed of parents. Here is how the editor describes it:

> At the present time no one can seriously demand that the quality of elementary education be set by the parents. The majority of parents have had little education themselves and as a rule are content with instruction in the three R's, though some might want a bit of language and others some history. But the present system needs an overhaul. Apart from noticeable bias and partiality at the official examinations against Christians seeking their teacher's certificate, an even greater grief is the legal requirement of maintaining religious neutrality in the public school. That is an impossibility and should no longer be required. Instead, the opposite should be instituted: teachers should be allowed to teach according to their religious (and political) convictions.
>
> But, some will ask, would that not deliver the schools up to teachers who are oriented to modernist theology and who cannot help but teach in that vein? Indeed it would; but is that not exactly what is happening quietly at the moment?
>
> However, the situation would greatly improve if one other measure were instituted: namely, to allow the public school to be separated out into variously oriented schools in keeping with local conditions. For example, when the number of pupils increases, the school should not be expanded with a larger facility and more teachers, but instead the number of schools should increase, each under a headmaster of a particular persuasion, who could be assisted by like-minded teachers if necessary. Nominations would be made by the parents whose children attend that school. Appointing a headmaster to fill a

---

1. Kuyper must mean 1857.

> vacancy would be done by a committee chosen by the parents and composed of people who meet certain legal requirements of fitness. ...
>
> In many, very many, localities, two—or even three or four—elementary schools could exist: two schools in places with 600 residents, three for 1,000 residents. Before long the variety of schools would exhibit a catalog of the religious persuasions in the land. In places where all parents are either orthodox or modernist, all schools would have either an orthodox or a modernist headmaster; but where the population is divided over both persuasions, there the schools would be separated. If the state and the municipality then had all schools share equally in public funding, the distinction between government schools and Christian schools would, after a suitable period of transition, disappear. The schools would all be public schools, but none would be a religiously neutral government school. Neutrality will have been replaced by the free expression of religious persuasions. We will have a variety of national schools that exemplify the religious diversity of our nation.

Let me add here that several ethical-irenical spokesmen[2] have expressed their sympathy with this proposal.

People are trying ever so hard to devise a solution to the schools question that will be acceptable also to the liberals, and they now think they have found it by proposing that the state remain the educator, even become the sole master in the world of education, on condition that parents will be allowed to nominate the headmaster depending on his religious persuasion.

For the editor of *De Banier*, we are convinced, this plan is the mature fruit of a long-cherished conviction. For many who now take his side, their sympathy for this idea is rooted in aversion to the Free University. They realize that in the long run the principle espoused by the Antirevolutionary

2. The "ethical-irenicals" were a loose grouping of opinion makers in the country, chiefly pastors and theologians, who favored national unity over divisive politics and who worked for restoring orthodoxy in the national church "medicinally" rather than "juridically" by pure preaching of the gospel instead of resorting to the ecclesiastical courts.

Party demands breaking with the state universities, government gymnasia, and municipal high schools.

Higher, secondary, and elementary education certainly differ in method and purpose, yet are on a par as far as religious principle is concerned. Hence before long every proponent of state education at the higher and secondary level will also favor it at the elementary level. And inversely, every opponent of state education at the elementary level at long last will reject it also at the higher and secondary level.

One can halt between two opinions for a long time. One can entangle oneself and one's followers in half-truths for a very long time. But in the end the logic of a principle will have its way. There is no question that as soon as the present confusion subsides, just one contrast will remain between two groups based on principle.

On the one hand, the group of those who seek safety in citizen initiative, but who then also will carry this through along the whole range of higher, secondary, and elementary education.

And on the other hand, the group of those who prefer to lean on the state, but who then also will once again wish to carry the principle now applied to universities and gymnasia over to the elementary school.

That is the direction things will take.

They who pin their hopes on state universities and neutral gymnasia are compelled—willy-nilly and gradually, yet on principle—to turn against the free elementary school.

Those on the other hand who on principle refuse to surrender the free elementary school cannot but gradually arrive at the conviction that they are also called to establish free gymnasia and free universities.

We are not saying that the latter are obliged to support the Christian gymnasium in Zetten and the Free University in Amsterdam. That is not the issue here. But we do maintain that the principled and consistent proponents of the free elementary school will be compelled in the end also to abandon the government gymnasium and the state university.

Otherwise—let people drum this into their heads—the free elementary school before long will be finished.

If the idea of *De Banier* were realized and its proposal became law, within three years all free Christian schools would in due course have been changed into public schools. After all, the idea is that by becoming government schools our free Christian schools would all of a sudden be rid of all financial burdens and be fully funded by the state without losing their right to preach Christ. And it stands to reason that it would be almost superhuman if our free schools would be able to resist such a tempting arrangement.

All of a sudden free of all burdens! No more financial worries! And above all, as state schools sharing in the esteem of the public school! With one stroke of the pen, gone will be all burdens, worries, and slander and abuse.

You can depend on it, well-nigh all our Christian schools would succumb to the temptation.

If it is the object of the unbelieving state once and for all, with a single stroke of the pen, to break and destroy the fruit of all our exertions thus far, then truly, it can do no better than to adopt this plan of *De Banier* without benefit of inventory. It would undermine the Christian influence and at the same time sanction blatant propaganda for the crudest unbelief, to lead our nation altogether away from Christ.

Of course that is not the intention of Rev. Tinholt.[3]

On the contrary, his sincere intention and his definite expectation, we are happy to assume, is that this would mean gain for the honor of Christ.

But for that very reason our warning has to be all the more solemn.

If this became law and the state set up this trap, luring us to enter it, our only salvation would be if our entire Christian leadership called out to our people: "Do not kneel before that Mammon!"

But when a Christian pastor, as editor of *De Banier* and in league with many ethical-irenic pastors, tells our people that entering this trap is a demand of higher wisdom, then of course our schools are finished.

Then it will not take three years before our energy is broken, our spontaneity paralyzed, our love of liberty extinguished. And seduced by the disastrous state trough, one private school board after another will allow its schools to be transferred to the public system, until at last not one of our free Christian schools will be found in the land.

It will again be solely the state, solely the government, solely the national education department and the local mayors, that will rule the domain of education. Worse, there will be overt preaching of unbelief in by far the

---

3. Rev. Lambert Tinholt (1825–86) was a child of the *Réveil*, an admirer of Groen van Prinsterer, and a defender of "Christian-historical principles." His many publications include "The Supernatural and the Laws of Nature," a paper in the German language read at the meeting of the Evangelical Alliance held in Amsterdam in 1867. He defended himself and his proposal against Kuyper in a brochure of 130 pages titled *Een Twistappel en zijne wegruiming; een voorslag tot oplossing der onderwijs-kwestie, tegen bestrijding verdedigd* (Utrecht: C. H. E. Breijer, 1885).

majority of schools in the country. And it will be accompanied by an ever-diminishing, flagging, failing level of energy and enthusiasm in our nation!

Poor Groen van Prinsterer, is this what you tortured yourself with your whole life long, that your followers could voluntarily surrender what was gained with so much sacrifice?

THE AMBUSH

The free Christian school is being lured into an ambush.

It was by no means the intention of the editor of *De Banier*, but his proposal amounts to a snare in which the free Christian school will soon be strangled.

In a friendly opponent one may never suppose even a shadow of evil design, hence we readily believe that none of the supporters of the proposal ever suspected that it amounts to an ambush, a snare, a trap. Rather, we assume that they in perfect good faith believe that the future of our Christian schools is best safeguarded by this measure.

But like everyone else, they too are subject to influences.

They wish to go back to leaning on the state. Begging for private funds tires them out too much. And they find public recognition more attractive. We noticed that in the case of higher education. When a free association establishes and maintains a privately funded university and on its own authority appoints men such as Rutgers, Woltjer, and Lohman to chairs in theology, letters, and law, they find little that is attractive in that. But when a minister of the Crown with the country's money appoints a totally unknown person to a chair in one of those faculties, they think it is mouth-watering privilege. To have been appointed by the Crown, to be entered into the official corps of professors, to receive one's salary from the public treasury, and to be assured of one's pension—all that is attractive and prestigious.[4] But if it is done through a private body, by free citizens, with pennies bathed in love, then that is not to their liking.

The Free University especially has brought this view to light. To the ethical-irenical leaders, the fact that elementary school teachers were a marginalized group didn't seem to matter in the past. So long as that situation would remain limited, they thought the world of the free school.

4. Kuyper may be alluding here to the appointment in 1874 at the State University of Utrecht of the Rev. Dr. Nicolaas Beets (1814–1903), a theologian, man of letters, and a leader of the ethical-irenicals.

But now that they might have to make the move themselves to private initiative, their old sympathy for public recognition awakens and their eyes turn again to the state trough and state meddling. We are not saying this about them personally, but about their system. They cling to their salaries in the national church. They stand by the state universities, detest the Free University, and decline to establish their own free universities. That the Christian school is a venture of private initiative is now felt as an inconvenient inconsistency.

Indeed, their stance is untenable.

There is a fork in the road here. The choice is between state meddling or citizen initiative. We choose the latter; it is the position of the Antirevolutionary Party. Their choice is for state meddling: in the church, in higher and secondary education, and now also in elementary education.

Oh, if only Groen van Prinsterer were still alive!

No wonder the liberals are already clapping their hands! Bravo! That's how you orthodox will break your own energy and enthusiasm.

Already other voices from among us are venting proposals similar to that of *De Banier*.

The liberals are right!

If this bad idea were ever realized, in three years' time our free Christian schools would be done for.

This is irrefutable, and *De Banier* with its usual candor has admitted as much. For if every free Christian school, simply by allowing itself to be transferred to the list of government schools, is instantly rid of financial worries, is paid from the public coffers, and even guarantees pensions to its teachers, without having its freedom in the least curtailed to preach the Lord Jesus—what school and what teacher would still be willing to make sacrifices for free and independent education?

That would be impossible.

That would be psychologically inconceivable.

There is no doubt that if this system were adopted, the very next day 90 percent of our schools would move over, bag and baggage, to the state trough. That is to say, in one stroke virtually all our schools with the Bible would fold as independent schools and turn into government schools.

"But," *De Banier* will ask, "what's so bad about that? Also in the case of the primary school, our struggle was a struggle for Christ, was it not, and not for some formal freedom. So why the alarm? Let the state take care of the whole of primary education, and pay for the whole of primary education, so long as the children come to the Lord Jesus Christ. In fact, if the Lord Jesus is preached with government sanction it will be extra attractive!"

That sounds good. That even sounds so pious that many run the danger of falling for it. The snare lies in that reference to preaching Christ. Therefore, for now we submit the following counterarguments to the supporters of the proposal:

1. At the university level you never showed any concern about the honor of Christ.

2. Your right to preach Christ in your government school would be bought with the price of allowing the crudest atheist to preach his godless creed in all the other government schools, at public expense, under the auspices of the government.

3. The very fact, brothers, that you were forced to erect and support your own school, to train teachers and sacrifice money for it, is precisely what made you grow in strength—while the liberals, who had only to eat from the state trough, diminished in strength. The practical school struggle, if nothing else, spurred on your national strength and made you what you are! Remove that spur, so that you no longer have anything to erect and support and sacrifice for, and you will sink back into your old lethargy, you will lose your pith and your resilience, and within ten years you will stand in the forgotten corner where you used to stand.

4. Once your strength is broken, your free organizations destroyed, and the desire to lean again on the state rekindled, Christians will soon have nothing to say anymore. The liberals will once again dominate the entire country, and not you but the liberal state will be the boss in your school. And finally,

5. When things have lasted long enough so that the liberal senses "the Christians won't offer any resistance anymore," then you can be sure that a small amendment to the law will be railroaded through Parliament, stipulating that the freedom to preach Christ will be taken away again.

Such will be the sad course of events.

Once we surrender our weapons and leave our trenches to enter the open field, you will find out how quickly they will "roll us up."

That's why we issue this warning, before it is too late.

This proposal, however well intentioned, comes down to this, that Groen's work, our party, our efforts and sacrifices will all be wiped out with a single stroke of the pen.

Know this well, brothers: if you take this lethal step and strike at the heart of the free school and the free church in the free state, we are finished.

THE FATAL PROPOSAL

The proposal of *De Banier* is a stumbling block that must not be allowed to lie in the way but must be removed.

Our intention is not to be hard on *De Banier*, let alone to say something nasty to its skillful and respectable editor. Our arrows were not directed at him or his paper, as our previous two articles have made abundantly clear. Our sole target is his proposal. Nothing more. But then the proposal in its full fatal consequence.

The proposal could be ignored if it were merely the hobbyhorse of one man, the monomania of one editor. But it had to be tackled the moment a small group of men declared themselves in favor of it and the [liberal] opposition joined that chorus. The editor whetted the sword, but others are now preparing to use it.

There is no question here of misunderstanding. The proposal is clear. We all know that it concedes virtually everything. It allows that you divide the children according to the choice of the parents; it admits that in the school of your children Christ will be honored without hindrance; it grants that all schools in the land will charge tuition fees;[5] it concedes that the choice of the parents will determine the choice of the teacher. On all these points the proposal is excellent—except that all schools will again be government schools and within two years all your free Christian schools will be administered by the authorities.

5. That is, no unfair competition, where private schools need to levy tuition fees while public schools are free of charge because they are funded from the public purse.

That is the fine point on which everything hinges, the pivot on which everything turns. That is the dead fly that spoils the entire ointment.[6]

Never mind if *De Banier* responds by painting the benefits of its proposal even bigger and brighter; it will leave us perfectly cold. We hold it to account on only one point: Will the school of its proposal be under the authority of the state, yes or no?

For whether I say that you may run your school as freely as you like, and I will hardly ever impose the slightest bit of my supremacy—the question is and remains: Whose flag will be flying at the top? Who ultimately will be in charge? Who in the end will be the boss of the show? Who will, now and in the future, have the right to draw up regulations for the school? Whose prerogative will it be to say: this is how things will have to be done!

Whichever way you put it, it is incontrovertible that the school which this fatal proposal will call into being, and in which all our free Christian schools will be swallowed up, will be a school under the banner of the state. Parents will have a say in it, but only so long as the state permits. The school that is envisioned will be, as far as its facilities and furnishings are concerned, the property of the government; it will be regulated at the pleasure of the government, and it will lack all sphere sovereignty.

In our free Christian schools we ourselves are sovereign. No one can tell us what to do. We are lord and master there. If the government should ever dare to intervene, it will be an injustice and we will challenge it in the courts.

But if this fatal proposal goes through, you will at first be treated ever so politely and ever so obligingly. The new arrangement will be made as free and comfortable for you as possible. No one will cross you. Your shackles will be set with polished rubies, and the lock on your cell will be of pure gold.

But if sooner or later the question should arise who has the final say in the school and you start acting like free Christian men, you will politely but quickly be brought down to earth and made aware that you are mistaken, that your freedom is over, and that you have renounced your sovereignty within your own proper sphere.

Like Esau, you will have sold your birthright for a mess of pottage.

That's how things will turn out once your private organizations are broken up, your enthusiasm extinguished, your habit of giving unlearned, and

6. Kuyper here reverses the image used by Jan Kappeyne van de Coppello (1822–95), a fierce opponent of orthodox Christianity, to describe the recalcitrant antirevolutionaries.

so your national strength broken. The noose on your head will quietly slide down over your neck and be drawn tight, until you suffocate.

The entire Antirevolutionary Party should be deeply concerned. For realize this well: implicit in this fatal proposal is a public policy, a political direction, and a political principle.

What do you want, brothers? A government as in France, one that does everything for you and so paralyzes your spontaneity, one that breaks your private initiatives and so snuffs your spirit of liberty? If so, follow the way of *De Banier* and its adherents; their course is direct, their idea is consistent: they want to give all education—higher, secondary, primary—back to the state. But if not, if you realize that this course collides with the spirit of free citizens, if you oppose state meddling with citizen initiative and public funding with voluntarism, and if you refuse to entrust the honor of the name of Christ to a state that does not confess him—then make sure that you are not seduced by the pernicious course of *De Banier* and its endorsers.

Bear in mind that its fatal proposal is up against the following considerations:

1. Our party's program states that the government should not be operating schools as a rule but only by way of exception, as a substitute or emergency measure, when parents default on their duty to rear their children. As well, it states that the government school should never give instruction in spiritual principles. — The proposal recommends the exact opposite.

2. The proposal, if the new arrangement goes wrong, will put our free schools in the position of being unable to go back to the situation that obtains at present.

3. The proposal implicitly opens government schools to abuse of Christ, to propaganda for atheism. Factually it means that in most schools atheism will have public license while only a small minority of schools will honor the Lord.

4. The proposal turns the primary public school into a kingdom divided against itself, since it allows itself to be opposed on principle within its own bosom.

5. The proposal will bring about that in every secondary and tertiary school run by the state, the propaganda for unbelief will

go forward at an even more dreadful and reckless intensity, because the false principle will be established irrevocably.

6. The proposal will all but destroy the immeasurable strength that was activated thus far by our people's sacrificial giving, and our current works of mercy will degrade into paying off a debt imposed on us.[7]

7. The proposal will increase the national budget by several millions, since public ventures are always more expensive than private ones.

8. The proposal will entrench the principle that the state will again have the initiative in church, school, and society, and so will sound the death knell for our entire antirevolutionary movement. The only choice will be between liberal and conservative policies, while the distinctive voice of the gospel will permanently retreat from politics.

This is no time to dawdle.

It is time to take action.

If you want to go the way of *De Banier*, then say so. Then we will bow out and try to organize on the old foundations a new Antirevolutionary Party in the land.

But if that is not the way you want to go, then be on guard against the incursion of a false principle.

The editor of *De Banier* means well. We do not doubt it. But his proposal is fatal.

7. That is, voluntary charitable giving will be replaced by welfare payments funded through taxes.

IRON AND CLAY

TEXT INTRODUCTION

The venture of a free Reformed university was for Kuyper of the same order as the battle for church reform. Both areas struggled with the indifference or else the passiveness of those who in his opinion knew better. The occasion of this address was the annual prayer service on the eve of the membership meeting of the Association for Higher Education on Reformed Principles.

In this lengthy address, intended to prepare his audience for earnest prayer for the Free University, Kuyper identified the same error in the academy that was contaminating the national church, namely the willingness to "mix iron and clay"—that is, to allow things to stay together that did not belong together. In the church it was creeping modernism next to orthodoxy; in the academy it was the secularization of higher learning alongside personal piety. He based his indignation about this unholy mingling on the words in Daniel 2:43: "They shall not cleave one to another, even as iron is not mixed with clay" (KJV).

In his impassioned peroration Kuyper outdid himself in laying the burden of the Free University on the hearts of those who had come out for the prayer service. As he prepared to lead in prayer, he asked his audience to join him in "storming the gates of heaven."

Following the opening paragraph, the translation picks up the text after page 10, after the speaker had assured his audience that praying for the Free University was not sinful just because prayers for their university, which represented a schism in the world of higher education, might aid and abet schism in the church (as nonsympathizers had charged).

Source: Kuyper, Abraham. *Ijzer en leem: rede ter inleiding op het gebed voor de eenige hoogeschool hier te lande, die op Gods woord gegrond staat.* Amsterdam: J. H. Kruyt, 1885. Pp. 11–15, 18–31. Translated by Nelson D. Kloosterman and Harry Van Dyke.

IRON AND CLAY

INTRODUCTORY ADDRESS AT THE PRAYER SERVICE FOR THE ONLY UNIVERSITY IN THIS NATION THAT STANDS ON THE FOUNDATION OF GOD'S WORD, JUNE 30, 1885

Esteemed Audience!

Our gathering at this hour is not a service of the Word, but solely to implore the Most High to bless the only university in this nation that is still based on Holy Scripture. I shall follow the laudable custom of taking a word from Scripture to indicate the main theme of what I should like to say in preparation of that prayer. To that end, allow me to refer to Daniel 2:43, to what is stated so firmly in that text about the incompatibility of iron and clay. We read there: "As you saw the iron mixed with soft clay, so they will mix with one another in marriage, but they will not hold together, just as iron does not mix with clay." I shall limit my remarks to those closing words: "even as iron is not mixed with clay," and leave the context for what it is since I am not called to exegete the word. I take from Daniel's lips only the fundamental idea of Scripture that also among men, things of a different kind cannot adhere, as little as iron and clay cannot permanently adhere. But in order that our help be in the name of the Lord as we closely examine this profound principle, may our communal prayer first be raised in the words of a psalm, so let us sing Psalm 65, the stanzas four and five:[1]

1. William Kuipers, 1931; William Helder, 1980/2009. ©2009, Standing Committee for

You are the hope of distant nations;
you by your strength and power
placed mountains on their firm foundations
and stilled the ocean's roar.
Those who make far-off lands their dwelling
all tremble at the sight;
both dawn and dusk, in praise excelling,
with joy acclaim your might.

Dear friends, the substance of all true religion consists in this, that God truly remain God and man never be anything other than a puny human being. Precisely because God created man in his image and summoned him to the most intimate and tender communion of spirits, we must carefully ensure that the being of a man and the being of God are always kept clearly separate. Every sin consists precisely in this, that people attempt in some way to intermingle those two beings, as when one attributes to God what belongs to man, or when man proceeds to sit in the seat of God. So an absolute boundary has been established, and that boundary naturally is manifest throughout creation by means of the golden rim surrounding the majesty of the Lord of lords. Because he is God, he consequently keeps his essence free from admixture with that of his creature. He is the Holy One!

So that man would be mindful of this line of separation, it has pleased God to reflect that line of separation in the fixed boundaries which he created between one creature and another. God created *kinds* of beings. He made a star to be altogether different from an angel; a stream very different from a lightning bolt; iron different from clay. So God's path does not run through the uniformity of chaos but through the rich diversity of life divided into kinds. Trees and plants were created "yielding seed according to their own kinds" [Gen 1:12]. In order that every being would have its own character and every kind its special nature, God the Lord worked by means of separating; what was initially intermingled he pulled apart; and he established for all things their boundary and limit. This explains the constantly repeated formula in the creation narrative: "And God separated" [Gen 1:4, 6, 7, 14, 18]. Separating light from darkness; separating the waters from the waters; separating the sea and the dry land. Always separating! Nothing must remain without order,

the Publication of the Book of Praise of the Canadian Reformed Churches. Used with permission.

all mixed together. Even within humanity there may not be any mixture of two kinds of life, which is why we do not find in Eve a duplicate of Adam, but another kind alongside Adam, as a helpmeet for him.

So it is established that God has engraved separations in all that is creaturely, as emblematic of that absolute separation that he maintains between the creature and himself. But with this we have not yet said enough. For he who established those separations also ordained connections. Creatures do not stand next to each other without connecting or touching. Rather, there must be connections; in such a way, however, that these connections might not be arbitrary and arise apart from God, but actually arise according to and by virtue of God's ordination. He who carved the boundaries also wove the bond that would fasten together what was separated. It would all be emblematic of his exalted command, both in the dividing and in the connecting. It was for God, who had separated all creatures, and not for the separated creature, to determine: "These may adhere but not those, this must be connected to that since they belong together, and this must remain foreign to that since they do not belong together." Man and woman shall cleave to each other, but not iron and clay. This is God's right, his ordinance, his law, which the psalmist praises: "I have seen a limit to all perfection, but your commandment is exceedingly broad" [Ps 119:96]. Here lies the glory of the divine harmonies. Out of Zion, the perfection of beauty, where in prophetic symbolism those separations and harmonies are restored, there God shines [see Ps 50:2]!

But things did not stay that way.

There is an altogether different world above, and in that higher world a break was introduced, a tear was made, a schism wrought, a revolt raised against God—and by means of that violent disruption of the boundaries and harmonies established by God, a power came into existence that God had not created—namely, the dreadful, terrible power of sin. The Evil One who had inspired that sin then invaded God's paradise and brought about a break within the heart of man, a break whereby he sought to mix together precisely what God had separated. "You, o creature, shall be like God!" was the slogan of this false mingling of God and man that caused the dreadful break between God and man. And then that tear, that break, that revolt was extended from the heart of man to all of creation, and the earth witnessed the deep sin that the creature broke asunder what God had joined together and mixed together what God had separated, thus positing a false law which directly contradicted God's exalted command.

And what did the Eternal One do? Does Scripture tell us that God acquiesced in that break, surrendered to that revolt, yielded to that false mingling? No, I tell you, but precisely the opposite: God the Lord set one break against another break, in order to check that ungodly mixing together. Grace arrived on the scene, but a grace that worked by means of separation and severance, by means of breaking and sifting, by means of election and conversion. For now the point was not only to disentangle again what God had separated, but also once for all to take whatever belonged to the Lord and separate it from that devilish quality that had penetrated the creature—namely, sin.

That is why God's law appears in polemical form: *Thou shalt not!* And it does so in two tables. The one is designed to keep apart what may not be mixed together—namely, the exaltedness of God and the arrogance of man. The other is designed to prevent separating what God had joined together by opposing murder, adultery, theft, and the like. Or stated more eloquently and spiritedly: over against Satan God placed the wonder of Immanuel, in order through him to separate what must be parted and to gather together what belongs together. And when Immanuel comes he tells us: "I have not come to bring peace, but a sword," and to set people against one another [see Matt 10:34–36]. And so at the foot of the cross the entire creation was split in two. Not gradually, but break against break: the chaff is separated from the grain, the iron from the clay, by intervening through miracles, above all by raising Jesus from the dead, and even now by having people be born again!

Not only this, but along the entire path leading to Immanuel, Scripture shows us a constant, restless separation, a breaking apart and a resistance to every false mingling. "With the seed of men"—that is, through the interconnection of families and clans—the false mingling constantly tried to assert itself, but the Lord allowed it no rest. Again and again, by means of his divine action and at his command, the clay had to be removed from the iron. No sooner had his brother's blood stained Cain's hand than he had to depart from Adam, just as after his fall Adam had to leave paradise when the cherubim flashed the sword of separation. And still the sons of Cain mingled again with the children of God, resulting in a dreadful outbreak of corruption—until in the flood God the Lord imposed his break on the entire world: he broke apart all continuity, he did not permit it to fester nor to run its course, but he created something new. He brought about the fearsome separation between Noah and his generation, a division and a schism through the entire human race, experienced with mortal fear by God knows how many thousands of souls! That separation continued onward and forward: in Noah's family between Shem and Ham; at the tower of Babel between all the nations; in Shem's offspring by tearing Abram from his father's house; in Abraham's own family by means of the break between Lot and himself, between Isaac and Ishmael, between Esau and Jacob; until long after Jacob's death, his posterity once again threatened to mingle with the people of Egypt. But that mingling too was stopped when the Lord pulled them out by means of a break, and settled them in Canaan.

Now for the first time, separation, if need be through a break, truly became a life-principle when God introduced it in this awesome command: "Do not mix together with those nations, but exterminate them, and in the bosom of your own people make division and separation and oppose false mixing together, for I the Lord am the one who makes that separation between the holy and the unholy"—a command that was impressed on Israel as many as seven times: see Exodus 26:33; Leviticus 10:10; 11:47; 20:15; and Ezekiel 22:26; 42:20; and 44:23. Nothing levitically unclean was allowed to be mixed together with the holy. Indeed, among Israel, two kinds of seed in one field, and two kinds of thread used for the same garment, was an abomination to the Lord!

No matter how strongly the iron and the clay always sought to cleave to each other, they would not blend or merge. Phinehas [Num 25:7–13] and Gideon [Judg 6:25–27], Jesse's son [1 Sam 17:37] and Elijah [1 Kgs 18:21–40], time and again tore apart the falsely joined garment. Isaiah called back "to the teaching and to the testimony" every soul that would have perished through that mixing together [Isa 8:20]. Ezra drove out those gentiles who had again mixed together with the holy seed [Ezra 10:8–11]. When Jerusalem broke Jesus on Golgotha, God brought breaks on Jerusalem: he tore the curtain in the temple and left not one stone on another. When later in the church of the new covenant that false mixing together crept in, people were told: "If anyone does not obey what we say in this letter, take note of that person, and have nothing to do with him " [2 Thess 3:14]; "If anyone comes to you and does not bring this teaching, do not receive him into your house" [2 John 10]; and, "What accord has Christ with Belial?" [2 Cor 6:15]—until finally on Patmos the command is heard: "Come out of her, my people, lest you take part in her sins, lest you share in her plagues" [Rev 18:4].

And that is how this separation continues, if need be through breaks: *spiritually*, when the double-edged sword of the Word pierces to the dividing of soul and spirit [see Heb 4:12]; *physically*, when the scythe of death cuts down the stalks and body and soul are broken apart; and *cosmically*, when, at the call of the Bride, Christ himself returns, and everything that was mixed together is broken apart and the goats are forever separated from the sheep.

Thus, in Scripture all uncertainty is removed. The power that constantly seeks to mix things together is sin, and in opposition to that false mixing together, God the Lord firmly establishes the demand for separation, even when it has to be done by means of making a break.

God first established that demand in the law; then with miracles; continuing in regeneration; and most powerfully in the prophecy of the second coming. God, who is your Sovereign, establishes that demand not merely in what he does, but just as decisively in what he commands. He upholds that demand in the old covenant, and renews and intensifies it in the New Testament. For faith and unbelief, like fire and water, are two elements that cannot be paired together but exclude and nihilate each other. And no matter how firmly you press together clay with iron, your God ensures that they will not affix together; they will always break apart.

The address continues by recalling that not only in Scripture but also in history, unholy mingling is broken up. For example, said the speaker, Christianity broke up the world of pagan antiquity, and the Protestant Reformation broke up the Roman church. The same beneficial rupture—"always under lawful conditions"—occurred in the Low Countries when they broke with historical continuity and broke away from Spain. It occurred in America when it broke with the British yoke and then with the "even more shameful" yoke of slavery. It occurred in modern Germany when it broke with a divided federation to create a unified empire. All this was accomplished not through gradual transition but solely through rupture and separation. Kuyper continues:

But now, brothers and sisters, let us talk about those *lawful conditions*. For obviously, we do not commend every separation, and even less every break. On the contrary, neither separation nor break may ever exist except where it is the fruit of unconditional obedience to the King of all kings, the Lord of all lords.

Let us see, then, how this single powerful condition comes into existence in the diversity of life.

Family and state must then immediately be sharply separated from school and church. In each of these, to be sure, God is the only sovereign and supreme commander. But this authority does not function in every area in the same way. Family and state are physically binding; school and church are free corporations. You are placed in the family, and nobody can reverse the fact that you are born from that mother and that father; so too in our country where we must all dwell together, for a state cannot exist within the state. But this is not the case with school and church. I belong to a school by virtue of a spiritual conviction and voluntary membership, hence I am not breaking apart any essential bond nor have to relocate my residence if I bid farewell to a formerly beloved school and establish another. Even though the matter is different with a church because most are born in the church, nevertheless the church is the visible gathering together, not of all the family members nor of all your fellow countrymen, but very specifically of believing confessors, so that differences about the confession must ultimately require breaking with that particular church denomination.

From this it follows, with respect to authority, order, and unity, that in family and state all who are in these institutions belong together, and unless something contradicting God's word is commanded, every member has to follow the head of the family or the head of the state. This is why the father in his family and the ruler in the state have the right to command, and why a person has the right and duty to break away from these divinely ordained authorities if and only if a direct conflict arises between obedience to the original King above and obedience to the appointed rulers on earth who are subordinate to God. This is why all mutiny or revolution in family or state that refuses to submit to the appointed authority, not for God's sake but from arrogance, is cursed of God and ought to be opposed in the name of the Lord.

But this same argument in no way applies to the school of science and the church of Christ.

Not in the school, since people belong to no other school than the one of their choosing, and in the school the sovereignty of the Lord is exercised in no other than a direct manner, by means of the force of logic, love of truth, and sincerity of conscience. In the kingdom of science kings exist only figuratively. In the school of science no yoke may be placed on anyone's neck. Here, separating from historic institutions and breaking from the leading authorities is far from being a sin, but rather a duty as soon as in that school the gold of the truth that belongs to God is tarnished by false mixing together.

Nor may this rule be applied to the church, for the simple reason that sovereignty within the church has been granted to no man but has been placed undividedly on Christ Jesus. Now people in the church must continue to submit to the ordained authority so long as it is understood that such ordained authority is neither a pope nor a synod but only and exclusively Christ himself. To separate from Christ, to break away from Christ, that is the only possible revolution in the ecclesiastical sphere. As soon as people perceive, as in our case, that this mutiny has indeed broken out among the ecclesiastical authorities, then this places the faithful and loyal subjects of King Jesus before the grave question whether separation and breaking from such a mutinous organization is mandatory by virtue of their oath of loyalty to their only lawful King.

In the church of Christ "iron and clay," unlike "wheat and weeds," must never be allowed to continue in a mingled state. Weeds and wheat point to the *internal* harvest, to whether one is converted or not converted, and woe to anyone who has sought, contrary to Jesus' explicit instruction, to break apart this spiritual mixture already in the here and now. Jesus has reserved that for himself in the day of judgment. So hands off. But that is not what "iron and clay" refers to. This figurative language refers to what is *external*. One can mistake wheat for a weed, but not iron for clay. Accordingly, a person's public confession and his public walk have to be evaluated. One who confesses God's truth may not remain permanently mingled with one who rejects God's truth. Unless separation occurs through gradual detachment, ultimately separation through a break becomes obligatory.

Not as though—and you will of course understand this—the decision to do this is to be made in a hurry. Profound movements are always painstakingly prepared. Before he reaches that ultimate point, no true reformer will despise whatever can still be done, whatever can still be tried. But if at last every paved route has been exhausted and every conceivable means has been tried, and the issue comes down finally to a principled opposition between the authority of our King and God's word, and the presumptuous authority of sinful men and their words of mutiny, then I declare—and I would be disgracing my forefathers if anything different crossed my lips—then I declare that remaining together would be sinful and breaking apart is mandated by God's justice.

To be concrete: if the synod, claiming the highest legislative, judicial, and administrative authority, refuses to distance itself from that presumptuous title on behalf of King Jesus, and continues to refuse to recognize the royal authority of God's word as the law of the church, then it becomes the duty of the churches to end this revolution and, just as our fathers brought out the churches from living under the pope, to lead those same churches out from under this tyranny. That is how faithful sons would constrain their father if he had become insane. That is also how faithful believers will defy the synod if it does not surrender, and evict the imperious intruder from our ecclesiastical terrain—not out of any thirst for revolution,[2] but precisely so that the offensive mutiny that has gone on now for years may finally be stopped. ...

These then are the necessary conditions attached to the imperative principle. Or rather, this explains the principle that our fathers invariably paid homage to and knew how to act on, the same principle that was advocated by Luther and Zwingli, by Calvin and Beza, and in the writings of all our Godfearing theologians, jurists, and practitioners. It is the principle to which our country owes its glory, England its flourishing, and America its liberation. It is the principle from which Protestantism derived its origin, the Reformed faith its incisive character, Puritanism its piety, and our Calvinism its irresistible resilience. Or if you will, these are the very principles which today we know as the antirevolutionary principles, the principles of which Groen van Prinsterer scattered the precious seed and which, after Groen's decease, are so often sprinkled by our aged Elout[3] with such refreshing dew.

To those antirevolution principles our Free University owes its founding as well. Not as though it would try to influence state and church *directly*. That is not its calling. It has to leave those spheres alone. Our university is and must remain a school. It is called instead to press with cogent arguments in theology and jurisprudence, indeed in every discipline, for the necessity of this sound principle; it opposes the revolutionary, Roman

2. The prayer meeting was held in the Walloon Church of The Hague after the Reformed church of that city had denied the use of its main sanctuary because it feared schismatic activity and revolutionary agitation on the part of Kuyper and the friends of the Free University.
3. Pieter Jacob Elout van Soeterwoude (1805–93), longtime friend and ally of Groen van Prinsterer and cofounder of the Free University, was seventy-nine years old at this time and probably sitting in the audience.

Catholic, Passivist,[4] and pantheist influences which today seek to gain the upper hand, in order to advocate in a scientific manner the glory of our Protestant, more particularly of our Reformed, pedigree. …

In truth, friends, it is by no means redundant to be reminded of this compelling argument not to mix iron and clay. For each of these influences can only lead to the complete destruction of Protestantism, notably of its Reformed branch.

Allow me to show you this by means of a brief summary of the four.

Let me first say something about the revolutionary influence. What is the aim of the revolution? Is it always bent on reversing the established order? Hardly. The revolution has that in mind whenever it finds in church or state an order of things established *according to God's will.* For it will not permit or put up with such an order, and if it sees no chance to quash it with violence, it jumps in to turn the foundations upside down, to force the wheel of life to turn in the opposite direction, and to put in its place an order of things established *according to its own will.* But once it succeeds in this, and its appointed authorities are in control, oh, then that same revolution exercises a far more terrible tyranny than the worst despots ever did. The almighty power of the state becomes its life-principle, the general welfare its guiding theme, and far from tolerating freedom of expression it suppresses the cry of the wounded heart and ignores the demand of the aggrieved conscience. The state is free to resist God, but for citizens to resist the state constitutes lèse-majesté. The action of the revolution always comes down to this, that a person, in his heart as well as in church, state, and society, does not experience liberty so much as a violation of conscience: God having been dethroned, the absolute authority that God had over his conscience is now exercised over him by violent men. The revolution has nothing to do with the liberation of the spirit which Protestantism finds in voluntary submission to God. It merely transfers the locus of authority from God to power-hungry men and proceeds to practice absolute despotism.

With well-nigh equal force the Romanist principle attempts to assert itself, right in our very own Reformed churches, which under God were at one time founded here in our country with such wonderful purity in martyrs' blood. Once again, just as in the days of Rome, human regulations and ordinances are elevated above and against the word of God. You need

---

4. Kuyper uses the term *legitimiteit* (legitimacy), in the sense of conformity to, or acquiescence in, accepted rules and established legal rights.

only observe how an exaggerated pietism once again restores works-righteousness to a place of honor; a misguided perfectionism offers "modern saints" a new chance; and a straying mysticism once again tempts people to embrace sick fantasies. But above all else, notice the main difference that was fought over between the Calvinists and the Romanists in the days of the Reformation. For what was this? What else, my friends, but precisely the issue that has surfaced once again: will the organization give way to the confession, or the confession to the organization?

In Rome's confession there always was the seed of truth, concealed under many wild branches, for God's word was still always held up as holy, and people did not meddle with the great and mighty mysteries of faith. As far as that is concerned, transformation and reformation from within had always remained possible. But that was not how it went with the organization, with the hierarchy, with the authority of the popes. For this was sacrosanct; this was not to be touched. Standing up for King Jesus against the pope, and for God's word against the papal bulls, was at that time called revolution. Everything was subordinated to unity. The kingdom of God stood or fell with the papal church organization. Whereas our fathers challenged this system of false mingling by insisting on "An organization corresponding to the confession!" today that old Romanist spirit again haunts our churches, and self-styled Protestant ministers defend the inviolability of the synodical hierarchy with the very same arguments used long ago by the followers of Sadoletus and Canisius in defense of the papal hierarchy.[5]

But the third cancer eats away even more severely, that of passivity, whose enervating effect is felt even in Reformed circles. How can one recognize this poison? This way, my friends: when someone presumes to substitute God's hidden will for his revealed will. A dreadful error, one that in the days of the Hattemists[6] and their antinomian brood ultimately tore down all the props of accountability, and amid the cry of "Lord, Lord!" sank down into the sludge of the most abominable sins! Well, that same passivity is once again rearing its head today, and whispers to you that

5. Jacopo Sadoleto (1477–1547) and Petrus Canisius (1521–97) were leading Roman Catholic apologists and polemicists in the Reformation era.
6. Hattemists were followers of Pontiaan van Hattem (1645–1702), a Reformed minister who was defrocked because he taught that pure religion deemphasizes dogma and instead emphasizes God's love, discounting any distinction between good and evil and branding guilt and the need for repentance as delusions. His followers practiced a pietism tinged with mysticism and were found guilty of libertinism.

"things are no different than what God has willed"; that "if things have to change, God himself will bring it about"; that "we must leave things alone and let them quietly run their course"; for "whatever situation arises, it is not man's place to do anything against the Lord's will." That is how the siren sings her song with pious tones, charming souls and seducing them. This is that ancient melody that suggests that the thief was predestined to be a thief and on that basis is called by God's will to thievery. This is a terrible heresy, which naturally undermines all Protestant and Reformed identity. For if God's hidden will and not the will revealed in his word is to serve us as guide, for what purpose then do we have the word, and for what purpose the law? God deliver us from this, brothers, for once that passivity is transferred to the spiritual arena, it will mean the death of all Christian living, all Reformed living, indeed, all responsible living.

And yet, you will not excise that cancer so easily, because a pervasive pantheism, which I mentioned in the last place, has already poisoned life at its deepest source among countless many; and precisely against this last danger our Free University must offer resistance with all its strength. Naturalism is not nearly as dangerous for Christians, for everyone who confesses Christ is automatically armed against it. But the danger is all the greater that the toxic fumes of pantheism will infiltrate and penetrate. Not the fumes of the pantheism that has been unmasked; none of our brothers would be attracted to that. No, but the danger lies in that veiled pantheism that whispers to you that "nothing should be *made*, but everything must *grow*"; that without the intervention of disciplinary measures "the truth will automatically overcome the lie"; that "there is a grain of truth in every error, and we must give that error some time for its germ of truth to sprout and develop";[7] and whatever other sweet-sounding and seductive sayings it has, designed to charm us by the beauty of an undisturbed and uninterrupted process in which everything is mixed together and intermingled, and truth ultimately includes the lie, indeed, in which virtue absorbs sin.

Oh, you do not know the dangerous seduction of this pantheistic notion of the "undisturbed, self-redeeming process of history." It erases God; it exchanges the creation for Darwin's evolution; it melts the Scriptures down into saga and myth; and it recasts the two natures of Christ into a third new entity, to end in deploring sin as merely a necessary transition toward

7. These sentiments were typical of the ethical-irenic school of thought.

holiness and extending the process of that constantly emerging newness to beyond the grave. Oh, let me exhort you, my friends, for the sake of your soul's salvation and for the certainty of the divinely ordained foundations: do not take this toxic poison into your own bloodstream, nor introduce it into the souls of others. For of course, with this terrible poison all devotion to duty becomes revolutionary; then there is no room for the wedge of God's word. And then you cannot but arrive at the point, as the Irvingians have in fact done,[8] of accusing your forefathers of rebellion and branding all your Protestantism as sinfully disturbing the historical process.

And so we are back at our starting point and in a position to expose the error to its fullest extent. We began by acknowledging the created order—namely, that God appointed boundaries and intentionally introduced separations by ordering the chaos into kinds, and for each kind a unique nature, all of which he did, not for the sake of the beauty of diversity, but so that in such beauty the absolute separation between God and man would be secured. This then is the order whose foundations are today being overturned. People are melting together clay and iron, and are making miry iron out of it! Or to say it without figurative speech: from God and man something "god-human" is supposed to come forth, and from "spirit and body" something "physico-spiritual" is supposed to emerge. And that is why people oppose all separation. They erase every boundary. They melt every kind together. They employ the theory of evolution to make all kinds flow together. At last, as even Schleiermacher's school of thought has dared to do in our country, they abolish the absolute distinction between God and his creation.[9]

And so you see how life can be infiltrated to its very core by that principle of "letting things run their course" and "never interfering" in the undisturbed process, and berating every break as "revolution." Before you realize it, Immanuel is turned from being "God with us" to being "God in us," and the God "in us" is then diluted into Hegel's "God unfolding within us"!

Therefore, as surely as there is a law of God that disrupts the process of sin, and as surely as there is a miracle of regeneration that interrupts

8. A revival movement in England around 1830, associated with Edward Irving (1792–1834) and leading to the founding of the Catholic Apostolic Church. Some of his followers repudiated the Protestant Reformation and reaffirmed the medieval church as their mother.
9. Friedrich Schleiermacher (1768–1834) is often recognized as the father of modern liberal Christianity.

the process of sinful development, and as surely as we await the return of Immanuel one day to destroy the entire process of Satan's sinful power—so surely do I now summon you, whether in your own heart and life, in your house and social circles, in your school and church, to intervene whenever and wherever you find a sinful process that resists the word of God by means of false mixing together. …

And so our defense has turned into offense, and your only prayer for our synod can be that it abdicate, and for our public universities that they repent. And you will pray with all your heart for the only university in our country that stands on the foundation of the word of God.

We know it is *lawful* for us to pray for our university provided our intention is to defend the Lord's cause. The Free University has received nothing but ridicule and slander from the world. It lives off voluntary gifts. Its strength is hardly a match for its rivals. What has kept us alive is the firm resolve that in the field of higher education the long-despised name of the Lord should no longer be without defense.

Moreover, it is *urgent* that we raise such prayer. For there is no time to lose if we are yet to succeed in turning the hearts of children to their fathers and to call a generation misled by false philosophy back to the word of God. The Christian primary school alone will not suffice; a free university had to be founded, for it is not just elementary education but still more higher education that determines the spirit that rules the mighty world of thought.

But above all we stand in *need* of such prayer. Our strength is so little, our scholarly output is still so insignificant, and the demands placed on us are so terribly high. Who else but the Spirit of wisdom and knowledge can raise up for us the men of talent and genius we so sorely need?

We need to pray because of the fierce opposition we face. Through the hands of mortal men we are targeted by the enemy, by Satan and his followers. This eats at our confidence; it sows dissension in our ranks; it even creeps into our student body.

Finally, we need to pray for our university because of the "mingling with the seed of men" [see Dan 2:43] by which we ourselves are so anxiously tied down. We may no longer fall prey to former temptations, but we have not yet made much progress on the new battlefront. Here the strands of life still lie interwoven; the vital links are still interconnected. Those whom we have to oppose today stood by us yesterday. The battle cuts right across the generations, is tearing families apart. We used to know one another, belonged together, should today be building together instead of fighting each other.[10] Never forget, at the Free University too we are human, susceptible to all that is human. That is why our prayers are so necessary. Pray that we remain faithful to the word, that we may never be told, "You that love the ties of blood or friendship more than me are not worthy of me" [see Matt 10:37].

Let me add, finally, that we possess *boldness* for such prayer. Our fathers, the heroes of the days of the Reformation, the martyrs burned at the stake, they all call on us not to simply look on and passively allow the pure word of God—for which they were ready to lay down their lives—to be once again suppressed in church and school and held captive to that false mingling.

Still more, we possess boldness because we realize, now more than ever, that the Holy Spirit himself makes intercession for us with groanings which cannot be uttered. The toxic mingling of iron and clay penetrates far deeper than any of us can see, and neither our protest nor our effort but only God's Holy Spirit can preserve feeble life and help us in our weaknesses, for we know not what we should pray for as we ought [see Rom 8:26].

And, to conclude, what ultimately gives us boldness in prayer is this, that neither for the synod nor for the public universities but only for the Free University are you able to pray *in Jesus' name*. For the issue, after all, is the name of Jesus—in your heart when you need to repent; in your family when he sets your child at variance against its mother [see Matt 10:35]; in your country when part of the nation rejects the Lord and his Anointed and cries: "Let us break their bonds asunder!" [see Ps 2:2]. The name of Jesus is at issue in your church when its authorities reduce Christ to a do-nothing king in his own church. And Jesus' name is at issue in the domain of science and scholarship when every man of learning rejects the King and Christ can no longer rule in the realm of truth!

But thanks to God's electing grace, in our university Christ does rule. To him we bow, to him alone. Unlike the charter and the curriculum and virtually all of the professors of our four public universities, our charter, our

---

10. Kuyper is perhaps alluding to growing tension with his colleague Professor Philippus Hoedemaker (1839–1910), who disapproved of organized action to reform the church. Hoedemaker's "theocratic" ideal was one united, biblically faithful, national church, favored by a national government that heeded the teachings of the church. He resigned from the Free University after the *Doleantie* was an accomplished fact, though not as an enemy, but as one who saw "a beautiful ideal grow pale."

curriculum, and absolutely all of our professors, governors, and curators repeat after the apostle Peter: "Lord, to whom shall we go? You have the words of eternal life" [John 6:68].

We know that we have an intercessor also for our school. And therefore, even if all the churches were closed to us,[11] let us gather I would almost say under the canopy of the forest or if need be out in the open field. For prayers *must* be raised for that small and menaced institution which ventured forth bearing the name of Christ.

The stakes are high, my friends, very high. Who are we that we could save the school? Only the Lord Sabaoth is able to break up that false mingling. Only his strong arm clothed with power and authority shall at the appointed hour separate the iron from the clay. So let us pray for our school from the depths of our soul. Let it be a storming of the gates of heaven. For truly, friends, our school is still engaged in anxious struggle. It could still collapse at any moment. Men aim at its demise.

But before I lead you in prayer, let us sing the closing stanzas of Psalm 74.[12]

> Remember, Lord, the scoffing of your foes;
> Hear how your Name is taunted by the wicked!
> Yield not your dove to beast of field and thicket,
> do not forget your children in their woes.
>
> Look to the covenant! Hold it in regard,
> For terror reigns in all the land's dark places.
> Let the downtrodden not endure disgraces,
> and may the needy praise your name, O Lord.
>
> Rise up, O God, rise and defend your cause.
> Ignore the taunting of your foes no longer;
> do not forget their shouts of raging anger,
> the uproar which continues without pause.

11. See above, n. 2.

12. William W. J. Van Oene, 1972; revised. ©2009, Standing Committee for the Publication of the Book of Praise of the Canadian Reformed Churches. Used with permission.

BOUND TO THE WORD

TEXT INTRODUCTION

The address "Bound to the word" depicts Dr. Kuyper in his usual teaching mode. In it he struggles to explain to a largely lay audience how a Reformed, Christian university and its teaching staff are to be unequivocally committed to basing all its instruction on "the word of God." Pivotal in Kuyper's explanation is his creative interpretation of the two-book view of divine revelation as expressed in the Belgic Confession. Kuyper argues that reading the book of nature, where God reveals himself in a clear and elegant way, is more directly relevant for the practice and pursuit of science and scholarship than reading the book called Holy Scripture, where God reveals himself more clearly in a salvific way. Kuyper glosses over the fact that the Confession makes the point that reading the book of nature still leaves the natural person "without excuse" (Rom 1:20); he prefers instead to emphasize that in the book of nature God "shares his thoughts" with humankind, thoughts which humankind can think after him, hence their relevance for scientific knowledge.

Meanwhile, this whole address must be read against a somewhat complicated background. Its central thrust, that God's word is found not only in Scripture but also in the creation, was hardly new but rarely stated so forcefully. At the same time the address is part of a series of events that marked a definitive break between descendants of the more evangelical Réveil movement of the first half of the nineteenth century and Kuyper's neo-Calvinism.

The Free University, which opened its doors in the fall of 1880, was not operated by a corporation but owned and supported by an association of 490 dues-paying members and 1,824 donors. (In 1899, the year of this address, these figures were 455 and 8,081 respectively.) This "Association for Higher Education on a Reformed Basis" was dedicated to basing all its instruction "solely and exclusively on the foundation of the Reformed principles."

When Alexander Frederik de Savornin Lohman, Esq. (1837–1924), a judge in a provincial court, was prevailed on in 1884 to join the faculty, he did so both as a proponent of scholarship pursued by Christians and as a well-known champion of freedom of education. At the same time he expressed his reservations about the tie to "the Reformed principles," personally preferring instead to be "bound to the word of God." He did not want to be forced to choose between Ethicals and Calvinists, and emphasized individual conscience over organized Christian action and institutions.

Ten years later, Lohman and Kuyper had a falling out over the political question of extending the franchise. A legislative bill to that effect was warmly supported by Kuyper in his newspaper, but Lohman opposed it in Parliament on constitutional grounds and was supported by the nine members of the Antirevolutionary Party who had a more aristocratic background, who shared Lohman's spiritual leanings, and who were happy to recognize him as leader of their caucus. Kuyper downplayed the constitutional objections of the dissenting antirevolutionary group and then dragged the Free University into the political disagreement by openly writing: "One wonders how a law professor at the Free University can be the mouthpiece of such a consortium."[1]

Next, rumors began to circulate among students at the Free University, inevitably followed by members of the association in the country, that Professor Lohman "wasn't really Reformed" in his teaching. Thereupon, at the behest of curators, the faculty sat down and in the spring of 1895 adopted 18 Theses sketching a roadmap for ascertaining the meaning of "the Reformed principles";[2] only Professor Lohman cast a dissenting vote.

The theses outlined how all professors, each for his field, should work out the Reformed principles by engaging in critical study of the history of Calvinism, its theology, its polemical and scholarly publications since the sixteenth century, its cultural impact, its response to the modern emphasis

1. A. Kuyper, "Het fatale Manifest," *De Standaard*, March 28, 1894.

2. *Publicatie van den Senaat der Vrije Universiteit in zake het onderzoek ter bepaling van den weg, die tot de kennis der gereformeerde beginselen leidt* (Amsterdam: J. A. Wormser, 1895). The main author of this document was Kuyper, with input from especially Professors Fabius and Woltjer.

on subjective factors in the acquisition of knowledge and the pursuit of science, and its reading of reality as created, fallen, and re-created. Lohman let it be known that he did not agree with this approach toward discovering and identifying "Reformed principles."

On June 27, 1895, at the annual meeting of the association, thirty-four members repeated the concern about the Reformed character of the professor's instruction, and a motion passed to strike a commission of investigation into the matter. Its report was presented at the next annual meeting by theologian Herman Bavinck (1854–1921) of the seminary in Kampen. The committee which he chaired had come to the conclusion that Professor Lohman's instruction "did not do justice" to the Reformed principles. Thereupon Lohman resigned.

Some members felt vindicated; others were very upset. To calm things down, Kuyper decided that at the next annual meeting he would address the question: How can lay members judge the instruction of a professor? His answer: only indirectly, yet reliably, by noting how he conducts himself in practical life.[3]

Three years later, Kuyper must have felt it was expedient to deal with the thorny question once more, but from a different angle: What does it mean to be "bound to the word"? The address set forth that the phrase had to be more specific by including God's "word" (lowercase) not only in Scripture but also in nature as defined in the Reformed creeds and accepted as one of the Reformed principles. Thus it was more honest and less ambiguous to bind professors not to "the word of God" but directly and explicitly to the more inclusive term "the Reformed principles."

Source: Kuyper, Abraham. *Band aan het woord. Antwoord op de vraag: Hoe is eene universiteit aan het woord van God te binden?* Address to the annual meeting of the Association for Higher Education on a Reformed Basis, held at Middelburg, June 26, 1899. Amsterdam and Pretoria: Höveker & Wormser, 1899. Translated, annotated, and edited by Harry Van Dyke and checked against a manuscript in the Dordt College Library containing an undated translation made by the late Rev. Conrad R. Veenstra of Sioux Center, Iowa.

---

3. The address was titled "De wacht bij het beginsel" [On guard for the principle] but could not be delivered at the annual meeting for lack of time. Shortly thereafter it was published in *De Heraut* of July 12, 1896. For the last clause, "by noting how he conducts himself in practical life," one might well read: "by noting what company he keeps and what he thinks of concrete issues such as extending the franchise."

BOUND TO THE WORD

HOW CAN A UNIVERSITY BE BOUND TO THE WORD OF GOD?

Esteemed members of the audience,

I have been asked to answer the question: In what way can a university be bound to the word of God? Behind this question, meanwhile, lies the more general one: How is being bound to that word to be applied to the entire world of human thought? Allow me, therefore, to address this more general question first, and then examine it more specifically as it applies to a university.

The question is of current interest also outside the circle of our university. You have heard how the "Merckens affair" has rocked the community of our Christian schoolteachers.[4] No doubt you have learned that this exceedingly important issue has brought to light a noticeable difference

4. H. Merckens, headmaster of a Christian elementary school, had published an article in which he deviated from the Reformed understanding of the inspiration of Holy Scripture by suggesting that when we read in the Bible that "God spoke" it was often

of opinion between the daily newspaper of Amsterdam[5] and the [free antirevolutionary] daily of Rotterdam.[6] And it will not have escaped the attention of those of you who are in the habit of observing the signs of the times that the two divergent answers to this question have gradually been narrowed down to two formulas. One side asserts that the basis of our organizations and associations is to be found in Holy Scripture, without any further qualification. The other side insists that this formula, once common, has become unusable today and that we should definitely opt for the more narrow formula, namely: on the basis of the Reformed principles.

I wish to state here that I am in favor of the latter formula and side with those who are opposed to the former. I do so, not as a party leader, but on the basis of exclusively scholarly considerations. This is the controversy I am going to address—not just to strengthen the conviction of those who agree with us but also to caution those fellow Christians who seek safety in the old formula, warning them against the danger to which they are exposing themselves and their followers.

In the debate about this question of principle a measure of unscholarly passion has gradually insinuated itself which came out most sharply when we were reproached: "We follow Jesus, you Calvin." That passion is uncalled for, and I will not rise to the bait. What exercises both sides is a complex issue that is of paramount importance for everyone who confesses Christ, in fact for all who fear God. Together we must exert every effort to come to a correct resolution, and we are to do so in quiet reverence before the majesty of God and in a spirit of brotherly love for one another.

You may have noticed that in the manner in which my address was announced I had the expression "word of God" printed without a capital *W*. I did so advisedly. I wish to go behind Scripture to God himself. We are

---

"through circumstances" and not "in an audible voice." After many discussions his membership in the Association of Christian Schoolteachers was revoked. His school board, however, maintained him in his position.

5. Editor in chief of the antirevolutionary *De Standaard* in Amsterdam was of course Abraham Kuyper. He had argued in his columns in favor of "the Reformed principles" as the basis of Christian education.
6. Editor in chief of the free antirevolutionary *De Nederlander* in Rotterdam was Alexander de Savornin Lohman (1837–1924). In this rival newspaper he had reiterated his stance that one's commitment to Holy Scripture should be sufficient. This stance had cost him his professorship at the Free University in 1895. A few years later Lohman went further and stated that a personal commitment to Jesus Christ should suffice.

not looking at a question about Scripture but are prompted by respect for God's majesty. Our concern is with God. We wish to submit ourselves to the Lord God. If it is the case that the Most High God has left us to grope around in the darkness in which we find ourselves, then nothing is left for us but to wander about on our own errant ways. If, however, God has sent light into our darkness, then we deem it our bounden duty to carefully catch every ray of that light so that we have a lamp unto our feet and a light unto our path.

Now, anybody who still believes in God in whatever way will acknowledge with us that God has revealed himself, and still reveals himself, and that we are to regulate our lives in accordance with that revelation. On this question even the modernist stands with us. Only, he maintains that God reveals himself exclusively in nature, including reason, conscience, and history. The impressions he picks up from reason, conscience, nature, and history, he proceeds to translate into a "word," and this to his mind is the real "word of God" to which he is bound. Not that he discards Scripture altogether, but he dissolves it into the everyday phenomena of life. Increasingly that is understood among modernists today in a pantheistic sense. That is to say, they refuse to recognize a self-conscious, personal God. To them, only in man's self-consciousness does the gradually self-realizing idea of the world spirit become manifest. This notion deprives them of the right to talk any longer of a "word of God." The expression "word of God" presupposes two things: a God who is a thinking being, and a thinking God who speaks his mind in such a way that we humans can understand him. On their pantheistic standpoint, neither is true. They no longer have a God who thinks in awareness of himself and who shares his thoughts with us. What they call the word of God is their own word on which they put a divine stamp.

To maintain our integrity, there should be no doubt in our minds as to the meaning we attach to the two terms "God" and "word." I shall not provide arguments for them; they are the axioms that I cannot do without as I present my case. My standpoint is that of virtually every Christian. By "God" we are to understand a self-conscious, personal Being, and by "word of God" the communication to our human consciousness of an idea that was in God.

Should anyone want to deny these two axioms, I am prepared to debate that question with him on some other occasion, but not now; today these two axioms are the basis from which I proceed, and I will only engage those in debate who declare themselves in agreement with me on this score. No other approach is appropriate for a debate that will inevitably be of a serious nature. There has to be some common ground for a debate to be meaningful.

I

The first step to take is to examine more closely how we are to understand the communication of God's thought to our human consciousness. We call it a word of God, but does that mean exclusively his written word, or if you will, the word expressed in concepts and sounds? Or does this phrase also encompass the communication of God's thought in events and phenomena? Indeed, it is undeniable that a word of God also comes to us in what God has made or has done and is still doing. It may be said even of humans, if they are serious, that their activity is inspired and guided by thought. Is it then conceivable that a personal and self-conscious God would act without thought? Speech goes out from what God does and has done. God speaks to us in nature. All history speaks of God. There is a word of God in our reason. There is a word of God in our innermost sense of the divine. This is what Scripture teaches, as does our self-consciousness and our experience. It is an undeniable fact, therefore, that whoever fears God and binds himself or his conduct to the word of God must at once reckon with that multifaceted speech of God that comes to us in nature—or, to define it more closely, in nature and history, in reason and conscience. The Reformed churches have always confessed that we know God by two means, namely:

First, by the creation, preservation, and government of the universe; which is before our eyes as a most elegant book, wherein all creatures, great and small, are as so many characters leading us to "see clearly the invisible things of God, even his everlasting power and divinity." ...[7]

This fact alone shows that to say, "I bind myself to Scripture" is a very incomplete formula. We have to begin, in fact, with a reference to that wholly other word, to God's speech in nature—a reference that is absent in the formula "on the basis of Scripture" but that is present in the formula "on the basis of the Reformed principles." Those principles, after all, contain, as an indispensable element, that primary reference to the word of God in nature.

7. Belgic Confession, Art. 2. The article continues: "Second, He makes Himself more clearly and fully known to us by His holy and divine Word, that is to say, as far as is necessary for us to know in this life, to His glory and our salvation."

But now a second question arises: Are we able to understand that word of God in nature, and is that all we need? Yes, says the modernist; no, says every believer in Christ—Catholic, Orthodox, and Protestant alike, and among the latter Lutherans and Reformed, Anabaptists and Methodists, Ethicals,[8] and Ritschlians.[9] What accounts for this difference? It stems from the difference in presupposition when assessing the phenomenon of sin. Modernists do not deny the reality of sin, but they do not see it as evidence of apostasy and guilt. Their axiom in this instance is that sin points to inadequate development. As believers in Christ, however, we reject this view and oppose to it the view that sin points to a fall and imputes guilt, and further that this fall had a threefold effect: a darkening of our minds, an impairment of our willpower, and a pollution of our desires. It follows from this that without spectacles, as Calvin put it, we can no longer read the book of nature, and that we can know neither from nature nor from the light of our reason whether, and if so how, we can escape the power and guilt of sin. This situation necessitated a special, further revelation, supplementing the general revelation in nature, and that for two purposes: to teach us to read the book of nature again, and to open up the way for us to be reconciled to God. In short, there is a twofold word of God: a word of God in creation, and a word of God supplementing creation.

Would it be proper, then, to say without further comment that next to nature we are also bound to Scripture? Without question, yes—if you say, "I take my stand on the Reformed principles." But no, if you deem it sufficient to say, "I bind myself to the word of God." For, apart from the fact that the latter stance does not reckon with nature as a source of knowledge of God's will and truth, history teaches that definitely not all Christians agree that the further revelation of God which supplements the revelation in creation is given to us exclusively and solely in Scripture. On the contrary, on this point Christ believers are completely at odds with one another. Roman Catholics, while fully recognizing that this revelation is found first of all

8. Reference to those Dutch theologians and churchmen who had opposed Kuyper's campaign for strict adherence to the confessional standards of the Dutch Reformed Church and who therefore refused to secede with him in the schism of 1886 known as the *Doleantie*. The self-styled "ethical-irenical" party represented a form of mediating theology that began to give in to some of the results of higher criticism.

9. Reference to sympathizers with the influential school of Albrecht Ritschl (1822–89), which stood for a version of theological modernism that grounded the Christian faith in the religious experience of the Christian community.

in Holy Scripture, place three other sources of knowledge next to it: the apocryphal books of the Old Testament; tradition, including the decisions of councils; and the *ex cathedra* pronouncements of the bishop of Rome. A similar though smaller difference exists between us and Lutherans. No doubt Lutherans stand by Luther's battle cry, *Das Wort Sie sollen stehen lassen*: "Leave the word alone!" Yet they too supplement Scripture with the Apocrypha, ascribe binding authority to the ancient ecumenical councils (not the later ones), call the clergy the *ecclesia docens*,[10] and regard the authority of the New Testament so much higher than the Old that they consider the New Testament their real Bible (at most enriched by the Psalms, which they print in the back of their New Testaments). Anabaptists are of a different view again. They too declare that Scripture is the source of divine truth, but next to it they place the "inner light"—in this sense, in fact, that the more one advances in spiritual maturity the more the authority of Scripture diminishes and the authority of "inner light" increases.

I omit the Ethicals, Methodists, and Ritschlians for now, confining myself to sketching the three great historic traditions that bear on this question and that evolved alongside the Reformed tradition.

It should be clear by now that you are not done by stating, "I stand on the basis of Scripture." That is what everybody claims to be doing. Something more needs to be said so that it becomes clear at the same time (1) how you see the relation between the Old and the New Testament, (2) where you stand with regard to the Apocrypha and the councils, and (3) what you think of "inner light."

Any such clarification will not be ambiguous if you choose the formula, "I take my stand on the basis of the Reformed principles." That formula contains a full explanation not only of your unconditional acknowledgment of the authority of Scripture but also of your stance with respect to those other things that Christians have put alongside Scripture. Again we can see that the formula "I bind myself to Scripture" is utterly inadequate and insufficient, whereas the formula we advocate offers both certainty and completeness.

Let no one say that this may be true strictly speaking, but that in practice this more narrowly defined position is redundant because the issue is to adopt a rallying cry for Protestants, and no Dutch Protestant honors

10. *Ecclesia docens* stands for "the teaching Church"—that is, the authoritative teachers of Christian doctrine.

a religious authority next to Scripture. I grant this, broadly speaking, but surely the choice cannot be difficult between a broad formula that might do at a stretch, and a precise one that hits the nail on the head.

Yet notice that those who use the broader formula do not say: yours is really more precise and better. Rather, they reject our formula outright and hold it up to public scorn. There must therefore be a reason why they favor the broader, inadequate one. Moreover, confessing the basis on which you build is done not only for the sake of those who join you but just as much for the benefit of those who turn away from you. In the interest of honesty alone, therefore, you are obliged to show your true colors in regard to the difference between you and them. While this is obligatory with respect to Roman Catholics, it is equally right to declare your position with respect to Lutherans and Anabaptists. When laying your foundation and the cornerstone for that foundation, it is crucial to make sure things are perfectly level and that no part is out of plumb. It must be one or the other: either our Lutherans and Anabaptists differ from their ancestors in their view of Scripture and have come over to the Reformed view; or they still confess the same view as their ancestors, hence have an altogether different view of Scripture from ours. If the former, our formula covers their present meaning; if the latter, the general formula referring solely to Scripture is of no use, for then we still disagree and will sow hopeless confusion by using a false rallying cry.

Thus, with reference to the two formal questions regarding the relation (1) of Scripture to nature, and (2) of Scripture to the Apocrypha, tradition, councils, and "inner light," the sole reference to Scripture tells you absolutely nothing and leaves everything undecided and uncertain. On the other hand, our reference to the Reformed principles not only does a better job of upholding the full authority of Scripture but what is more, closely defines the relation of Scripture to all those alternative (true or false) sources of knowledge.

However, the difficulty of this complicated problem is not limited to these formal questions. The material aspect of the question, too, requires further definition, namely: the interpretation of Scripture and its content. Now then, people who are not born again cannot even see the kingdom of God, so what they say about Scripture's meaning cannot even be considered. But what about those who are born again? Am I suggesting that just any convert, so long as he opens his Bible and reads it, is able to tell us what it says—what Scripture teaches us and how we are to obey its testimony by believing it and acting on it? To be sure, that is how we proceed when reading the Bible for personal devotions. As well, Scripture (as our fathers confessed) is clear and sufficient so that every child of God can find in it the way of salvation. But, as everybody will agree, that is not our goal when we set up associations, leagues, societies, organizations, and a political party. What we need to know in those cases is the correct view of man, of domestic life, of social and civic life, and so much more, so that we can propagate the principles that God has ordained for them and follow them for our collective action and collaborative efforts in every area of life. That goal requires a fundamental, coherent, and praxis-oriented knowledge of the content of Scripture. Then it is not enough to say: we agree that Scripture must be our guide. You need to define how you can come to know what the Scriptures demand and intend.

This may appear superfluous if you take Scripture juridically as a law code and read its clear pronouncements as legal prescriptions. Even then the task is not easy, for judges and lawyers themselves often disagree on how to read legal clauses. But I grant that if Scripture is a law code, a good Bible concordance will go a long way toward ascertaining its meaning. You then look to see whether a subject occurs in the concordance and you look up the various texts listed there. But to go this route we must first agree that Scripture is such a law code. And about that we disagree. On the contrary, anyone who is at all knowledgeable on this point will reject this approach as totally antiquated and useless; professionals do not take it seriously. That is not what Scripture is. It rarely offers definitive pronouncements, and then only by way of exception; by far the greater part of the Bible is history, expressions of praise and lament, prophecies about vanished nations, or laws and regulations for cultural conditions altogether different from ours. When you compare one isolated text with another you repeatedly run into contradictory statements, and we are reminded of the saying that the devil can quote Scripture for his purpose.

In actual fact, this antiquated method, condemned by all biblical scholars, comes down to this, that one first thinks up what one would like, and then tries to find out whether there is a text in the Bible that sounds as if it confirms one's idea. Serious thinkers have therefore always realized that this method gets us nowhere. We cannot do without a well-considered hermeneutic. To make headway, there has to be agreement about whether Scripture can be read purely according to the literal and historical meaning, or also according to the allegorical and mystical sense; whether Scripture's authority applies only to what is explicitly stated, or also to what can be logically deduced from it; and, to mention no more, whether every verse stands on its own or whether Scripture is to be explained according to the "analogy of faith."

Besides these questions there arose the threefold possibility that biblical exegesis is bound, as Rome contends, to the pronouncements of the church, or as the Anabaptists maintain, to the inspiration of the inner light, or as the Reformed confess, subject only to reverent scholarly inquiry, provided always that such inquiry be free. So how helpful is it if you bind your organization to Scripture and it turns out that from the same Scripture different people deduce totally different opinions about man, his relation to the world, and the rule for civil society and the various societal relationships? Then you do not agree, then you cannot work together, and you cause the authority of Scripture, which you both say you believe in, to become a bone of contention between you instead of being a source of unity. But if instead you take the Reformed principles as your basis, you have settled all these questions of interpretation and you all know how together you understand the sense and meaning of Scripture about man and his God-given place in the world.

It is sometimes objected that this is replacing Scripture with a human system. In reply we ask: Is God's revelation a system, or is it a jumble of unconnected parts? Everybody will admit that even to entertain the possibility of a chaotic confusion in God and in his revelation would be to deny his wisdom. God is the supreme Artist and Architect, and not even among men does a builder just lay one brick on another, but he builds in a particular style, according to a blueprint. Scripture reveals a system of which the parts are arranged in orderly fashion. Our only problem is whether we can come to know this "system of God" from Scripture. That problem confronts us squarely with our human limitations and the willful darkening of our minds. Indeed, we have forfeited the ability to know God's system with any completeness. We know it only by approximation, with slowly increasing clarity. And the difference between persons and nations is so strong that in the course of the centuries multiple versions have arisen of the system embedded in God's word, and under the influence of German philosophy the present century has added still another version of the "system of God," that of the Ethicals.

Now, the conception that a person develops about the system with which God created and governs all things is called someone's *life- and worldview*;

and the fixed starting points for the lines of such a conception are called someone's *principles*.[11] It is in this sense that we speak of Catholic principles, Lutheran principles, Anabaptist principles, Reformed principles, and today also of Ethical principles, or if you like, of the Catholic, Lutheran, Anabaptist, Reformed, and Ethical worldviews. And at least in the first four cases no one takes that to be a system made up by people but exclusively people's coherent conception of God's system, which they, on different standpoints, believe can be derived from divine revelation.

We must be careful, therefore, not to confuse two widely different phenomena. Particularly in the nineteenth century a variety of philosophical schools have sprung up. Adherents call themselves Kantians or Hegelians, Herbartians, or Fichteans, while others are known as Darwinists or Pessimists; and each of these schools propagates a system that is supposed to help us understand the world and how it functions. And it is perfectly true of these philosophical systems that they are the figments of the human heart—human systems in the most literal sense of the word, derived from human brains. But we must never put these schools of philosophy on a par with the great religious traditions. They differ patently. The schools start by denying God's special revelation, whereas the great historic traditions have nothing else in mind but to interpret the content of revelation. Second, the schools erect their own system, whereas the religious traditions intend no more than to give an outline of God's system. Third, the schools construct their systems on the basis of abstract thinking, whereas the religious traditions arise from life, labor with the works of God as their building blocks and with the blood of martyrs as their mortar. Hence the schools rise and fall as their inventors come on the scene and are pushed aside again, whereas the religious traditions rule the ages. It is therefore unscientific and at odds with the facts and with history to look on Luther as a kind of Kant and on Calvin as a kind of Spinoza. The fathers of these religious traditions have nothing in common with the founders of the philosophical schools. Even when Augustine, Aquinas, and Calvin plot the lines for a Christian philosophy, they always indicate the two scriptural coordinates that are to determine the direction of each line.

Once this is properly understood it cannot be difficult to demonstrate the difference between the standpoint of those who deem the general Scripture formula sufficient and of those who emphasize their place in one

---

11. Orig.: *beginselen*; some may prefer to translate: "first principles."

of the great historic traditions. Thus in France they choose the Catholic, in Germany the Lutheran, and in our country the Reformed principles. Their difference comes to light in three things.

In the first place, the champions of the general Scripture formula lack unity and cohesion in their conception. They appear to form their opinions haphazardly, citing this or that Bible text that superficially sounds like proof for a variety of positions. Thus they never possess a rich organism of ideas to work with. They are like a person who enters a garden to gather a bouquet: he picks a flower here and a flower there and then ties them together with a ribbon that has no organic link with the bouquet. By contrast, those who profess their solidarity with one of the great historic traditions possess a worldview that is firm and unified because it wishes only to be an interpretation of the system of things that God has put together in creation and has revealed to us.

In the second place, those who retreat into the general Scripture formula act as if a Christian in the nineteenth century relates to Scripture in exactly the same way as a Christian in the days of Constantine. He reads Scripture, ponders it privately, and then tries to form a conception for himself of the world and how it functions. While he admits that this is not the task of a single individual and that the whole church of Christ has worked at this gigantic task for more than fifteen centuries so that it behooves us to profit from that labor of centuries, yet on his standpoint he cannot reckon with it. Were he to do so, he would with irresistible logic always end up having to choose from among the great historic traditions. And that is a choice he refuses to make. He denies the legitimacy of those traditions and insists, on the basis of his general formula, that there is only one tradition, which he calls the "Christian" one. The advocates of the narrower historic formula, by contrast, will tell you that if you want to travel in a foreign country you do not risk finding your own way but you consult guides who can tell you which routes earlier travelers have taken and how they have fared, and you then choose the guide who inspires you with the most confidence.

In the third place, the defenders of the general Scripture formula are unable to show a relationship between their conceptions, loosely strung together from Scripture, and the historic life of the nation. Their conviction about things sacred is like a dripping cloud that passes over the land but lacks a channel dug out in the life of their country. All fundamental connection with the history of the country and the distinctive character of its people is lacking. By contrast, those who choose the historic formula and therefore refer to the basis of Reformed principles are shaping their own lives in continuity with the life of their forefathers and link their confession to the unique character traits of their nation. By so doing they arrive at a conception about things sacred that fits in with the life of their people.

The threefold contrast, therefore, comes down to this, that the general Scripture formula is neither coherent nor historical nor attuned to national life, whereas Reformed principles yield a conception of things sacred that has organic unity, profits from the lessons of history, and goes on to further develop the thought patterns of their ancestors. And those who embrace Reformed principles confess that these characteristics must not be detached from the providential guidance of the Father or the reign of the Son or the enlightenment of the Holy Spirit. It is God who determined our place of birth and line of descent. It was under the kingly rule of Christ that these pluriform outlines of God's system arose in his church from Scripture. And it was under the instruction of the Holy Spirit that men realized with increasing clarity which ways lead to dead ends and along which paths the believers can go forward from strength to strength. And therefore they refuse to unravel again the fabric of previous generations in order to start new patterns each time, but quietly and calmly carry forward the old patterns of thought.

Should you ask, finally, whether truth is not one, after all, and if it is, whether it can be placed side by side with three or four conceptions of the truth (albeit not all equally correct), then this is our answer. One and the same ray of light, passing through panes of red, yellow, and blue glass, colors whatever is in the room in a different way, and since we humans are too limited to catch the white light without color, these differences in hue are inseparable from our human limitation. In a certain sense, therefore, it behooves us to be always mindful of the fact that others may have part of the truth and a portion of the power that we were unable to grasp. But this is far from saying that we put the other traditions on a par with our own conviction; rather, each on his own standpoint, if he is in earnest, cannot and may not confess otherwise than that he is personally convinced that his own confession is the highest and purest and most adequate expression of what God has revealed in his word.[12]

12. Here Kuyper circumscribes, in passing as it were, his doctrine of pluriformity in Christendom.

Having demonstrated why the general Scripture formula in and of itself must yield to the historic one, and how the formula "on the basis of the Reformed principles" satisfies all those further conditions that we cannot dispense with if we are not to deceive ourselves when basing ourselves on Scripture, we must now sound a warning against the danger posed by the biblical criticism of the Ethicals, which in the school of Ritschl has already led to casting Scripture aside. Notice that I am not talking about the biblical criticism of the modernists. They no longer swear by the Scripture formula, but the Ethicals still do. You know where biblical criticism has brought them. One of them, Rev. Hulsman,[13] has made this very clear. In all of Scripture, they say, barely a few statements remain about which there is certainty that Jesus did say them in that way, with those words. What the apostles wrote, however profound, has no binding authority. And as for the Old Testament, first it has to be completely rearranged, and once this and that has been established by guesswork that the course of Israel's religion was such and such, then prior to David nothing is historically certain, and everything that comes later may be rich in deep religious insights and exalted ideas but there is no longer any question that Scripture is invested with divine authority. What they continue to call "inspiration" is nothing but mystical prompting and mystical persuasion, such that every interpretation of those impressions remains fallibly human.

This was the inevitable outcome of the standpoint of Ritschl. At first the slogan was: Not the Three Forms of Unity but only the Heidelberg Catechism plus the Belgic Confession, without the Canons of Dort. Then: The Forms, yes, but *quatenus*, not *quia*.[14] After that: Not the confessional standards but Scripture. Still further: Not Scripture but God's word in Scripture. Till finally Scripture as such was done away with, to make room for the slogan: Not Scripture but Jesus. And Jesus here means not the Christ as the apostles confessed him but a Jesus whose image has to be constructed from what criticism has left standing of his life and his sayings. This extreme position

---

13. See G. Hulsman, *Moderne wetenschap of bijbelse traditie* (Utrecht: Kemink, 1897).
14. The use of these Latin terms was the common shorthand for referring to the dispute over the form of subscription in the Dutch Reformed Church. In 1816 this form was deliberately rephrased to create latitude in interpreting its intention. The new wording allowed an office bearer in the national church to know himself bound to the confessional standards insofar as (*quatenus*) but not inasmuch as (*quia*) these standards accorded with Scripture. This ambiguity frustrated efforts for church reform by the orthodox party in the church.

has today been adopted also in our country. Those who attack our position have already made the transition from Scripture to Jesus.[15]

If the Ethicals were open and honest in their attack on us, the danger would not be as great. But they are not. Rev. Hulsman, a born-and-bred Ethical and a trusted figure in their circles, has provided documented proof that what they teach from the pulpit often flatly contradicts what they teach in their seminaries. Hulsman puts it this way: "If the faithful in the pew, listening to the preacher's Christmas sermon, were able in the same moment to hear what the preacher really thought about it, they would pick up stones and with holy indignation hurl them at his head."

Do not forget, meanwhile, that if you look for security in the general Scripture formula these Ethicals will for the time being take your side and say, "We are with you in your protest against the Reformed principles." Well, then it is completely obvious that in the current situation the general Scripture formula stands condemned and is of absolutely no use because it includes those who undermine and destroy everything that our forefathers, and hence also the men of the *Réveil*,[16] understood by the authority of Scripture.

I will go a step further and state frankly that anyone who has read Rev. Hulsman's book and knowingly persists in defending the general Scripture formula for the sake of including the Ethicals shows thereby that he himself no longer confesses the absolute authority of God's word. This judgment has nothing to do with a failure to appreciate the many good things that were preserved among the Ethicals. Mysticism is rich, and by withdrawing into mysticism they can delight themselves and warm others with their ardor. That is how it was with Gerson and his followers toward the end of the Middle Ages. And yet, it was not they but Luther, Zwingli, and Calvin who saved Europe and ensured a new future for the Christian religion.

For this very reason, brotherly love toward the Ethical believers obligates us to withstand them to their face on the question of the authority of Scripture. He who does not do so hardens them in their deviation and shares in the sin which they are committing against Scripture. The men of the *Réveil*—Bilderdijk, Da Costa, Groen, Elout, Mackay, to whom they now

15. The wording is similar, yet this extreme reduction was not the position of Lohman, even though some people in Kuyper's audience, upon hearing this, may have associated Lohman with it.

16. Early nineteenth-century revival movement with which some leading members of the Reformed aristocracy in the Netherlands identified, many of whom later came to oppose Kuyper's neo-calvinism.

appeal and who in their day could still use the general Scripture formula in good faith—these men would today, with all the wrath that sacrilege arouses, protest vehemently against the deeply false notion that they, given their absolute confession of the authority of Scripture, would ever have intended to include such undermining of Scripture.

Summing up, I conclude this first part of my address as follows:

1. The general Scripture formula can suffice as a slogan for a few philanthropic and social organizations whose activities are inspired by those general scriptural principles about which all Christians in the main think and believe alike.

2. That formula is useless, however, both in and of itself and increasingly so when it is to function as a rallying cry for united action inspired by our worldview and hence by the principles that are to guide us. Therefore the formula "on the basis of the Reformed principles" is the obvious and only adequate slogan for all who are Reformed by history and birth, by ancestry and personal conviction.

3. In this formula the expression "Reformed principles" refers in the first place to what a Reformed person believes concerning Scripture in order that its authority may rest on unshakable grounds.

4. When this formula also entails a leading and systematic conception about man, nature, and the world and how it functions, it does not intend to honor a human system but only and exclusively the correct, scripturally based conception of the framework and order, which God himself has instituted for and in the creation and re-creation of all things.

5. Further, the general Scripture formula formally does not say anything specific about the relation of Scripture to nature or about the competing authorities of the apocryphal books, tradition, the councils, and "inner light," and just as little about how to judge the authenticity of the holy books, their interconnection, and their interpretation. The formula "on the basis of the Reformed principles," by contrast, declares itself decisively on all these points.

6. Materially the general Scripture formula includes the most contradictory and mutually exclusive views about rules of conduct in the domestic, civil, and social domains, whereas the formula we advocate offers guidance and direction for all these domains.

7. The general Scripture formula leads to disjointed opinions instead of coherent views, to a priori vagueness instead of historical continuity, and to loose generalities instead of integration in national life. Our formula, by contrast, assures us of unity, historical continuity, and national compatibility.

8. Finally, whereas in former times the general Scripture formula at least still guaranteed a clear acknowledgment of the authority of Scripture, this formula has become utterly useless now that it is even recommended by those Christians who first undermine all scriptural authority and then set it aside, to fall back on a conception that is still further removed from Scripture—namely, a conception of what they conjecture Jesus must have taught and meant.

II

Having thus far discussed the general meaning of "being bound to the word of God," I now come to the further question how such a bond can govern a university. Here too, "one size fits all" gets you nowhere. A church has to be bound to the word through its confession, backed up by disciplinary measures. For a philanthropic organization the general Scripture formula may perhaps be enough. For associations that deal with the deeper issues of life, however, you will only go safely by stating your belief about Scripture, both formally and materially. But how do things stand when it is a question of a university, an academy of science?

Until quite recently, people thought very differently about the nature of a university. Both during the Middle Ages and in the age of the Reformation it was simply assumed that a university had a confessional basis. In the Middle Ages this was less obvious, simply because there was only one church with a single confession. But no sooner did the Reformation shatter that unity than three types of universities arose: Catholic universities as in Louvain, Lutheran universities as in Wittenberg, and Reformed universities as in Leiden. Nonconfessional universities were unknown. That is how in our country, too, the three older universities in Leiden, Utrecht, and Groningen were established on a confessional basis. The same was true of our academies in Franeker and elsewhere that have since folded. Things stayed that way until the turn of the last century. For the longest time since then [1800] the official rule was that a university was not allowed to be bound to anything. In reality, however, it had to be opposed to all religious confessions. At present the tide is turning again, and confessional universities have reappeared in Switzerland, England, America, and here. The dominance of religious indifference has had its day, for which it has only itself to blame since it abandoned its own principle. That principle, after all, demands that the most competent scholars should always be appointed quite apart from their religious convictions. In practice, however, partisanship ensured that apostates were favored and that stars of the first magnitude, such as Bilderdijk and Groen, were forced to let their light shine outside the academy. Thus in point of fact the university did have a religious basis, but it was bound to the religion of unbelief.

Looking at it from a loftier vantage point, what are we to make of this? Does a religious basis have the right to bind a university, or does it not? A university is not a seminary or vocational school. It does have, to use somewhat popular language, a "retail outlet" or store, but at heart it is a "factory" or workshop—a workshop of science and scholarship. In the life of a nation, in the life of humanity, there is an irrepressible urge to extend our knowledge of nature and our control over it, and to increase our knowledge of the whole life of man in such a way that we gain insight into the forces and ordinances of that life and are able with the aid of that knowledge to give shape to it. To devote itself to that task is a university's true calling. It follows from this that its goal can be no other than to acquire knowledge of real states of affairs and the true order of things, something that can be expressed as a search for truth and nothing but truth.

Now, if it were granted humans to know objective truth, this search could never be other than the very same for all time and all people and each and every scholar. But that is not how it is. God alone knows objective truth; we can never advance beyond our subjective conception of the truth. That conception is related to our fundamental conviction, and that fundamental conviction is determined by our inner state, by the lingering effect of the past, and by the ideal that inspires us. And since that inner state, that lingering past, and that inspiring ideal differ widely from person to person, as a result of which one person's fundamental conviction is altogether different from that of another, therefore we all have different points of departure. You may call that point of departure your axioms or, if you will, your life-principle, or the root of your belief—but there is always something that you take with you as you embark on your research—namely, your *self*, and with yourself something dominant in your consciousness. The very question whether you believe with all your soul in God, or else are a pantheist or an atheist, is decisive for the whole of your scientific work.

Now then, will it do to put to work in one and the same university people who believe in the Triune God next to others who believe in a cosmic All-Soul, and before long next to people who deny all existence of God?

That depends on your view of a faculty and a university. If you take them to mean that every professor is capable on his own to study all the scholarly literature that he needs for his area of study, then there would be no objection to this. But if you sense that this would exceed all bounds of human capability and that the one scholar cannot do without the help and support of the other, then a university too has to have a division of labor. Thus a faculty is really a group of men who collaborate in investigating one part of the great field of academic learning, and a university is a combination of faculties who together aim at investigating the whole field. But then it is a foregone conclusion that those men must proceed from the same fundamental conviction, otherwise the work of one does not square with the work of another, in which case they would make no progress. Imagine how the palace in Amsterdam's central square would have turned out if three architects had worked on it at the same time, each according to his own plan.

If this fact alone shows that unity of fundamental conviction is indispensable, what I called the "store" next to the "workshop" requires the same thing. Unity is an indispensable requirement for vocational and professional training. A student must become acquainted with all sorts of schools and theories, but he has to learn to critically evaluate them in terms of a unified viewpoint.

A third argument is that a university costs money, a lot of money. If that money is acquired largely from voluntary contributions, then it stands to reason that no one will want to sacrifice anything for the scholarly work of two men of whom the one systematically pries loose every brick which the other has just inserted with great effort. If you reply: "Let the government fund the universities," well and good, provided the government does not reserve for itself the right to appoint the professors, for then only those professors will get appointed who belong to the prevailing school of thought, while the conviction of the country's minorities will continue to be without scholarly elaboration.

If the above arguments have persuaded you that an effective organization of a university demands that it should have a fundamental conviction on the basis of which all its research is carried out, then the next question is: How will you bind a university to such a basis? All Christians will of course say: it must be bound to God; the university too must serve God and glorify his wisdom. To specify further, one may say that the university is to be tied to the word of God—in every way in which God informs us of his word: in nature, in history, in our own hearts, and in scriptural revelation. Bear in mind that a university not only has a theological faculty but also investigates nature, history, the sphere of law, and so much more. To say therefore that you bind it to Scripture is not enough. A university has to listen and follow no matter where or how God speaks. Thus there need not be any disagreement about the question at hand: always and everywhere the university is to be bound to God and to God alone, whenever and wherever God reveals his wisdom, his will, and his ordinances, or makes these knowable through investigation.

Yet recall that I said a moment ago that our knowledge is never objective, that it can never be anything but subjective. What our "I" sees is not the thing itself but only an image of the thing reflected on the retina of our eye. Thus to say: bind a university to nature and Scripture, does not carry you one step further. For then all those differences in fundamental conviction are back: a Catholic, a Lutheran, an Anabaptist, an Ethical, and a Reformed scholar all say the same thing, but they all understand something different by it. And those differences exercise such a decisive influence on every aspect of academic research that, given the division of labor, the moment the research is related (as it should be) to your fundamental principle all unity of investigation is out the window, unless you have made sure that everybody's understanding of nature and Scripture, both in their mutual relationship and in their meaning, is the same as far as the basic principles are concerned. Only men who have arrived at one and the same worldview on the basis of nature and Scripture can work together as architects in building the common house.

Now then, that unity of worldview should not be a casual one. A university lives on through the centuries, so you need to designate a unified worldview that is not the fortuitous result of a momentary agreement but one whose continuity with national life is assured by its very nature and its historical roots. Accordingly it must embody one of those sharply differing schools that have emerged historically in the life of the nation.

It is for this reason that having a university bound to the word of God is only possible by binding it to the Reformed view of the world and to the Reformed outlook on life, or to put it more briefly, by binding it to the Reformed principles. These principles alone, after all, express for all involved what are everyone's fundamental convictions concerning the word of God that comes to us in nature and Scripture. When you insist that the tie to Scripture is enough, you leave out nature and you leave undecided all those critical questions that I presented in the first part of my address. As I said, they are questions, both materially and formally, which perhaps need not be settled in the case of a few philanthropic associations but which demand immediate answers particularly in the case of an academic institution; and if the answers diverge from one another the university will fall apart.

But what now is meant by binding a university to the multifaceted word of God via the Reformed principles? Does it mean that you present your professors with a broad syllabus of propositions for each scientific discipline, which they have to accept, which they may not touch, and which they have to repeat like parrots? Of course not. Then there would be no research and no scholarship. No; on the contrary, the intention is that the scholars will first of all thoroughly investigate the multifaceted word of God in nature and Scripture in order in this way to demonstrate the scientific soundness of the Reformed principles and where necessary to refine and carry forward their historical lines.

As the fruit of my own research I published my *Principles of Sacred Theology*,[17] but do I speak like a parrot on any of its pages? Are my conclusions not drawn from the deepest root of our communal life and thought? No reviewer has ever asserted otherwise. And if you now wonder if that does not leave everything unsettled again, then my answer is: your guarantee against that lies in the unity of fundamental conviction as expressed in the communal confession of the Reformed principles. For, to repeat, a university is an academic institution, and no professor there has the right

17. A. Kuyper, *Encyclopaedie der heilige Godgeleerdheid*, 3 vols. (Amsterdam: Wormser, 1893–94). A partial translation by J. H. De Vries is found in *An Encyclopedia of Sacred Theology: Its Principles* (1898; repr., 1954, 1963, 1965, 1968, 1980, abridged 2001, revised 2008).

to arbitrarily pass off something as a Reformed principle. On the contrary, he has to prove his claim. He has to demonstrate that his view of the Reformed principles is historically the correct one. He has to combat scientifically what is passed off as a Reformed principle but in reality is not. And if he finds that in the Reformed tradition something was viewed as truth which is not in accordance with the multifaceted word of God in nature and Scripture, then he is duty-bound, for the Lord's sake, to cast the misconception into the crucible and purify it.

Thus a professor at our university is charged with four things:

1. He is to solemnly declare that the Reformed fundamental conviction is also his.
2. He is to investigate which leading ideas in the area of research assigned to him were historically derived from the Reformed principles.
3. He is to vindicate with the authority of God's word in nature and Scripture the Reformed principles and the lines drawn from them, or else to correct them if they are at variance with that word.
4. He is to carry forward the lines from the past into the spiritual struggle of today.

And so I trust I have shown you clearly, first, why the general scriptural formula is absolutely inadequate for serving as a university's bond to the word of God; second, why we can attain that firm bond to the word of God in no other way than via the tie to the Reformed principles; and third, why this neither conflicts with the scientific standpoint nor clips the wings of scientific research, but much rather allows scientific research to fully come into its own.

None of the arguments that have been raised against our formula affects the standpoint I have indicated.

Should you ask me more concretely, finally, in what manner at the founding of such a university the bond can be laid so that it will stick, then some formula or other would have to be included in its charter or bylaws. We discussed that in our morning session. I would like to point out, however, that the best formula in and of itself is a dead letter, hence powerless, if it is not connected with life. Living by the Reformed principles is concentrated most intensively in the institutional churches, and therefore a university is to be congratulated if it has a connection with these churches such that those churches support it in confessing and upholding God's word according to its purest interpretation. It is to bind all faculties to this connection, yet in such way that the knot—of course a knot composed of the ends of two cords—is tied in the appointment of the professors in the theological faculty, since that faculty is assigned to a field of research that is directly related to the task and calling of the institutional churches. It is certainly no easy thing to tie that knot, because both church and academy have to insist on their rights. But that knot will be tied if those who are called to the task pray to God for the gift to do so, having no other goal than to be obedient to God's ordinances.

Yet even though the chief contact between church and academy is found in the theological faculty, the bond must also be laid with the other faculties to the extent that its professors too may rightly be required to seek the communion of the saints in a church that lives by the Reformed principles, not just nominally but also spiritually. Transitional circumstances are certainly conceivable, and I can well imagine a situation in which a zoologist or a botanist is impeccably Reformed as far as the principles pertaining to his discipline are concerned and yet is more Lutheran than Reformed on the question of the perseverance of the saints. But as circumstances become more normal, surely it is not too much to ask of a man of science that he be a man of one piece and not appear two-faced before the public but rather allow his basic conviction to suffuse his entire worldview.[18]

Granted, it can quite well happen that a man of science who sincerely believes he is living by the basic conviction that is embodied historically in the Reformed principles nevertheless arrives at contrary scientific results. But in what field does that not happen? There are people who once were Catholic but later became Reformed or Lutheran. Others are born Protestant but later turn Catholic—and, if he is a pastor, resigns his office, as was done in a recent case. There have been politicians who withdrew into private life when their convictions changed. Also army officers who became followers of Tolstoy and surrendered their commission. This is hard, but always less hard than what our martyrs suffered for their convictions on the gallows

18. *Note by the author:* Of course, the Free University, which I have the honor to serve, does not in the least claim that by binding itself to the word of God in nature and Scripture it has already attained the ideal as I have sketched it.

or the stake. And however painful this may be, one must never demand that, to avert this pain when convictions change, a church or a university should on that account wander about without any convictions, lacking any bond—and that bond taken as binding—to the word of God.[19]

I thank you.

19. Lohman replied the same year with a brochure entitled *De waarheid bovenal* (Utrecht: Kemink, 1899), to which Kuyper responded in the weekly *De Heraut*, nos. 1141–1166, 1171–1174. The address *Scholastica II: Om het zoeken of om het vinden? Of: het doel van echte studie* (Amsterdam/Pretoria: Höveker & Wormser, 1900) may also be considered an (indirect) response to Lohman's position; for an English translation of this address, titled "The Goal of Genuine Study," see below in this volume.

SCHOLARSHIP

TEXT INTRODUCTION

In 1889, and again in 1900, it was Professor Kuyper's turn to function as rector of the Free University, which included welcoming the students at the start of the academic year. He used the occasion each time to give advice on how to study effectively and how to model the life of scholars-to-be. At the same time he sought to inspire them by expounding on the guiding principles of the university they had chosen to attend. He held forth on the divine purpose of scholarship for human culture and emphasized the calling of the *Vrije Universiteit* to be an "Opposition School." At its start in 1880, the university had been "embarrassingly small to the point of blushing," but twenty years later it was still an embarrassment in terms of size: a small student body, taught by half a dozen professors. Nevertheless, the rector believed their university had every right to exist. After all, it based itself on a centuries-old worldview and stood for a viable alternative to the reigning paradigms of the day.

Source: Kuyper, Abraham. *Scolastica, of 't geheim van echte studie*. Amsterdam: J. A. Wormser, 1889. *Scolastica II. Om het zoeken of om het vinden? Of het doel van echte studie*. Amsterdam/Pretoria: Höveker & Wormser, 1900. Translated and annotated by Harry Van Dyke.

SCHOLARSHIP

TWO CONVOCATION ADDRESSES

THE SECRET OF GENUINE STUDY (1889)

Esteemed Students,

Whether you are a returning student or a new recruit, on behalf of the senate of this university: welcome to our academic auditorium!

The oppressive summer heat at times made the atmosphere too sultry to demand much exertion from your brains, but now that the air is becoming cooler your head too is gradually clearing up, and the joy of study excites you with renewed urgency. Our friend "Bruin" busies himself in the summer and goes to sleep when winter approaches, but your lifestyle is exactly the opposite. You take it easy in the summer, but when the sky rises and the thermometer sinks you enter your true element.

I still recall from my own student days how the start of a new academic year beckoned us. In June we yearned to get away. Our head was tired, the courses finished, our wallet usually empty. This couldn't go on. The arrival of a long summer vacation was an exhilarating prospect. To quit the stuffy city and enter the country, to leave the solitary room and travel home, no more lectures, no more exams, master of our own time! How we would enjoy "home sweet home" and drink of the pleasures of life.

In June, yes, those summer holidays opened up visions of true bliss. But then, when June was behind us and July had passed and August had gone by, the best days were over and memories of the good, happy days in the academy rekindled in our imagination. The holidays seemed empty and without purpose. No, this could not go on either. At last we longed for the end of summer and the start of a new school year.

And when the day finally arrived that we returned to our alma mater and the lecture halls and got reacquainted with our fellow students, then we looked with affection even on our professors behind the lecterns and were happy to see them back, the men who had made us slave away at their courses and who during oral exams had looked like veritable inquisitors. We realized keenly that the university was our real life and that the academy was our real element. Enthusiastically, as though from now on it would be clear sailing and we would hit the books like never before, we embarked on the new semester without a care in the world and hungry for more knowledge.

I hope that all you returning students have come back with similar feelings. At the end of the holidays a student is like a fish on dry land, and to greet the academy again is for him to meet the flood tide that surrounds him, lifts him up, and bathes him in fresh waters. As for you first-year students, you may not be familiar with such delights, but you will experience even greater riches. To become a university student for the first time is for you to enter into a new, mysterious world, a world that fascinates you precisely because it is so mysterious.

So greetings and welcome to you all, whether you are already acquainted with these riches or will experience them for the first time.[1] Let there be a tremor of noble intentions in your hearts! Open your eyes wide and muster all your strength to really study hard this time. We your professors, we too have our hearts beating more rapidly now that we see you back. A lot is expected again of you and of us. Much will be demanded again from all of us this year. Very well; let us resume our task with manly courage and Christian sense. And in case difficulties await us, let us begin not

1. The Free University, begun in 1880, by this time (1889) had eighty students, five professors, and three part-time instructors.

with presumption but in humility. For our help is in the name of the Lord, who made the heavens and the earth and therefore also made the world of thought and for that thought the world of study.

Since by way of introduction to that study I now offer you some words about the nature of study, please give me your still undivided attention for what I am going to say about the *disciplina scolastica*. If you were not students I would add: don't let the sound of the word *scolastica* frighten you just because it reminds you of nothing so much as arid concepts and overly subtle distinctions. But a university student does not go by the sound of a word, and old specters do not frighten him. In the word *scolastica* you detected the root *scola*, and so you understood immediately that the *vita scolastica* is the life of the school and has nothing to do with the disputations of the old scholastics. Yet even then you do not reach deep enough for its meaning. *Scola* is not a school of learning. *Scola* is the *res publica litterarum*, the entire republic of letters, that distinctive sphere in society which indeed centers on the university yet pervades the country with young men who thirst after knowledge and with men of learning who illumine our towns and villages like bright stars.

In the days of the Synod of Dort in 1619, our Reformed polymath Alsted[2] dedicated a marvelous book to the States General.[3] It was a book of more than four thousand columns that saved a poor student the cost of acquiring a library, since this single quarto served as a handbook for all the subjects. It was a library in itself. It even contained a Hebrew, Greek, and Latin lexicon, and did not omit a manual for music. But, what I wanted to get to: in this quarto Alsted also dealt with *Ethica*, and after completing it he says that he would now move on to *Symbiotica*—that is, to the sciences of symbiosis or living together, of which there are, he says, three in number. There are three spheres in life, each drawn with its own compass: *Economica, Politica,*

---

2. Johann Heinrich Alsted (1588–1638) was a professor of philosophy and theology at Herborn in the duchy of Nassau, Germany, and later in Transylvania, today part of Romania but at the time an independent principality with a strong presence of Hungarian Calvinists. Alsted is renowned as an encyclopedist, and Kuyper possibly refers here to Alsted, *Scientiarum Omnium Encyclopaediae*, 4 vols. (Leiden: Huguetan and Rauaud, 1649). The topics Kuyper refers to are contained in volume 3.
3. The States General in 1619 was the governing body of delegates representing the United Provinces of the Netherlands, also known as the Dutch Republic. It should not be confused with the present-day States General of the Kingdom of the Netherlands, which is a bicameral parliament in a constitutional monarchy.

and *Scolastica*. *Economica* is the science of domestic life; *Politica* is the science of the life of the state; and then follows *Scolastica*, the science of the republic of letters, or if you will, of the circle of scholars.

In those good old days, all those who devoted themselves to scholarship or completed a classical education were regarded as constituting a separate life-sphere, a distinct order in society. People were still aware that men of science lived by a distinctive principle, moved in a separate world, and were called by God to fulfill a special task in the whole of human society. A professor would therefore address his students as *ornatissimi commilitones*: distinguished comrades, fellow conscripts in the army corps to which he himself belonged, companions in the war against the same enemy, in the service of the same country.

This was already understood in ancient Israel. Men of learning were regarded as a separate family, where every teacher was called "father" and his pupils were greeted as spiritual "sons." You know those names, "father" and "sons," from the wisdom of the writer of Proverbs. That awareness of having a distinctive calling in life and a special God-given task—how gloriously it speaks to you when you read there:

> My son, if you receive my words
>   and treasure up my commandments with you,
> making your ear attentive to wisdom
>   and inclining your heart to understanding;
> yes, if you call out for insight
>   and raise your voice for understanding,
> if you seek it like silver
>   and search for it as for hidden treasures,
> then you will understand the fear of the Lord
>   and find the knowledge of God.
> For the Lord gives wisdom;
>   from his mouth come knowledge and understanding;
> he stores up sound wisdom for the upright;
>   he is a shield to those who walk in integrity. [Prov 2:1–7]

This was originally the basis on which the whole concept of a university rested, for it did not denote then what was made of it later, a *universitas scientiarum*, a community of the sciences. Rather, it had an altogether different meaning: a university was a *universitas docentium et discentium*, a community of teachers and learners united in a single corporate body. That is why men spoke of a "republic of letters" as a commonwealth that transcended all states and empires and formed its own sphere throughout the world. That was also the particular reason why this republic had its own language: not the Latin of Cicero, but a Latin which it had itself forged out of the old Roman tongue.

True, this high and holy conception of a university was soon falsified. Young men whose object was not the study itself nevertheless coveted the privileges attached to the order of the learned and began to penetrate our sacred garden like veritable parasites. And then the sense of constituting a separate order bred stupid and foolish self-exaltation that stamped everyone whose name simply appeared on the registrar's rolls as a scholar, while everyone who did not belong to the elect, to the "men of the gown," was booed and reviled as a philistine or a "man of the town." Especially when the order of scholars still had external privileges—a student could with impunity defy the "constables" during nightly raids on shop signs and doorbells, and a student paid no import duty on his wine—then that privilege once again, as everywhere else, worked its evil effect. Not studying but creating a nuisance in public and carousing and drinking their fellows under the table became the base occupation in which students sought their honor. And of course, from their student days this false pride accompanied them into life. Because they had once attended university they thought they could forever look down with contempt on all those who had never gone to university. The holy laurels of learning fell into the mire, and the renegades' faces were wreathed in the vines of wild creepers.

This behavior came home to roost, and the outcome was that the sphere of scholarship lost its native impulse, tore up its charter, and put itself in the service of the state, so that *Scolastica* dissolved into *Politica*. Worse, a desire to break down the faith instead of shoring it up became for many the principal motive for doing scholarship. At last the evil, narrow-minded selfishness arrived that sees no higher purpose in the academy than to assist its visitors as quickly as possible in preparing them for what is called a "position." The first stage caused the academy to forfeit its freedom, the second set it in opposition to God, and the third lowered it to the level of studying to pass the exams. And who knows, maybe they have also sneaked into our own university already—those young men who supposedly are devoting themselves to academic studies but who have only one goal in mind: once and for all, and as quickly and cheaply as possible, to be done with bookish learning. They are parasites who come in order to pursue "success" but whose parched lips have never tasted one sip from the holy grail of scholarship. They are not looking for silver and do not search for hidden gold in the mine of scholarship: their only goal is to acquire a steady position and a guaranteed salary.

Do you see now why I wanted to talk about *Scolastica*? At the start of the new year I wanted to put this question to you before the face of God: *What should be the goal of university study and the goal of living and working in the sacred domain of scholarship?* I wanted to see whether I might perhaps rouse in some of you a more sanctified passion.

To have the opportunity of studying is such an inestimable privilege, and to be allowed to leave the drudgery of society to enter the world of scholarship is such a gracious decree of our God. Nature out there (God's word says: as a punishment for sin) is hard for 99 percent of the human race. Of the 1.4 billion people who live on this earth, there are at least 1,300 million who literally have to eat their bread "by the sweat of their brow"—on farm or factory, at lathe or anvil, in shop or office, forever occupied in wresting food, clothing, and shelter from nature by processing, shaping, shipping, or selling it. And the real man of science does not look on this with contempt. On the contrary, he senses that to live such a life should really have been his lot too, and that he, bowing under God's ordinances if that were his occupation, would have found happiness and honor in it. But God created, in addition to the world of nature with all its elements and forces and materials, a world of thoughts; for all creation contains *Logos*. You are familiar with what the apostle John testifies in the opening of his gospel: *en archē ho logos ... kai di' auto ta panta egeneto kai chōris auto egeneto oude en ho gegonen.*[4]

Now, the deeper meaning of this Logos is only disclosed to us through the revelation of God's mystery. He who does not worship God as the Triune One does not understand this mystery. But even if for now we do not try to remove the curtain from this holy place of worship, this at least is clear: there is not only a creation but also a Logos in the creation, and man, created in the image of God and therefore a logical creature, has the capacity and the calling to use his logical thought to reflect on this Logos which shines in all creation. And this, students, is the beautiful, exalted, sacred task of science.

4. That is, "In the beginning was the Word ... and through him all things were made and without him nothing was made that has been made." See John 1:1, 3. Kuyper appears to be quoting from memory.

Now if nature were not so hard and life not so cruel, many more people could have the enjoyment of that sacred calling. But things being what they are, only a few are granted that honor, and by far most people are deprived of that privilege.

But you and I have received this great favor from our God. We belong to that specially privileged group. Thus, woe to you and shame on you if you do not hear God's holy call in the field of scholarship and do not exult with gratitude and never-ending praise that it pleased God out of free grace to choose you as his instrument for this noble, uplifting, inspiring calling.

It is for God's honor that there should be scholarship in the land. His thought, his Logos in the *kosmos*, must not remain unknown and unexamined. He created us as logical beings in order that we should trace his Logos, investigate it, publish it, personally wonder at it, and fill others with wonder. This too proclaims the glory of his name. Without scientific research that treasure remains hidden in the world and does not rise to the surface. As the Zulu for centuries walked over the goldfields without suspecting what treasures the miners of Transvaal would one day dig up, so too the nonscientific person treads on the soil of God's creation until the man of science discovers the mine of knowledge, opens it up, descends into it, and searches there for silver, to bring out the gold of God's thoughts.

Of course, man can live without science and scholarship; witness the native peoples of Botswana, Mongolia, and North America. But not until a higher form of consciousness awakens in people does human life receive its nobility from the thoughts of God. Then man increases his power over nature and moves from the dark cellar to the bright upper room flooded in light.

Thus there are three wonderful things about science: it brings to light the hidden glory of God; it gives you joy in the act of digging up the gold that lies hidden in creation; and it grants you the honor of raising the level and well-being of human life. So, whatever made you think that you can become a scholar merely by studying and cramming for exams? No, I tell you, even if you had stuffed your brain full of facts and theories and had passed every examination summa cum laude, you would still be no more than a hewer of wood and a drawer of water in this elite corps of scholars—unless you had entered that world of God's thoughts with all your heart and all your mind and in that world of God's glorious thoughts you had heard the voice of him who had ordained you a priest of learning and anointed you with consecrated oil for that holy priesthood.

Every man of learning should be fired with a zeal to battle against the darkness and for the light. The glow of gas lay hidden for centuries in the dark coal mine, but not until that coal was dug from the mine and processed by human art did it reveal its luster. Similarly, it is your high calling to wrest the light of God's splendor from the hidden recesses of creation, not in order to seek honor for yourself but honor for your God.

To be sure, God has caused light to rise in our darkness also along avenues other than science. His is not the cruelty of our age that had generation after generation wander in darkness until at last in this nineteenth century the lights could go on—and then only for the aristocracy of the intellect. God is gracious and compassionate, and by means of his revelation and the founding of his church he had from the beginning ignited a glow that faith imbibed and that enriched an Abraham and a Moses far beyond what any nineteenth-century learning is capable of—rich in their heart, rich in their soul, rich in those more tender sensations that bear the mark of the eternal. And scholars, far from being able to do without that faith, must begin by being rich in that faith if they are ever to feel their heart stir with the holy impulse that drives them to engage in true scholarship.

Still, scholarship is something all its own—not something higher, but a work of our minds during which the minds travel along other paths. Even if there were no salvation for sinners and if God's wrath plunged us all into eternal perdition, even then our race would not be absolved from the obligation to investigate the Logos that God has hidden in his creation and to bring it to light. God must not be robbed of this honor. Science is bound to religious belief only to the extent that an unbelieving man of science causes science's beehive, as much as depends on him, to degenerate into a wasps' nest. He does this unintentionally, simply because he cannot act otherwise, in order to rob God of that Logos and pass it off as a product of his own thoughts. That defines the school of science in this century, which wants to be something outside God, apart from God, in opposition to God, and to seek its glory in ridiculing the Christian faith. But even this derailed science brings gain, for what it correctly observes is observed and what it properly investigates is investigated. Nevertheless it contains a dangerous element by wandering off into materialistic science or else by setting its hypotheses in opposition to the *thesis* of God's revelation. Either way, it deviates from its sacred calling to be God's minister, God's priest in his holy temple.

The suggestion that men of faith for this reason would have to flee from the world of science is one that can only be maintained by the unscientific person. For that would amount to forsaking one's duty, abandoning science to unholy secularization, and personally forfeiting the influence that men of faith must exercise on the thinking of our generation. Instead, given this state of affairs, it is imperative—and this will give you a clue as to why the Free University was founded—that a warmer, bolder interest in science and learning should awaken among God's people, in order to get derailed science back on its God-given track and to refute the lie that faith hates science. At the same time we need to be encouraged not to disdain the scholarship of others but together with others to contribute to mankind's great scholarly task, provided only that it can do so in its own institution.

But I hear you! I understand your barely concealed laughter asking me whether students are already PhDs and whether I would want to see you parading on Amsterdam's streets, thrusting out your chest and proudly proclaiming, "Here goes a man of science." No, I do not. I would rather that you keep alive the old tradition of dressing down every conceited young man who may have stolen into your ranks. Whoever cures a fellow student of this academic leprosy will have rendered a service to his country. Genius of genuine gold, as Fichte[5] put it so beautifully, does not know its own beauty. Real talent has the fragrance of a flower without being aware of it. The true scientific spirit possesses its ornament with blushing naïveté. Academia nurses little hope for young men who notice too early that they are smart and who leave their village and sail into the university town as prodigies. Indeed, I go further and tell you that a youth who sits in his room calculating whether he might be made of the stuff that professors are made of should never even have enrolled and should be struck from the registrar's rolls for covert misconduct. I also know very well that no one person can learn all knowledge and that one can sooner empty the North Sea with an oyster shell than that a student with the shell of his brain could drain the ocean of science. For a single discipline alone, the studies are so voluminous that the successful defense of a dissertation, even if passed cum laude, means little more than the declaration that the newly minted doctor can now at least begin to realize that he still knows or understands almost nothing. Europe has only one Mont Blanc, and the intellectual world too has ever so many stretches of plains, then broad mountain ranges, and only here and there a lonely Alpine peak. So if the *scola* does not want to decimate itself, it must not use a few men of genius as its standard. That would end in a

5. Kuyper refers here to German philosopher Johann Gottlieb Fichte (1762–1814).

deluge with barely eight souls in the ark and also much cattle. No, its rule must embrace the entire body of scholars and so must also be geared to the emergency personnel in the field hospitals. But to study any discipline at all takes such a huge effort that even if you make no higher demand than to be a half-decent participant, there is just no time left to feed the tiniest microbe of self-conceit. Solid study is the natural antidote for those parasites, and the remedy never fails.

But if a recruit—say, a child of the regiment—has just joined the colors, that does not yet give him access to the council of war, unless it be to hand a book or a map to the commander. Yet for all that, he is a member of the regiment! And if the next day the entire army is routed and this recruit is the only one left, then the recruit, if he is a man, will pick up the colors and wave it till his last breath; it will not drop from his failing hands until it is captured by the foe.

This is the holy awareness that I wanted to kindle in you students as you enter the fortress of science. For whatever modest place you take up at the back of our corps, you are nevertheless inside the boundary that separates the domain of science from what lies outside it. You are recruits, not yet with the marshal's baton in hand, yet fully inducted into the corps. Your aspirations and intentions should merge with the aspirations and intentions of that corps. You are wearing its uniform and therefore the spirit that inspires the corps to victory must not be foreign to your spirit. Just as a commander sins if he risks the battle without lifting up his divine vocation before the face of God, so the conscript is wanting in godliness if he takes up his guard duties without being conscious of the divine nature of his vocation and without praying to God for his blessing. Do I mean that you should pray before opening the pages of Lysias[6] or memorizing the Hebrew alphabet? Most certainly you should do that, too, but what I mean reaches deeper. I mean that you place yourself with all your academic hopes and dreams before the face of God in such a way that praying for your studies flows naturally from it and is not attached to it as an afterthought.

What I ask of you is that you realize something of the reason why God for the sake of his work wants there to be scientific learning among men; that you begin to see how on account of sin only a few are elected to be engaged in scholarship at various levels as a calling from God; that you will

6. Lysias (ca. 445–ca. 380 BC) was an Athenian speech writer and orator in classical Greece.

be jubilant with praise and thanksgiving for being privileged to take your place among the ranks of the elect; and that you will be impressed from the outset with the fearful thought that every person who has received this as his calling can only say that his study is wasted and his life lost if he dies without having contributed his share to the honor of God. Or, to say it with an allusion to a word of our Lord: I want you students to realize that the man with the spade and the man of the leather apron, if they have thought about their vocation, will enter the kingdom of God before you.

This is not to suggest that someday you should all write fat tomes or advance the frontiers of science. Only the peaks above the snow line form lasting glaciers; what lies at lower levels melts anyway. Yet each of you has the calling to live life as a scholar and to gather honey for the great beehive of life in the interest of the environment into which you will eventually be placed. A single educated man in a humble village is for that village the hub of a higher life. A scholar's mission in life should be to serve and not to be served. Our maxim will always be: "You received without paying; give without pay" [Matt 10:8]. Indeed, the point is that you are open to receive, that you are receptive. Not necessarily so that you may receive much. The rock shelf where the waterfall clatters down receives less than the loose, sandy soil that is normally watered from the clouds by droplets only.

The "receiving" that leads to knowing is expressed etymologically in almost all languages with a metaphor derived from procreation. The unchaste woman becomes a mother only by accident; the whore as a rule dies childless; only the chaste, respectable woman conceives and so receives. But that is exactly why you are required to embrace science in love, why your blood should stir passionately for science, and why you should be ravished by her beauty not in the marketplace but in discrete privacy. In your mind lies your glory as scholars. That is your field of labor. Not merely to live, but to know that you live and how you live, and how things around you live, and how all that hangs together and lives out of the one efficient cause that proceeds from God's power and wisdom. Other people, when evening falls, have to have sown and plowed, counted and calculated; but you have to have thought, reflected, analyzed, until at last a harvest of your own thoughts may germinate and ripen on the field of your consciousness.

You too for your part must feel called to be a nurseryman in this consecrated garden. And if others plant a cedar or a vine while you perhaps make only cuttings of lilac or hyssop, that does not matter. Even mint, dill, and cumin belong to the plant world. Just as long as something is growing, and as long as that something is not a weed.

And how does this sense of calling become evident? From the very outset, if study is your delight or your burden. Time for relaxation may intervene—I would say, must intervene. But the kind of relaxation that you look for marks you. If you are one of those who, when the books can be pushed aside for a while, seeks recreation by descending hastily to what is base and making up for lost time by indulging in coarse entertainment or debauchery and drunken revelry—no, then you are not a man of the colors on this sacred battlefield but a wretched trespasser. Only when it becomes evident that you seek your relaxation in things noble, honest, pure, and lovely will you be given your commission for this holy war.

Your sense of calling also becomes evident when you take up your studies again. For how you study is crucial. Is this how you study: first finish the general program to get to your major, then go fishing for the questions usually asked on the oral finals, and then with the diploma in your pocket heave a sigh of relief: "Thank God, I'm done with books for the rest of my life!" In that case, what have you, trained racehorse, divined of God in the study of languages, in mathematics, in the beauties of classical studies, in the finer details of your chosen discipline? Eyes open, you saw nothing; ears open, you heard nothing. You took in ballast, sailed with ballast, and now you throw the ballast overboard. You toured the country in a hooded carriage, took lodging at nightfall in village after village, but now that you have reached your destination you know nothing about the countryside because you saw nothing and observed nothing.

Students, a farmer who has studied his draft horse and knows how to handle it is more scientific than a "learned" graduate whose whole academic achievement consists in a scrap of paper that was handed to him upon graduation, a certificate that will accuse his conscience for the rest of his life.

Real study takes time. Not a year, or a year and a half, of frittering away the days, and then working up a sweat at the pump like a fireman. He who has a love of scholarship is like the worker bee that leaves the hive early in the morning, forages for flowers, and comes back in time with honey as its prize. Such a student studies more than what has been assigned for the exam; he loves to crack open a book, wants to get a general education, and picks up, say, the *Iliad* in the original, not in order that he might give a half-baked translation of it if it were ever asked, but to enjoy it for himself because it is beautiful, and to get a sense of what it is that makes it so beautiful.

The pseudo-student builds a house of blocks, like a child, and when he has finished it he puts the blocks back in the box. The true student builds a proper house and takes care that his studies are done properly: the beams have to be real beams, the iron bolts of real iron and not of tin, and the cornerstone a real stone that can bear the necessary weight. This causes him to develop a sense of what is truth. Not guessing at it, and by chance coming up with a tolerable answer. Not bragging and showing off with what is not asked and what is not relevant, but really knowing what you know, every argument a genuine argument, every opinion an opinion that has merit, checking every link in a chain of ideas to see whether the argument is watertight. After all, the man of science does not play fast and loose with the facts, but it is granted him to track down the gold of God's thoughts, the gems of divine wisdom, a labor that requires real discernment. Then you may at times know much less than the braggart and look shabby next to the dandy; but is the woman who can adorn her throat with one real diamond not richer than the trollop from the music hall who has bedecked her bosom with the glitter of costume jewelry?

I pray that this quiet conviction of having a sacred calling may more and more govern your whole academic life! I hope it will govern your relationship with your professors. It is the sneak who bows and scrapes before them to avoid difficulties at exam time, and it is he who picks on the "bookish" student as his favorite target for the arrows of his ridicule. The serious student, by contrast, sees in his professors what the soldier values about his officers, not in the barracks but on the battlefield: men who know a little more than he and can lead him to where he otherwise would never arrive. Professors are not your commanders but your fellow soldiers—the concept of fellow soldiers, after all, is necessarily reciprocal. They are men whom you don't avoid, but seek out. You are not blind to their faults and failings, and you gently poke fun at them in order to improve them. But in the end you know that they share one holy calling with you.

That sense of calling should be no less evident in student life. Because we form a *scola* together, a distinctive sphere, a distinctive class in society, the motive for which God called that sphere into being should also govern your social conversations. A hunter loves to talk about his partridges, his dogs, his adventures at the chase. A mariner will talk about port and starboard, windward and leeward, halyard and bowsprit. A good housewife talks almost too much about her children and her maids. And that is how you will also hear students talk: sometimes about a pretty girl they spotted, yes, or a perfect carom in billiards; but in general their talk will be a discussion of an issue in the world of thought, a skirmish which at times resembles a real fight. Small-town squabbles and petty jealousies will be cut off by their fresh tone and candor. Students state frankly what they think; they tell each other the plain truth. But talk behind someone's back they leave to the philistines.

Their sense of calling becomes evident even in the way they handle their money and take care of their body. I know, money is always a student's weak point. But it makes such a difference if a student carries home in triumph, like a hunter his partridge, the book he won at an auction thanks to a skillful bid, or if he spends even his book money on fancy shawls or absurdly priced cigars or rides in a fancy carriage. I am not ridiculing anyone's small means; there are students who crave books and feel nostalgic when they look at their empty shelves. But at least they don't squander their money, and that very nostalgia speaks of their love of study.

When I mentioned care of the body, I was again serious. The apostle Paul pointed out how the Greek athletes and wrestlers made certain to strengthen their muscles in preparation for the match [see 1 Cor 9:24–27]; and our gymnasts, cyclists, and rowers model for us how a sensible treatment of the body enhances the use of their muscles. Now, would a student be responsible before God if he thought about everything except his body and thoughtlessly neglected it? Such unholy spiritualism will not get you very far. If you want to be devoted to things of the spirit, then make sure you don't begin to look like a spirit. If you are called to reflect on how things are interrelated, can you overlook the relation between yourself and your body? And is it not peculiar about our *scola* and your role in it that *study* stands in contrast to *bodily movement* and that it concentrates all your exertions on that part of the body which you call your brains and which controls more powerfully than any other part the well-being of your entire body and can exhaust it through overexertion? That is why you need to make a study of your body. You have to exercise it; you have to keep it fresh. A *sana mens* dwells only in a *sano corpore*.[7] And whoever thinks that fresh air, vigorous movement, nutritious meals, and regular sleep are of secondary importance for scholarship should read Bilderdijk's *The Disease of Scholars*[8] and be cured of his presumption and madness by this gigantic beacon at sea.

---

7. See Juvenal, *Satires*, bk. 10, line 356: "A man should pray for a healthy mind in a healthy body."
8. Willem Bilderdijk, *De Ziekte der geleerden* (Amsterdam and The Hague: Allart, 1807), a didactic poem in six cantos.

Your method of studying, too, must be inspired and directed by that sense of being enlisted in the world of scholarship. You are to build, and building demands a structured course of action. No futile Sisyphean labor, in which the rock, rolled uphill, forever rolls down again. No pointless task as of the Danaids, filling jars riddled with holes so that the water flows out again as fast as it is collected. Look at lambs skipping in the meadow, how they go about rehearsing in a fashion. If you keep on studying without ever rehearsing and reviewing, in the end you will know nothing. You have to be methodical about your study. Scientific study, if nothing else, must be approached scientifically. Don't just work, but think about how you work. Why this and not that? Why this first and that later? Don't just work through the books on your shelf, but proceed as demanded by your ability to absorb, in keeping with the organic interconnectedness of knowledge. Read widely, but remember that mere browsing yields knowledge that evaporates quickly. So, if you manage your time and know how to make the most of your hours and minutes, you will double your work time and have more free time to boot. The watchword of science is order. If you study chaotically you will get lost in the chaos. It is the mountain climbers, not the loafers and the drifters, who have taught us *Qui va piano va sano é qui va sano va lontano*: slow and steady wins the race.

Finally I come to form. By themselves, I agree, form and design belong to the world of art; but the world of science too calls for the beauty of design. Consider the Father of lights! Is his creation ever without design, and do the smallest leaf and the tiniest insect not display the most artful finishing touches? So would it be proper for the scholarly elite to view the requirements of form as falling beneath their dignity and to regard the restrictions of design as undermining their freedom and independence? I realize that sensitivity to design is not given to everyone equally, so I will not insist that every student's digs be tastefully furnished and that the cut of everybody's coat be well tailored. But there is one demand that comes to all students without exception: that you pay attention to outward form. The ancient lesson *Non scolae sed vitae*[9] means that each of you in your own way, as men of learning, will soon have to take up a position in society in order to serve, bless, and inspire your fellow man, which you cannot do if you neglect the form. Form and design are the hydraulic drills with which you

9. That is, we learn "not for the school but for life." See Seneca, *Epistulae morales ad Lucilium*, Ep. 106.

penetrate the public with what you have to say. Suppose two men appear before the bench, at the lectern, on the pulpit, on a dais, or in a panel: one of whom is less talented yet whose appearance is pleasant, whose thoughts flow clearly, whose style and diction are refined, whose voice is pleasing, whose enunciation is pure, whose manner of speaking is compelling, and whose gestures are well timed—this man of few talents will have far greater influence than the man of ten talents who is carelessly dressed, has a poor style, speaks with an accent, has an awkward posture, and waves his arms like a windmill. Outward form is therefore crucial. You cannot dispense with it; your success, your future, your influence depend on it. Proper form will determine whether you will waste your time and energy in the world of science or make a lasting contribution to it—that is, whether you will answer to your God-given calling or forsake that calling. Of course I know that form can be hollow, artificial, false. God preserve you from it. But may God also preserve you from that levity that thinks: "The form will take care of itself." That may be true for men of genius, but to those of you who are modest enough not to fancy yourself a genius I say: devote some time to studying these things, in the knowledge that it is no less true of form and design that *pour savoir quelque chose, il faut l'avoir appris*: in order to know something you have to have studied it.

I have come to the end of my address and go back to where I began. The *scola*—or, if you prefer, the circle of people with an academic education—is a God-ordained order in society by virtue of a divine calling. If you keep that in mind, you know that it implies pure living and sincere piety. Scholarship is not abstract learning separate from life. The saying that "great men have great faults" only reminds us also in academia that great powers of genius and talent have been lost for service in the temple of science through pride and dissoluteness. Brilliant minds and sharp intellects may impress you, but if moral truth is absent, so also will be the anointing of priestly love and dedication. *To alēthes* and *to agathon* cannot be separated.[10] Whoever fails to honor God's laws in the temple of science only raises clouds of dust that darken his view of truth. So live clean lives and hate what is base and immoral. Light does not illuminate the field of science except for the righteous—provided, and I would emphasize this, provided it is not the righteousness of the Stoic but the tender purity of the child of God. Only from faith does the spark fly upward that lights the passion for science in

---

10. That is, the true and the good are inseparable.

your breast—the faith which feeds on God's revelation and submits to it, and which personally gives you the blissful knowledge that you are a child of God; but as applied to the *scola*, also a faith that makes you serve the Lord of glory in your studies and gives you the unshakable conviction that God elected you for these studies. To have the *cor ecclesiae*, the doctrine of election, applied to your studies, is the goal of every Reformed university. Not even the least among the brothers may say, "I am a reject," and even if you did not choose this life yourself but had it chosen for you by your parents, still you will hold fast to the calling of your God, despite this mediated decision. It is he who has ordained your life for this order, this sphere, this academic world, and woe betide you if you stop your ears to this call or resist it. He called you by name, and you have only to answer, "Here I am," and to be faithful in this service of your God till your last breath.

Students, let this faith set the tone as we embark on a new year. No doubt disappointment awaits us also this time, but the blood of the Mediator has atoned for sin also in the world of science and scholarship. Only take care never to do one thing: to give up on your ideal. In your studies, always leave your calling the way God has ordained it and do not spoil it in accordance with your own limited ideas.

I thank you.

THE GOAL OF GENUINE STUDY (1900)

Aestumattissimi, Ornatissimi Commilitones!

Latin may be dying out, but allow me to address you according to academic tradition as *distinguished students, esteemed comrades in arms*, and to bid you once more, on behalf of the senate, a warm welcome in the army camp of our studies. Welcome first of all to you upperclassmen as you rejoin the colors for a new campaign, but just as warm a welcome to you first-year students, fresh recruits from the gymnasia, presenting yourselves for the first time under the university banner.[11] Going home at the end of the academic year may elicit rich sensations of relaxation, especially if you've earned your leave after passing your courses. Nevertheless, come autumn, a longing for our academic army tent rekindles your fighting spirit. And that our novices yearned to join our ranks is all the more understandable at a university where no dread of malicious initiation rites comes to deflate

11. In 1900, fourteen new students enrolled, bringing the total to 126 (all male; the first coed would not be registered for another five years). Of the three departments, the majority of students were enrolled in theology, a dozen in law, and a few in letters.

high expectations and where proper modesty ensures a safe conduct against any molestation at the periphery.

Thus the start of a new school year always makes for a positive mood in our circles—also among us, your professors.[12] We have dedicated our lives to the struggle for a sacred principle. It is our passion to hunt down the lie in the world of academic scholarship and to dislodge error from its hiding place. After a period of rest, the vow to press onward burns on our lips. It is like a brook that swells and wants to flood the fields. And what scene can be more desirable, what sight more striking, than to see you all lined up again in front of us, eager to listen to our words if well-founded?

Students, we are supposed to form you, but you in turn form us. As the child makes a woman into a mother, so the student makes the professor. Time and again your curiosity elicits from us what might otherwise never have passed our lips, and for all our delight in inspiring you, you also inspire us. As well, our hearts are still somewhat heavy when we contemplate our small numbers, and although the sexagenarians among us are not yet ready to retire, still we feel we need assistance, soon replacement. Without new recruits an elite corps dies out. And where else but from your midst are they to come who will before long take our place? That is why you are *spes nostra*—our hope. Today you are our listeners, tomorrow the mouthpieces of our word, and someday—this is our quiet prayer—more than just our epigones.[13]

Spes nostra, but no less *spes patriae*, the hope of the fatherland. For the spirit of our forefathers that has taken hold of us continues to meet with hostile resistance among the leading circles of our nation. And although our faithful God still spared a remnant, that remnant cannot strive for victory, can barely hold its own, and will be defenseless if it does not acquire, *also outside the church*, heroic men who can bear arms in every domain: the one the sling and the bow, the other the sword and the lance. Our Christian folk are crying out for such men; they hope to see such men come forth from among you in ever larger numbers. And if our people give generously to our school and have given our Free University the love of their hearts, then it is because they expect us to teach you the indispensable skills, and for

12. The faculty at this time consisted of six full-time professors and the odd part-time instructor.

13. That is, more than just followers or imitators.

the brightest among you, the fundamentals of military science, for waging our sacred struggle.

All the more do we trust that this high-minded expectation will not be disappointed because your passing up other universities and choosing to come here in itself already demonstrates your willingness to make a considerable sacrifice for your principle. Our young institution lacks so much of what is offered in abundance at other schools. Our departments are few, our faculty is pitifully small, we are without academic institutes worthy of the name, and the degrees we confer still lack any *effectus civilis*.[14] To have studied here has never yet been a recommendation for public office; to dare to have studied here still bears a mark of dishonor. But that is precisely why your coming here is a moral act that compares so favorably with other people's love of ease and abject betrayal of principle. It is the moral character of your choice that automatically creates a bond of spiritual kinship between you and your professors and gives real meaning to the title "comrades in arms." And so long as the flame of that holy principle continues to burn in our breast, our paucity of numbers cannot discourage us and the heat of day does not daunt us.

Nevertheless, students, studying at an opposition school need not be made more onerous than necessary. It borders on cruelty to strew your difficult path with stumbling block after stumbling block, and in this opening address I am therefore going to try to remove at least one of those nasty obstacles. Or is it not offensive, and is it not calculated to dampen all your courage, when you put up with sacrifices and then to hear them yell at you from the opposite side: "You won't find scholarship at the Free University anyway, just indoctrination in time-worn propositions. 'Filling station' is perhaps too banal a name, but your would-be university will never be more than a drill school, a cramming school for regurgitating ancestral lore." This evil recrimination, which is even echoed in the major liberal papers, might easily become too much for you first-year students, too much in any case for you to be able to respond to it with a principled refutation. You can stop your ears to it, but that is not how you defeat it. That is why I am going to use this opportunity to put your mind at ease at least on this point. If I spoke eleven years ago about the secret of genuine study, let me on this occasion

14. Until the revision of the Higher Education Act in 1905, graduates from the Free University with a degree in law or letters did not qualify for office in the justice system or a teaching position for classical languages in a public school.

speak to you about the goal of genuine study, focusing on the all-important question: What is the point of scientific study? Is it to seek or to find?

The difference between seeking and finding as the goal of scientific study is best illustrated by pointing to analogies taken from daily life. You have heard of the recreational activity of the hunt. What is it that drives all those gentlemen who normally live a life of ease (a few not even all that steady on their feet owing to rheumatism), to spend hours upon hours chasing across the fields and crawling through the woods? Is it to catch a hare for dinner or a partridge for supper? Apparently not, because any poultry shop can supply the most pampered palate with a wide assortment of game; and to have game on the menu for a whole week no doubt costs far less than a whole day of hunting with dogs and loaders. No, what matters for the true lover of the chase is not to taste or eat game, but to hunt. His passion is for the activity of hunting as such. Eating game is a bonus, but the thrill he is looking for is the actual chase.

That's how it is with the huntsman, and it is no different with the angler. Stepping out when it is still half dark, baiting the hook, lowering the float, and waiting for a nibble, striking at just the right moment and then landing a pike or a bass, that is the real pleasure of the recreational fisherman. The sport is the search, and the search is the angler's bliss. Buy a fish in the store or receive one as a present, marinated in the finest sauce—that too is a treat; but for a real sportsman nothing can compare with personally angling for a fish in a stream or canal. Our Frisians know how wealthy Englishmen cross over to Frisia just for the pleasure of fishing in the well-stocked Frisian lakes. That is how it is with hunting and fishing, and that is how things stand, though to a lesser degree, for all those who find joy in their daily occupation. Money lightens toil, but money does not inspire. Rembrandt and Frans Hals created marvelous paintings that today are worth their weight in gold, but they were fobbed off with a hundred shillings, if that much; and Vondel, our "prince of poets" as he came to be called, worked as a clerk in a hosier's shop and as a teller in a savings and loan bank.[15] Painters who today paint for a living see their talent visibly drying up. But poets and painters who are artists by the grace of God are those who write verse because they can't stop themselves and who create paintings because it is

15. Rembrandt van Rijn (1606–69) and Frans Hals (ca. 1581–1666) belong to the "old masters" of Dutch painting, and Joost van den Vondel (1587–1679) was a famous Dutch poet and playwright.

their passion. And although this holds especially for artists, it is no less true of our artisans. A mason, a carpenter, a house painter, an upholsterer, if they think only of their weekly pay and derive no pleasure from building, decorating, and upholstering, are not held in high regard by their bosses or their coworkers. Even the farmhand who plows and sows, disks or harrows, should find his enjoyment and passion in the work itself, or his boss will not take him seriously. Small wonder, then, that a real student does not make any progress until the study itself gives him pleasure. The joy of academic life is no longer to have to finish assignments on time, as formerly at school, but to be free to study for the sheer pleasure of it. And the person who graduates and is allowed to assist in the search for truth at a more advanced level, to grope for light in much that is dark and to hunt and dig where no one has gone before, that person relishes his good fortune: he tastes the pleasure of study, indulges his passion with rejoicing, and feels great delight as he engages in research.

Accordingly, I have no intention of disputing the delights of seeking after truth. I welcome it with gratitude as a token of God's common grace. When we lost the luxuriance of paradise and were burdened with eating bread by the sweat of our brow, it was a blessing that along with that burden we were given pleasure in work as a spur for that work. A thoroughbred finds pleasure in the race and a pedigree hound takes delight in the chase. A purebred husky can scarcely be held back from dashing forward. You need a whip only for those animals that lack nobility. To have to till the ground in order to have bread and to plow and sow not slavishly but with joy—that is grace. Without passion for work, all that work would debase us. And that the flames of enthusiasm leap even higher when not the hand but the head has to perform the work—that is an even richer gift of grace from God, something which even the pagan poets acknowledged when they explained their irresistible urge from divine inspiration: *Est Deus in nobis, agitante calescimus Illo.*[16] It is that wondrous urge to which our generation owes its richest benefits, its greatest treasures. And without doubt it is also true of the pursuit of science that the urge to seek truth is from God and that even if you make no discoveries the search itself elevates your person, and that here too *laudanda voluntas*[17] remains a patent of nobility.

---

16. That is, "There is a god within us, and we glow when stirred by him." See Ovid, *Fasti*, bk. 6, line 5.
17. That is, "The mere will is praiseworthy." See Ovid, *Epistulae ex Ponto*, bk. 3, Ep. 4: *To Rufinus*, line 79.

With one proviso! Provided science aims to serve, never to rule. Seeking should be in the service of finding. The ultimate purpose of seeking is finding. Only from this lofty goal does seeking derive its reason for existence. The shepherd who had lost his sheep did not rejoice in searching for it but in finding it; it was then that he called together his friends and neighbors and exclaimed: "Rejoice with me, for I have found my sheep" [see Luke 15:6]. Jesus expressed the same thought about the woman who had lost a piece of silver. And when the prodigal son finally returned home, the emphasis was so exclusively on having found him that the father did not mention a word about seeking; he could only shout for joy: "This my son ... was lost, and is found" [Luke 15:24]. Delight in searching is priceless, and without it you won't succeed; but finding must be the goal and motive and therefore the main thing above all, for science that seeks truth.

When you are really thirsty you do not seek a spring for the sake of seeking but for the water that can slake your thirst; and once you find water, seeking is furthest from your mind. When a traveler through the desert locates a well with bubbling water, he does not withdraw at dusk to forget about its whereabouts, to look for it again the next morning; instead he lies down next to it and falls asleep, to refresh himself with the water at dawn before moving on. Thus when people say that in the field of academic scholarship not the possession of truth, not the finding of truth, but the search for truth is the principal motive, then evidently the thirst for truth has flagged in their hearts, and not the desire to possess truth but the pleasure of seeking it is paramount with them. They do not seek in order to find; in fact, too much finding would spoil it for them. The angler who has a bite every minute grows tired of landing fish after fish and no longer finds pleasure in the sport.

And yet, that is all too often how modern scholars approach their studies. They quote the bold words of Lessing: "If God were to hold all Truth concealed in his right hand and in his left only the steady drive to seek Truth but with the proviso that I would forever go astray in the search, and He would bid me choose, I would humbly take the left hand and say: Father, give me this one—the pure Truth is for you alone."[18] Thus for Lessing, the search for truth is more glorious than the possession of truth. But let no one be misled by this pithy saying. For if you were to say that even Lessing after all

18. G. E. Lessing, "Anti-Goetze" (1778), in *Werke*, ed. H. Göpfert (Munich: Carl Hanser Verlag, 1979), 8:32–33.

did ultimately hope to be in possession of truth provided it were the result of his own searching, your objection would not stand up for one minute. Call truth one hundred; what Lessing's contemporaries knew of it, nine; and what he himself along with his adherents could add to it in a lifelong search, one-hundredth (which is of course far too high an estimate); then it still is true that he would rather die without ever having known nine-tenths of the truth than to have found the truth as a result of his searching for it. Lessing's statement runs perfectly parallel in the intellectual domain to works righteousness in the moral domain. To want to earn one's own salvation and not receive it by grace is perfectly on a par with the desire to seek all truth by oneself and spurn any revelation of higher light. To prefer to dispense with nine-tenths of the truth rather than to receive the light of truth humbly and gratefully from God's hand is to want to pick from the tree of knowledge in order to be like God, and to owe one's knowledge to no one but oneself, and to own it thanks solely to one's own effort.

You all know the fundamental contrast between knowledge in this life and in the life to come. In this life it is a question of finding by seeking, gradually knowing more and more, but always a knowing in part and never otherwise than through a glass, darkly. In eternity, on the other hand, it will always be knowing the essence of things, knowing face to face, knowing God even as we are known by him, a knowing that is immediate, exhaustive, perfect, and for that reason without any seeking. And the knowledge which is our possession without seeking and which the prophets and apostles say is the most exalted and the most glorious of knowledge—that knowledge is rejected by Lessing and all who follow him, rejected as unworthy of the human spirit. However, those who with us rank the possession of truth above all else, and who honor immediate knowledge as the highest knowledge, feel deeply how humbling it would be if we in our sinful state could not gain even the bread of knowledge except "by the sweat of our brow," by dint of our own efforts. We therefore thank our God that all our exertion in seeking after knowledge is attended by delight in studying and that the search itself has its own attraction.

This contrast in standpoint has three direct consequences: If for you the pleasure of seeking truth surpasses the possession of it, then you cause to be lost what is not lost; then you will seek again what others have found long ago; and then you will rather grope in darkness than open your eyes to the light of the revelation that has been given us. If on the other hand you seek only in order to find, you will take care not to lose what you already have;

you will no longer seek what was found long ago; and you will gratefully accept what is thrown into your lap without ever having to search for it.

Let us examine each of these three contrasts more closely.

The first contrast is that you must not lose, or cause to be lost, what was not lost to begin with. You know how a cat plays with a mouse: when it has caught the mouse it deliberately lets it go again purely for the pleasure of catching it again. That is how a cat plays, but it does not behoove the man of science to play like that with the truth. All knowledge proceeds from fixed presuppositions, not as artificial hypotheses that fell from the sky but as simple expressions of our existence, of our consciousness, of our perceiving and thinking *I*, including axioms, including *perception* as perception and *being* in ourselves, in the cosmos, and in that which transcends the senses and is experienced immediately by our soul. This is the common belief that is foundational to all knowledge.

For example, it is by means of discrete numbers and adding, subtracting, multiplying, and dividing them, or taking their square root, that we acquire the sums that we make ourselves by induction. But you have to start with these discrete numbers; if you commence your computation with zeros you will always end up with zero. Any lessening of the certitude that is rooted in this fundamental belief can only lead to doubt, to skepticism, and at last to insanity. I do not deny that afterward it is humanity's duty to analyze, plumb, even x-ray the thinking subject. In that respect all of us are in debt to Kant. But analyzing the fact presupposes that the fact is there to begin with. And what is never legitimate is that we imagine that we ourselves have to prove being itself and that we willfully discard what we know immediately in order to regain it as the product of our own thinking. The absurd notion of our mind as a tabula rasa began with Descartes, who thought he could make not just knowledge, but also being, hang by the flimsy threads of an intellectual formula. And ever since Descartes, that process of doubt in one form or another has carried on its destructive work without letup. People are no longer sure whether we even have a soul. And if these thinkers, these neglecters of what is immediately given, did not time after time deny their own intellectual constructs once outside their ivory towers, then these gentlemen would be of no earthly use in the practical world.

To inspect a precious seal ring that is not lost but that you clasp in your fingers—to assay the karats of its gold and appraise the value of its diamond—is something altogether different from throwing it deliberately into the vortex for the sheer pleasure of retrieving it again. The art of every age mirrors the aspiration and the self-awareness of the age; so it is not an inaccurate characterization when a man of letters, himself a modern of moderns, wondered only recently what the art of the nineteenth century betrays other than an age of feebleness, flabbiness, inconstancy, and insipidity. "Future historians," he exclaims, "will not see anything else in our art but the somber index of the spiritual state of our self-abasing century, the mark of our moral impotence, the melancholy testimony of the bankruptcy of our energies, however much we may boast of our energy."[19] That is the just punishment for people who cause to be lost what they already possessed by casting it into the vortex and who then dive into that vortex in vain hopes of recovering it. As real children of Pilate, they are left with not one fixed starting point for their thinking, not a single pillar in their temple of justice, not one firm rule for their moral code.

For this reason it is not an unscientific standpoint, but a sine qua non for any science which is to enrich humanity, that we in our university resist tooth and nail that wanton rejection of certitude, and, honoring religious belief as a foundation also for science and scholarship, use our common sense and hold fast to man's immediate knowing of the basic elements of all being and all thought.

The case is no different with the second contrast that I pointed out: no longer seeking what was long found—or if you will, keeping to our historical standpoint, over against hypercriticism and its penchant for always starting afresh. The edifice of scholarship is so enormous in design that if the pursuit and practice of science had no order, no collaboration, and no recognition of the historically prepared foundations, the building would never be put under one roof. Then everything that was ever discovered would be lost again and the search each time would have to start all over again. Every scholar now living would have to begin afresh, on his own account, and cover the whole field. And every published result would only arouse your suspicion. You would want to look for possible mistakes by former scholars and to show them up for those mistakes. You would claim to be a free, independent thinker, and even as a professor you would need to take no notice of anything or anyone. If after ten years you were to topple like a house of cards the results you once dished up with great show of learning, even then, both what you first assembled and what you later discarded would still have to be lauded as "great feats of scholarship."

19. Leo Clarence, in *Le Monde moderne*, no. 68 (August 1900): 241.

We refuse to go along with this critical individualism. It is contrary to the very nature and purpose of science. It speaks of the play enjoyed by people who delight in the search, but not of the earnest desire for humanity to advance to ever-clearer light of knowledge. If science were concerned with the material world only, with things that can be weighed and measured, there would be no danger in that mania for criticism and that atomistic self-conceit. After all, an experiment can be repeated at the drop of a hat and a mathematical result can be checked at once. But however important the discovery and the manipulation of the forces of nature may be, all disciplines devoted to their study can never yield more than the lower levels of science. You do not ascend to the higher levels of knowledge until you delve into the spiritual sciences of invisible human life and in the relation of that life to the law which it obeys and so to the single mysterious force which causes it to come into being and to pass away again and which directs it to its goal or end.

That higher, nobler science is so intricate and complex, and so surpasses what a single century, let alone a single thinker, can encompass, that there can be no question of progress in science unless the next century is prepared to continue spinning the thread as it slips from the failing hands of the dying century. The result of that historical labor has been that this higher science has produced fundamentally different positions, which history itself has worked out in blood and tears. Here, subjective differences rule out unity of vision and, depending on a person's mind, one of these historic positions matches that person, and that person matches that position.

Given that scholars cannot work together unless they share a common starting point, we at this university collaborate exclusively with those who take the position of our Reformed forebears. The way they viewed things strikes us too as the truth—matches the way we too view life. That is why we refuse to take to the streets and put the torch of criticism to everything that has been built up, to start building all over again. We inhabit the Reformed house bequeathed to us by our forebears, and that is where we carry on our lives. If that is called unscientific, then notice how those who label us with that stigma factually do the same thing, only on less solid grounds. Among them, too, there is not one who has devised his own world of ideas and has investigated every foundation of knowledge. They too float on corks that others have launched in the water. They adjust to the dominant pattern of thinking and simply repeat its slogans. They are Kantians, or Hegelians, or Darwinians, and so on. They spawn school after school, each with its own catechism, and they swear by the creed of their favorite mentor.

Our alphabet has never numbered more than five vowels, and among the critical atomists, too, the consonants, which have never given a sound of their own, account for the bulk of their speech. In other words, they too inhabit a house with others and proceed from a position that others have found. With this difference only, that the position on which we take our stand bears the stamp of centuries, whereas they adjust their kaleidoscope almost every decade. Plus this difference as well: we for our part openly acknowledge that we proceed from what others have found, whereas they deceive themselves by claiming that they never come out with anything other than fresh produce from their own greenhouse.

The third point I indicated is even more important. The first was not to cause to be lost what is not lost to begin with, and therefore to maintain the elementary things that are sensed through immediate knowledge. The second was our historical standpoint: not to seek again what others already found long ago. Now to add the third point: stop seeking if God graciously reveals to you what you were seeking.

This too is a reasonable demand. The opposite is the way of the schoolboy who has to practice his arithmetic. Even though the answers to the problems he is assigned are in the back of the book, still he has to find them for himself. And that makes perfectly good sense in his case, since the problems themselves are never taken seriously by him. His goal is to learn arithmetic. But if you could cable Lord Roberts the current whereabouts of De Wet,[20] that cunning commander would not for a moment consider tearing up your telegram without first reading it simply for the pleasure of continuing the search. And that is how it is in every domain. When someone is roaming the mountains and just cannot find the right path, he is delighted when he meets a guide who can show him the way; and he would make himself a laughingstock if he were nevertheless to say to the guide, "I won't listen to you because I want to go on looking for the path myself." No captain of a ship that is driven off course will, when hailed by a pilot's boat, hoist all sails and steer clear of the pilot in order to look for the course himself. To continue searching when someone else brings you what you are looking

20. Lord Roberts (1832–1914) and Christiaan De Wet (1854–1922) were opposing generals in the Second Boer War, which was raging at the time.

for is contrary to everything that is reasonable, and what is unreasonable should not be called scientific.

So here. Science too encounters questions in life that scientists never give up trying to solve but without ever solving them. What is the origin of things? Who rules this world and gave the world its law for life? What differentiates organic life from mechanics? Where did sin come from? Is there life after death? How can right triumph over might? How is reconciliation possible? What is the unity of history amid the multiplicity of events and phenomena? And so on and so forth. All of them are questions that continue to exercise the human mind, and the answers to these questions determine our energy, our courage to face life, the motive of our supreme devotion, the peace of our heart, and our heroism in the face of death. Nevertheless, all that questioning, all that searching has been of no avail. Results have remained as scanty as thirty centuries ago in India, Greece, or China.

But now God has revealed himself. He has spoken in a variety of ways to the fathers through his prophets and apostles [see Heb 1:1]. He sent us the One who said, "I am the way, and the truth, and the life" [John 14:6]. He has sealed his faithfulness to us in his word. And he continues to call out to all who seek but never find: "Come, everyone who thirsts, come to the waters; and he who has no money, come, buy and eat! Come, buy wine and milk without money and without price" [Isa 55:1]. Or to speak with the learned scholar from Tarsus: "For since, in the wisdom of God, the world did not know God through wisdom, it pleased God through the folly of what we preach to save [that is, to enrich, also in knowledge] those who believe" (1 Cor 1:21). Thanks to this revelation, a generation arose that no longer wavered in fear nor sought in vain, but that dared to say: "We know" [1 John 3:14]. It was a generation that possessed certitude and whose firmness of conviction enabled them to show forth invincible power. Earlier, Jesus had said of these heroes of firm conviction: "I thank you, Father, that you have hidden these things from the wise and understanding and revealed them to little children" [see Luke 10:21]—that is, to those who are willing to be children in matters of the spirit.

Where do we see here, I do not say erudition, but true science that aims at genuine knowledge? Is it found in the vain groping and guessing of those who mock this revelation and keep on searching without ever getting beyond agnosticism? Or is it found in our standpoint, whereby we gratefully accept the God-given solution to those profound questions and through our studies continue to build with boldness and inspiration on the foundation laid by the prophets and the apostles?

Now, all this is governed by the fundamental question I raised at the outset: *What is the goal of genuine study?* Is the goal of science to open up a hunting ground for a few scholars to indulge in their critical investigations? Or is it to endow people with confident certainty, with firmness of conviction, with *knowledge*? And if it follows from this, assuming you opt for the latter, that to cause to be lost what was not lost, to search anew for what our forebears already found, and to keep on seeking what God has revealed—that all this cannot possibly be reconciled with a reasonable understanding of science's goal. Why then, from the point of view of science, is the standpoint of the Free University objected to when it favors thirst for truth above the pleasure of study, when it prizes finding above seeking, and when it thus upholds both immediate knowledge, results once obtained, and the solution given in God's word to otherwise unsolvable questions?

But we are not there yet. Our threefold starting point may be vindicated, but it is not yet clear what scientific studies are meant to do. The immediate pronouncements of one's consciousness come naturally; the guiding principles of the Calvinist worldview are more or less known; the answers that God's word offers for the great questions of life are summed up in the Apostles' Creed. So what is left for science to do?

My answer is that science is to fulfill the threefold task that constitutes the calling of every university: first, to establish; second, to deduce; and third, to systematize. Science is to establish the wealth of truth that we acquire either immediately or by induction. Next, it is to deduce from these firm data the implications for our present life and our current state of consciousness. And finally, science is to take this wealth of truth and its implications and bring them into coherence, to raise them into a system. I will not detain you with a discussion of the last two tasks. No one suspects the seriousness with which we at the Free University work at these tasks, nor does it occur to anyone to dispute, given our declared standpoint, our right or our ability to deduce and systematize in keeping with the rules of science. We stand for three principles—confidence in our consciousness, historic Calvinism, and scriptural revelation—from which implications for every relationship in life can be deduced with logical rigor. Likewise, no man of science can resist the urge through systematization to elucidate the essential coherence of his principles and the organic link of his various deductions to those principles. Thus I have never heard that where our deductions and our systematization are concerned, the scientific nature of our work is disqualified.

But I strongly emphasize that first task: establishing the wealth of truth from which we proceed. That is the point where we are attacked. The allegation is that we certify unproven assumptions arbitrarily, hence unscientifically, and that we merely parrot traditional dogmas. Exactly here lies the misunderstanding. On the contrary, establishing the truths we possess demands wide-ranging studies that penetrate to the root of the matter. Not as though we would still want to *prove* the certainty of the axiomatic pronouncements of our consciousness. That would be a contradiction in terms. No school of thought entertains such an absurd argument. Even Descartes took his *cogito* as a given starting point and tried from there to ascend to his *ergo sum*. And, inversely, it is no secret for us either how easily a *common opinion* that is accepted for a time in certain circles can be mistaken for the immediate pronouncement of our consciousness. What is real has to be separated from what is imagined, and to be able to do so we have to investigate the nature of this certainty, explain it psychologically, and confine it to the elementary givens. We confess, more than other schools, that false lines have been drawn across our immediate consciousness by the darkening effect of sin. Thus the allegation is simply ludicrous that we believe having a firm starting point excuses us from examining it more closely.

The case is no different with respect to our historical principle. Or do people think that the Reformed worldview has been slipped into our hands in a secret document, ready to hand and fully worked out? Is Calvinism in its rise and flowering not a historical phenomenon which just like any other configuration in history has to be mined from the sources? And does finding its leading idea not require that we remove its time-bound features, separate the leaven from the flour, and trace the unity behind its multiple forms? And if this is as clear as day, why should establishing the Reformed principle be judged less scientific than establishing the spirit of India or Greece?

And the case is again no different when we come to the principle of revelation from Scripture. Here too it is an altogether false idea that Scripture offers a ready confession and a cut-and-dried catechism for life. What Scripture reveals can only be established after thorough study. And although belief in the truth of Scripture is a fruit of the *testimonium Spiritus Sancti*, which is surer than anything else, *knowledge* of Scripture and its contents can only be the fruit of study and research. So much so, in fact, that there is no book in any language that has been subjected to more thoroughgoing, comprehensive, and unremitting study than Holy Scripture.

For us too, therefore, establishing the truth that we possess has nothing in common with drawing up an inventory of known truths without having to do any serious scholarship. On the contrary, only psychological, historical, and biblical studies that go to the root of things can enable us to establish in an informed way just what we possess. The confidence in our consciousness needs psychological study; our Calvinist standpoint needs historical study; the revelation of our God needs biblical study. This is all the more important since by far not all Christian thinkers reach the same conclusions as we do, either now or in former centuries. On each of the three topics mentioned, divergent schools of thought have arisen, leading to friction and controversy. And this controversy, in which we are obliged to demonstrate the soundness of our conclusions over and over again, compels us continually to test and inspect the way we establish what we know, an inspection that does not spare a single detail.

But even then the task of establishing is still not complete. Non-Christians and anti-Christians time and again allege that much of what we store in our treasury of truth as gold and diamonds is tinsel and paste. Now, nothing is further from our mind than to say that we couldn't care less what others say about us. Our bond with our fellow citizens is felt deeply by us and includes those among them who oppose us. Science and scholarship is a common human endeavor, and he who shuts himself up within his own circle without ever having it out with those who think otherwise leaves the refreshing stream and ends up in a stagnant bog. We have to engage the objections of those who oppose us on principle and attack their notions that we deem false—attack them, not in bitter hatred, but from love of those who are misled by them.

Only, we go about this with level heads and a discriminating eye. So long as our strength is so little and so much still needs to be done to build our own house, we shall concentrate our energies first of all on the positive, deductive, and systematic investigation of our principles. How we divide our time and energy is our decision. If you rush to spend all your time as an apologist, you will always lose in influence, you will be mostly disappointed by a poor reception and a poor outcome, and you will have your studies dictated to you by your opponent. Your studies will lose focus, and every morning you will have to be ready to answer what has been brought against you this time. You will be tied down by an unproductive series of ad hoc arguments. That first of all. And then in the second place, we refuse to waste our energy refuting for the umpteenth time what has so often been refuted already. Many of the objections raised against us are worn-out theses that have been fully answered long ago. Staging a gladiator's match too frequently makes it unpalatable: it is *oleum et operam perdere*.[21] And one more thing, in the third place: by far the majority of these objections are inferences from contrary premises that are governed by a philosophical idea. Now, it is always fundamentally unscientific to wage the battle in the area of inferences so long as the starting premises have not been thrashed out. Why engage in an argument, for example, about Christian doctrine with someone who denies it, so long as you haven't come to agreement on the authority of Scripture? Or again, why argue with that person about the authority of Scripture so long as you haven't agreed on the meaning of the concepts of sin and revelation? But although on that account sound scientific method indeed demands that you settle an argument about the source of a river high up in the mountains and not down by the seashore, nevertheless where the fundamental premises are at issue we too have to join battle, even in the case of a Nietzsche. A scientific school that declines to give account of itself commits suicide.

Thus we do not in any way shirk the strict demand that scientific verification should extend to the most critical level. Not that we close our eyes to subjective differences in fundamental convictions. Aesthetically, you will never convince a deaf person of the beauty of Beethoven's symphonies. Ethically, a Nero could never be convinced of the sacredness of marriage. Similarly, in the domain of truth Jesus judged that "unless one is born of water and the Spirit, he cannot even see the kingdom of God" [see John 3:3, 5]. But even then that subjective element itself remains open to scientific debate, and we are prepared in that respect to demonstrate the legitimacy of our standpoint.

Assuming that this is so—that we are obliged and prepared, at least at a time of our own choosing, to give an account of everything, even of our deepest convictions—if you should now ask, finally, in what way we differ from others and why we concentrate our studies in a university of our own (after all, one can debate about certainty of consciousness, Calvinism, and Scripture at any university), then this is my threefold answer: The first is that although the state universities are said to be religiously neutral and

21. That is, a waste of time and trouble. See Plautus, *Poenulus*, act 1, scene 2, line 333.

admit every opinion to their forum, the fact is that for many years already only one school of thought has set the tone, and even Bilderdijk, Groen van Prinsterer, and Da Costa[22] were debarred from their faculties. In the second place, the university also aims to form and mold its students. Now then, pedagogically speaking, an education that calls a lie in Tuesday's lecture what was recommended in Monday's lecture as the truth mocks the primordial demands of a formative education. Moreover—and this I want to note in the last place—there is proof and proof. There is a kind of proof that settles the question once for all. But there is also a kind of proof which, when it fails to convince or even when it fails outright, nevertheless in your eyes leaves unimpaired the truth that was truth for you before the proof was ever undertaken. A judge does not accept the truth of a fact until the evidence submitted is complete; what is not proven adequately he may never accept as truth nor act on it. But that your mother is your mother and that you were begotten by your father is so much part and parcel of your experience of life that the fear of being a baby switched at birth or a child born of adultery can never enter your heart. You never searched for a document to prove it. But suppose an inheritance has to be divided, and an evil person fastens suspicion on your family connection, then you won't sit still; then you hunt down whatever proof you can find. But even if you did not succeed in that, the truth of the matter would never be shaken in your mind.

And this difference holds also here. Every rationalist wants to put you in the dock, and in the absence of proof that in his eyes is complete, he will contest your right to hold your conviction. Now, when you face such a denial you too will collect all the evidence available to you and argue your case as thoroughly and powerfully as you can, but also in such a way that you firmly believe the truth of your own basic conviction not after but before the debate takes place. In fact, even if the debate is called off, that basic conviction is still not weakened in your soul by a millionth of a milligram. This is not just so among us, but among all men of principle. Everyone's

22. Poet Willem Bilderdijk (1756–1831), historian and statesman Guillaume Groen van Prinsterer (1801–76), and Netherlands-born messianic Jewish poet Isaäc da Costa (1798–1860) were early nineteenth-century pioneers of the revival (*Réveil*) in the Netherlands of evangelical Calvinism.

basic conviction is the axiom of one's self-consciousness that will defy every wave of attack: *Saevis tranquillum in undis*.[23]

So long as your own consciousness, therefore, is not a mirror that by turns reflects every color, but has a center that sends out its own strong searchlight, two things will stand out: first, your basic conviction has nothing to fear from the most thorough investigation; and second, our basic conviction actually demands that all scientific research should go down to the root of the matter. And therefore, as resolutely as we reject the scholarly pride of a Lessing, who organized the pursuit for truth merely for the pleasure of the pursuit, so strongly do we urge you to pursue your studies with scientific rigor, but only on condition that thirst for truth be your incentive.

Am I reassured about that? Allow me to share an observation with you. At other universities I have sometimes noticed, especially among theology students, a measure of enthusiasm for study that I have often missed among you. But what was it that accounted for that impulse at those other schools? The impulse arose from the passion to negate: to contribute personally, if possible, toward prying loose a stone from the walls of God's holy Zion that was still held in place. It arose from the critical spirit to outstrip others in unraveling the Christian confession. What accounted for this drive and incentive was the impulse of the spiritual vandalism that will not rest until the last pillar is pulled down. That is how those students joined the ranks of the intellectual iconoclasts, how they became a little Strauss, a miniature Bauer, and how they dreamt of being a disciple of Renan. For this they reaped approval and praise. Their professors gratefully drafted them into the light cavalry of the elite army of critics. Their name sometimes became known in other countries. Such promising young men! And that goad did wonders, for in our younger years—why deny it?—we have a lot of untamed energy; moreover, a revolutionary trait runs through every scholar's soul, and joining in something brand new can cast a dangerous spell.

Oh, those innovators of yesterday! Such laurels will not be reaped by you. We do not train you in demolishing what is standing, nor are we set up for that. As well, our respect for the holy is too powerful not to label these attacks on God's truth as sacrilege and so appeal to the conscience of those who perpetrate them. No, if the spirit of study is to awaken more strongly among you, then your motive must not be self-exaltation but the exaltation of the glory of God, and your focus is to be on shoring up whatever is

23. That is, calm amid the fierce waves.

tottering. Then your critical exactness must be balanced by your historical sense. Then in your estimation Augustine must rise high above Strauss, and Aquinas far above Renan, and not the creeping tendrils of Wellhausen[24] but the laurel sprays of Voetius[25] should keep sleep from your eyes. Then the passion of your soul should be for God, for his cause, and what should rouse you to holy jealousy is to sweep skepticism and negation off the pavement of his holy temple, even if only from a single slab in it. That will not be easy. To declare a psalm to be Maccabean or to excise another chapter out of Isaiah is much more clever, and the cheerleaders from the gallery of critics will start applauding even before you have finished. And yet I know you will not shirk this holy task. Soon it will become apparent among you that thirst for truth is a more powerful motive for study than the appetite for negation. The love of God's people will compensate you for the applause that will pass you by. And the God of truth, whose honor laid hold of you, will, if you have not forgotten the holy art of prayer, sharpen your mental powers, enhance your talent, and in his holy name will prosper you.

There are already quite a few who have graduated from your noble circle. May many of you in our audience today follow in their footsteps. Let the academic year begin! May it do its part in contributing toward that lofty goal, and let us take up our studies tomorrow as those who know that only that which is begun with God has meaning for eternity.

I thank you.

24. David Friedrich Strauss (1808–74), Ernest Renan (1823–92), and Julius Wellhausen (1844–1918) were pioneers of higher criticism and wrote a "Life of Jesus" from a naturalistic standpoint.
25. Gisbertus Voetius (1589–1676) was a Dutch theologian and a champion of orthodox Calvinism.

PART THREE

A PLURALISTIC PROGRAM FOR NATIONAL EDUCATION

IDEAS FOR A NATIONAL EDUCATION SYSTEM

TEXT INTRODUCTION

Following the Prussian example of the eighteenth century, in the nineteenth century the race was on among the nation-states of Western civilization to erect a universal public education system. While universities and their preparatory schools continued to fend for themselves, systems of elementary education for all classes of society were slow in coming and not seldom were achieved only after bitter wrangling and less than successful experiments.

In the Netherlands the compromise School Act of 1857 failed to settle chronic grievances among dissentients of a creedless Christianity imposed on a "common" or "mixed" school. By the 1870s a government inquiry revealed in a report that the education system needed drastic reforms, in terms of quality as well as content. At this, progressive liberals campaigned to put a definitive end to the school struggle by installing a national school system acceptable to all "right-thinking" people, if need be at the expense of minority rights.

But in the spring of 1874 Dr. Abraham Kuyper took up his seat in the lower house of Parliament. He had promised the longtime leader of the antirevolutionary movement and his own personal mentor, Groen van Prinsterer, that he would take "a position not behind but in front of today's liberalism," and that he would offer "a *modus vivendi* also to the opponent."[1] Accordingly, in the two speeches on the following pages, given on December 7 and 8, 1874, while baiting the minister to reveal his plan for education reform, he ventured to propose a plan, in places quite detailed, for a national education system that he felt all fair-minded people should be able to support.

Source: Kuyper, Abraham. *Naar aanleiding van het onderwijs-debat in de Kamer*. Amsterdam: J. H. Kruyt, 1875, pp. 3–22. Reprinted from the Dutch Hansard, *Bijblad* of the *Verslag van de Handelingen der Staten-Generaal*, 21 Sept. 1874–18 Sept. 1875 (The Hague, 1875), pp. 488–93 and 514–16. Translated by Nelson D. Kloosterman. Edited by Harry Van Dyke.

1. See Kuyper's "Memorandum," dated Feb. 4, 1874, in *Groen van Prinsterer. Schriftelijke Nalatenschap: Briefwisseling* (The Hague: Instituut voor Nederlandse Geschiedenis, 1992), 6:735–38.

IDEAS FOR A NATIONAL EDUCATION SYSTEM

SPEECHES AS A MEMBER OF PARLIAMENT, DECEMBER 7 AND 8, 1874

Mr. Speaker, I hope that I am not responsible for fostering national indolence when I ask leave, in connection with this line [in the national budget] to state my initial, and perhaps my final, opinion regarding the issue of primary education. In this context I appeal all the more to the indulgence of the Chamber, because everyone will agree with me that it can surely be said about this material: *Facilius est incipere quam reperire finem.*[2] Be assured that where I am able I shall abbreviate my remarks.

2. It is easier to start than to find the end.

Let me say at the outset that it is not at all my intention to present a partisan agenda in the bad sense of that word, as though I had in view to advance the interests exclusive to a single group, a single school, a single movement that is manifest in our nation. I believe a political party answers the demands people should make of it only if it knows how to derive an agenda from its principles that appreciates and promotes not only the interests of its sympathizers but first of all the interests of the nation as a whole.

My intention as well is not to defend from this podium the exclusive interests of the Christian school, but rather the interests of the primary school in general. I would even think to be falling short of the duty resting on me as a representative of the people were I to focus only on the sixty thousand children enrolled in private schools, without my heart beating with equal warmth for the hundreds of thousands who receive their entire education in the public system.

But it is precisely for that reason that I will not let myself be confined to the dilemma: either religious schools or the education system based on pseudo-competition. That dilemma has had its day. At least it seems to me that this contrast is outdated; it was very much to the point decades ago; it fit entirely in the context of the struggle waged here between the liberal and the conservative parties; but it can no longer be thrust on us now that it is becoming apparent how our political development is seeking other paths.

I reject this dilemma all the more because I am firmly convinced that the 1857 school law and the system embedded in it, rather than bringing the expected blessing to our fatherland, has instead driven a deep wedge throughout our national life. It should have been possible to provide our nation, too, with a school system that was not subject to partisan politics. Education in my opinion is not first of all a political issue but a social issue, and I endorse without qualification the sentiment of the British secretary of education, Mr. Forster, who, when he made a "motion for leave to bring in the Bill for Elementary Education," declared in Parliament: "There never, I believe, was any question presented by any Government to this House which more demanded to be considered apart from any party consideration."[3]

Again, I reject the dilemma all the more because I concur with the honorable member from Utrecht who addressed the chamber this morning (although some difference between his viewpoint and mine may perhaps

3. William Edward Forster (1818–86), in *Hansard's Parliamentary Debates*, vol. 199 (London: Buck, 1870), 439.

become evident), to the extent that also from a pedagogical perspective the school system of 1857 has not borne the fruits that one might have expected of it.

I shall not repeat what he said, but I would like to refer to several figures by way of comparison with an outcome obtained elsewhere. In England, the new school system has been in operation for almost three years, and what results are already evident? According to the most recent report to Parliament, the school population in England and Wales in 1869 consisted of 1,824,306 students, and under the operation of the new school system that number increased within less than two years to 2,369,000 students. Similarly, under the old system there were 14,404 schools; under the new school system this number has climbed within three years to 17,506. When one compares these figures with the results obtained among us as they appear in the report on the ten-year operation of our law, then one finds that in those ten years, 70,000 children and 251 schools have been added, thus approximately 7,000 children and 25 schools per year.

I shall not weary the Chamber with mathematical calculations; you can check my computations, but comparing the results here and in England head for head, I think that if we were keeping pace with England our school population should have increased by about 20,000 children and 215 schools per year. So there is hardly any reason to brag about the excellent functioning of the prevailing school system. This does, however, provide me with a reason—before I come to the question about what improvement in the existing school law I consider possible while maintaining Article 194 of the Constitution—to want to raise that other question: What education system is most suitable for our nation? After discussing both these questions, I will conclude briefly with an answer to a more immediate question: Can we look forward to enough clarity on the part of the minister?

I

Regarding my first question, *What education system is most suitable for our nation?* I would in the first place press the need for education to acquire, once and for all, the right of an independent position.

Initially, primary education could not capture that position, and naturally so. For primary education, at least in the sense in which we understand that phrase, dates from the fifteenth century. Shortly before the Reformation, one finds the first traces of a public school in the proper sense of the term. The Reformation thereupon conscripted those schools for the church, and in my opinion misused them at least in part as a means for advancing and propagating its ecclesiastical ideas. I am not saying that it did this with wrong intentions, nor that it should not have done so; rather, its action was a blessing. But it cannot be denied that the dependence of the schools on the church had to lead to the result that on the school menu the religious meal gradually became the main course, and in the nature of the case instruction in secular subjects could not reach its full potential. That's how things remained until 1789. For the first time around that year—in one country earlier than in another—a revolution occurred in ideas about schooling, with the result that, at least in our country, the state now conscripted the school, thus committing, in its own way, the same mistake that the church had formerly committed: it emancipated the school for service to the state. About this, too, I say: at that point in time the state did well; somebody had to take an interest in the neglected school. But the inescapable result was that once again the school landed in a position of dependence. For in the nature of the case, the state now attempted to do the very same thing that the church had done earlier: to propagate its own ideas by means of the school.

As I see it, this does not need to continue, nor should it. Education is a distinct public interest. Education touches on one of the most complicated and intricate questions, one that involves every issue, including the deepest issues that invite humanity's search for knowledge—issues of anthropology and psychology, religion and sociology, pedagogy and morality, in short, issues that encroach on every branch of social life. Now it seems to me that such an element of cultural life has the right in every respect to an absolutely independent organization; always in the sense that education should function in the spirit of what the British call *a body corporate*.

This could be achieved, I think, if parents, to the extent that they pay tuition for their children, in whole or in part, elect a *local school board*, concerning which I will leave open the question whether a government representative should be appointed to that council and in what manner teachers should have seats in it. From those local school councils, then, one could proceed to *provincial school boards* and from there in turn to a *national school board*. To this hierarchy I would assign the mandate: (1) to be responsible for the entire administration of the school system; (2) where the right of freedom of conscience requires, to establish schools that are strictly neutral; and (3) to enforce compliance with the regulations that the government has established for education. Please understand me well. What I have in mind is not at all a hierarchy in the sense of the French Académie, but on the contrary, a hierarchical school council in the sense of the British school boards. The difference is well-known. The French law states in Article 10 of the 1850 statute: "Four members of the general council, of whom at least two from their midst, shall be elected by the general council *from nominations by the Ministers*"; whereas the British bill of 1870 states in Article 29: "The school board shall be elected in the manner provided by this Act, in a borough *by the persons whose names are on the burgess roll* of such borough for the time being in force, and in a parish not situate in the metropolis *by the ratepayers*." Do I wish to exclude state involvement in the sense that the state as state will have to view education not to be an activity of the government? On the contrary, I fully agree with those members of this Chamber who judge that a state would utterly ignore its calling if it did not provide itself with a guarantee that those now living, in their link to the coming generation—that is, the nation in the continuity of the generations—are raised and maintained at a level of intellectual development as is required for our nation to continue to compete successfully with other nations.

The difference, then, involves only this question: *In what manner* is the state to carry out its task? The honorable member from Haarlem[4] recently spoke briefly about education; and today the honorable member from Utrecht, upon hearing it, gave a response. At which point I wondered whether I had perhaps been mistaken in my assessment of the Haarlem proposal. Since that honorable member is my senior, I am inclined to believe that he saw the matter correctly. Nevertheless, the member from Haarlem will prefer to have me as the interpreter of his words. Therefore I will tell him how I have understood his words. I consider it more prudent not to shoot as long as I don't know where the quarry is. As long as I cannot determine with certainty where the honorable member takes his stand, I wish to wait for further information.[5]

And I must admit: it struck me that in his program so much was applauded and acknowledged of what used to be defended with such talent from these very benches by Mr. Groen van Prinsterer. As I listened

4. That is, Johannes (Jan) Kappeye van de Coppello (1822–95), a self-styled progressive liberal, tipped by many as the leader of the next government. In a speech on Nov. 24, 1874, he suggested that the country's political culture ought to be suffused with the "modern worldview."
5. Kappeyne expounded further details of his school program the next morning.

to his speech, I thought I might rejoice that the antirevolutionary ideas are indeed making progress. I refer to just two points, constantly opposed with logical consistency by Mr. Groen van Prinsterer: to the false idea of a *social contract*, and to what is inconsistent with a sound constitutional polity—namely, proceeding from the *individual*. The honorable member led us back to the days when a powerful party in the land actually harbored those views, and he commented: "If we look back twenty-five years we see that the general view was this, that the state is nothing but a giant police force that has to provide only for the security of the persons and property of those residents temporarily living together under its care, and that each individual had to sacrifice a portion of his freedom and his possessions in order to purchase this protection of the state,"[6] and he passed sentence on that viewpoint when he added: "But that argument is no longer valid." This differs little from giving up on the idea of a social contract and the individualistic principle so wittily stigmatized and castigated by Renan when he wrote: "The Revolution's code seems to have been made only for those born as foundlings and dying without offspring."[7]

But there is more. From these benches Mr. Groen van Prinsterer always insisted forcefully on the *historical* principle; and now I find again in the address of the honorable member from Haarlem that he too is earnestly arguing for the continuity of the generations in our national life. I shall not repeat his extensive comments; everyone who heard them knows that he urged the recognition of the *solidarity* of the nation's [past and future] generations. Nevertheless, that does not yet decide the issue. The French Revolution went through two stages, one in 1789 and one in 1793; the first overemphasized the individual, the second exaggerated despotic authority, the absolute power of the state.

In a recent work on the philosophy of the French Revolution, the author acknowledges that other side of the Revolution in so many words: "The revolution," he states, "wanted to achieve justice and *only knew how to employ force*, so that at the very time that it sought to establish justice *it violated it*."[8]

---

6. This fairly sums up early nineteenth-century liberalism on the Continent.
7. Ernest Renan (1823–92), a French scholar of religion and politics. This quotation is from the preface to *Questions contemporaines* (Paris: Michel Lévy Frères, 1868), iii: "Un code de lois qui semble avoir été fait pour un citoyen idéal, naissant enfant trouvé et mourant célibataire."
8. Paul Janet, *Philosophie de la révolution française* (Paris: Germer Baillière, 1875). Kuyper quotes the sentence in French.

Now then, if the Haarlem program turned out to help introduce that second stage of the French Revolution, the phase of absolutizing the state, then my fundamental opposition would have been decided; but even then I fear nothing, for then I stand with Mr. Messchert van Vollenhoven[9] in the firm and unwavering conviction that nothing of the kind could possibly succeed in our good Netherlands with its age-old spirit of civil liberty which has always been the coronary artery of our politics.

Meanwhile, I shall not make up my mind just yet. Regarding the special issue of education I find in the speech of the honorable member from Haarlem much that has my sympathy. He wants constitutional revision; so do I. He acknowledges: "The state cannot itself provide everything," and he says that it must be done through private initiatives organized in associations, and he wishes that these would have a statutory character. "Naturally," he observes, "all of that cannot be undertaken by the State alone; it must call upon private initiatives for help, and those too will come up short if they cannot make use of the instrument of association. Such association functions as a corporate body: it always possesses a public-legal character, even though it remains civic and social."

With this, the speaker was referring to *material* interests, but would he object to applying this same idea to *moral* public interests? If the honorable member's answer to this question is affirmative, then I in turn gladly endorse his words when he says that the state "cannot leave to chance the matter of providing for education." I also agree with him that "competition in this matter is impossible." As he put it, one should not talk about competition, "for in my opinion competition between private and public education is as inconceivable as competition between decisions by arbitrators or between judicial verdicts by magistrates." If therefore he too can arrive at a system whereby the state must watch over education but nevertheless, being unable to provide it itself, must call on private initiatives for assistance and grant these initiatives public-legal status because they function as corporations, then he comes close to the British system that appeals to me, a system that will succeed here even better because we possess what is absent in Britain—namely, the regional, provincial link between the national government and the municipalities.

I would want to present the state with a right and a duty.

---

9. Jan Messchert van Vollenhoven (1812–81) was a conservative politician who served in both the senate and the lower chamber of the Dutch parliament.

The state has the right (1) of indirect compulsory education (more about this in a moment); (2) of legislation, including stipulating the level of educational outcomes; (3) of supervision and inspection; and (4) of certification, or if you will, the right to issue teacher's licenses.

But then the state also has the *duty* to issue certificates of competence to those who want to become teachers. This is a duty based on the right of the state to indirectly compel schooling. Note carefully: *indirect* obligation for schooling, which means that I view the state as entirely authorized to make the full enjoyment of the rights it grants citizens dependent on certain conditions that its citizens must meet. If nobody contests the right of the state to deny certain rights to someone whose mental capacity has broken down, rights which the state grants to others, then I do not see why one would not be permitted to make the full enjoyment of those rights just as dependent on fulfilling certain minimum requirements of mental development.

But then a duty flows from this as well. If the state requires, albeit indirectly, that everyone who wants to enjoy the right it grants shall receive primary education, then the state ought also to take into account the fact that not all parents have the financial ability to provide for the costs of education for their offspring; and therefore acknowledge its duty to provide financial aid, in the sense that, assuming the average cost per child were twenty-five guilders—an estimate far higher than obtains at present—the state would be obligated to pay the parents all or part of this sum in proportion to their inability to pay. Thus not, as is the case now, in order to divide the members of society into two classes, the rich and the poor. That division is not accurate; in reality one finds very different situations: parents who can pay the entire cost, others one portion of the cost, still others two or more portions of the cost, and finally, those who cannot pay anything. Instead, the members of society should be divided by rates, so that each receives aid from the state according to his ability.

If that system could be implemented, then I would ask the opponents this: What more do you want for the state? For under that system you would have the certainty that all the children of your nation received education, and that education met the requirements established by the state. I think only one answer could be given to that question, but I hope it will not be given. For you could respond by saying that then you would still be without the one advantage you enjoy at present—namely, to imprint on our youth Kantian deism. I do not believe that will be the response, but note well: if it were to be given it would prove that there was some truth buried in the characterization of the government school given by Mr. Groen—namely, that it is *the privileged sectarian school of a certain religious system.*

I would point you to a second duty of the state: to guard freedom of conscience. To have a good system, we need a guarantee that freedom of conscience in the field of education can never be violated. My proposal would offer little danger of that, but if it occurred the state would have to do its utmost to secure that freedom, in four ways: (1) by ordering school councils to establish *strictly neutral* schools, (2) by homeschooling, (3) by providing alternatives, and (4) by erecting regional residential schools (and here I am thinking in particular of a very small number of our Jewish countrymen who live spread out across the countryside and who still value religious education for their children). If one were to look at the financial aspect of this system, one would see that the extra costs would only be one million guilders. At this moment, the national, provincial, and local governments together are already paying 5.5 million for public primary education. If we add to this the approximately ninety thousand children who are currently outside the education system, then of course the expenses for education would multiply by about one-fourth. This already brings us to seven million. The salaries for the primary school teachers, which currently come to about 2,980,000 guilders, need to be increased. The desire is to raise the minimum from 400 to 900 guilders. Add to this the fact that classroom teachers will be increased, and a rise in costs of two million is certainly not too high an estimate. Assuming that the present system were implemented properly and consistently, causing the number of free schools to dwindle again, which would require new expenditures from the state, one could safely estimate the budget at around eleven million, whereas the system that I am proposing would cost around twelve million.

If I am asked what the advantages of this system would be, my answer is: (1) people would return from the abstraction of theory to the requirements of concrete life. When it comes to education the state is dealing with *children*, and it is true especially for children that their lives cannot be divided into compartments. Only adults, and then the educated ones, possess the capacity to deal with abstractions whereby a person separates his various life-expressions. A child does not do that. For the child, both the social and the moral, the religious and the intellectual dimensions of life, are all bundled together. I readily admit that the natural scientist, for example, has the perfect right to say: when I observe nature my heart is silenced, I lay aside my real personality and simply use my instruments for making observations and drawing connections between them later by means of my intellect. But what I consider to be permissible for the natural scientist (as long as he does not commit the error so often committed, of constructing systems involving spiritual matters, concerning which nature teaches him nothing), I contest the state's right to make such a separation already with the child. How is one to develop the moral, religious, and intellectual life of the child if not by accepting it in terms of that which makes up the only reality in the life of the child?

The honorable member from Utrecht mentioned that under the current school system, the moral standard of our national life has not advanced. I will leave aside whether there is indeed a basis for laying such an accusation at the feet of our school system; it will always be hard to settle such a claim. But it is undeniable that when the lower classes of the populace reach a deeper awareness of their power thanks to the increased knowledge they are provided with, the question deserves serious consideration: Is the growth in knowledge not a weapon in people's hands that can be used safely only if those hands are also at the same time being guided in a moral direction? Note the report in this month's *Quarterly Review*, where it is acknowledged that collecting the latest statistical data for the criminal courts in London revealed that the decrease in crimes is attributable largely to the influence of Christian philanthropy. You can find a summary of those statistics, among other places, in *Het Vaderland*.

Moreover, a second, no less important advantage [of the education system I propose] is the emancipation of instruction in the history of our country. If our nation is not to degenerate gradually into a collection of global citizens and our genuine national life is instead to be continually fostered, then—and who would disagree?—instruction in the history of our fatherland is the obvious means for that purpose. Recall a recent example. I will cite it *sine ire et studio*.[10]

In the first session last week, Mr. C. Van Nispen[11] asked in response to my claim that the period of William the Silent and of our republic represented a glorious page in our history: "How can you ask me to view as glorious a period when my fellow believers were persecuted?" I respect his conviction completely. But notice the logical inferences that follow from his position. He judged that period less glorious not because they were fellow believers

10. That is, dispassionately.

11. Carel van Nispen tot Sevenaer (1824–84) was a leading Roman Catholic politician.

of Mr. van Nispen who were persecuted, of course, but because they were citizens who were persecuted on account of their faith. But now think back. In the period just before this one, persecution on account of faith was rather more intense in nature, no matter where it struck; and back in the eleventh and twelfth centuries, when we were ruled by counts, we find evidence of persecution upon the discovery of heresy. So too, after 1789, in our contemporary history, we find once again traces of similar persecution, this time of those who seceded from the national church. Giving all due respect, as I do, to everyone's convictions and taste, I still ask: What is left of your instruction in the history of our fatherland if, as the law requires—and rightly so, in my view—such convictions have to be avoided in the neutral public school?

A third advantage would be that our politics would improve. Our politics—who does not recognize it?—is corrupted precisely because the education issue has become the axis around which politics turns. If that is so, then not until the parties become reconciled on this issue and justice and freedom of conscience have been guaranteed for every group, can the possibility be created for our political life to be liberated from the straitjacket and twisted context in which we are currently constrained. Only then will a new and fresh stream spring forth from which new models and programs, and with them more consistent party formations, can come to life.

Finally, in the fourth place, only by means of this kind of system will justice be done to the parents. At present, the school and the parents are two separate entities, and very questionable results flow from that separation. Is it any wonder that the bonds of obedience and submission that should bind children to their parents are weakened by the present school system? Children who attend school are for the greatest part of the day under the guidance of the teacher. If now this teacher holds to ideas which in many respects differ from those of father and mother, then will not that child, who by nature has already begun to resist the ideas of his parents at home, necessarily find support *against his parents*, and will that not necessarily result in diminished respect that children owe their parents? These are not chimeras. Everyone can be convinced about such facts when he looks at families. Is it, or is it not, of the utmost importance, especially now that the social question is becoming more urgent, that the principles of order and authority that find their origin in the society of the family are strengthened rather than weakened?

I would add only this: the system that I am recommending rests on genuine Dutch principles. Recently in this Chamber, Mr. Tak[12] demanded, in connection with the discussion about our water management, that here Dutch principles be maintained and French ones banned. Correctly, in my judgment. For more than anything else, by means of its free and corporative administration of dikes and polders, of water boards and polder reeves, our water management has shaped our national character. When I now intend nothing other than to apply the same free and corporative model to education, you will not ask for any further proof that what I am recommending truly rests on Dutch principles.

Only two objections against my system could arise in your mind: either that it would cost too much, or that it would require a revision of our Constitution. To the first, I answer, along with Mr. Haffmans:[13] we are wealthy enough to live properly. To the second, regarding constitutional revision, I reply: whether we want it or not, it will happen.

II

This brings me to the second point that I wanted to discuss: What can already be done now to improve the situation by revising the school law?

The system of a public-legal corporation, obviously, cannot be achieved under the present Constitution. Article 194 upholds the right of the state not only to legislate and superintend public education, but also administratively to function as teacher; second, it maintains the system of pseudo-competition; and third, it is doubtful whether it would allow a conscience clause that fully guarantees freedom of conscience.

Now I do not wish to provide, with respect to the school law, any partisan agenda in the bad sense of this term. However, adopting the position of the Constitution, I ask in good faith: What can be improved at this moment, given the limits imposed on us? In the well-known speech that sounded like the loading and firing of a cannon, I was reproached by the honorable member from The Hague for not being sufficiently precise. I promised a rejoinder, so during the present debate I would like to refute that charge, in the safest way I think, by being very precise this time.

Which demands would I want to make of the present school law? Am I still requesting that the word "Christian" be scrapped? Mr. Speaker, I forgo

12. J. P. R. Tak van Poortvliet (1839–1904) was a liberal politician.

13. Leopold Haffmans (1826–96), a conservative Catholic member of the Second Chamber for the southeastern district of Boxmeer, 1866–96.

that demand, and I will tell you in what sense. *Lucus a non lucendo.*[14] Given the light it throws on the question, it [the word "Christian"] may stay as far as I'm concerned: everybody knows today that it stands for *christiana a non christianisando.*[15]

Was the initial agenda of Mr. Groen van Prinsterer for that reason pointless? On the contrary, his goal has been achieved; it was to open the nation's eyes, and today the entire nation knows what remains of the Christian character of our state school. Then people demanded the revision of Article 194 of the Constitution, and now they are demanding a general constitutional revision. Is that a contradiction? No, provided we keep in mind that what is in play here is not merely a political principle, but the all-determining principle governing all of politics.

What is the profound grievance that our Christian-historical movement has against the present institutions of the state, a grievance shared by many who do not even belong to our movement? It is this, that our present-day public institutions grant the right and the authority to a coterie or party, once it has ascended to the highest level of power, to exploit the entirety of state authority for its own benefit. Note well, in this sense that such a party can devote the entire, immense power of the state's authority in order to indoctrinate the nation with its principles by means of the school. That is not fair; that should not be so; and if the honorable member from Utrecht, when he spoke of "tyranny," meant it in that sense, then I wholeheartedly agree with him. Against that system I too register my protest. Precisely on this depends the great all-governing political principle as to whether you will provide the minorities in the state with the safeguard that such an unbearable tyranny will never happen. If you want that safeguard, you must expand as much as possible the range of statutory law, severely restrict the arbitrariness that remains in the administration, and so restrain the power of the majority with the bonds of justice. Conversely, if you praise the system that is currently functioning among us, then restrict the reach of the law as much as possible and expand the area where partisan influence can dominate.

But then you should also disregard the inescapable consequence that this latter system imposes on you. For once you've put your foot in the

---

14. That is, an absurd inference, as in: "It is called a grove [*lucus*] because it does not shine [*lucere*]."

15. That is, it is called Christian because it does not Christianize.

stirrups you cannot shrink from having your spurs rip open the face of your opponent. For this you know, if he succeeds in pulling you out of the saddle and so unseats you, he in turn will have the right to tyrannize you and employ against you that same universal power of the state which was initially at your disposal—to indoctrinate the nation with principles that are inimical to you.

Therefore, revising Article 194 of the Constitution or a general revision of the Constitution is, in a political sense, completely the same agenda. Both represent a protest against the deficient guarantee of freedom of conscience of which we are accusing our political system.

Permit me now to identify the special changes that I would think can already be made in our school law. They are of two kinds: changes that are mainly pedagogical, and changes touching on the principle of justice.

Regarding the pedagogical principles, I desire:

1. that advanced primary education[16] be adjusted to fit reality so that it satisfies the needs of people's lives. After all, the people don't exist for the school, but the school exists for the people. Therefore, advanced primary education must vary depending on whether it is being provided in rural areas or in the cities. In rural areas, it must serve (a) the city folk that are found in our villages, and (b) the theoretical training of the farmer. In the cities, by contrast, it must satisfy (a) the need of some further education for the lower middle class, and (b) the need of theoretical training for the trades by means of technical schools;

2. that three ranks for teachers be introduced in the primary schools. This, too, is a demand derived from the real situation in our national life. A village school of 120 to 150 pupils is something altogether different from a city school with 500 students, the latter coming from a population that usually ranks higher intellectually. The freedom to assign assistant teachers to be headmaster of a school does not increase the number of ranks. Article 20 of the 1857 school law is rather a blemish on our legislation. And if there are in fact two kinds of schools, then a dual rank of teachers is indispensable. If people want to call the one

16. A kind of middle school, called U.L.O. or M.U.L.O., lasting four years after the first six primary grades. It was created by the Act of 1857 and abolished in 1968.

rank that of headmaster and the other that of teacher, it makes no difference to me, as long as the requirement is met that the teaching personnel for our cities achieve a higher intellectual development as expressed in their qualifications;

3. that the school hierarchy be restored. At the present time, an assistant teacher is added to the headmaster by the local council. This conflicts with the monarchical character of the unity of the school, and therefore I desire that assistant teachers not be appointed except by nomination from the headmaster;

4. that school hours be set at different times for the rural areas and the cities, so that the education provided in rural areas can accommodate the needs of field work and so end the bad practice that village children skip school for weeks on end without feeling in their conscience that there is anything wrong with it since the nature of rural life requires it and public opinion does not frown on it;

5. that minimum salaries be raised, but not in the sense as requested, for example, by the Association for Public Education, which commits the same mistake as the school law—namely, to assume the same minimum for all the municipalities throughout the land. With a minimum salary of nine hundred guilders a teacher in Amsterdam or Rotterdam would starve, while another teacher in many a small village would be able to live off that with relative ease. What is needed, therefore, is a schedule of minimum salaries that identify not only the minimum salary for a village, but also the minimum salaries for places where the cost of living is far higher, such as cities;

6. that the number of students per teacher be reduced by simply assigning fifty students rather than seventy; but also that the same teacher be prevented from having to teach several grades at the same time. It is a serious mistake in our school law that it sometimes allows a teacher, aided by at most a single teacher trainee, to teach four or five grades at a time;

7. that, finally, curricula be regulated by law. A school's curriculum is an index of the level of instruction it provides. This

should never be left to an Order in Council but must be regulated in law.

This all concerns the pedagogical aspect; I turn now to the principles of justice. On that score I have four demands.

1. Let us write into Article 16 the imperative mandate for all local boards to maintain in readiness as much school accommodation as is required for the number of children whose parents or guardians desire admission[17] to the public school for their children or wards.

   Tuition fees should be made mandatory by law. That demand is also fair. At present, arbitrariness rules. Think of a recent example of what happened not long ago in a municipality near Leeuwarden. At 5,780 residents, it had thirteen public schools for primary education, and the local council proposed to build a fourteenth in addition. Where? In a hamlet where sixty-seven families were living, of which virtually all the children attended a private school, so that a public school was needed for the children of only three families, and that public school was already available in the community hall of the hamlet. Indeed, what is even worse, the parents of those children were housed so that the distance from their home to the already existing school was just as far or even closer than the distance to the center of the hamlet where they want to build the new school. Nonetheless, in order to kill the competition (which shows you again to what degree any fair competition is impossible), the municipality went through with its plan to build the fourteenth school[18] and—whether rightly or wrongly I shall not say—the appeal lodged by the interested parties to the provincial authorities and even to the king was unsuccessful.

2. Revision of the abstract theory of Article 23 into a concrete conscience clause. As the article now reads, it appears to

17. School attendance was not compulsory.
18. A public school with low or no tuition fees, making it more competitive than the private school.

grant safeguards for the conscience, but in fact it does not.[19] So I desire that the abstract formula be removed, and replaced with a concrete indication of the boundaries within which the teacher must function in the school.

3. No subsidy; for when it comes to education people should not have to ask for alms, as Mr. Groen van Prinsterer has said. I ask for restitution. Restitution is the term that is used when asking for justice; subsidy when wheedling for charity. Therefore, restitution, in the same sense in which it already exists, for example in Amsterdam, where the city council grants restitution to the Jewish hospital for the expenses that the city saves because the Jewish community provides for its own hospital. Recently Mr. de Mol Moncourt[20] showed the city council of Groningen with statistics that by establishing private schools, private individuals were saving the city a sum of four hundred thousand guilders, expenses that the city itself would have had to pay if private initiative had not manifested itself so well. The same applies to all of our large cities. And for that reason I ask that all municipalities begin to provide ample *accommodation* (I use this foreign word because it expresses exactly what I mean) needed for its public schools, but that they next inquire how many more children would have to be provided for if private schools did not provide for their needs, and then put the money that this would require, guilder for guilder, at the disposal of those who have lifted part of these expenses from the shoulders of city council thanks to their private initiative.

4. Finally, a reward of a fixed premium to be paid to each teacher who has trained a candidate who passes the examination for assistant teacher or headmaster. We are starving for teachers, and for that reason the state ought to encourage every available means aimed at increasing the number of teachers.

---

19. "The teacher shall refrain from teaching, doing or permitting anything that is inconsistent with the respect due to the religious beliefs of those who think differently."

20. Jacobus Christoffel de Mol Moncourt (ca. 1818–83) was a grain merchant from Groningen and was involved in the founding of a Christian school there in 1851.

I shall stop here. These are demands that have been honed very precisely. They are not misty ideas, but crystal-clear water droplets that you need only to collect, and behold: the stream is flowing.

III

With this I come finally to my last question: Can we hope to benefit in any way from the overabundance of ministerial ambiguity?

But first a word of thanks and appreciation to the present minister. When I compare what was recently stated in the speech from the throne with what former ministers in succession declared here, then there is indeed reason to be content. If you ask to see this minister you no longer hear, as with Thorbecke: "Please come back tomorrow!" or as with Fock: "The shutters are closed, no response, regardless," or as in the case of Geertsema: "The doorbell has been disconnected to prevent neighborhood noise."[21] No, instead, you are greeted courteously at the door and led to the antechamber. You will, however, be asked to wait a while, because the professors are still inside. But once they're done and a higher education bill is ready, you too will be shown in.

A word of thanks also for the fact that the minister has taken up our cause in the First Chamber. That body, in its reply to the speech from the throne, had expressed the wish that the principles of the school act might be maintained and safeguarded. The minister was silent about that, and I will not conceal that this silence surprised me for a moment. But that surprise lifted quickly and turned into satisfaction, even gratitude, when I heard the minister declare in response to the question of Mr. van Zuylen[22] in this Chamber: the only principles that I defend are *no revision of Article 194*—of course, I knew this already, and although I might wish otherwise, I must quietly acquiesce in this—and *the public school usable and accessible to all*. Of course that declaration might have slipped out in the heat of improvisation, without fully expressing his *pensée intime*.[23] But no, in the minister's memorandum of response, the same words have been repeated literally, with the added comment that in the bosom of the government the matter had been

---

21. Johan Rudolph Thorbecke (1798–1872), Cornelis Fock (1828–1910), and Johan Herman Geertsema (1816–1908) were prominent politicians whose service included time as minister of the interior. Jan Heemskerk Azn (1818–97) was minister of the interior (as well as prime minister) at the time of this speech.
22. Julius van Zuylen van Nijevelt (1819–94) was a conservative politician and former prime minister.
23. That is, private reflection.

decided in the same spirit. This last point may be tacitly assumed; after all, no ministry can presume to sit at the council table with the intention of revising the school law without knowing beforehand on what basis that is to be done. If then the school law will be revised in accordance with the interests of the nation, with the single proviso that the public school be "usable and accessible to all," then I ask: What more could I wish for? I am completely satisfied with that. I must even declare that if from my side I had to identify a minimum of principles that should be retained in the law, my minimum calculation probably would not have dared to go that low.

Is there no ambiguity then? None whatsoever, I think. I find the declaration crystal clear. When I read and reread the declaration I have no more questions. Nevertheless, people generally do not think about it this way. Some think it still contains a certain indeterminacy, a certain obscurity. For that reason I could wish that the minister agree to provide an affirmative answer to this question: Is the principle that you have identified, *the public school usable and accessible to all*, the only principle in the existing school law that you wish to maintain?

If, however, the minister is of the opinion—for in governmental matters the requirement of prudence applies—that it is not advisable at this time to offer a direct answer to that question, then I am prepared *to wait*. But if we have to wait anyway, we should spend the time efficiently. For example, by appointing what the English call a *royal commission*, a measure which the importance of this issue certainly merits. In his "Letter concerning the Gelder polder regulation," Mr. Thorbecke judged that even for that issue, appointing such a commission—not simply a government advisory commission, but a commission to which every interested party can make known their desires and interests—would have been highly desirable, even necessary. Very well, with respect to the issue of education I make his words my own:

> Should such a procedure not have come before consideration of the regulation bill by the [Provincial] States? Especially regarding measures that impact many special interests, the British legislators feel they should broaden such consultation as widely as possible, away from the halls of Parliament. What a contrast between this great and modest wisdom and the rash haste of your assembly![24]

24. J. R. Thorbecke, *Brief aan een lid der Staten van Gelderland over de magt der Provinciale Staten uit Art. 220 der Grondwet* (Leiden: P. H. van den Heuvell, 1843), 5.

Mr. Van Zuylen, one and a half years ago already, in this Chamber, expressed the same idea [of appointing a royal commission] for the government's consideration. And so I would say: the sickness has been identified; vigorous action is needed. If you are unable to make the specific declaration that I desire, and if you are unable to give voice to your own advice, then *consult others*.

But my preference would be to receive a positive, categorical declaration now, for the sake of the benefit it would provide to the nation, the Chamber, and the minister himself.

Benefit to the nation. Public opinion is preoccupied with the issue, but it talks "thirteen to the dozen," as the saying goes; the nation drifts about rudderless on the waves of an undisciplined discussion; it does not select a fixed point on which to focus its eyes. Not until the minister is willing to speak authoritatively will they have a beacon to steer toward. Then public opinion will be able to complete its task, before the Chamber takes up its own task and causes an opinion to ripen in the nation that the Chamber will have to decide on.

But benefit for the Chamber also. It will be important, I think, that the public come up with a specific declaration of their viewpoint. We are only a few months away from the elections. There is now an opinion circulating in the press and throughout many groups in the country that the Chamber is no longer quite representative of the ideas fermenting in the bosom of the nation, and that for this reason we no longer enjoy the undivided confidence of the nation. I am not saying that I hold this view, but I am merely observing the fact that some do.

How can this be resolved? The best way, it seems to me, is through the periodic elections, provided they are as pure as gold, by which I mean that during election campaigns people in every district are made fully cognizant of the principles to which the candidates are committed in regard to this all-dominating issue. Partly for this reason I have for my part been very precise about my ideas about the school law, so that the public will be able to evaluate them, leaving it to my voters to decide how well those ideas please them.

Finally, benefit for the ministry as well. I deem a clear, unambiguous declaration absolutely indispensable. A government must lead and not be led. I was therefore pleased to hear from the minister that in his opinion the authority here proceeds from the Crown, and he added: "We, the government, do not cut ourselves loose from Parliament; we come with our considerations and ideas, and leave it to the prudence of Parliament to judge whether our proposals can obtain their approval." But then, if the cabinet is to be rooted in the trust of the nation, the guiding political idea must not be lacking by which people can evaluate the efforts of the government.

Recently the minister employed, after the fashion of our unpoetic age, the less aesthetic image borrowed from the steam engine: "Put on the brakes in the East Indies, fire the engine in the Netherlands!" So, we shall be traveling by train. But then I have a request. At the larger stations, at least for the express trains, there is the excellent custom of hanging on the side of every train car a sign that you can read from a distance, identifying the train's destination. Your Excellency, before we board your ministerial train, please write on the cars, with words incapable of double meaning, where you want to take us. You have promised us a royal express train. All the better. Better to have an express train than what people in France call a *train omnibus*. We make only this plea: if it must go that fast, then let's not travel all too long in nocturnal darkness.[25]

During the debates of the following day, December 8, 1874, Kappeyne van de Coppello announced that the ideal education system for him and like-minded liberals was compulsory elementary education, free of tuition, in religiously neutral schools, for the entire population. Other schools were free to operate but would always have to be privately funded, thus as a privilege for the rich and a form of charity for the poor. He explained further:

Should the church or the state assume the task of education? If the church, then it must have a monopoly, for the church cannot tolerate a school that is not placed under its ecclesiastical oversight. In that case, not only the state school, but the private, free school as well, are impossible. By contrast, if the state undertakes the task it will be happy to see both free private schools and religious schools emerge alongside its own schools; for the state is really interested only in worldly instruction. That this worldly instruction is not corrupted even when permeated with a religious leaven that leans in this or that direction, I will not dispute. On the contrary, I recognize that there are many religious schools whose instruction is better than that in the public schools.

So I am dealing only with worldly instruction. The honorable member from Gouda [Kuyper] has understood me very well when he expressed no doubt that I did not in any way want to place state schools opposite religious

25. The minister did not table an education bill until two years later, on Dec. 6, 1876.

schools as the enemy. A state school mandated to disseminate a so-called natural religion covered with a Christian veneer is an abomination to me as much as to him.

Thus, if the state can entirely satisfy the demands in this way, arranging its education appropriately while tolerating the free private school as well as the religious school alongside its own, then this alone demonstrates that in our society it is the state that must look after education and not the church, all the more so because in actuality we are not dealing with the church but (especially when it comes to conscientious objections) mainly with just one party in one particular denomination, and this party can never make a claim on the public school, given its position. For instance, if the honorable member from Gouda counters with the argument: "You have banned the Bible from the school," I could ask him: "Do you want the Bible interpreted at school by me?" When the eschatologist admonishes the rich who "have heaped treasures together for the last days" to repent [Jas 5:3], the honorable member thinks it proves that the Netherlands needs a labor code; but when it is pointed out to him that the same chapter prohibits the oath he gives us an interpretation that undoes the prohibition. I believe he has more of the gift of interpretation than I have, but I ask: Does having your Bible in the school mean anything other than having that Bible interpreted, applied, and used in the way you desire? Is it any wonder then that no Bible is allowed in the school unless that school is specifically a religious school?

But if education cannot be left to the church—and this is so because, even though she is not averse to enlightenment, she fixes her eye especially, and if need be exclusively, on the salvation of the souls of its children, not on their earthly interests—then I ask whether, if the state is able to establish and maintain an appropriately organized educational system, the demand is not legitimate that each child *must* make use of primary education?

I am told: that conflicts with the right of the parents. I don't understand that right of the parents. The honorable member from Arnhem complimented me in connection with my general views by saying: your understanding of public law is classical. That is true; I have learned it, as he has, from Justinian's *Institutes*. But he added: Christian society is built on marriage, hence on the family. Leaving aside whether the church in the first centuries showed itself to be an advocate of marriage, I am not sure that the ecclesiastical definition of marriage was derived from Roman law; but I do know that the ecclesiastical (the Christian, if you will, though I prefer to say the Germanic) conception of law completely altered the legal relationship between parents and children. Whereas according to Roman law the child was the legal possession of the father, Germanic law wanted that legal relationship to be regulated according to the obligations of the parents toward the children. The child is not someone's legal possession but an object of love. Now I ask you: Can any father claim that it is his duty to withhold the first level of education from his child if the school where that education is provided is made available by the state at no cost? If I am told, "if that's what you want, you will oppress the minority," then I would almost say: then that minority will just have to be oppressed, for then it is the fly that spoils the entire ointment and has no right to exist in our society.[26]

During the same session that evening, Dr. A. Kuyper responded with the following:

After hearing the honorable member from Haarlem explain his school program, I hope he will never become a leader of the government so long as he professes the principles he defended this morning. Still, I would like to appeal, not to his head this time but to his heart, and ask him: Is the word "compassion" no longer able to tug at your heartstrings? If it is, then how could you declare here, in the parliament of the Netherlands: my system would have to organize the country, and the education in this country, so that only those gain freedom of education who can pay for it? Does the poor man, the not so well-off, not also have a heart, convictions, wishes with respect to his offspring? And will it really do to still use the word "liberty" in a program that offers *freedom for the rich, compulsion for the poor*?

The honorable member summed up his rebuttal [of my proposals] with this—and I say this with deep concern—appalling expression: "Then the minorities will simply have to be oppressed if need be, for then they are the fly that makes the apothecary's ointment stink." That single sentence fully answers the question I put to him yesterday: Esteemed colleague, where do you stand? Are you really in that gloomy corner where despotism, tyranny, state absolutism has pitched its tent? To be absolute means to have no limits or boundaries, or no other boundaries than those that the body wants to assign to itself. Now I ask him: Where, according to your theory of the state, are the boundaries that limit the power of the state? He can identify them so poorly that when an ultimate limit to the state's power presents itself as

26. Allusion to Eccl 10:1.

people's conscience, he says: smash that minority, and remove that fly that would spoil my precious ointment!

Over against this—he asked for system versus system—I say: The power of the state certainly has its boundaries, and those boundaries must be the product, the resultant, of the wrestling that goes on between the state and the life-issues of society. In that society there exist independent spheres whose unique authority is not derived from the earthly king but from the King above, and in their wrestling with the state, they are the ones that determine the boundaries within which the action of the state has to confine itself. When a father demands love, respect, and obedience from his children, he derives the authority to do so not from a political constitution but from a divine ordinance, for he is a father over his children "by the grace of God," just as much as our king rules by the grace of God over the kingdom of the Netherlands. If now the honorable member says that the power of the state accordingly must be expanded until at last even the conscience should be subject to it; and if you then ask me what would be my ultimate point of support against that endeavor, the unwavering constant whereby the free life of society can be safeguarded, then I reply: that is what *faith* offers you.

Faith—not a confessional document, but the faith that constitutes the inner bond of my person in the depth of my heart to the God who dwells above and from whose almighty power I through faith can derive the power, should the state turn its full power against me, to stand alone if necessary and to demonstrate that in my conscience, when bound through faith to a higher authority, a boundary has been fixed which even the authority of the state cannot permanently cross. One need only consult history. Whenever the authority of the state has attempted to rule over that internal authority, it may have triumphed temporarily, but in the end it has always had to yield.

Mr. Speaker, should the day ever arrive when a minister of the Crown announced this member's program as the program of the government, saying that if need be he would oppress the minorities and kill the fly that might spoil the prepared ointment, I would cry out: then also remove from the Dutch coat of arms the lion, proudest symbol of liberty, and replace it with an eagle clutching a lamb in its talons, the symbol of tyranny!

Earlier in this speech Kuyper had replied[27] *to two other objections to his proposal:*

27. This section is taken from A. Kuyper, *Eenige kameradviezen uit de jaren 1874 en 1875* (Amsterdam: J. A. Wormser, 1890), 239–40.

The honorable member from The Hague ... has tried to show that the law of 1857 is recommendable in particular because it satisfies two demands: that it promote the *unity of the nation*, and that it save us from the *secular* school.

The unity of the nation! There is unity and unity. As you want. Is it the unity of the house painter who covers everything with the same color, or that higher unity in the harmony of colors which the artist pursues with a rich diversity of shades and gradations? The first kind is the unity that the honorable member wants by casting everybody in the same mold; the unity that I aim at is the unity of the flowerbed whereby each flower retains its peculiar form and color from which is born that higher harmony.

The system of 1857 avoids the *secular* school! For, as the honorable member points out, after school hours the church may enter the classroom. The honorable member, through his contributions here and through his career in society, has shown that he loves the child and knows a child's world too well that I can let him get away with this assertion. Surely he will concede, if he has ever watched children coming out of school—children who have worked at their desks for a long, very long time, from nine till twelve, and who had to sit still, squirming under the school's rules—that they are hardly eager to go to *catechism classes* in their free time. They want to have a sandwich, have time to play with their favorite toy, have fun with their friends. I ask the honorable member to inquire of teachers of religion sometime whether they have not discovered that wherever this system was in vogue it was virtually impossible to arouse the least interest on the part of the child. Seriously, when a child's mind is tired is it a suitable time for discussing the highest, dearest interests not only for this but also for eternal life? And if the church is then called to enter the school at such a time, then I think she will answer: "I would rather wait till Sunday and give my Sunday school a new boost; then at least I will have fresh minds." No, if religious instruction is to be given under those conditions, following the regular lessons, the result will not be love of religion but aversion to it.

The Act prescribes moral education. But the state cannot teach morality because morality involves principles of anthropology and psychology of which the state is incompetent to judge. That is why Mr. Groen van Prinsterer fought tooth and nail against the education bill of 1857 because it would of necessity lead to the state's teaching its own brand of religion and so create a kind of state church disguised as the public school.

GRIEVANCES AGAINST THE SCHOOL LAW

TEXT INTRODUCTION

This bellicose series of articles was written during a critical phase in the school struggle. A younger generation of Liberals, till then held back by older and more careful, conservative forces among their ranks, was preparing to end the school struggle once and for all by updating and modernizing the government schools and so pricing the private school out of the market and ensuring an absolute monopoly for the so-called religiously neutral but increasingly secular public school. In the coming general elections of June 1875, they hoped to achieve this goal by appealing for the vote of the "thinking part" of the electorate during the campaign, in which they planned to make the public school the key issue.

The past few years had seen the growing strength of the more progressive Young Liberals, among whom figured the convinced agnostic and fierce debater Mr. Kappeyne, who was prepared to ride roughshod over the conscientious objections of the minority in the interest of a new and improved common public school for the entire nation. On the left this group was even surpassed by the self-styled Radical Liberals who advocated compulsory school attendance for all children between six and fourteen years of age and a truancy law that would punish delinquent parents with fines and jail terms.

Kuyper's newspaper editorials in response to these threats are by turns playfully sarcastic and deeply serious. In a merry-go-round of images and metaphors, they show Kuyper at his polemical best or—depending on your taste—his worst. He composed them as he was serving his first term as a member of Parliament, during which he worked at a feverish pitch, kept up with the daily newspapers and studied the official documents far into the night, spoke up in the Chamber perhaps too often for a rookie, and incurred much derision and hostile reactions to his ideas, which he "preached" with great passion. Within the year he collapsed from nervous exhaustion.

Source: Kuyper, Abraham. *Grieven tegen de schoolwet en het geheim verraden*. Amsterdam: J. H. Kruyt, 1875, pp. 2–32. Earlier published in *De Standaard* between January 11 and March 26, 1875. Translated by Arjen Vreugdenhil and Nelson D. Kloosterman. Edited by Harry Van Dyke.

GRIEVANCES AGAINST THE SCHOOL LAW

THE COMPETITIVE MODEL FOR EDUCATION

Our contention has been all along that competition in the area of education [between public and private schools] will prove untenable in the long run and cannot produce a healthy educational model. This view has come in for much criticism. We would ask that this criticism be reconsidered. In order to avoid misunderstanding, we will first give a clear presentation of our thoughts on the subject.

As long as Article 194 of the Constitution remains as it is, one cannot avoid the competitive model. It is therefore erroneous to think that we hoped to have the competition removed without an amendment of that article. As long as the government on the one hand is required to ensure that adequate primary education is available everywhere, and on the other hand maintains the liberty of private persons or groups to organize free schools,[1] there will be competition in the area of primary education, not

1. The two requirements were prescribed in Article 194 of the Constitution of 1848, which read: "Public education is an abiding concern of the Government. The organization of public education is regulated by law, while respecting everyone's religious beliefs. *The Government provides adequate public primary education throughout the*

simply in fact, but by force of law. Our opposition to the competitive model is therefore based on the firm conviction that sooner or later the "wretched clause" in Article 194[2] will be removed and our schools will be protected from the suffocating embrace of politics.

The state cannot teach, since it has neither pedagogical principles nor a religious confession. As a result, it is bound to pursue neutrality, which in practice ends in favoring [theological] modernism and opposing Christianity. Yet the state would undeniably be remiss in its duty if it failed to ensure that education of sufficient quality were available to all. Combining these two factors, the only solution we see is the free and independent, private organization of primary education, under the supervision of the legislative authority.

Education by its very nature is not a political but a social issue. Not in the realm of the state but in the realm of society does one find the natural intersection of the educational interests that are equally important to parents and children and church and state. Only the acknowledgment of this truth will put a definitive end to the stand-off between state and church in the matter of the state school; only in this way can one arrive at a model that promotes the free school as the rule, and perpetuates the official neutral school merely in a supplementary role.

Now what objections to this idea can the supporters of the current competitive model have? And even assuming that no organization of education will be perfect, do their objections to the social model outweigh the dangers of the competitive model?

What, then, are those dangers of the competitive model? We point out four dangers in particular.

1. The School Is Reduced to a Stake in a Political Game of Chance

It is often said that because of our irascibility, we antirevolutionaries have introduced the issue of education into the political debates. As if the

---

Kingdom. The provision of education is free, subject to government inspection, and moreover, insofar as secondary and primary education is concerned, subject to an examination of the competence and moral character of the teacher, to be established by law. The King shall cause an annual report to be presented to the States General on the state of the higher, secondary, and primary schools" (emphasis added).

2. The "wretched clause" are the words italicized in note 1 above.

education model provided by the Conservatives in the Act of 1857 did not compel us to undertake this political intervention![3]

No one would disagree if a similar model obtained in the realm of commerce, where competition more properly belongs. Suppose the government were required to maintain a sufficient reserve of food in every municipality; would it then be fair to accuse our bakers, butchers, grocers, and so on of undue agitation if during election campaigns they tried to reduce this impossible competition to the smallest degree possible? Who is to blame, we or the Conservative lawmakers, if we try to utilize the ballot box as the only effective means to prevent the competition of state-run schools from turning into large-scale suppression of ours?

The law itself turns the public school into a political issue par excellence. It is a political issue for our liberals, who for lack of party unity now rally around the neutral public school to protect this precious instrument which Conservative myopia had handed them for liberalizing the next generation. It is a political issue for our Conservatives, who, realizing their mistake of 1857 at the eleventh hour, have been using the education issue to ensure support from the opposition parties. It is a political issue for our Roman Catholics, who, because they are less inclined to make their political agenda transparent, have made a rare tactical retreat to the rear of the battle over education.

And similarly, it is a political issue for us, antirevolutionaries. So much so, that for many years the most elementary study of general government policy was pushed to the background. Reduced to a political issue, the schools

3. The most controversial provision of the Primary Education Act of 1857 was Article 23, which read: "The instruction in the school shall be made serviceable, while learning suitable and useful skills, to the development of the intellectual faculties of the children and to their training in all Christian and civic virtues. The teacher shall refrain from teaching, doing or admitting anything that is inconsistent with the respect due to the religious beliefs of others. Religious instruction is left to the church denominations. For this purpose the school facilities can be made available outside of school hours for the pupils who attend the school." Article 16 meanwhile expressed the ideal of the mixed or common school in these words: "Every municipality shall provide education for its population in a number of schools adequate for existing need that shall be open to all children without distinction of religious persuasion." In his defense of the bill at the time, the minister had explained in Parliament that the state cannot teach religion and that therefore the phrase "training in Christian virtues" must be taken in no other sense than that it removes from the state school "every dogmatic element, in a word everything that belongs to the definition of Christianity, its truths, its facts, its history."

question in the last decade has been the single issue during elections, the main difference between the parties, and the sword of Damocles for every new government.

The resulting corruption has been reciprocal. The school corrupted politics. Politics corrupted the school. One may seriously wonder whether, among the causes of our national deterioration, anything compares to the wretched Education Act of 1857.

2. The Influence of the Parties That Oppose the State School Cannot but Hinder It from Flourishing

If a competitive model is to be commended, then the competition must be fair. Is fairness conceivable in the case of the primary school? Fair competition means that in a race the chances are equal for the entrants. Equal chances! What do you think? The public school has the following advantages: (1) the full weight of government; (2) the support of nearly all inspectors and supervisors; (3) unrestricted access to the pocketbooks of all citizens; (4) job security for its teachers; (5) teacher training in well-endowed colleges; (6) a pension plan for retired teachers; (7) an unclear law, which therefore can be made to condone anything; (8) tuition-free education.

In contrast, the free school, having nothing, literally nothing, is compelled to row against the stream of administrative superiority, financial preponderance, and clever misuse of the law.

You who support the competitive model, let me put three questions to you: (1) Is competition not supposed to be fair? (2) Does fair competition not presuppose equal chances? (3) How would you ensure that the free school has the same chances as a state school?

Only one means of resistance is left to the supporters of the free school. To the extent that they have the right to vote, they can vote for members of Parliament who will mitigate the constant tendency to increase the inequality of chances. The legislative power decides about the state school. In that process of decision making our members of Parliament have a voice. To keep their seat, what else can they do except refuse an allocation of funds that would increase the power of the state school, a power whereby the free school would be oppressed even more?

3. The Competitive Model Places the Life or Death of the Free School in the Hands of an Artificial Parliamentary Majority

Recently, in the latest debate on education, the supporters of the state school revealed their plan to (1) increase the costs of education significantly, (2) hire a large number of additional teachers for the state school, and (3) significantly raise the costs of free schools. Note well: with the express declaration that they had no intention whatever of addressing our grievances.

Already at this moment the free school is struggling with the impossible. It lacks stability, money, personnel. One can safely predict that unless there is relief the free school will succumb.

Yet the agenda is being proclaimed publicly of increasing its burden threefold, and whether that agenda can be stopped or will succeed under the triumphant cheers of the liberals, depends ... on a single vote in Parliament; on the outcome of a single election; on the possibility that the conciliatory faction in our parliament dare to go that far.

4. The Competitive Model, as It Currently Functions, Will Not Provide the Competition Needed to Improve Education

We readily acknowledge that a few cases can be identified in which parents, who in principle favor the free school, choose the state school because of its excellence, and that there are also parents who in principle favor the state school but send their children to the free school because of its superior education.

But these are exceptions to the rule. Only very few towns and villages feature educational competition between the public school and the free school. As a rule, the decisive factor is the principle one believes in. Christian parents send their children to a Christian school, even if it has difficulty finding teachers, rather than entrust them to a state school. Conversely, other people care so little for pedagogical excellence that, without the slightest research, they tend to hate every Christian school as a religious plague and a hotbed of intolerance.

Thus the competition shifted from the realm of pedagogy to the realm of principle and politics; not the pedagogical but almost exclusively the political competition led to the debate about the nation's education system. Therefore, so long as "competition" continues to mean competing with the state, it appears to us untenable and harmful; and it is only that competition that we opposed.

It goes without saying that there might be competition also in the social model of public education, and that in fact only in this model would competition provide the incentive for pedagogical excellence.

But to the point! What our opponents defended and praised as the crown jewel of national wisdom was not the free social competition but exclusively the competition of private schools with the schools of the state.

SCHOOL INSPECTION

One of the most serious and persistent grievances against the educational model of 1857 has always been the one-sided nature of school supervision, which was mandated not so much by the letter as by the spirit of the law.

School inspection, in its various branches, extends to education in all its forms; as such, it is aware of the distinction between public and private education only in the technical sense; its operation must encompass both equally. It is to investigate not which kind of education is preferred in a given municipality, but only whether the education offered complies with the requirements of the law.

This supervision is not insignificant. Inspectors and commissioners are vested with a fair amount of power. Moreover, the well-being of the school as well as the individual careers of teachers depend, sometimes quite heavily, on their favor or disfavor. In this way they exert a moral influence that reaches beyond their formal authority, and in the matter of education they have decisive power for the future, more than the school boards, more even than the provincial authorities.

Can such government influence[4] be placed in the hands of a supporter of the free school? Will a supporter of the free school be equally welcomed to the position of school inspector, at any level of the hierarchy, and will he be considered an equally reliable commissioner for the government as a zealot for neutral education? Can we be sure that when these officials are appointed none will receive preferential treatment on account of his support of the public school?

Naturally, the occasional appointment of a free-school supporter, loudly trumpeted to the nation to disprove and fend off any complaints, does not contradict the rule but is the exception that confirms it. Besides, even such exceptions are extremely rare.

In spite of the theory of neutrality, it did not take long before the same practical result was achieved nearly everywhere: as much as possible, school inspection was placed in the hands of supporters of the public school, interpreted in a very partisan sense. The advocates of neutrality realized that, although an opponent of the state school would not wish to violate the law and no doubt strive for impartiality in his office, yet the flourishing of the public school was a matter of the heart, of dedication and affection, and a school inspection without that ingredient would eventually cause it

4. School inspectors and supervisors were appointed by the municipal government.

harm. Thus, they themselves were not satisfied that "professional impartiality" was good enough; nevertheless they felt that the free school should be able to put up with this "professional good will." They would challenge us: "Why do you feel disadvantaged? Speak up, if you have a complaint! Are our inspectors, both of higher and lower rank, not impartial and humane?"

But tell us (we would like to respond): Have you ever detected partiality or inhumaneness among those few members of the "learned college" of inspectors who agree with our position? And if not, why does your party systematically exclude our men?

Recently it happened again, in the city of Groningen. Mayor and aldermen had, more than once, proposed to include in the local school committee one or two supporters of free schools. There was a reason to do so: half of the educational offerings in Groningen was of the free-school variety. A very acceptable candidate was available. Nobody would have rejected Prof. Gratama[5] as an unfit or biased candidate. His appointment would have removed longstanding grievances which a large part of the citizenry have nursed against the city council for years. There was no risk: if he had been chosen, Prof. Gratama would have had only one vote, and would have stood alone in the committee.

Yet the proposal to appoint him was strongly opposed by the Groningen city council. Mr. Leopold preferred not to declare any of the alleged complaints inadmissible.[6] However:

> Even if some people had grievances, one would still have to consider their nature. Meeting them would still not lead to any practical result. These grievances concern neutral education: that it is not neutral. One might think that if education were made neutral it would also be used by that party; but that party does not want that: it wants positive Christian education. The proposed solution could never satisfy their grievances. Speaker uses the following analogy. He imagines that the state plans to provide good drinking water, and that the government proposes to realize that idea. That government says that the water should be cold. But one party says that it should be warm. This party does not get its way, so what does it do? It says: you

5. Bernard Jan Gratama (1822–86) was a law professor at the University of Groningen.
6. What follows is in the typical shorthand style of city council minutes.

want the water to be cold, but it is not actually cold. Speaker believes such resistance toward state education to be dishonorable. What interest could that party have in the degree of coldness of that water, while it has objections of conscience against its use to begin with?

Mayor and aldermen address the matter of equity. There is something to be said for it, but one should not give in too much. It is desirable that every party should do what it considers best, and that is precisely what the Antirevolutionary Party is doing. This party, according to the speaker, excludes everything that is not of its stripe; the recent church-related events here in Groningen are the best proof of that. Without asking whether this would turn away the most skilled and noble part of the population, the party pursues what it considers the right goal by electing people who would bring it closer to that goal. Therefore the speaker has much respect for that party. He desires to see that same exclusiveness in the other parties, and cannot imagine a wholesome situation otherwise.

Mayor and aldermen want to see the principles and opinions of the Antirevolutionary Party represented in the school committee. Speaker is willing to accept that this statement is a slip of the tongue: principles may play a role in the making of a law, not when implementing it.

Mayor and aldermen suggest what the speaker views as utopian, namely that an anti-state school supporter might change his mind. Speaker believes no proper distinction is made here. We are not dealing with an anti-state school person, but with an antirevolutionary: the former simply flows from the latter. But if there were to be any changes of mind, the entire committee might come over to his view, something that the city council of Groningen would likely consider undesirable. Change or no change (the latter being more likely), all this would result in an endless fight within the committee, and the one who tired of it first would terminate his membership.

The outcome of the debate was that half of the twenty-four council members expressed support for Prof. Gratama, while the other half, apparently on the basis of prior collusion, voted unanimously for the teacher named Rijkens.

This must be pointed out: *either* this exclusion, the passing over of a man like Prof. Gratama in spite of his public nomination by the mayor and council members, stems from the spirit of the Education Act of 1857, which then stands condemned because of its own fruits. *Or else* it conflicts with the spirit of that law, but then worse still, a shameful insult was perpetrated against all the supporters of the free school in the rejection of an outstanding sympathizer like Prof. Gratama.

What side does the liberal party come down on? Its statements are becoming increasingly more suspicious. What to think of the following sentences in the *Amersfoortse Weekblad*?

> The people opposing the School Law are more vocal here than anywhere else, and under the guise of morbid fanaticism they fight against the existing order in the state. One should commend the state for its forbearance: although it has the perfect right to do so, in the interest of public order it has not denied such associations their right to exist.

That we are still tolerated is supposed to be a case of forbearance!

AN EVEN WORSE CULTIVATION SYSTEM

From the point of view of a liberal partisan, one can scarcely imagine anything worse than the cultivation system that Conservatism introduced on Java.[7] Javanese society should not have been forced. Such paternalistic meddling necessarily resulted in the death of the people's vitality. The Javanese should have been allowed to decide for themselves what crops to grow. For a government to take over an entire country and make it serve a system of production which the people would not have chosen themselves is criminal. This is not up to the state; this does not belong to its legitimate authority; this cannot be the task of government! A government engaged in agriculture ignores its own dignity and the future of the nation. For a time it may appear to yield impressive results, but ultimately it will end in national decay.

---

7. The cultivation system, known in Indonesia as *tanam paksa*, "forced planting," was a government policy in the mid-1800s in the Dutch East Indies that required part of agricultural lands to be devoted to cash crops for the European market; see also *OP*, 302–6.

To a large extent we always went along with our liberals in this condemnation of the cultivation system in the colonies. One might even say that the antirevolutionaries were the first to come out and say that this compulsory system was indefensible. At home and overseas, in motherland and the colonies, we always protested against inhumane compulsion and warned against the confusion of entrusting to the state what is the sacred task of society. We felt that the liberals could not but stand with us by virtue of their *formal* principle, and in our view their battle against the cultivation system was justified especially by that principle.

Will our favorable opinion of the liberals be able to survive? Actually we are beginning to doubt that it will, and we freely admit that we are at sea now that our liberals are promoting even more offensively in the motherland the very thing they had condemned so implacably and so justly in the Conservative policy in the colonies.

Seriously, tell us: On closer inspection, is the new *school program* of our liberals any different from the threat of introducing an even worse cultivation system in the territory of the kingdom of the Netherlands here in Europe? Does it not appear as if the apostles of this system, such as Kerdijk and Moens,[8] are trying to have their names immortalized in the national history books alongside that of Johannes van den Bosch?[9]

In the cultivation system Java had to produce not what it chose but what the colonial governor deemed expedient. And what else is the purpose of the liberal school program than to have the nation produce, by means of the state school, not what the nation itself wants but what the liberal zealots want it to produce? A nation also labors in a spiritual sense, and in a free nation the product of that ceaseless labor must be determined by national choice and inclination.

The liberals want to put an end to this. The nation will have to continue to labor, even more strenuously than before, but the product of that labor will be predetermined by our liberals. The miracle performed by the government coffee plantations on Java must be repeated by the government schools in free Holland. Because the government needs coffee, the Javanese are compelled to grow coffee trees. Similarly, because liberalism needs the

8. Arnold Kerdijk (1846–1905) was a liberal politician and journalist; Antony Moens (1827–99) was a modernist preacher who later became a prominent school inspector.
9. The cultivation system was introduced on Java by Count Johannes van den Bosch (1780–1844) when he was governor-general of the East Indies from 1830 to 1834.

dechristianization of the nation if it is to survive, the next generation must be made ripe for this secularization in the state school.

Our governors take counsel together. In their tribunal they determine the quantity and quality of spiritual fruit that must be produced by our nation within a certain time frame. Next, they misuse the strong arm of the state to compel a free nation to deliver this product, contrary to its own inclination, with no regard for its past, and in spite of its stated unwillingness.

Here too we are surely dealing with a cultivation system, but one that is even worse. On Java, at least the rice paddies were spared; but the Liberals are aiming precisely at the destruction of our plots—of what we cultivate in our free schools. On Java, a cultivation system was implemented to replenish our treasury; but the cultivation system of the Liberals is on its way to ruining our treasury.

Last but not least, the colonial cultivation system disrupted the free course merely of material interests, but the cultivation system of our Liberals is an assault on the nation's spiritual development. The stated purpose of this newfangled cultivation system is to utilize the nation's resources to turn all our boys and girls into little liberals.

Like most people, Liberals tend to entertain their special wishes concerning the next generation. Now then, allow the nation to develop freely, and none of the Liberal ideals will be realized. On the contrary, things will develop in the opposite direction, and then Liberalism has no future. That is intolerable. That must be prevented. The nation must be liberalized. And the primary school must accomplish that. Therefore the primary school must be smuggled into the hands of the Liberals.

But that still won't be enough if people don't make use of that school. Two solutions are available. First, the Liberals will try the least obvious approach: make the private school impossible; then the children will automatically come to your government coffee plantations. But if that too fails, the Liberals have another approach up their sleeves: close the private school and station police officers at every home to see to it that the boys and girls emerge every morning, to undergo daily from 9 a.m. to 4 p.m. the required molding in the "state factory of little liberals."

THE OBLIGING NATURE OF ACTUAL PRACTICE

Article 23 of the Education Act is intended to guarantee freedom of conscience. "The teacher shall refrain from teaching, doing or admitting anything that is inconsistent with the respect due to the religious beliefs of others." In a previous article we showed that this article accomplishes the exact opposite of what it intends: it does not protect the conscience but puts it in a stranglehold.

Back in 1857, there simply were a number of communities whose population was too diverse and too small to have an alternative to the one, single, mixed school. This restriction was applied to the entire country, even though in many places other alternatives were viable. And so we ended up on the wrong track.

Yet, as we also mentioned, it turned out once again that nature was stronger than the doctrine. We pointed to the Veluwe and the regions south of the Moerdijk.[10] The law requires that the public schools in those areas may be no different in any way from those in, say, Rotterdam or Arnhem. The law knows of only one kind of public school. Throughout the country the public school must have a uniform character. Deviation from this rule is a violation of the law. There ought to be so little variation that it should be indifferent to a Roman Catholic citizen whether he sends his child to a public school in Groningen or to a public school in Boxtel; conversely, it should make no difference to a Protestant whether he entrusts his child to a public school on the Veluwe or to one in Tilburg.[11] Such are the requirements of the system, the pretense of the theory, the force of the law.

Does actual practice correspond to this?

Let us begin with the church affiliation of the teachers. Naturally, this has nothing to do with the public school. To a public school it is completely irrelevant whether the teacher is Catholic or Protestant, Jewish or Muslim. They may not even be asked about it. Recently our school inspection was "indignant" about the misbehavior of a city council that dared ask questions about it—rightly so, in our view.

Based on this, one would therefore think that an inventory of the placement of teachers with regard to their church membership should reveal the most variegated mix. You would expect it to be entirely random. Since any causal relationship has been declared unlawful, you should not find any patterns. Statistically, it should be the most balanced distribution imaginable.

---

10. The Veluwe was, and still is, an important part of the Dutch "Bible belt," and the regions "south of the Moerdijk" are still nominally Roman Catholic.

11. Boxtel and Tilburg are towns in the predominantly Catholic southern province of Brabant; the province of Groningen and the region of the Veluwe are predominantly Protestant.

Take any region in the country, and you should find in village after village a Catholic headmaster next to a Reformed one; here a village with a Lutheran teacher and there one with a Jewish teacher, regardless whether you are in the middle of the Veluwe or in the heart of Brabant.

Yet how mistaken your expectation would be! To the contrary, the data would allow you to formulate a fixed rule, so that you could predict with great certainty to what church the man belongs who teaches the youth in the public school. For entire provinces you can be almost certain that the vast majority of the teachers are Roman Catholic, and for other regions you can predict with confidence that they are Protestant; in some areas you could even guess to which particular Protestant denomination the teacher belongs.

A coincidence? No one would dare to claim that. But if it is not a coincidence, then apparently candidates are quietly assessed also as to their church membership. And that is a violation of the law.

Now then, what do our Liberals say about this? If a single city council dares to be open about this and adds to its advertisement of a position the letters "P. G.,"[12] then these men are indignant. But when several city councils, although they do not blaze it abroad, make no appointments without first ascertaining that the candidate belongs to the desired church, then the Liberals say nothing. Or rather, something is said about it, as the daily *Het Handelsblad* did two days ago, but nobody finds any fault with it. Could one find a more apt illustration of the paradox of "sifting out the gnat while swallowing the camel" than this factual accommodation?

If only that were all! But this accommodation goes much further. The entire country, from north to south, knows that the schools in the heart of the Veluwe are of an entirely different character from the schools around Maastricht in the Catholic province of Limburg; likewise, that the school in Limburg is entirely different from the school on one of the islands in South Holland. Ask around (unofficially) among your acquaintances in all denominations; inquire of your Liberal friend, your Roman Catholic dinner guest, your Conservative confidant, and they would smile if you pretended that you might not agree about these facts. Anyone who would defend the thesis that the public schools in the Veluwe, Limburg and Brabant, South and North Holland, are identical would become the laughingstock of public

12. That is, Protestant, *Gereformeerd* [Reformed].

opinion; he would show that he does not know his geography and that he needs to be called from the mists of theory back to the hard facts of reality.

Has there been an official investigation into this well-known fact, in order to restore respect for the law? On the contrary, the authorities close their eyes to this fact. They see it, but pretend not to see. The law was a means, but something else was the end ... and that end was not violated but rather promoted by these obliging accommodations in practice.

Was this intentional? Was this situation brought about deliberately? Certainly not. There simply was no alternative, and this singular option had much to recommend it. "The end justifies the means. ... What objection could you possibly have?"

What objection do we have? It is this. If the theory of your law, however well designed, runs up against the facts of life, then you should be a legislator who is both honest and wise, and change the stipulations of a law if it is incompatible with the actual situation in your country.

Throughout, we have taken your standpoint. Very well, on the basis of that standpoint, too, we call out to you: make Article 23 concrete!

THE SECRET BETRAYED: A MISCALCULATION

The grafting of liberalism onto our nation was not an easy process. An improved variety was flourishing on French soil and had to be imported and grafted onto those wild plants in the Dutch nursery. The public school in particular was assigned this large-scale task. It was of no benefit that the artificial light of liberal thought had already enlightened the upper classes; under a constitutional government one had to reckon with the influence of people of all social classes. Therefore there would be no lasting triumph until the grafting was completed throughout the entire nation. This explains why so much attention was paid to the primary school.

The years 1806 and 1857 were two milestones on the route that was to lead to a conquest of that national power center. At both times the uniform state school was promoted at the expense of the free school. In 1806 it was done under the banner of a bland Protestantism, in 1857 under the flag of a watered-down Christianity.

Another two days' journey, and the destination toward which the principle is leading will be reached. Just as a bland Protestantism turned into a diluted Christianity, so the latter will continue to turn into a colorless religiosity, and ultimately this process must lead to an open assault on all religion. Poulin dared to say it: *La vraie religion c'est de n'en avoir aucune!* which means, "Only those are truly pious who have broken with all religion!"[13]

Yet none of this animosity toward all religion showed at the surface. The evil lies in the principle; and also among our Liberals no more than one out of ten is a man of principle. Rather, the press as well as the general public and the legislator thought they were promoting true piety by engrafting the improved variety of liberalism.[14] They thought they were not fighting against true piety but against false piety; not the church but the sect; not the revelation of heavenly grace but of hellish hatred.

We must therefore make the charitable assumption that most supporters of the school law truly envisioned the national well-being through a national education system. They were convinced that the old-time religion would be harmful, but the new religion of humanity would be beneficial. They designed an elegant system. Our school law was to be a law of liberty: it would respect the convictions of all; it would increase the benefit of general education and foster all Christian and civic virtues. Seriously, what more could one ask for?

But consider the flip side. Favoring a "Christianity above sectarian differences"[15] deftly shut the door to all revealed religion, to Scripture, to the name of Jesus Christ as the Redeemer—but it left the door ajar for the self-willed religion of modernism, for the catechism of the Society for the Common Good,[16] and for presenting Jesus as a religious genius. The demand to respect all convictions prevented teachers as well as students from protesting against the atheist, but it did not go so far as to spare the sectarian hatred of believing Christians.

Education was to be free, ostensibly for all—but in reality it excluded 80 percent of the nation, which, after paying taxes for the state school, had no money left to pay for a second school at its own expense. Thus they succeeded in creating a primary school that seemed to fit the system of freedom. This system included competition and excluded compulsory

---

13. See Paulin Poulin, *Religion et Socialisme* (Paris: Librarie Internationale, 1867), 15. See also A. Penjon, "L'Autorité," *Revue Philosophique de la France et de l'Étranger* 74 (1912): 458.
14. That is, by incorporating the ideals of the French Revolution.
15. "Nonsectarian" education was originally meant to exclude *confessional* or *denominational* distinctives, but Kuyper argues that it developed into secular education.
16. See elsewhere in this volume "The Society 'for the Common Good.'"

attendance.[17] And so, trifling with the title Christian, it could reach its goal without overt compulsion.

The popularity of this system was so great that some prophesied loudly that now for the first time the development of the nation would take off. Just think ahead to that next generation, raised in that wondrous school; you may have heard of Dutch glory in the days of the republic, but the national prosperity that is about to arrive will be beyond imagination!

Almost twenty years have passed, and what has become of that grandiloquent fanfare? Religious strife was to have ended for all time, yet the battle has never been as fierce as at this moment. We were supposed to be united into a single nation, but we have never been more divided than today. Commerce and shipping were to reach record highs, but they have never languished as much as at this time. Morality and family life were to grow stronger, but the revenue from the tax on liquor has never been as high as in the past years. There was supposed to be universal contentment, especially among the lower classes; but never before did we see a greater social crisis on the horizon.

Even if one looks only at the quality of primary education and the flourishing of education in general, the disappointment of our Liberals is enough to stir one's pity. Even at the twenty-fifth anniversary of our Constitution [in 1873] they were drunk with joy; but now [in 1875], sobered up, they have grabbed the lyre and sing lamentations about the sad state of our teachers, about the miserable state of education, about the inferior quality and quantity of teachers and pupils. Their dirge is so touching, so lifelike, so heart-wrenching, that their cry for help sounds warranted: *our public school is in peril!*

In a situation like that, intelligent reflection would readily lead to self-examination and raise the question: "If the prediction of my opponents came true, could it be that I was a false prophet? Could it be that the fault lies with my starting principle, with the impossible principle of well-intentioned yet practically unattainable and thereby invalidated '*neutrality*'?"

Rather than even considering that possibility, Liberalism suppresses the question and tries to regain its lost self-confidence through political excitement by declaring: the problem is not the principle but the system. Our system, to save the appearance of freedom, was based on competition and left school attendance voluntary. That system must be abandoned,

17. That is, officially the state school was treated on a par with the private schools.

the sooner the better. There must be compulsory school attendance, and competition must ultimately become impossible. There is counsel to be had from Abednego,[18] provided that one first agrees on the matter of primary education.

Three systems stood alongside each other:

> *Old Liberals*: Competition. Therefore moderate costs for education. Voluntary school attendance.
>
> *New Liberals*: Competition effectively squashed by severely raising the cost of operating schools. Mandatory attendance.
>
> *Radicals*: All competition forbidden by law. State school for all, free of tuition. The free school closed.

Let the reader judge whether the term "about-face" is too strong for these reversals. In the past, stubborn resistance to any change in the school law; today, a demand to amend it immediately! In the past, opposition to compulsory education; today, universal promotion of it. In the past, a system on the basis of competition; today, competition declared untenable in the long run.

Christian Netherlands! Remember, you have been forewarned! You still imagine that the attack will come in the front? Take a look; you are already surrounded from the rear!

ENDS AND MEANS

Het Handelsblad, too, has joined the debate about the schools issue that we reopened. That makes us glad. At least in that paper one is safe from the vulgar, flippant attitude with which other publications so often spoil an exchange of thoughts concerning matters of national importance. Even more so than *Het Vaderland*, whose dignified language we have often appreciated, *Het Handelsblad* almost invariably maintains the proper tone and remains within the bounds of good manners. For this reason we wish to follow closely its latest three articles the moment the current discussion

18. Pseudonym of a self-styled radical liberal who had proposed a revision of the Constitution in order to make free schools impossible; see his pamphlet *Herziening der Grondwet. Het Programma der Radicalen* (Groningen: L. van Giffen, 1871).

gives us but leave.[19] But at this moment the debate does not concern that part of the old educational program of the liberals (which they still maintain), but solely that other part in which they now reject what they promoted in the past; or also, in which they now devote themselves to what they used to condemn and by which they dare to launch a second, even more vehement war on freedom of education in our country.

Above, we indicated the contrasts. They all focus on competition and compulsory school attendance, or more concisely, on the issue of money.

The future has disappointed our liberals. They seriously thought that with the Act of 1857 in place they had arrived. On the one hand, they relied too much on the soundness of their own agenda; on the other, they thought too little of private initiative.

Their fortified palace has already been compromised. They no longer feel safe within its walls, and this compels them to find a stronger position, one which they hope can withstand any siege.

It does not enter their minds to investigate whether their lack of educational success should be blamed on the system itself. Their faith in the soundness of their system remains unconditional. In their minds, the poor results are caused exclusively by excessive forbearance on their part. They did not demand enough for themselves. They still gave us too much latitude. Their reverence for "freedom" cost them too much. Hence they now want to go ahead with their *sharp resolution*;[20] and if that fails, they firmly intend to continue the sharpening of that resolution until opposition is no longer possible and the public school will with mathematical certainty have accomplished its goal—the liberalization of the national spirit.

We ourselves have acknowledged that an even sharper resolution is possible. Compared to Abednego, the Association of Public Education is as backward as it is ahead of the law of '57.

---

19. This promise was kept in another series of articles titled "Het Redmiddel"; these eight articles appeared in *De Standaard* between March 1 and 25, 1875.

20. *Sharp resolution*: a famous epithet in Dutch history that refers to the decision by the States of Holland in 1617 to arm its towns with mercenaries to preempt a possible coup by Prince Maurice, commander-in-chief of the armed forces of the United Provinces. The resolution was part of the policy of government leader Oldenbarneveldt to restrict the activities of the orthodox party in the Reformed Church and to resist the convening of a synod to settle the dispute over the doctrine of election. Kuyper uses the epithet to characterize the liberal plan, announced by its leader, Kappeyne van de Coppello, to amend the Education Act in favor of the public school, in disregard of any minorities.

Yet the designation "sharp resolution" is not too strong a description of the new educational program.

The teachers of the secondary school in Amersfoort wrote: "The state has still been too forbearing with the free schools."

Mr. De Veer cried out at the meeting in Amsterdam: "Stop negotiating with those fanatics and get down to business!"

Mr. Kappeyne van de Coppello declared in the Second Chamber: "Then let the minority be oppressed, for then they are the fly that spoils the ointment!"

Mr. Godefroi testified: "I wish to strengthen the state school, but admit your grievances? Never!"

These are ever so many signs of the times that warrant our conclusion that the new liberal program resembles Pharaoh's answer: "Let more work be laid on the men!" Or, if you will, Rehoboam's counsel: "Our fathers beat you with whips, but we will discipline you with scorpions!"

The means to accomplish this are remarkably simple and may be summarized in that monotonous request which they direct to the government: *Give us more money!*

All programs of the liberal politicians boil down to that one demand for more money from the public treasury.

More money to pay our teachers better.

More money to appoint more teachers.

More money to train more and better teachers.

More money to build even more and even bigger schools.

More money to provide even more generously for the needs of state education.

We say this not to blame them, but to prove how weak their position is whenever they try to cast doubt on the moral quality of our effort by pointing out that on our part the school issue can be reduced to a question of money.

In order to present their demand for an additional two million guilders from the treasury as imperative, they eagerly show us the deep wounds of the state school. They invite you to go with them into their schools, to persuade you that the number and quality of the teaching staff leave much to be desired, or that the products of the education are still very inadequate, or that such a state of emergency requires immediate provision.

Of course, no one disagrees. And the public school teachers utter not a peep in response to such an insult to their reputation, for that would ruin everything. And superintendents and inspectors, rather than defending their schools, are taking the lead in this campaign. And we least of all have reason to make an apology in defense of the excellence of the public school.

And thus, with remarkable unanimity, all agree that the state school urgently needs improvement; and according to the arguments of the trailblazers of Abednego, this is irrefutable proof that the state simply must give more money. Once lack of funding is no longer a hindrance, they are confident that (1) better educators will become available, (2) the training of those educators will improve, and (3) the education given in better schools by better and more educators will mean true progress for the nation. They do not deny that this will put the free school in a difficult position; but who will require them to be sorry about that? If you, supporter of Christian education, are to pay significantly more than currently for the state school, which is useless to you; if, to keep up with the competition, you nearly double the salaries of your own teachers; if even for that increased salary, despite your tripled advertising, you can no longer find more applicants; if in this unequal competition you see your school fall behind every semester and its deficit increase at an alarming rate; and when your attempts to raise funds fail because your Christian brothers can spend their contribution only once and now have to spend it on the state school; then, undoubtedly, the sharp resolution of the liberals will succeed in killing your Christian school—but can they help it? This was not their intention, even though it was the inevitable consequence.

This was not their intention. They are not just saying that; we believe they are sincere. At least, this is true of the vast majority of the voters who are being groomed for this sharp resolution. It is also true of the majority of the teachers and school boards, who are too busy with their own schools to give a thought to our schools. And this may also be the case for some members of the press.

But this does not mean that liberalism itself is innocent. In this system the clearing away of the free school is a very real goal. The leaders realize this perfectly well. Yet they persist in their agenda. At least Opzoomer[21] and De Veer make it unnecessary for us to prove this point. While outsiders are

---

21. Cornelis Willem Opzoomer (1821–92) studied philosophy, law, and theology, and was appointed professor of philosophy in the University of Utrecht. Christianity, according to him, was "a sublime and singular phenomenon." He wrote that Jesus is but one of many teachers of humankind, that miracles are absurd, and that prayer is meaningless. Nevertheless he was offended when people refused to call him a Christian.

made to believe in good faith that this proposal [increased funding of state schools] is the goal, in the counsel of war it is merely a means to an end.

THE PUBLIC SCHOOL: WHAT A DISAPPOINTMENT!

The supporters of the public school suffer from something that is often seen in sick people. For a while they do not feel well but keep up appearances, deflecting any comment about their pale face and dull eyes with the pumped-up response that they are doing just fine ... until they have to give in and, overwhelmed by sickness and feeling down, retire to bed; and now, going to the other extreme, they suggest that their sickness is much worse than it actually is.

The same happened with our public education. For a long time the physiognomists had been saying that something was wrong with the health of the public school, that its gait was slow and uncertain, that its face was telling. But don't think that this caused any concern among the foster parents of that school. On the contrary; they proudly maintained that this alleged sickness existed only in our imagination, in our jealous mind. Their foster child was the very picture of health, tingling with fresh and vigorous life, the envy not only of our private school but also of the entire educational system in Europe.

But suddenly all this has changed. Now you hear nothing but complaints; there are aches and pains everywhere; nothing functions as it should; the school lies prostrate on its sickbed and people speak sorrowfully of the possibility that the disease may take a turn for the worse.

Of course, neither the former show nor the latter display is true to actual fact. The public school was already sick when it boasted of its good health, and currently it has nothing serious to fear, despite its imagination that without heroic intervention it might be close to death. Neither its former boasting nor its sudden complaining is a psychological mystery. Even less so because one can observe the unmistakable signs that all is not well. Not just when you go by your own impression. Not just when you pay attention to the groans of the patient itself. But also when you take into consideration the scientific diagnosis presented in the *National Report on Education.*

We will not mention the evidence of "complications," as physicians call them. For us lay people it is enough to know the chief ailment. Especially because you would never have guessed what that ailment is.

Imagine, the public school suffers from—wait for it—atrophy of the brain! It is contributing to the intellectual deterioration of our nation!

Seriously, whatever one might have suspected, not this! We would have guessed that the religious and moral life within its walls was weak or sometimes lacking altogether. And rumor had it that the teaching of Dutch history was more about trivial knowledge of numbers, names, and commonplaces rather than about solid insights. But a regression in thought?

Thought: the free expression of informed judgment! But that was the very goal of our school system. That was really the heart of the school law. If it was not the end-all and be-all, at least it was the primary goal, and they had guaranteed that we would reach it.

After all, to form and shape autonomous, self-confident citizens, trained in critical thinking and able to form their own judgments and insights—that would be the salvation of our country, and this was precisely why political priority was given in our electoral law[22] to the "thinking sector of the nation" and why those who protested for conscience's sake were not even granted a hearing.

Who would not expect the public school, at least in this respect, to earn a top grade for its accomplishment? Who in the world could have imagined that the public school would not produce uniformly fine, outstanding graduates?

Now read these statements from the official *Report*:

> As to composition in the Dutch language, one may expect of young people who sit for the final exam that their compositions reflect independent thought. — Most of those examined failed to show this.

And this:

> The poor results in the history exam would seem to be attributable in particular to the lack of thoughtful reflection on the events of the past by those who were examined.[23]

---

22. Reference to *census suffrage*, that is, the right to vote based on the amount of annual taxes paid, often combined, as in this case, with the level of education one had completed.

23. These quotations from the *National Report* refer to final examination results in secondary education.

Or this:

> The majority of candidates lacked confidence in theoretical knowledge of the language and its grammar.

And add to that:

> Most candidates received a failing grade for knowledge of grammar ... and in some cases it was childishly inadequate. The organization of sentences, rules of spelling, gender of nouns were for nearly all those examined a veritable *terra incognita*. Only very few attained an appropriate level in the art of presenting their thoughts in an orderly, clear, concise, and fluent manner. The ignorance of some concerning the literature of their own country fell below all standards and was in fact most shameful.

One could not give a worse testimony concerning the formation of intelligent thought, also in one's native language, which is the first vehicle of thought.

Now you might think that this statement perhaps addresses the situation of "a bunch of farm boys," the next generation of "dumb" Veluwe folk. But no, this statement reflects the accomplishments of the select few. It refers to that exquisite section of our national youth that advanced from the first to the final grade, from elementary to secondary school, completed all grades, and then sat for the final examinations. One of these statements even relates to the very top students, who afterward would apply for a position as teacher in our secondary schools.

Perhaps you still cannot believe what you are hearing. You say, "Surely this statement is a lie published by those who slander public education!" But that is not the case. These statements carry the signatures of those who administer the exams: loyal supporters of the school law. "But then this report has been kept out of the public eye!" Excuse me, but it is printed in the *National Report* that is submitted annually to the States General by no one less than the king himself!

CONFESSIONS OF ONE WHO IS DELIRIOUS!

Yesterday we compared the state school to a sick person who, after a long period of denial, finally gave in, and is now depressed and fearing for his life. This alone is, in our opinion, the key to the puzzling psychological fact that the state school, which until recently boasted of its superiority, is now supposedly so sick and close to death that its end is near unless it receives a powerful stimulus.

It is worth considering the reasoning that brings the sick state school to this pessimistic conclusion. But this is well-nigh impossible, given that in its feverish moments, while delirious, it confesses things that one would have never guessed from its usual talk.

It cannot be denied that the state school always claimed that it held the heart of the nation; that the vast majority of the nation as one man would defend it; that *our* schools were forced on the nation; and that, if only we relented, virtually the entire nation would automatically bring its children to the door of the public school.

We have never made it a secret that we simply did not believe this. Rather, it seemed to us that the nation, if only it were again given freedom of choice, would hold on to positive Christianity and our national heritage, at least in the rearing of its children.

Naturally, the supporters of the school law resented our doubts concerning the popularity of their darling child. Our language was labeled "populist deception," and whatever arguments we presented for our position, they maintained their boastful attitude. The nation, they said, did not want to have anything to do with us: it had given its heart and soul to *the school without positive religion*. And so, for many years, our no stood over against their yes, and no progress was made.

But what is happening now?

We publicly expose their sharp resolution, their horrible decree, their intention to discipline us with scorpions instead of whips, their scheme to take our one little ewe lamb, their spiritual compulsory cultivation system—and as soon as we do so, they suddenly change their language and admit that they were wrong.

First they thought it best to apply the technique of divide and conquer; they eagerly publicized every dissenting voice that was heard among our ranks. When they noticed that this no longer worked and that we were united on nearly every point, they reached for the weapon of mockery and published in *Het Vaderland* that strange letter about "Bet" and "Gees."[24] But now that this strategy has also failed, the fever rose and the sufferer became delirious, confessing to us things we had never counted on.

---

24. This reference could not be traced.

"Restitution system! Restitution system!" cries the sufferer continually, "then my school is gone!"[25]

What do you mean, your school is gone if we implement a restitution system? Gone, if we introduce a restitution system that gives back to every father, partially and gradually over a period of several years, the free choice to have his God-given child educated in a school after his own heart. Will that finish off your public school? Your school, which you said was beloved by virtually the entire nation? And you suppose it would be abandoned as soon as the nation could follow the desires of its heart?

Poor school law supporters! How you reveal your deepest thoughts in that delirium! So now you admit that your public schools contain children of parents who would rather not send their children there. Not just one child now and then, but many, very many children. So many that if those who are currently with you against their will would walk out, your schools would empty out significantly.

We gratefully take note of this admission. Now you have admitted yourself that your school has been imposed on our nation, not through the free love of your people, not through the free choice of the parents, but through compulsion, through the removal of alternatives.

"If our opponents were to desert us, the mixed school would cease to exist!" This precious sentence is printed in a leading publication of the liberal party. You must admit that it is no hallmark of freedom to prevent your opponents from leaving. And now you have admitted that you wish to force opponents to stay with you.

How clumsy, such an admission! It reveals utter lack of care in prudent policy and choice of words. Apparently the school law party counted on our naïveté. It reckoned that, even after its sharp resolution, in spite of its horrible decree, and despite the about-face in its system, we would stubbornly stand guard by our spiked gun[26] like crude Russian soldiers. Then their

25. By the "restitution system" local governments would pay parents or private school boards the money they saved by not having to teach those children who attended a private school. It was for a time the system of choice defended by Kuyper and his friends.

26. The "gun" they voluntarily "spiked" for tactical reasons was the old proposal to remove the word "Christian" from the School Law; the new campaign would be to work for a general revision of the Constitution to cleanse it of everything "that tends to make the State carry on a religion of its own which in nature and essence can only be anti-Christian."

coup would have succeeded beautifully, and soon the death knell would have sounded over the Christian school.

But now that the keen eyes of Groen[27] delivered us once again from danger, their fury at such a bitter defeat knows no bounds. Let there be no gloating on our part, but let there be gratitude for what we owe, once again, to our *leader*.[28] Through the carelessness of their leader Moens, the liberal party has ruined much in its own game. Naturally we may take advantage of this. Liberals are proving to be opponents of liberty!

IS THIS RESPECT FOR THE PUBLIC SCHOOL?

The liberals fiercely attack our threefold demand. On the surface, this seems to be proof that we could have made a worse choice.

In particular the idea of restitution is a thorn in their side. There is no limit to their bashing of it, and they literally wear themselves out to prejudice our nation against this idea by presenting a caricature.

So be it. It is one's duty sharply to oppose that which one condemns or fears. As far as we are concerned, such opposition may be taken rather far. But we ask in all seriousness: May one go so far in the defense of one's educational system as to disrespect the school itself?

Yet the liberals do precisely that. And if nobody protests, it will soon become their daily bread. The daily *Nieuws van de Dag* started it; the very next day the *Nieuwe Rotterdamse Courant* followed suit, and *Het Vaderland* gave its approval.

To what, do you think, do our liberal newspapers compare the public school? No, you will not guess it.

They go so far as to compare it to a pump. Or a gravel road. And, by way of variation, to a crane, a lamppost, or a railroad sign. Because they think that a restitution system would be foolishness when applied to a city pump, a brick road, a stretch of pavement, and so on, they conclude that it is also useless for a school.

Imagine what would have happened if *we* had made such a crude comparison! How quickly would the word have been spread to present our low,

27. See G. Groen van Prinsterer, *Nederlandsche Gedachten*, vol. V (Amsterdam, 1874), 360. See also Harry Van Dyke, "Abraham Kuyper between Parsonage and Parliament," in *Calvinism and Democracy*, ed. John Bowlin, The Kuyper Center Review (Grand Rapids: Eerdmans, 2014), 4:184–85.

28. Kuyper uses the English word "leader" to refer to the unique role of Groen van Prinsterer in the antirevolutionary movement.

dishonoring view of the public school as proof of our animosity toward the education of our nation!

To compare the public school with a stretch of roadway! Not figuratively, not metaphorically, but to express the level of concern our state should have for it. Can one imagine a more disrespectful, crude, and materialistic view of the school? Does the state in its care for the school have no other motivation, no other considerations, no other duties than those that apply also to the construction of a lift-lock or a water pump? Would you actually paint the school, in which our future generation receives its education, with the same brush as those trivial material needs? Is a school essentially no different from a municipal slaughterhouse? Does the school have no more nobility, no finer organization, and is it subject to no higher (and therefore different) laws from a gas plant or a sewer system? Does that which applies to city property—water treatment, communication lines, garbage disposal—apply equally to the school? Obscurantists though we may be, in the face of such disrespect we will defend primary education, and even the public school!

Surely they will not be so blind that, if we did not protest, their partisanship would go so far as to try and encourage the people of the Netherlands to mention their schools in one breath with abattoir or streetlight. We should think that the more noble school-law supporters must feel irritated by this complete loss of regard for primary education. No doubt this despicable move could be effective in misleading the crowd of unthinking people, precisely because of its crudeness: "Do you get your money back if you are sick and therefore do not use the street?" But those among the liberals who appreciate tastefulness more than demagoguery will surely have grumbled inwardly at that crude article in the *Nieuws* and wondered how it could so forget itself and lose all sense of propriety? All the more so, since the effect of such trivializing is never lasting. Believe us, even the lower classes of our nation have too much taste and propriety to fall for such vulgarity. At first, perhaps, they might not know how to protest. But beyond what people know what to say, their instinct still functions. And that is all we need. The nation's instinct knows full well that a school and a city pump are not to be treated as equals. Yes, those simple folk may laugh occasionally about some tasteless silliness. But if you think that such laughter means that you have won, then you are mistaken. In our nation the sense of respect is still alive. It demands respect for its king, for its government, for its history, and also respect for its school. Even now it realizes that the liberal press has wronged that respect in its crude, materialistic comparison with pumps and cranes.

And the national conscience will agree with us, not with them, that in honor of our primary schools and in the name of national respect we had to raise a protest against such banality.

HOW THEY BETRAY THEMSELVES!

The liberals are wailing and raging, because—yes why, do you suppose? Because they fear that justice will be done.

Justice! Namely, that no village populations will any longer be compelled to waste thousands of guilders on a state school which, due to the absence of children, is empty and an object of mockery.[29]

Justice! Namely, that a quietly tolerated violation of law will no longer serve as a safety valve to make an impossible law appear practical.[30]

Justice! Namely, that opponents of all positive religion will no longer have a monopoly on the state's treasury to serve only their own interest.

And the odds (if there be any) that this justice may soon be served sows panic in their ranks; the entire camp of our liberals is afraid, and their hearts are filled with dread.

What does this tell us about their conscience? Do they actually fear that, if justice is restored, their school without positive religion will bleed to death? Are they keenly aware that, if justice is served, they will be gone? Having been compelled to self-examination, do they now realize that for years they have, in violation of justice, oppressed the nation and subjected it to the tyranny of an un-Dutch, antinational system that eradicates Christianity?

We still cannot believe it. We cannot believe it because our regard for our opponents' character is still too high—too high to believe that a political party would engage in such oppression, intentionally opposing justice.

But then there is no escaping the conclusion that their concern is pretense, their fear a show, their cry for help artificial. Then their alarm is merely a meaningless tactic, a ploy to shift the focus away from their lethal

---

29. Local authorities would sometimes continue a tuition-free public school even when few or no children attended it, as was done, for instance, in the Frisian villages of Wons, Schraard, and Gaast.
30. That is, to allow a school to have a modicum of religious instruction, even Bible readings, in harmony with the local preference, to discourage any efforts at starting a separate Christian school.

plans against the Christian school. Then it is a trap to catch you in their nets if you were to respond to their cry for help.

This is how it will be, from now on until the elections in June. If we allow ourselves to be baited, if we fall asleep, if the watchman is not alert, they will jump you before you see them; you will be overwhelmed, and in shameful defeat you will lament your unforgiveable carelessness.

As often as we suspect danger we will sound a warning, as we do now. Let everyone spread that warning within his own circles. But our warning might come too late. And therefore: follow your general! Groen has never made a wrong choice. See for yourself how his proven tactics have once again upset their calculations.

Indeed, had they not been our fellow citizens and countrymen, your indignation against such an unpatriotic, partisan strategy would be pushed to the limit. One can hardly imagine it. The position of the Christian school has become practically untenable due to the miserable system of the school law; and at that very moment the liberals present their proposal, not to meet your grievances but to kill you financially, as they compel you, on pain of incarceration, to entrust your children to a school that you disapprove of. And if you resist this clenched fist and struggle against it with every power of conviction and indignation, and dare to strike back and by your cries awaken the national conscience from its slumber, then they resort to terms of abuse in order to chastise you for being such a spoilsport and ruining the game, just because you were not stupid or cowardly.

For a child on Java they have compassion: it should not be compelled against its will to pick coffee beans. Toward the East Indian who is far away there is a sense of justice. But when in our own country a poor Christian father from the lower classes of society asks that his child should not be compelled to go to a school without Christ, then this sense of justice is suddenly blunted; then the intention is to expand rather than shrink an even more unbearable cultivation system, and whenever the oppressed tries to escape a worse fate it is condemned as national treason.

Had we demanded anything that would grant us even a semblance of advantage over our opponents, we would be able to understand this uncompassionate attitude. But what more did we ask than to be treated as equal with the others? Are we not also children of our country, Dutch citizens, as much as the liberals and the radicals? Does not the state belong to us as little or as much as to them? Who gives them the right to speak as if they were the real citizens but we mere sojourners, a bunch of helots who do not count?

And yet, in actuality we asked for even less than equality. We still left them many advantages. Far from it that we should desire a privilege at the expense of our fellow citizens! Or is it a privilege if we demand that no more tax money be used to build schools that will remain empty; schools that serve nothing but the spiders who hang in their webs and the cleaners who earn a day's wage for removing those webs? Is it a privilege if we demand that Article 23 of the school law no longer be violated, with the connivance of the government, in vast regions of the country? Given that the liberals and radicals have spent a great deal of money from the treasury on their schools, is it a privilege if we ask for our modest share because after all we too are Dutch citizens?

That, and nothing more, is the demand of justice, against which the wrath and fury of part of the liberal press is currently burning. It is fortunate for our country that numerous liberals, and among them not the least noble, themselves disapprove of this uncompassionate attitude.

Don't forget, the liberal press and the better liberals are two different groups. Will they finally change the direction in which they are headed, for the sake of the fatherland, for the sake of justice, and (allow us to add) for the sake of rescuing their own strongly fragmented party? We do not know. June is approaching. Disappointment has brought despondency. Most likely, the press will continue to be the only speaker. The liberal party is uneasy; it hangs together like a rope of sand; it is paying too severely for its former failures. In this state of affairs, the issue of education offers a welcome expedient to bring the party together. They are beating the big drum!

IS THERE AN ULTERIOR AGENDA?

The school should belong, not to the church, not to the state, but to the parents! What objection can be brought against this demand? "Simply this," came the reply. "Parents lack the necessary motivation, the necessary concern for education." In our experience, these words are too strong. Yet we readily admit that a public school supported solely by the involvement of parents risks failure.

But how would this be an argument against our system? Would you continue rocking your child, keeping him on your lap and carrying him down the stairs, because he falls over when you first start teaching him how to walk? Moreover—and this definitely defeats the objection—did we ourselves not emphasize that the state must remain active *as long as* and *insofar as* parental initiative is in any way wanting? No, there was no reason to fear for the quality of education.

Yet this did not satisfy them. Did that not show that the quality of education was not the only intention behind their state school, but something which the school law supporters neither dared nor wanted to say and which they would not get if the parents had a say? That there was something of this nature was easy to guess; but it was not so apparent that it could be officially established. It was therefore impossible to discuss it in any concrete detail.

No longer today. What has changed? Now that debates are being held about amending the school law without changing the system, the same pattern emerges. Once again the supporters of the school law say: "Just guarantee quality education!"—but when you have done so they are still not satisfied and fight back with increased passion.

They cannot deny that this is happening again. They have publicly said, in so many words, that their only concern is the quality of public education, without serving any other interest of their own.

You ask whether we, on our part, have provided assurance of quality of public education. Judge for yourself. We have declared our willingness to collaborate in (1) improving teachers' jobs, (2) increasing the staffing of schools, (3) reforming the training of teachers, (4) raising the quality of instruction. We have stated our belief that the state must see to it that there is always ample opportunity to receive public education, everywhere and always, for the children whose parents or guardians desire so. We have declared that all parents or guardians who desire a different education for their children should be able to obtain this in such a way that the excellence of education would not suffer. Finally, we have expressed our view that the state ought to exercise the strictest quality control over all schools, public and private, and that every school that failed to meet quality standards must be closed.

Now may we ask our opponents: What is lacking in this approach for the quality of education? Would education not gain in quality at every point? Where would there still be a gap in ensuring excellence in education?

We ask this with some urgency, and we fully expect that at least one of the many periodicals available to the supporters of the school law will clear up this matter for our nation.

It is their duty. After all, they say that this is the reason why they purported to oppose us. This is their concern when they call the entire country to arms. *The quality of education is threatened.*

However, unless we are completely deceived, an honest opponent will find it impossible to prove this. We have made their quality standards our own, and added a guarantee for private education which they could not give. Therefore, if he proves that our standards fall short, then in doing so he condemns a fortiori his own program as well.

Just like last year, when we defended the model based on the principle that "the school belongs to the parents," we discover once again, oddly enough, that the supporters of the school law, even with the most solid assurance of quality education, remain discontent, and become even more passionate in their rejection of our model.

What motivates this? Obviously, the only reason can be that there is something else, something they are not mentioning, for which they have even more zeal, at least comparatively speaking, than for the quality of the education. They must have an ulterior motive.

What that motive is can be established with reasonable certainty. It is not the desire to foster tolerance. If that were an accomplishment of the public school, it would be appropriate to sentence the entire crowd of school-law supporters, including their press, to a three-year program in such a school. Its tolerance at least is aptly characterized as the "cat's paw." You remember what De Genestet said about that![31] Even Thorbecke admitted the uselessness of the mixed school for fostering tolerance.

There is something else behind this, and *Nieuws van de Dag* has given us a helpful hint to find out what that something is. This most useful of liberal papers writes: "The school must also serve to oppose dogmas and prejudice."

Ah, there! Now we understand more. Of course, then you cannot use the private school. On the contrary: then you have to crush it. After all, private schools often teach as life's wisdom what you dare call "prejudice."

Still, this is not quite it. It helps, but the real motive lies deeper. That did not become clear until *Het Vaderland* carelessly published a remarkably early editorial, far in advance of the elections, giving us some insight into the meaning of the mission trips undertaken in our country by circuit

31. P. A. de Genestet (1829–61) was a pastor who published much poetry. The reference here is not entirely clear but may perhaps be his poem "De Handdruk," which includes the line: "The hand may shrivel that caresses so false / I'd rather feel teeth or a claw."

riders Messrs. Kerdijk and Moens. At that moment, the motivation became clearer. It was announced openly that the education issue would be the key issue in June.

The consortium of political groupings called "Liberal party" has fallen apart. Nonetheless, Kappeyne and Levy must be able to go to the voting booth together in June.[32] Voters must not be able to notice any internal dissension such as exists between the followers of Thorbecke and Van de Putte, between Vissering and Van Houten, between *Het Vaderland* and the *Nieuwe Rotterdamse Courant*. The more so because "the party" is still suffering from its more recent ministries,[33] which removes all possibility of its exercising any moral influence.

That is why the issue of education is being pushed to the foreground—that is to say, in the version of Moens and Kerdijk, thus in the way the radicals like it. Old liberals had to come along, willy-nilly, and even Godefroi[34] was quick to show his docility. They also emphasize this issue because it naturally turns the public schoolteacher of every town and village into a political agent, and because it may help to gain support from the left wing of the Conservatives.

From this we conclude that there must be a connection between the struggle for the public school and the well-being of the liberal party in the month of June. It has nothing at all to do with the quality of education, but is of decisive importance for the supporters of the school law.

So be it. They have a right to choose their own position. We demand but one thing: do not allow the Pharisee to speak! That ongoing pious talk about "the quality of education" is becoming too hypocritical! Be a man, and call things by their name!

---

32. Jan Kappeyne van de Coppello (1822–95) was a progressive liberal politician who stood poised at this time to become the next party leader and prime minister; he was a fierce opponent of orthodox Christianity. Isaac Abraham Levy (1836–1920) was a political commentator and a social liberal. His sympathies were not with Kappeyne.
33. The liberals had headed short-lived governments in 1870–71, in 1871–72, and in 1872–74, none of which had been particularly successful owing to lack of internal unity.
34. Michel Henry Godefroi (1813–82) was a more conservative liberal member of Parliament.

IS THE RESTITUTION MODEL IMPRACTICABLE?

TEXT INTRODUCTION

This series of eleven leading articles in *The Standard* is a continuation of Kuyper's preelection press campaign on behalf of the schools issue.

Thanks to Kuyper's oft-exhibited delight in working with numbers and statistics, his articles give us a glimpse into conditions of primary education in the Netherlands by 1875: the state of school staffing, categories of teachers, average number of pupils per school, class size, and so on.

Relying on his detailed study of operating a school and of educational systems in other developed countries, Kuyper compares the Dutch situation to what obtained elsewhere. At the same time he tries his hand at sketching specific legislation to demonstrate concretely how a restitution system could be workable.

His defense of some form of restitution to private schools is marked by a plea for fairness and the conviction that the nation would be spared growing resentment among its citizens.

Source: Kuyper, Abraham. *Is het restitutiestelsel onuitvoerbaar?* Amsterdam: J. H. Kruyt, 1875, pp. 3–31. Reprinted from *De Standaard*, April 19–28, May 27–31, 1875. Translated by Arjen Vreugdenhil and Nelson D. Kloosterman. Edited by Harry Van Dyke.

IS THE RESTITUTION MODEL IMPRACTICABLE?

I

Over against the *sharp resolution*[1] we placed the demand of *fair restitution*.

It was an attractive concept! It had been expressed earlier, in general terms, by Mr. Gratama, professor in Groningen; by Mr. Mol Moncourt, city council member in Groningen; and later by Messrs. Van Vollenhoven, Van Gestel, and Kuyper. But thus far it received little attention. So little in fact, that Mr. Messchert van Vollenhoven at a meeting in Amsterdam, with birth certificate in hand, maintained his paternity of this child, apparently unaware of what others had already written along the same lines before he did.

Today you hear more about it. We will not discuss who is responsible for that increased interest. No one will contradict the fact that this idea, which in the past was only briefly mentioned and quickly forgotten, is now alive in the hearts of thousands and on the tongues of all. It has set many pens in

1. See above, p. 186.

motion, provided material for newspapers, and is on the way to becoming the shibboleth at the voting booths in June.

For the advocates of the idea, including us, this creates a duty to recommend it, to bring it among the people, to show its excellence, and to refute as much as possible the objections that may arise against it.

The latter has been easy. Not a single serious, adequate, meaningful objection has been brought against it. We need not refute what refutes itself. Also, anything concerning the school issue in general that does not specifically touch on the restitution system may be excluded from the discussion. Likewise, no sane person will require that we treat the expressions of faulty logic or the utterances of an angry spirit as if they were arguments.

Out of weakness, opponents have turned to *practical objections*. Very well, we shall face these and investigate whether the implementation is in fact so difficult.

One should not be surprised about this weakness of the opposition. A system that so thoroughly commends itself to common sense and to conscience because of its fairness, justice, and modesty is too strong. It does not pretend to be a definitive solution of the controversy, and only partially separates the political issue from the pedagogical issue. It does not violate the Constitution, but merely provides a temporary compromise of opposing interests, as we await the political debate about the foundations of our state, allowing all parties to engage without bitterness.

It also leaves untouched the principles of the School Law of 1857. The government will provide public primary education everywhere, to the extent required to meet existing needs. The public school will remain a school accessible to children of all backgrounds. The French system—a school established and maintained by the government without involvement of the citizens—will be continued for the time being. Supervision and inspection remain as centralized and bureaucratic as they have been until now.

In other words, the restitution system has nothing to do with our principal opposition to the dominant educational system. The service it must provide for us is only this, that it prevents an unbearable law from becoming even more unbearable.

If our school law could remain as it is, we might have been able, despite our unequal chances and with the greatest efforts, to continue our principled opposition. But that is now impossible. Now all parties agree that our public school in a general sense needs urgent improvement. Our opponents themselves are the first to acknowledge the inadequacy of the existing law.

As a result, the liberals have proposed amending the school law, which will come down to increasing the financial burden by several millions. In light of this, if at this moment we would stubbornly continue with our principled opposition, it would be reckless foolhardiness, thoughtless overconfidence, and premeditated suicide.

The more so because the liberals, apparently counting on such naïve foolishness on our part, are trying to push their demand for school improvement with almost wanton levity, by means of the unbelievable brashness of the sharp resolution and the *horrible decree*.[2]

In these circumstances there was only one thing that we could do as proof of prudent leadership. Before anything else we had to defend ourselves against this boundlessly tyrannical assault, to protect ourselves from being overrun. We had to save the life of the free school and then look for ways to resume our political opposition with hope of success.

Nonetheless, there are some enthusiasts among us who would rather smash their head through a wall, and afterward sing their lamentations on the ruins of our Christian schools with the refrain of Article 194. This phenomenon is seen in any popular movement, and no one who knows history should be surprised.

Let us be content that the vast majority of our sympathizers were willing to listen to caution, and did not wish to continue traveling the route to a harbor that was no longer accessible. Recognizing that a mine had been dug against us, they diligently joined us in digging a mine in response.

II

Before we discuss the implementation of the restitution system, first a word about the proposal in general.

We were not at all surprised that our restitution proposal found support also outside the circle of our sympathizers. If anything surprised us, it was rather the fierce opposition from the liberal side.

The liberals—why deny it?—especially through their concern for the people of our East Indies, had accustomed us to the impression that they were actually concerned for justice. Now that it appears that this impression was mistaken, is it to be taken ill of us for having had too high rather than too low an opinion of these our fellow citizens? Are we to be reproached for ascribing to the majority of our liberals such a strong sense

2. See above, p. 186n20, concerning the "sharp resolution" of the liberal party.

of fairness and justice that we thought it a real possibility that they would unquestioningly accept a fair proposal such as the restitution system? That this was not the case pained us for the sake of the good name of the liberal party. Its harsh and unreasonable opposition to our proposal leaves a rather poor impression of its moral attitude. It has now become quite clear, at the cost of its honor, that this party, too, has adopted the slogan "might makes right."

The attitudes of the conservatives, conservative-liberals, and Roman Catholics were very different. The conservative-liberals, whose most telling publication is the *Amsterdamsche Courant*, at least admitted this much: that the implementation of the sharp resolution without finding relief for the free school would be unfair and therefore undesirable. The conservatives, realizing that the restitution proposal violated neither Article 194 nor the principle of the School Law, declared their willingness to grant us this measure of justice. And the Roman Catholics, aware that Damocles's sword hung above their free schools as well as ours, did not hide their view that some provision had to be made in this untenable situation.

Add to this the rather large group of private educators, and headmasters of nonconfessional schools—and without fear of exaggeration we may conclude that there is still hope that the free school may escape the lethal blow administered by the faction of Moens and Kerdijk. All the more shall we foster that hope if, from now until June, our sympathizers will persevere in their attempt to promote unity among our sympathizers, to organize the forces available to us, to make the lukewarm hot and the slow quick, and to impress on all the grave peril in which we find ourselves.

Especially the modesty of our demand should help boost our moral strength. Our demand intends to enable the improvement of the primary school. We follow as closely as possible the program of the pedagogues. To the public school we leave in every respect the advantage it has over the free school.

We can do this and dare do this because, unless our life is cut off, the principle on which we rest gives more than sufficient strength to sustain, within certain limits, even an unequal fight. With one battalion against a half-brigade one can at least remain standing. Over against an entire division or an entire army this would be impossible.

Only in one instance, we readily admit, might the restitution system do damage to the public school: if it turns out that the vast majority of the nation does not care for the public school. But if that were the case, would it not serve as a commendation of our system if this were settled for once and demonstrated in numbers and expressed in terms of financial sacrifice?

Does the state exist for the sake of the nation, or the nation for the sake of the state? Throughout the centuries, the Pharisees hold that man exists for the sake of the Sabbath—that is, the institutions of society must not serve man but oppress him. Translated into politics, this false principle results in this rule of political Pharisaism: that man exists for the sake of the state, the nation for the sake of the state, and society for the sake of the government. This rule is the source of all despotism and tyranny, of government meddling, caesarism, in short, of every attempt first to trim down the liberty of citizens, then to cut it off.

Therefore, if it were shown in fact that the vast majority of the nation does not give the public school the enthusiastic support needed to assure its increasing success, even under extremely advantageous circumstances, then we doubt seriously whether this should be a reason for us to regret our restitution proposal.

What advantages will be left to the public school?

1. Anyone who desires public education for his children needs only to say the word in order to get it; while the father who desires free education has to organize everything, must try to manage it somehow, and if there are not many in his town who share his view is forced to give up all hope of getting for his child what he desires.

2. Teaching personnel in the public schools have job security and many career opportunities, which will cause it always to have the best teachers.

3. School inspection in principle favors the public school.

4. Public education, thanks to all the years since 1857, has at its disposal an endless collection of beautiful school buildings that will serve it for many more years.

5. The public school, even when the restitution system is adopted, will continue to receive full financial support, while restitution will profit the free school only partially.

6. Public education is unified, while the free school is split up, so that public education still receives more money for its schools than what the free schools must share among themselves.

How weak the position of a liberal party must be if with such an incredible advantage on its side it still cries wolf, as if its school were all but lost? Until now it fought us with a saber and gave us nothing but a reed as our weapon. Well, that was still bearable. But now it wants to assault us with a halberd, and would prefer that we wield only our walking cane. Now that it discovers that we wish to exchange the reed for a baton, these brave knights tremble with fear. Engaging with a halberd against a baton—no, that is asking for too much courage.

III

When we introduced the idea of restitution[3] we described it as follows:

> When we speak of restitution we exclusively mean: a refund to the free schools of the expenses they save the state.
>
> As long as Article 194 of the Constitution remains in effect, the state has the obligation to maintain in all municipalities a sufficient educational system for the needs of the population.
>
> Now suppose that your municipality has 5,000 children of school age; then your local government should open ten schools, each of them serving 500 children. The construction of these schools would amount to 500,000 guilders, and their maintenance would require 70,000 guilders annually. Thus your local government would have to budget about 100,000 guilders annually for primary education. That expenditure would not depend on the whim of your local government, but be prescribed by law.
>
> Suppose, however, that in your municipality the free school becomes popular, and grows so much that ultimately half of the children receive sufficient and excellent education, as required by the law, in the classrooms of the free schools. Instead of ten schools for 5,000 children the local government needs to maintain only five schools for 2,500 children; for primary education it has to spend only 50,000 guilders instead of 100,000 guilders annually. The government is spared these expenses by the parents who established free schools.
>
> It is natural that these free schools cost more. Instead of five schools with 500 children each, they have twenty schools,

3. Here Kuyper quotes from his editorial in *De Standaard* of March 3, 1875.

> designed for 50, 75, 100, or 150 students each. They require relatively more personnel. The school provides more opportunity for personal involvement with the students. The pedagogical quality will be noticeably higher. The harmony between the upbringing at home and in the schools will be much stronger than was ever possible in a state school.
>
> Yet in the nature of the case the municipal council need not take any of this into account. It has no obligation toward these extra expenses. Those extra costs belong exclusively to the parents who decided on such more expensive schooling. Perhaps they pay 90,000 guilders, while the government would have refunded only 50,000 guilders; then the difference of 40,000 guilders is a relative luxury, to be paid by those who enjoy it.
>
> But it is different with those 50,000 guilders which the local government would have to spend by law but which it now saves. Justice and fairness require that this should be viewed as an expense to which the government is obligated and from which it is exempt merely through a fortuitous circumstance. It would be highly unreasonable to spend this money on other causes; after all, it would be taking advantage of parents who put up with spending almost twice as much on their children.
>
> If the legislator were to repeal freedom of education, nothing could be done. But now that the legislator acknowledges the existence of the free schools, and regards it as a pedagogical force of national development, it would be unfair and irresponsible to reduce the budgeted costs for education at the expense of the parents.

We did not pretend that this indicated sufficiently how to implement the system, knowing full well that the execution of such an idea must change steadily depending on the different circumstances of life, and that therefore this idea for its practical implementation should be supplemented with legislation that regulates how to deal with those different situations. Therefore we added:

> Without entering into a debate about the implementation, which would result in more than one stipulation, we therefore wish for now to focus on the core principle: let every

> municipality pay back to the collective free schools within their boundaries the monies they save the government.
>
> Subsidy is an alm; restitution is a reimbursement of expenses made for someone else. No interference in others' households is allowed, nor any arbitrariness. This principle of restitution intends only to solve the problem of enhancing the quality of our national education without condemning the free schools to commit suicide.

We continue to stand by this. The ballot box does not decide on the details of legislation, but on a general idea. The forum of our voters should not be confronted with anything that lies outside their reach. Our voters have no degree in constitutional law, and certainly are not called to dictate the articles of legislation. As soon as you turn a national issue into a political issue it eludes people's comprehension.

By doing that in an evil hour the liberals broke the force of Groen's cry of conscience concerning Article 194. The entire nation, even the humblest citizens, had to know whether in the name of our past and our future they wished to stand up for the rights of religion and our national heritage in the primary school. When the liberals declared that a serious discussion of Article 194 of the Constitution was out of order, Groen rightfully put the cry on the lips of our nation: "In that case, this wretched article must first be revised!" But instead of halting at this key principle, it was decided at the critical moment that the question of revising the Constitution should likewise be laid before the court of the citizenry. This smothered that cry of conscience.

This compels us to be doubly cautious not to fall again into the same error of forfeiting a constitutional issue that we were initially winning as a result of confusion about a cry of conscience.

Make clear that it is outrageously unfair to make the chances of the free school even worse than they already are. State that if there were no free school the municipalities would have to spend a good deal more money on public education. Ask whether it is not fair, or morally required, to refund at least this saved money to the free school. Raise the issue whether citizens of our country who desire a religious education for their children have a lesser right to state protection than other citizens who do not want to hear about religion in the school. Limit yourself to clear points, which are within the reach of every voter—and you will be invincibly strong because you will be presenting them with a question they can answer.

On the other hand, if you allow yourself to be sidetracked from that standpoint, if you lose yourself in legislative details, if you descend onto the winding trails of constitutional law—the nation will no longer understand you. It will leave you to your arguing and bickering. It is willing to believe that the issue is addressed, but the nation's conscience will no longer resonate with you. Stay with the principle, and you have the nation as your audience; debate details of legislation, and your audience shrinks to a handful of journalists and a club of politicians.

Understand well, therefore, that in no way do we intend to bring a detailed legislative proposal to the voting booth in June. Let the nation herself be the judge between justice and injustice, between freedom and tyranny. Let her choose between a boring list of dates or a vibrant national history. Let her speak up about compelling people to attend a school without religion who don't want to be there. Let them make a Solomonic judgment about the child, judging between the state and the parents!

That is her bailiwick. That keeps her within her limits. For decisions on matters of implementation we have a legislative body.

We want to watch out for only one danger. Our nation is also practical. And if the word were to spread that the restitution proposal is impracticable and that no legislation can be found or designed for it; in short, that it is an impossible proposal—then that might indeed turn many voters away.

That these big words, impracticable and impossible, are but a scarecrow to keep the birds away from the grain, is obvious. It would take any expert, say Messrs. Kerkdijk or Moens, less than a day to sketch out a complete, well-organized implementation.

"Impracticable," they say. Our response is that one could easily design ten different implementations. We have no desire to showcase our skill in finding such an implementation, and we certainly have no intention to bind the nation, the legislators, or ourselves and our sympathizers to it, but we shall now proceed to sketch one such possible implementation. We do solely in order to convict our opponents publicly of their error.

IV

As long as the wretched clause remains in Article 194 of our Constitution, the government must provide adequate public primary education everywhere in the country.

According to the debate, written and oral, about this article of the Constitution and about Article 16 of the School Law, this does not mean that the public school should have room for all children of school age. It was known and acknowledged that some children would never attend the public school. This concerns children who are chronically ill, children who are homeschooled, children who are sent to boarding school outside their town of residence, and finally children who go to a free school. To build a school for all those children, as Messrs. Moens and Kerdijk and their followers demand, would be absurd, a waste of money, and playing with the country's treasury.

Thus far, government, Parliament, and press have realized this. Nobody made such a senseless demand. Even Blaupot ten Cate[4] and others who debated the school law have readily admitted that the law is satisfied as long as lack of room in the school is never the reason why a child should not receive a decent education.

Therefore, in order to determine the number of public schools, the local government consults the existing free schools. At least, that is how it was formulated in the past:

> The schools of the Society for the Common Good,[5] of diaconates, almshouses, charitable organizations, and the like, the flourishing institutions and quality free schools as they exist in large numbers in this country, which are not inferior to the public schools but surpass them in more than one respect, ought to be regarded by the local government as adequately supplying part of the need.

Thus the local government is already required to determine of each free school whether it counts or not; to assess whether it is good or inadequate; to discern which schools, in the words of the then government, "are established on sound foundations and are in a flourishing state." And while the local governments are duty-bound to answer this question before they can make a plan for public education, our sloppy school law withholds from these governments any means to arrive at a fair, balanced, mature judgment in this matter.

---

4. Steven Blaupot ten Cate (1807–84) was a Mennonite preacher and liberal politician.
5. See "The Society 'for the Common Good,'" in this volume, pp. 3–14.

For this we must make a provision. Not only for the sake of the restitution system, but also apart from it.

Had not our school law been so inadequate and incomplete compared to those of other countries, both as the product of legislation and in its administrative and pedagogical aspects, this provision would have been made already in 1857. An expression such as that found in Article 16, "in a number of schools that is sufficient for the population and the need," may pass muster in a schoolchild's essay, but it disfigures any school regulation and does not belong in a law. It is a vague generality, which in its current form cannot be implemented and opens the door to arbitrariness, shirking of duty, and bullying.

Therefore our school law needs to include regulations that remove any uncertainty for the local governments, and allows them to decide according to a fixed rule how much school space they must provide.

This requires regulation of the following: (1) how many cubic meters of space every child should have, (2) how many children will be enrolled annually in the public school, (3) the maximum number of children in a single school, (4) the minimum number of children living at more than forty-five minutes away from an existing school who are required for the opening of a satellite school in their own neighborhood, and (5) the minimum number of children for which education can be given in an auxiliary classroom. If the law provides firm guidelines, then it is clear what should be done; the administrative inspection is easy; and in this respect we will move from the realm of arbitrariness to the state of justice.

For example, if it were stipulated that (1) in a normal primary school the space available to each child is three cubic meters;[6] (2) that the academic year runs from October 1 to September 30; (3) that in January a list will be made of children who will be enrolled in the public school in the next school year; (4) that the local government will ensure that by November 1 the required space for this number of students, increased by 5 to 15 percent, is available; (5) that a school may not have more than four hundred students; (6) that as soon as there are more than twelve students a school building must be erected, and as long as it remains below twelve an existing building should be rented and used as a school, subject to requirement (1) above; and (7) whenever in a hamlet, at a walking distance of forty-five minutes or more from the center of town, there are for three successive years at least

6. Kuyper uses the old unit of length of an "ell" (roughly one yard).

thirty children who desire public education, a school must be built in that hamlet—if stipulations like these were included in our law, then we would seriously ask both friend and foe whether our so-called school law would not look more like a proper law than in its current form.

School laws in other countries have long taken this road. For instance, the law in Wurtemberg contains more than thirty articles about the construction and furnishing of the public school, and some of these articles are an entire page in length.

It does not matter whether the numbers we mentioned are increased or decreased. If you think that a child younger than fourteen years needs five cubic meters of air rather than three, that's fine by us. If you want to limit the size of a school not to 400 but to 300 or 450 students, we do not mind. If you want to erect a school for ten children instead of twelve, or a satellite school for twenty-five instead of thirty, it does not detract from our main point. We are not quibbling about numbers, but simply demand that the law provide a clear norm for all questions that are raised. Provide a rule rather than arbitrariness.

V

As with the location of the school, the local governments must also decide about the teaching staff according to a fixed rule. We already have such a rule. Article 18 of our School Law stipulates that in every school there ought to be

> for 1–70 students: one principal [or headmaster = the more historical term]
> for 70–100 students: one principal and one intern
> for 100–150 students: one principal and one assistant teacher
> for 150–200 students: one principal, one assistant teacher, and one intern
> for 250–300 students: one principal, two assistant teachers, and two interns, and so on.

Article 20 allows that in a village school of fewer than seventy students, the principal may be replaced by an assistant teacher.

This law may be considered sufficient insofar as it removes any uncertainty, and for every situation directs what the local government is to do.

It is clear from the law what decisions must be made concerning the teaching staff. In contrast to Article 16, Article 18 is not a clause that allows for arbitrary interpretation but provides a fixed norm. Still, we believe that this rule too should be amended. Although there is a rule, it is pedagogically untenable. As soon as the number of children assigned to one teacher exceeds a certain limit, it is harmful for instruction, discipline, and supervision.

Moreover, a small school with just a few pupils of different ages will be divided into different grades, each of which will be working simultaneously on different subjects. If a single teacher must instruct them all by himself, the pupils will spend only part of the day in live interaction with the teacher. Experts all concur about this disadvantage. There is no doubt that the law is deficient in this respect. Teachers say: "The law must be changed!" The apostles of the sharp resolution intone: "Things cannot stay this way!"

We too have pushed for change: a change in the direction of an increase in teaching staff, and more consideration for the different cases that may occur. The details of this change do not matter to us, provided it goes in the right direction. So keep in mind that when we mention numbers they are given only by way of illustration. With this explicit provision, we could be satisfied with a rule along these lines:

> for 1–12 students: one assistant teacher
> for 12–50 students: one principal/headmaster
> for 50–70 students: one principal and one intern
> for 70–100 students: one principal, one assistant teacher, and one intern

and furthermore one intern for every thirty students, and one assistant teacher for every fifty students. For every school of over two hundred students, one assistant teacher with a principal's/headmaster's diploma. For a school of 350–400 students, a teacher with an even higher diploma than today's principals hold.

By way of explanation: If a village has no more than twelve children for whom public education is desired, no school can be provided. Suppose that typically of these twelve children, two of them, owing to distance or bad weather or illness, do not make it to school, then there are ten students left. These ten are divided into two children of the age of six, two of seven, two of eight, two of nine, one of ten, two of eleven, and one of the age of twelve. Now try dividing this into grades. The result is no different than a kind of homeschooling, when a father has his large family taught by a governess in a learning room. If you want to build a school for this and rent a house for the teacher and appoint a principal, then you would have to pay:

interest on building capital	*f* 400
rent of teacher's dwelling	*f* 250
school supplies	*f* 100
salary	*f* 1,000
	f 1,750

It would be absurd to set these requirements even if there were only three or four, maybe six or seven children: you would pay per child for primary education as much as 400 or 500 guilders. To avoid such absurdities, a line must be drawn. If we draw the line in such a way that no more than 100 guilders should ever be spent per child, then nobody can accuse us of being unwilling to spend money on education. The amount our best families in the country consider adequate for their children should also be adequate for the average citizen. If you reckon 150 guilders for the rent of a classroom, 50 guilders for school supplies, and for the assistant teacher 700 guilders' salary, then you still get a total expense of 900 guilders for nine to twelve children.

Large schools with 350 to 400 pupils are almost exclusively found in our cities, or in towns that are on a par with our cities. For such schools it might perhaps be good to have a teacher with more education than is currently required for the diploma of a principal.

Our opponents have tried to exploit this idea subversively, suggesting that we are attempting to lower the quality of education. But on the contrary, our intention is to increase, not decrease this quality.

Seventy pupils is already too much for one principal. That is why we ask for an additional intern already at fifty to seventy pupils. Fifty pupils can be managed by a single assistant teacher, but only if he has an aide who either looks after the class that he is currently not teaching, or helps with grading and supervising the pupils. For this reason we ask for an intern for every additional thirty pupils, and an assistant teacher for every additional fifty pupils. We are confident that any expert will agree that such an arrangement would enable teachers to provide quality instruction.

The requirement that in schools with more than two hundred pupils, one of the assistant teachers must have the diploma of a principal is based on the fact that such a school will be split into two divisions, and it is desirable to have a supervisor in the lower grades with more training than the other assistant teachers and interns.

VI

Organization of teaching staff also requires determination of the minimum annual salary for the teachers. The legislator in 1857 understood this, and accordingly wrote in Article 19 of the School Law that the income of teaching staff should be at least

for a principal	*f* 400 (plus housing and a small acreage)
for an assistant teacher	*f* 200
for an intern	*f* 25

There are two serious objections to this stipulation. It is (1) too low, and (2) too uniform.

The amounts are too low. No teacher can live on four hundred and two hundred guilders. You will not get teachers for this amount of money. Even if this salary were doubled, it would be difficult to find enough teachers.

But also, this law is too uniform. Four hundred guilders in Strijp[7] is not the same as four hundred guilders in Amsterdam. While one can find a boarding house at two hundred guilders in the Achterhoek,[8] this would be absolutely impossible in Rotterdam and The Hague. Many foreign legislators understood correctly that legislating a minimum salary either is a meaningless clause, or should depend on where the teacher will be living.

In Austria the schools are divided into three groups, and the minimum teacher's salary assigned to these groups is six hundred, seven hundred, and eight hundred Austrian guilders, respectively. In Saxony a teacher receives a minimum salary according to this rule:

in municipalities with a population below 5,000	500 thaler
between 5,000 and 10,000	650 thaler
over 10,000	800 thaler

7. A rural area in the south, near the border with Belgium.
8. A rural area in the east of the country, near the German border.

In the canton of Geneva the salaries for the three divisions are twelve hundred francs, fourteen hundred francs, and sixteen hundred francs.

Moreover, in several countries a second subdivision is made according to the number of pupils who attend the school. For instance, in Schaffenhausen the teacher in a school with two grades receives 1,300 francs, with three grades 1,350 francs, with four grades 1,400 francs, with five grades 1,450 francs, with six grades 1,500 francs, with seven grades 1,550 francs, and with eight or more grades 1,600 francs.[9] Elsewhere the teacher is paid a percentage of the tuition.

Finally, another factor often taken into account is the number of years of service. In Saxony, for instance, the salary increases

after 5 years to 280 thaler
after 10 years to 310 thaler
after 15 years to 340 thaler
after 20 years to 370 thaler
after 25 years to 400 thaler

Who would deny that these distinctions are much fairer? Who does not notice how poor and hollow the phrases of our school law are compared to such practical stipulations? What objection would there be, now that the school law will be changed anyway, to deal with these omissions as well?

After all, life is not uniform. In an outlying village life is less expensive than in a town; and in a town it is less expensive than in one of the bigger cities. A man needs more skills for a school of 200 pupils than for a school of 40 pupils. And a school of 400 pupils requires yet a very different man than one with 150 pupils.

Finally, the needs of a man who has been married ten years and has children are greater than those of a beginning teacher who is still single or has just married.

Consequently, we consider it an essential improvement if our school law were also to divide the municipalities into four classes. The first class for municipalities with a population below six thousand. The second class for municipalities with a population between six thousand and fifteen thousand. The third, between fifteen thousand and fifty thousand. And

9. Kuyper lists 1,400 francs for two grades and 1,500 francs for four grades, but these numbers appear to be incorrect.

the fourth for our big cities of more than fifty thousand population. We would then consider the following rule reasonable:

	I	II	III	IV
principal	*f* 700	*f* 900	*f* 1100	*f* 1400
assistant teacher with principal's diploma	*f* 600	*f* 650	*f* 700	*f* 750
assistant teacher	*f* 400	*f* 450	*f* 500	*f* 550
intern	*f* 50	*f* 75	*f* 100	*f* 125

If a dwelling for the principal is not provided, he ought to receive the following allowance for rent: for the first class, 150 guilders; for the second class, 200 guilders; for the third class, 250 guilders; for the fourth class, 350 guilders.

According to the size of the school we would propose that for every additional fifty pupils beyond 100 pupils, the principal receives an additional 25 guilders; for schools of four hundred children, the principal's salary would increase to 850 guilders, 1,050, 1,250, and 1,550 guilders in the four classes respectively. Likewise, the assistant teachers should receive an increase of 10 guilders for every additional fifty pupils. Their annual income in schools of four hundred children would then increase to 460, 510, 560, and 610 guilders respectively.

Finally, a gradually increasing financial remuneration based on years of service could be established simply by increasing the salary of a principal by 25 guilders and of an assistant teacher by 10 guilders for every five years of service. In schools with four hundred children in our big cities, this would increase the principal's salary to 1,700 guilders for thirty years of service, and that of the assistant teacher to 670 guilders. In villages the same thirty years would result in 1,000 guilders for the principal and 520 guilders for the assistant teacher.

If we are not mistaken, this practical arrangement of salaries and the prospect of promotion has, more than anything else, the double advantage that there will be more teaching staff available, and teachers will not move as restlessly between schools as is currently the case.

VII

And now: How does the restitution system work?

This country's constitutional arrangement already knows of restitution to lower levels of government for expenditures on care of the poor, public schools, police services, traffic measures, and so on. This restitution is made to municipalities or to water boards or to private individuals.

Extended to the free school, restitution should bring to realization this concept: the municipality ought to pay out to the free schools, at the end of the school year, all the money it would by law have had to pay extra if there had not been any free schools.

It is already known at city hall which free schools exist within its borders, because Article 37c prohibits anyone from providing private education unless in possession of a certificate issued by the mayor. Likewise, municipal governments already know how many pupils are enrolled in each of these schools, since they file a report with this information to the national government. City hall or, if you will, the school committee also knows how many children need placement in a public school for the coming school year.

Combine those three pieces of information; if indeed the law regulates the duties of the local governments as we indicated above, we really do not think there could be any difficulty in implementing restitution. After all, with the law in hand they will never be at a loss to know when, to whom, and how much they ought to pay.

The school year is set to run from October 1 through September 30. To determine the number of pupils one need only the available statistics about attendance on January 15, April 15, July 15, and October 15, and then divide their sum by four to obtain the average. Because the payment is a restitution, it is made after the school year is over, or if you will, at the end of each quarter, as reimbursement of expenses already paid.

For instance, if a free school has a total of thirty pupils, the municipality is spared hiring one teaching intern; for every fifty pupils, an assistant teacher; if it has two hundred pupils, a teacher with a principal's diploma; and for every four hundred pupils it saves the municipality a principal plus the rent of his dwelling.

If the public school has more than twelve pupils and the free school fewer than thirty, no money is saved, and the free school receives nothing. But if the public school has fewer than twelve pupils and the free school has, say, sixty pupils, then if these sixty pupils were added to the twelve, the municipality would be required to appoint a principal instead of an assistant teacher; thus the free school saves the municipality the difference in salary. If there is a free school in a village or hamlet where the municipality should by law have established a satellite school, then the free school saves the municipality these costs. Should the number of pupils in the free school, added to that of the public school, increase the total above four hundred, then the municipality saves the establishment of a second school and the salary of a second assistant teacher.

In short, in every situation one need only inquire: If there were no free school, and the municipality was obliged to add the pupils of the free school to the public school, how much additional expenses would the law require? These monies ought to be reimbursed.

For every principal, assistant teacher, or intern saved because of the free school, the combined free schools in that municipality should be paid the salary enjoyed by teachers of the same rank in the public schools. If there is no public school teacher of the same rank, then the minimum salary prescribed in the law should be paid, increased by the same percentage as the other teachers in the municipality earn above the minimum salary. The free schools should be reimbursed for the teacher's house, which the municipality is required by law to provide when no other dwelling is available.

School furniture and school supplies must be regulated according to how many pupils attend the school. The amount needed must therefore be divided by the number of pupils attending the public school, and that amount must be reimbursed for every child who attends the free school. The expenses for light and heat come into play only when the free schools have so many pupils that they save the municipality from having to build an extra classroom.

Finally, the expenses for establishing, maintaining, and renting school buildings can lead to restitution in only two situations: (1) if the municipality is saved the establishment or rental of a new school building; or (2) if the volume of the available school buildings is less than the total number of pupils in the public and free school combined, multiplied by three cubic meters. In both cases, the reason for the difference in volume determines how much money the free school saves the municipality in expenses on this account.

In this way one has a perfectly clear and fair norm in every possible situation, to calculate, down to the last guilder, how much more money the government would have to spend if there were no free schools. That additional money should be paid as restitution. Nothing more, nothing less.

One should not complain that we have invented such a precise schedule about buildings, teachers, and salaries only for the sake of this restitution system. You would be proven wrong by the legislation in Wurtemberg and elsewhere, where all these aspects are regulated even more precisely without a restitution system. That precise regulation is an administrative and pedagogical requirement, which is always necessary, whether one has restitution or not. That demand is not our private property, but we share it with our opponents.

That without such a precise regulation the restitution may raise objections must not be blamed on the restitution system, but on the fact that any regulation, of whatever kind and quality, will prevent a sloppy, incomplete, bad law. Indeed, the reason why implementation of the restitution system would lead to difficulties is not to be blamed on the system but on the sloppiness of the law.

Finally, we repeat that the schedule we have sketched is not the only one imaginable. We do not want to bind ourselves or anyone else to these precise numbers. It makes no difference if our figures are replaced with different figures. We provided this sketch only to silence our opponents, who would discredit the very concept of restitution with their cries of "Unfeasible! Impossible!"

That concept, and that alone, is what we lay before the national conscience. Is it just, is it right, can it be called fair, if the municipal treasury, which belongs to all, profits from the financial sacrifices of parents for the religious training of their children? If not, then reimburse the saved monies. More we do not ask. Our demand is just, fair, and modest!

A RESTITUTION SYSTEM AT WORK

I

Many people, even among our sympathizers, did and still do consider the alleged unfeasibility or impracticability of the restitution system a serious objection against it. They do admit that our series of articles, "Is the Restitution System Impracticable," presented a very straightforward and workable implementation; but even after reading it they still wonder: Will it be as smooth in practice as it appears on paper?

We would like to invalidate that objection. Not by refutation. Nor by detailed calculations based on our earlier proposal. But simply by revealing what an *existing* restitution system is based on.

We are thinking of the school system of England. One can hardly deny that this system has implemented restitution. Indeed, what are the three obvious features that distinguish restitution from subsidy? These:

1. Restitution is reimbursement of monies already spent.
2. Restitution presupposes a right to demand payment provided certain legal requirements are met.
3. Restitution requires that the level of payment for public and private schools be equal.

Wherever these three conditions are met there is a system of restitution. Restitution provides a right, a right after expenses paid. The standard for that right is the expenses of the competing school. If a school law meets these three conditions, it honors the idea we promoted, regardless of the form or implementation given to it in various countries.

Last month already, we wrote that one could easily sketch out ten implementations to prove its feasibility. This may have been considered boastful exaggeration, but wrongly so. The various components of the system—the definition of the beneficiary, the conditions for this right, the rules for the competing school, the supervision of both schools, the fluctuations in both types of school within the same municipality, the distinction between schools that charge full, half, or no tuition, and so on—can be correlated in so many different ways that within the strict boundaries of the three defining characteristics of the system, a whole slew of proposals for a law could be made, all of which, however different they might be, answer to the fundamental idea of restitution.

The English law is one of these. Misled by the terminology of the Act of 1870, and of the New Code and Regulations for 1875, many (including students of British law) imagine that that system is based on subsidy rather than restitution. But this opinion is seriously mistaken.

Without doubt the English legislation employs the word "grant," and it seems natural to translate this as "subsidy." But keep in mind that "grants" are always cited as "parliamentary grants." This shows that the English law means "grant" in a similar sense as when we say: "The Chamber grants these monies to the minister." Likewise, the monies for England's board schools (our public schools) are applied for to the houses of Parliament under the same name of "grants in aid." Anyone can sense the absurdity of speaking of "subsidy for the public school" in the sense we normally do in this country. This proves beyond dispute that "grants" are not like our "subsidies" but refer to the constitutional act of "making funds available" by Parliament. See Article I of the New Code: "A sum of money is annually granted by Parliament for Public Education."

We emphasize this all the more because a "subsidy" for a primary school is not unusual among us, but rather a long-known, often-used, almost worn-out term that has acquired its own cachet, a specific connotation, a sharply defined meaning. *Verba valent usu*—the meaning of words is defined by their usage. Because "subsidy" has acquired the historical meaning [in our country] of "a favor granted to a school that is willing to forfeit any religious character," this word should no longer be suddenly substituted in a completely different sense, even though we readily agree that one could conventionally call "subsidy" that which we prefer to label, more powerfully and eloquently, "restitution."

For England as well, the only question is whether the system of parliamentary grants has the features of the restitution idea. In other words, does it assign a right? A right after expenses paid? A right on equal footing with the public school? These questions can be answered only in the affirmative.

1. Does it assign a *right*, a "claim," as Mr. Heemskerk[10] rightfully called it? — See Article 19 of the New Code, which states: "The managers of a school which has met no fewer than 400 times, in the morning and afternoon, in the course of a year, as defined by Article 13, *may claim* at the end of the year, etc."[11] Or Article 22: "The managers of a school which has met no fewer than 45 times in the evening ... *may claim*, etc." Or Article 21d: "No grant *may be claimed* under this Article on behalf of any scholar, etc."

2. Is it reimbursement of payments made? — Reread Article 19, and note the end: "may claim *at the end of the year*." Recognize further that the school children had to submit to an exam before they could count toward the claim—and this point too is beyond dispute.

3. Finally, is there equal footing with the public school? — Yes. Under the term "managers of schools" the board schools and

10. Jan Heemskerk Azn (1818–97), leader of the conservative cabinet at this time, which made way for the Kappeyne Cabinet in 1877.

11. Italics added by Kuyper.

the private schools are placed on a par throughout the financial arrangement; see Article 15c, which recognizes as ruling boards:

1. the school board of any district
2. the managers of a school appointed by a school board
3. the managers of any other public elementary school

By "public elementary school" is meant any "voluntary" school that meets the following conditions:

1. that the parents have the right to exempt their children from the religious instruction in that school;
2. that no child will be compelled to attend, or be excluded from, any religious ritual;
3. that school inspectors are given access to it. (See Section 7 of the Act of 1875.)

Beyond doubt, then, the system of "grants-in-aid" introduced in England is a restitution system.

II

What regulations were followed in England for the implementation of the restitution concept?

For the answer to that question, imagine that you live in Norwich, say, and that for the sake of promoting Christian awareness among the youth you establish ten schools: two kindergartens, seven primary schools, and one college for the training of teachers. Assume that in each of the nine schools for children you have about two hundred pupils, and your college trains thirty young people to become teachers. How much money could you then claim from the treasury?

The answer is as follows.

1. According to Article 19 of the New Code, for the year 1875, four shillings for each child; one additional shilling if they also learn to sing; and one extra shilling if there are no disciplinary problems. For every child, a maximum of 6 shillings = *f* 3.60; multiply by 1,800 pupils, then the total is *f* 6,480.

2. For each child who attended at least 250 school periods, from 4 to 7 years, 8 to 10 shillings = *f* 5.40; from 7 to 10 years, 3 shillings for reading, 3 shillings for writing, and 3 shillings for arithmetic = *f* 5.40. On average, *f* 5.40 for each child; therefore for 1,800 pupils, a total of *f* 9720.

3. For each child who made good progress in grammar, history, geography, or needlework, 4 shillings per year; for 1,800 pupils, this amounts to *f* 4,320.

4. For every school that, within a distance of three miles, is the only usable school for a population of 200 to 300 persons, five to ten pounds. For the nine schools, assuming they are functioning well, this is *f* 150 each, for a total of *f* 1,350.

5. For every teacher in training who meets the legal requirements, 40 to 60 shillings annually; for four times nine trainees, each taken at 50 shillings = *f* 30, giving a total of *f* 1,080.

6. For the courses in extended primary education, 4 shillings per child for every two subjects. Suppose that 400 out of 1,800 children take these courses, then the school receives for 400 children, at *f* 2.40 each, a total of *f* 960.

Recapitulating, we find that for nine schools with a total of eighteen pupils one can claim 6,480 + 9,720 + 4,320 + 1,350 + 960 guilders = 22,830 guilders, or 12.68 guilders per child.[12]

And now the college for teachers. We assumed that there are thirty teachers in training. According to English law, the training takes two years. Therefore we may suppose that fifteen out of thirty students annually take the exam. For each of these students, provided he passes his exam, one can claim 100 pounds, or 1,200 guilders (for female students, this is 70 pounds, or 840 guilders). See Article 86 of the New Code: "Grants are placed to the credit of each college of £ 100 for every master and £ 70 for every mistress, who having been trained in such a college during two years, completes the prescribed period of probation, etc." For a teachers college with thirty pupils this would yield 15 × 1,200 guilders = 18,000 guilders annually.

12. Note that Kuyper does not include the contribution of item 5 above, which applies to the teachers college, not to the nine schools for children.

Thus one may expect, under the most favorable of circumstances, 22,830 guilders for the nine schools for children and 18,000 guilders for the college, for a combined total of 40,830 guilders.

This amount decreases, of course, if the teachers in training live in the same town; it may be decreased further if some conditions are met only in part. There may be a slight increase if there are more than two extra courses in the extended primary school. But if one wants to get an impression, without entering into all these details, of the maximum amount which as a rule is available, then we believe the budget sketched above may be viewed as quite high.

Of course, those forty thousand guilders have to be supplemented. Undoubtedly, the budget for the ten schools in Norwich would be about sixty to sixty-five thousand guilders. Thus only two-thirds of the budget is provided by the grant-in-aid. Indeed, Article 3 expressly states that the purpose of these grants is "to aid local exertion." The citizens must first take the initiative. Only then follows the grant to support that initiative.

Compare this to the neat calculation of the restitution system as applied to the city of Groningen and not only published in the *Groninger Courant* but also acknowledged by that paper to be perfectly convincing, and you will find that the amounts allowed by the English system and the amounts we proposed are virtually equal.

The conditions for such grants, or if you will, the organization of supervision in England, we will discuss in a later article. Here we merely point out that, according to a unanimous declaration of experts, after the introduction of this system [in England] "the religious difficulty has ceased almost to exist." The objection on religious grounds was removed from the English school issue once and for all, thanks to the restitution system.

III

We saw that the grants-in-aid of the English School Law are a form of restitution, because they (1) give a right, (2) after expenses paid, and (3) are based on equality of board schools and voluntary schools—that is, state schools and free schools. We also saw that this restitution system, applied both to public schools and teacher training colleges, takes care of about half of the costs.

What remains is this difficult but interesting question: How did the English legislator succeed in, on one hand, maintaining the freedom of the schools, while on the other hand providing a guarantee that the grants of money resulted in qualitatively good education?

Although the solution adopted in Great Britain in this respect is only one of many possibilities, we believe it is both ingenious and practical. The English legislator took his starting point in this idea: (1) that uniform restitution kills mutual competition, while an extremely elastic restitution is an incentive; (2) that every school must be free in its choice of pedagogy and curriculum, and free to accept restitution or not; and (3) that the evaluation of the education, because it relates to expenses made, should concern not the education itself but its fruits.

To start with the last item: restitution of educational costs is granted only after the exams are taken. Naturally, this requires hard work, but it is exceedingly profitable. Had we mentioned such an exam for the Netherlands, we would have been branded as halfwits and utopians. But in England this system actually exists. Exams have been taken for many years. All children of four years and older for whom restitution was claimed were given exams, yielding a figure of over 1.5 million.

The requirements for these exams for primary education are divided into six ranks, corresponding to the six grades. For the first grade, the requirements are as follows:

a) Reading: Reading a short paragraph, which also features words of more than one syllable.

b) Writing: Copying a line of print in large letters, on slate or paper; writing a few words from dictation.

c) Arithmetic: Adding and subtracting with no more than four digits; the tables of multiplication up to six.

For the second grade:

a) Reading: With comprehension, a simple sentence from an easy reader.

b) Writing: A sentence from the same book, read aloud once, then dictated word for word.

c) Arithmetic: Subtraction, multiplication, and division.

d) Grammar: Identifying the nouns in a sentence.

e) Geography: Definition, compass directions, shape and movement of the earth; the surface of the earth and the principal phenomena of nature.

And so on for the third, fourth, and fifth grades; the requirements of the sixth grade are:

a) Reading: At a good speed and with expression; reciting from memory 50 lines of prose or 150 lines of poetry, assigned beforehand by the school inspector. Familiarity with the meaning of the words and with allusions.

b) Writing: A short composition or letter of correspondence; attention will be given to the flow of the argument, the rules of grammar, spelling, and penmanship.

c) Arithmetic: Equations; fractions and decimal fractions.

d) Grammar: Parsing of sentences.

e) Geography: Asia, America, Africa.

f) History: British history from Henry VII to George III.

In a similarly precise manner, the level of the exam is specified from year to year for all subjects of extended primary education, including Latin, and for the teachers colleges; and wherever uncertainty remained, an authoritative interpretation of the law has been provided.

The results thus far have shown that over 90 percent of the examined children meet these requirements, and the outcome is twofold: (1) the quality of education has increased in all schools, and (2) in many schools additional courses have been taught at a decent level. This system of examination even allows for the appointment of teachers who have not been examined. The only requirement of the English law for claiming restitution is that in day schools at least the principal/headmaster has passed the exam.

To allow for the actual need of small villages, a number of "ambulatory schoolmasters" (traveling teachers) have been appointed, who visit a number of schools in turn, and the results of these village schools where a private person did the teaching (they were called "group children") were so outstanding that an even higher percentage of pupils passed the exams than in the state schools.

Second, this restitution system provides a guarantee against truancy. For Article 19 of the Code of 1875 requires that the school provide at least 400 class periods—that is, six times in the morning and four times in the afternoon for forty weeks. Only if this condition is met does the school receive as such, independent of the progress or diligence of the pupils, restitution in the amount of four to six shillings per child. Also, for children who attended at least 250 school periods, an additional eight to ten shillings per child is reimbursed. For children who work half days in shops or factories, this number is lowered to 150 periods.

Thus the restitution itself unwittingly provides an incentive and a guarantee for quality of education, order and discipline, good school attendance, and use of accredited teachers.

Meanwhile, everyone's overall freedom to establish and maintain a school of any kind, and to teach what and how one thinks best, remains untouched. But if the school does not produce the fruits the English state wishes for its citizens, then it does not save the state any money, and there can therefore be no restitution.

Conclusion

In the English restitution system there was no overall equivalence between state schools and free schools.

Both schools can draw the same amounts of restitution from the parliamentary grants, provided it is not more than half [of their expenses]. But in other respects the interests of both kinds of school are different. The free school must itself provide for the other half of the costs, while the state school is provided for through taxes.

This has disadvantages for both schools. For the free school, because it must compete with a school that has greater access to funds. But also for the state school, which lacks the incentive of the free school, is indifferent about the grants-in-aid, and therefore does not perform as well as the free school.

However, this danger is reduced by the way in which school boards are composed. As you know, they are not appointed by the government but by the local citizens, with two consequences: (1) for the sake of their own finances, the state schools also try to get as much restitution money as possible; and (2) they do not misuse the state schools as a means to kill the free schools.

England does not yet have regional and national school boards. But they will be established also there. Dr. Rigg, the great pedagogue, has written about it in his pamphlet. He writes: "Thus I expect that soon provincial districts will form with provincial school boards."[13] Likewise: "The institution of a national school board will be the main instrument to unify the national education in England, and ensure the free, yet stable progress of the entire mechanism of education."[14] This proves that Mr. Farncombe Sanders is not as familiar with the views of the English pedagogues as the tone of his criticism might suggest.[15]

Now this social character of the school boards—that is, through the single fact that the nation may give its input concerning the direction of primary education—has led to the following result:

1. In England they have what Thorbecke and our liberals, before their about-face, made out to desire for us as well: state involvement only where private initiative is wanting. Of the 1,600,000 children examined in the day schools, only one-twelfth, namely 138,000, attended the state schools.

2. The free schools, far from being oppressed by English law, rather found in that law, with its restitution system, the incentive to make giant steps forward. The Wesleyan schools, for instance, had only 119,000 pupils before the law of 1870. In 1872 this had increased to 166,000, and today (in 1874) it has climbed to 180,000, an increase of more than 50 percent in four years.

3. Both school buildings and educational methods, as well as the quality of teachers and instruction, have all improved incredibly since 1870.

4. Through the free choice of the population, the religious character is retained, even in nearly all state schools, both primary schools and teachers colleges. All school boards, except for two or three, not only allow but also promote prayer, singing, and Bible reading. Even in London. Only Birmingham, a particularly

13. James Harrison Rigg, *The Natural Development of National Education in England* (London: Training College, Westminster, 1875), 12.

14. Rigg, *Natural Development of National Education*, 18.

15. Apparently A. J. W. Farncombe Sanders (1833–96), member of the Second Chamber in the Dutch parliament, had publicly responded to previous installments in this series of articles.

materialistic city, has a school without religion like we have, but it was desired only by a small sector of the population. For these folks in Birmingham, Holland is their El Dorado. Nearly everywhere else, people are convinced with Briggs that all education, "if separated from Christian doctrine and principle and aim," is bound to remain "mutilated and incomplete." England still knows very well what Dr. Rigg recently wrote to Mr. Macgregor: "Holland is the only country in the world that has introduced a system of primary education separated from any religion."

5. The right given to parents to take their children out of school during the hours devoted to religion is almost never exercised, even by unbelieving parents.
6. The only remaining difficulty lies not in the desire for a-religious education, but in the dominance of the established Church of England.

Liberals have often asserted that the most pious Christians in England agreed with them and favored state schools. Nothing is further from the truth. A handful of Dissenters who in their hatred of the Church of England sometimes went too far in their utterances stand alone, are disavowed by their coreligionists, and have not the slightest influence. Rather, most Dissenters in England are loyal and warm advocates both of the free school (the voluntary principle) and the religious school. Their objection does not serve to promote the state school, but actually opposes the board school. They objected, but not because of its a-religious character (for it does not have that: it is a school with the Bible), but because of the excessive influence of the Anglican clergy, which in many places causes the school to be in fact an Anglican school.

This shows once again how dangerous it is to appeal to the public opinion in other countries without correct knowledge of the situation. It is very true that the small radical party in England had hoped that Forster and Gladstone[16] would imitate our nonreligious school. But neither Forster nor Gladstone wanted it, and even if they had wanted it, they did not dare

16. William Edward Forster (1818–86) and William Ewart Gladstone (1809–98) were leaders of the Liberal Party in England.

or were not able to pursue it. The English nation did not want a neutral school, because it knew that such a school corrodes religion and plays into the hands of unbelief.

The Dutch nation did not want it, either. But she has been misled; she has been blindsided. How long will we stand alone with our un-Christian public school, and be the laughingstock and an offense in the midst of Christian Europe? The years 1871 and 1873 reduced this evil! Why not remove it altogether in 1875?

Citizens of the Netherlands! Christian Europe, especially England, is looking at you. The question is: Will you return, with your public school, to Christ?

THE REMEDY

TEXT INTRODUCTION

The following eight lead articles from the daily *De Standaard* made up the fourth of six series that Kuyper wrote in advance of the June 1875 general elections, when education was sure to be a key campaign issue.

In 1875, newspaper editor Abraham Kuyper had been a member of Parliament for one year. In the series "The Remedy" he uses his daily to plead for a fair deal for supporters of nongovernment schools, arguing his case on the basis of civil liberties, to be reinforced in the national ethos by mutual respect and accommodation of differences. In passing, he makes an important distinction: in a just state—a constitutional commonwealth under the rule of law—citizens respect the right of others to hold ideas they do not agree with, but they cannot be forced to respect those ideas themselves.

According to Kuyper, a revision of the 1857 School Law or Education Act is more imperative than ever, now that looming education reforms may saddle Christian schools with new and possibly crippling financial burdens. The act must be amended in order to put an end to the arbitrary application of its clauses by local ruling elites favoring public over private schools.

But only as a first step. This critical phase in the school struggle does not set aside the ultimate goal of achieving a revision of the Constitution, one that would allow for conscientious objectors in the realm of education. That, in the long run, would be the only remedy that could pacify the supporters of Christian schools and put a definitive end to the school struggle.

For all his political intuition and foresight, the thirty-seven-year-old Kuyper could not know in 1875 that this dream would be partially realized in 1889, more closely approximated in 1905, and at last fulfilled in 1920, the year of his death.

Addressing in turn sympathizers and detractors of private Christian schools, Kuyper's chief effort at this time appears directed at achieving a united front in the school struggle, an essential coordination of strategy which he defends and undergirds with quotations from his former mentor and fellow publicist, the aging leader Groen van Prinsterer (1801–76).

In the course of his argument, Kuyper emphasizes that private Christian schools offer quality education and welcome government inspection. At the same time he warns them in the strongest possible terms never to jeopardize their freedom in exchange for a system of subsidies. Instead he makes the case for a system of restitution as the only just solution to the systemic discrimination of private-school supporters.

Source: Kuyper, Abraham. *Het redmiddel*. Amsterdam: J. H. Kruyt, 1875, pp. 2–24. Reprint of eight articles in *De Standaard*, March 1–25, 1875. Translated by Arjen Vreugdenhil and Nelson D. Kloosterman. Edited by Harry Van Dyke.

THE REMEDY

HOW CAN THE CHRISTIAN SCHOOL BE SAVED?

The situation is grave. This year [1875] an attempt will be made to execute the *sharp resolution*.[1] Will Parliament prove to be a reassuring bulwark against this assault on our civil liberties?

Certainly not the First Chamber, which revealed its maniacal support of the state school already in its Address in Reply to the Speech from the Throne.

And what about the Second Chamber? It has forty-one members who belong to the coalition of radical liberals, men who will not hesitate for a moment to dress up their favored school at our expense. In addition, there are four "conciliatory" conservatives, members who will never go out of their way to redress our grievances. The remaining thirty-five members[2] consist of sixteen Roman Catholics, eleven antirevolutionaries, and eight conservatives. Accordingly, if the general elections in June do not alter these numbers, it is already impossible to stop the *sharp resolution*, and we will have to get ready for the woeful task of burying the education issue under the ruins of our Christian schools. For this reason alone we need to point out, without entering the election debate as yet, that the voting booth in

1. For "sharp resolution" see p. 186.
2. Apparently, at this time twenty seats were vacant in this chamber of one hundred members.

June will be of crucial importance for the free school and that, whatever the outcome, the advocates of the *sharp resolution* must be turned away if our school is not to go under. If they claim that the education article in the Constitution gives them the right to threaten us with increased burdens, then naturally we on our part must work twice as hard to protest against this un-Dutch element in our Constitution. We must not relent in this protest if we are ever to lead "a quiet and peaceable life" as Christians in this good land.

We must protest, first of all, against the fountainhead of all this evil under which we and our children have already suffered and which now poses an even greater menace: namely Article 194, in particular that wretched clause.[3] On the strength of the same basic principle we must protest against any authority which the state derives from the Constitution for the purpose of obstructing the moral-religious development of our nation in a Christian direction.

We must protest, in short, against the general means provided in the Constitution that allow a coterie [of liberals] to abuse the vast influence of the state as propaganda for their pestiferous principles.

We must protest, not by fruitless writing or formal debating, but by concentrating all our actions and all our alliances on the goal of *revising*, along the shortest route possible, this untenable thing.[4]

What does that mean concretely for today? What position should the Antirevolutionary Party adopt toward the *sharp resolution*, which will soon be debated in the context of the proposed amendment of the school law? We will have to adopt a firm position on this matter. Whoever hesitates at the decisive moment in such a precarious concurrence of events will lose.

A decision is inescapable. Like it or not, the question is not whether we should propose an amendment, but what our strategy should be now that the school law will be debated.

If there were a proposal along the lines of De Brauw[5] the choice would be simple. We would vote it down, unwilling to be fobbed off, as has become

3. The "wretched clause" stated: "The Government provides adequate public primary education throughout the Kingdom."
4. That is, the objectionable article in the Constitution.
5. Willem Maurits de Brauw Sr., Esq. (1810–74), a member of Parliament, was a conservative with sympathies for the antirevolutionaries and a fierce opponent of liberalism. On May 14, 1867, De Brauw had moved in the Second Chamber that the School Law of 1857 be amended, on the grounds that there should be "justice for all,

a tradition. But that is no longer at issue. The situation has changed and is now totally different. Today, the pressure to change the school law comes from the side which until recently was the fiercest and most stubborn opponent of any change: it comes from the liberals.

This time the push is not at all for redressing our grievances, but for replacing whips with scorpions. It is not for doing justice to the Christian segment of the population, but for deliberately oppressing the minorities. Their hand is outstretched to take our lamb.[6]

Hearing this, a simple citizen might think that the question "What should we do?" is easily answered. "Take those scorpions away from your opponent! Resist the oppressor! Protect your lamb! And vote down every law along those lines!" But however simple and natural this reaction may seem, such talk reveals ignorance of the situation.

For what is the case? The Antirevolutionary Party always prided itself on standing at the front lines in the battle for the formation and development of our population through improved education. It always firmly resisted any attempt to lower the quality of education. It did not want it to deteriorate!

May our party now become unfaithful to its past? None of us would dream of it. But you should realize how this situation puts the squeeze on us. For what the liberals are asking of you is (1) that you acknowledge that our public education is not good, and (2) that you help them to improve it. Would you like to be on record as the one refusing to pay the teachers a decent salary? Could you bear the accusation that, in a school that needs two teachers, you force one teacher to overwork himself in an overpopulated classroom, thereby also harming the children? Do you want to be the man who denies funds to provide the proper training of teachers?

The coin, we realize, has a flip side; we ourselves have presented an analysis of the label *sharp resolution*.[7] But that side is not shown to the Chamber. There the question is simply: for or against a good salary for teachers; for or against sufficient school staffing; for or against adequate training!

---

especially where freedom of religion and conscience is concerned." The proposed amendment read that "local governments may give financial support to private schools." The motion was a noble but empty gesture, since everybody knew it had no chance of acceptance, and even if accepted it left the issue unsettled owing to the use of the word "may."

6. Allusion to 2 Sam 12:4.
7. See above, p. 186.

For the conservatives and the Roman Catholics this is not a big deal. They judge these demands to be nine-tenths exaggeration. But for us, anti-revolutionaries, who do not believe this and who agree strongly that our primary education requires improvement in every respect—for us the choice is precarious.

The school law advocates remonstrate against their own school law. If you read between the lines, their Remonstrance means the demise of our Christian schools. How, in what manner, ought our Counter-Remonstrance[8] then be formulated, on the one hand so as to avoid the reproach that we are enemies of improving public education, and on the other hand so as to save our Christian schools?

The *sharp resolution* contains three articles. Which three demands should we then make on our part to disarm its lethal implications for the free school? Could we not demand: (1) that from now on, rules instead of arbitrariness should govern the proliferation of public schools; (2) that the fatal Article 23[9] lose its sting; and (3) that the brute force of money be put aside?

We happen to be of the opinion that from the vantage point of fairness these demands are reasonable. Would they also be effective? Would they comport with our own principles? No doubt they keep the door open to a revision of the Constitution's article on education, which would otherwise be irrevocably slammed shut.

RULES INSTEAD OF ARBITRARINESS

We presented three ideas for fending off the imminent danger: (1) let there be rules instead of arbitrariness in determining the number of schools (imperative mandate); (2) for the sake of fairness, let local governments pay us the money we save them (restitution); and (3) let Article 23 be fleshed out more (conscience clause).

---

8. "Remonstrance" and "Counter-Remonstrance": a play on the names of the two parties in 1618–19 whose dispute over salvation was dealt with at the Synod of Dort. Readers of *De Standaard* would know immediately which side was in the right.
9. Art. 23: "The instruction in the school shall be made serviceable, while learning suitable and useful skills, to the development of the intellectual faculties of the children and to their training in all Christian and civic virtues. The teacher shall refrain from teaching, doing or permitting anything that is inconsistent with the respect due to the religious beliefs of those who think differently. Religious instruction is left to the church denominations. For this purpose the school facilities can be made available outside of school hours for the pupils who attend the school."

Not that this would achieve the goal of our struggle. How could it, since a system so hostile to us would remain in full force? If we are to replace that system with something better, a general revision of the Constitution is unavoidable. As long as that does not happen we remain trapped in the liberal prison. We may therefore not let up for one moment in our demand to be released from that prison through a change in the Constitution.

Still, this does not mean that while in prison we must put up with everything. We certainly may protest against the secret plan to convert us while in prison. Even a prisoner has rights in the face of extreme caprice and tyranny. Although you long for the moment that you will be able to leave as a free man, nobody can demand that in the meantime you put up with every wrong.

This was always the position of our party. The demand to liberate the Christian school was already made in 1869, but at the same time the request was made (1) to remove the word "Christian" from Article 23, (2) to put restrictions on tuition-free education, (3) to prohibit teachers from holding part-time positions in the church.[10]

Why did we insist on this? Because this threefold demand of ours had to be granted *even from the point of view of the school-law advocates*, assuming that they would judge fairly and consistently.

Our intention was not to give up the fight once these demands were met. The goal was a provisional acknowledgment of our right, the removal of the worst aspects, and the excision from the school law of that which was contrary to the system of the school law itself.

This prompted Dr. Lamping to argue in his well-known pamphlet[11] that even these three "absurdities" could be defended within the system of the school law. It was this epitome of scholarly arrogance that caused Groen van

10. To reduce the cost of the local public school, some Reformed churches would appoint teachers to salaried part-time positions such as janitor, gravedigger, bell ringer, and so on. This indirect support of the religiously neutral public school by the national church aided municipalities in reducing or waiving tuition for the public school, thus adding to its competitive advantage over the private school.

11. J. A. Lamping, *Kerk en School. Een woord aan het volk van Nederland* (Rotterdam: H. Nijgh, 1869).

Prinsterer to cry out: "If you are not willing to give us even this minimum, then onward to the fortress of the Constitution!"[12]

It is in this sense that we would like our sympathizers to reconsider the three demands that we mentioned earlier. If you think that a prisoner who resists the jailer's attempt to starve him to death is giving up on his goal to be released the sooner the better—in this case, giving up on his goal to see a revision of the Constitution—you would be ascribing to us gross naïveté. Our aim, in short, is to ensure, no more and no less, that the Christian school in the Netherlands will not be crushed before we can initiate a revision of the Constitution.

If others believe that the earlier demands should still be maintained as well, well and good. But do not forget that Mr. Groen already came to the conclusion that removal of the word "Christian" had become relatively meaningless.[13] As well, the evil of part-time positions in the church has in part been resolved, and the preference for free schools has increased rather than decreased. But, as we said, if our friends wish to maintain the earlier demands—we do not expect much benefit, but we are not opposed. Just don't let it hold us up. Rather, let us concentrate together on the new demands, which we must use as a shield against more recent arrogance.

Until now, as you know, the authorities have complete power to expand the public school system as they please. The most recent case is still fresh in our memory. A municipality of 5,463 persons already had thirteen state schools; yet a fourteenth had to be added, and that fourteenth school was to be the battering ram to beat down the Christian school.

Must this continue? Is it unreasonable that we demand, with urgency, that this arbitrariness be replaced by a fixed rule?

The "wretched clause" in the Constitution requires that "the government shall everywhere provide sufficient primary education." And in line with this, Article 16 of the School Law requires "that in every municipality primary education shall be provided in a number of schools sufficient to meet the size and demands of the population, accessible for all children, without distinction in religious persuasion." Is it right that, for lack of a

12. Groen discussed Lamping's pamphlet in his *Nederlandsche Gedachten* of September 9, 1869, pp. 18–24. No such direct quotation is found there, but its sense seems expressed on pp. 19 and 33.

13. See J. L. van Essen, "Groen van Prinsterer's Tactics in his Campaign for Freedom of Education," in van Essen, *Guillaume Groen van Prinsterer: Selected Studies* (Jordan Station, ON: Wedge, 1990), 79–88.

detailed rule, the wretched consequences of this miserable clause continue to result in double misery?[14]

Blaupot ten Cate,[15] a school-law advocate par excellence, recently characterized the requirement of the school law as follows: "No children may suffer from lack of primary education just because there is no more room for them in the school." He failed to add: "It would be unreasonable to have a public school for every small number of children in every village or hamlet." And he reiterated his warning against the perceived threat: "We must prevent any situation in which parents lack the opportunity to send their children to a school governed by the core idea of the public school."

Clearly, even in this form the demand is absurd. We would like an answer to this question: Why must the threat be averted when parents have no opportunity to send their children to a neutral school, but not when parents lack the opportunity to send their children to a Christian school? Are not all parents in the Netherlands equal?

But even if we were to adopt this partisan position, we would still insist: Make this demand subject to clear rules, and stop playing with us!

The outer limit of your demand is, in your own words, that there must be room in the schools for all children whose parents desire that they attend a state school. Now write something to this effect into the law, to prevent the scandal that schools are built for children who are not there, or whose parents do not want them to attend your state school.

When it comes to levying taxes or enumerating voters, the statistics of each household and business are determined with great accuracy; what objection could there be to inquire of your city officials for how many children public education is in fact desired? We realize that such numbers are always fluctuating, but that is a common problem in all government administration. It is no real obstacle; approximate figures are workable. Why then grab at straws when the subject is education? Surely, national and local administrative bureaus know the magic effect of charging fees? This objection merely concerns the implementation of the law and should be no obstacle for a skilled legislator.

---

14. Public schools were provided on the basis of population numbers, not on the basis of need or demand.
15. Steven Blaupot ten Cate (1807–84) was an Anabaptist preacher and a liberal politician.

The only question is this: As long as you keep us captive, will you at least treat us according to the prison's rules? Or will you leave us to be a prey to the most outrageous arbitrariness practiced locally by little despots?

Why not reformulate the core idea of the school law, as follows: "The government of every municipality shall see to it that sufficient room be available in schools for those children within their boundaries whose parents or guardians desire public primary education." The principle would then remain the same (and therefore still strongly objectionable), but at least it would put an end to the arbitrariness.

Furthermore, the law should spell out: (1) how many cubic meters of school space are required per child, (2) how many teachers should be present per how many children, (3) how much fixed additional space there may be on top of the calculated value, (4) at what age children should be enrolled, (5) what minimum number of children should be required in a village or hamlet in order to justify opening a satellite school, and (6) within what proximity municipalities may be combined.

These are minor points of implementation that could quickly be put in place. They do not affect the key issue. The key issue is this: Should we demand that arbitrariness be replaced by a fixed rule, to put a definitive end to the scandals that happened recently in Wons, Welsrijp, and elsewhere,[16] scandals that have become especially urgent in the light of the sharp resolution?

I think we have no choice. What do our readers think?

RESTITUTION

As long as attempts are made to increase the quality of our national education, one need not fear opposition from the Antirevolutionary Party, provided that it does not at the same time induce us to commit suicide. If our country's educators need higher salaries, lighter workloads, and better training, then we are willing to allow all of this, as long as it does not follow the rule "One man's meat is another man's poison."

Accordingly, we have proposed the following threefold demands as life insurance for the free school: (1) specification of the space in school buildings that should be available for public education, (2) specification of the conscience clause in Article 23, and (3) refund of monies saved by the state.

16. See above, p. 29.

Previously we explained the first demand. We hope to address the second demand next; now we address the third demand: restitution.

To begin, we wish to remove a misunderstanding that might easily arise among our friends. From the sound of it one might think that we propose a return to the former but now abandoned system of subsidized education.

We are fiercely opposed to subsidies. None of us wants to hear of it. The very mention of it makes us sick. We are fighting for justice and desire no handouts. Our fight is a noble struggle for a sacred principle. That battle we will not cease for the sake of some financial favor. The opposition will never have us asking for a subsidy in any shape or form.

Why are we so opposed to subsidies? Why do we despise them with all our might? The reason is obvious. A subsidy is an arbitrary allowance given by the rich to the poor, depending on his whim and caprice. Moreover, a subsidy creates obligations toward the giver and results in a kind of administrative interference that is incompatible with a proper understanding of freedom and independence. A subsidy assumes that an inventory is made of existing needs and an account is submitted showing that the allowance has been spent in an effective manner. Both are unthinkable without affording the subsidizing state such a control over our schools that it would thoroughly destroy any concept of a free school.

Anyone, therefore, who jumps to the conclusion that we essentially propose to demand such subsidizing of education has misunderstood our intention and is attributing to us a view that we strongly oppose.

Likewise, our view of restitution is not that the state should refund part of the tax monies to the free-school advocates. To those who think that this is what we want and who oppose this view, we readily concede that this would be repugnant to the nature of our government institutions, and that it arises from a confusion of public law and private law, which we wish to avoid. There cannot and may not be a settling of accounts between the state and the taxpayer. The government levies taxes by virtue of its supreme right to do so; it must not be viewed as a creditor who is paid by the taxpayer in exchange for certain services. To hold such a view, one would have to hold to a theory of popular sovereignty. We, at least, do not hold to that theory.

When we speak of restitution we exclusively mean: *a refund to the free schools of the monies they save the state.*

As long as Article 194 of the Constitution remains in effect, the state has the obligation to maintain in all municipalities a sufficient educational system for the needs of the population. Now suppose that your municipality has five thousand children of school age; then your local government has to open ten schools, each serving five hundred children. The construction of these schools would amount to 500,000 guilders, and their maintenance would require 70,000 guilders annually. Thus your local government would have to budget about 100,000 guilders annually for primary education. That expense would not depend on the whim of your local government, but be prescribed by law.

Suppose, however, that in your municipality the free school becomes popular, and grows so much that ultimately half of the children receive sufficient and excellent education, as required by the law, in the classrooms of the free schools. Instead of ten schools for five thousand children the local government needs to maintain only five schools for twenty-five hundred children; for primary education it need spend only 50,000 guilders annually instead of 100,000 guilders. The government is spared these expenses by the parents who established free schools.

It is natural that these free schools cost more. Instead of five schools with 500 children each, they have twenty schools, designed for 50, 75, 100, or 150 pupils each. They require relatively more personnel. The school provides more opportunity for personal involvement with the pupils. The pedagogical quality will be noticeably higher. The harmony between the upbringing at home and in the schools will be much stronger than is ever possible in a state school.

Yet the municipal council cannot take any of this into account. It has no obligation toward those extra expenses. Those extra costs are incurred at the expense of the parents who choose such more expensive schooling. Perhaps they end up spending 90,000 guilders where the government would have spent only 50,000. The difference of 40,000 guilders is then a relative luxury, to be paid by those who benefit from it.

But the case is different with those 50,000 guilders that the local government would have spent by law but which it now saves. Justice and fairness require that this amount should be viewed as an expense to which the government is obligated and which it escapes only through an accidental circumstance. It would be highly unreasonable to use this money to reduce the cost of providing public schools. That would be taking advantage of parents who spend almost twice as much on their children.

If the legislator were to repeal freedom of education, nothing could be done. But now that the legislator acknowledges the existence of the free schools and includes them among the pedagogical forces of national development, it would be unfair and irresponsible to reduce the budgeted costs for education at the expense of the parents.

Without yet entering a debate about the implementation, which could result in more than one stipulation, we wish to focus on the core principle: let every municipality pay back to the collective free schools within their boundaries the monies they save the government.

Subsidy is charity; restitution is a reimbursement of expenses made for someone else. There must not be any interference in the households of others, and there must be no arbitrariness. This principle of restitution intends only to solve the problem of increasing the quality of our national education, without forcing the free schools to commit suicide.

A NEW WARNING

That others also begin to see the threat to the free school is obvious from the serious warning in Dr. Bronsveld's column:

> The struggle about education has entered a new stage. It is no longer the members of the Christian-Historical party that propose to change the law. Dr. Jan ten Brink declared in the January issues of the magazine *Nederland* on page 4: "The law on primary education, while violated almost daily by those who promote evangelical sectarian hatred, nevertheless remains untouched despite all those biblical lamentations"—when he wrote these words he not only proved himself a heartless and hateful judge of conscientious objections (which is not uncommon for doctors in theology), but he also revealed himself as poorly informed even though he is personally involved in education.
>
> No, if you want to hear a devastating condemnation of our primary education and a fervent exhortation for changing the law, you should sit at the feet of [liberal politicians] Mr. Kerdijk and Mr. Moens, who travel around the country like prophets, preaching: Oh, please help us improve our bad primary schools!
>
> Thus spoke Mr. Moens recently in Rotterdam, in response to an invitation by a riding association. Good education, he said, is the only remedy for our social problems, and the primary school provides the most important education of our youth.

Currently [so runs the newspaper report of Mr. Moens's address] the question is: What should be demanded of that school, what are the needs of a citizen in our society? The short answer is: a certain amount of knowledge. Reading, so that he understands what he reads. Writing, so that he can express his thoughts on paper as clearly as he would like. [Mental] arithmetic, so that he need not reach for pen and paper every time but is able to do the calculation in his head. History, so that he knows to praise the deeds of our ancestors and also strives to perform better deeds today. Geography, so that he can find his way at least in his own country and not just be able to name a few towns but also know how to get there and what can be found there, so that he can go there if he needs to find a new job. Civics, so that he can make up his own mind without relying on others who promise gold but seek only to enrich themselves. Drawing, so that he can represent in a few firm lines what he sees. It is not enough to possess knowledge, but he must also know how to put it into practice. These are the requirements for anyone who wishes to get ahead in our society. And these are the things he has to learn in elementary school.

But then the school must be organized well. Skillful teachers, well-ordered classrooms of thirty or forty pupils maximum. The teacher must not only be able to oversee all his pupils, but also know them personally, which he will not be able to do if the number of pupils is too high.

Furthermore, the pupils must be at least seven years old. There must be good kindergartens, where children learn to see, hear, feel, and observe. Let children go to school when they reach five years of age, but until their seventh year the school should essentially be a well-organized kindergarten. Then, from seven to twelve years old, give them more formal training than material content; let the subject matter be used to promote thinking, and let those who will not continue on to a secondary school receive education until they are fifteen years old by extending and reviewing what they have learned thus far; a schooling in which there is more emphasis on the subject matter, even though mental development remains the primary concern. Would this not lead to the desired goal?

> It could be like this, but currently it is not. The speaker illustrated this with numerous proofs, and sketched the sad state of our primary schools. He referred to the insufficient number of teachers, their low salaries, the poor structuring of the grade levels in many schools, the chronic problem of truancy, and so on.
>
> Thus a change of the law is much needed, but we must also consider the costs: given that many municipalities already have difficulty bearing these costs, the central government will have to contribute a significant portion. Only then can the schools be organized as needed.
>
> The law must be such that it cannot be interpreted in different ways and avoided at whim, but it must impose firm rules. Next, the law must ensure that pupils show up at school regularly and until a certain age. Compulsory attendance is the only way to accomplish this. The only people who will consider this undue compulsion are those parents who neglect their children. For the sake of the true freedom of children, parents must be compelled to send their children to school.
>
> Since compulsory school attendance cannot be implemented as yet, let us start by establishing a sufficient number of schools and by appointing a sufficient number of qualified teachers earning decent salaries.
>
> The speaker strongly recommended the establishment of chapters of the Association for the Improvement of Public Education,[17] whose endeavors are fully in line with his views.[18]

It goes without saying that we, too, desire education to be as good as possible; those who regard us as patrons of ignorance are slandering us. But we emphatically object to the unbelievable tyranny that is expressed in this program. Mr. Moens[19] talks about the state school as if there has never been any other kind. By perfecting that school at the cost of millions of

17. The *Vereeniging tot Verbetering van het Volksonderwijs*, established in 1871, was an association that strongly supported the religiously neutral public school.
18. A. W. Bronsveld, "Kroniek," *Stemmen voor Waarheid en Vrede* 12 (1875).
19. Antony Moens (1827–99) was a modernist preacher who later became a prominent school inspector.

guilders, he wants to make it even more difficult to establish and maintain free schools. For whose benefit does he demand this? For the benefit of the state. But is this "state" the same as the people? I would ask of this former teacher of religion who is now a school inspector: please consider seriously whether our nation is truly served by a nonreligious school. Surely we may not overlook the thousands of Roman Catholics; and surely Mr. Moens remembers that among the Protestants the majority of the lower classes for whom we opened primary schools do not subscribe to the modern notions and prefer a school with the Bible to one without the word of the Lord. If he does not remember, the modernist preachers can provide him with all this information. Yet they want to compel us to help erect, with our taxes, schools that are desired neither by us nor by the majority of the lower classes for whom they are being erected in the first place. Wherever there are free schools, the state school is not able to win the competition for pupils, even though its tuition is less. And many parents continue to send their children to the public school only because necessity compels them. — And yet, the liberals now plan to act as if none of this were the case. The school law advocates know of only one school: the religiously neutral school; and because they love this school they want to compel us to help pay for it. Is this not tyranny? Does this not speak of hatred of religion? Is this not "sectarian hatred"? Instead of accusing us of lust for power, should they not rather accuse themselves?

As far as I can tell, it was never the design of Mr. Thorbecke[20] to kill the free school, even though out of his mouth the word "free" to describe our schools sounded somewhat ironic. We shall carry on, regardless. Much is gained, now that we know one another's intentions. Let us inform people more forcefully than before; let us show them the crucial importance of the current battle. Although we applaud the zeal of Messrs. Moens and Kerdijk,[21] we must oppose them, not because they want to improve education but because they want to curtail our liberty.

And we call out to our friends: do not recklessly rush into a public debate, as is currently happening in several localities. The education issue should not be addressed with just a few quotations from the writings of Mr. Groen, a plethora of Bible texts, and amicable lectures. It requires more in-depth study. Ask Mr. Groen. Ask Mr. Van Otterloo, whose excellent "Contribution

20. Johan Rudolph Thorbecke (1798–1872) was a leading liberal politician.
21. Arnold Kerdijk (1846–1905) was a liberal politician and journalist.

to Clarifying the Schools Issue"[22] we would like to see in everybody's hands. Our opponents are seasoned champions who have the right to demand that we do not attack them with paper helmets or rubber swords. You point to David? Realize that the accuracy of David's slingshot was also the fruit of much practice. "He who does not work shall not eat" [see 2 Thess 3:10] is a saying that applies to more than one situation.

THE CONSCIENCE CLAUSE

As soon as you bring together two incompatible things, you must find a way to establish a bearable situation. When the decision was made to try to bring together in one common school children from homes that are Catholic, Lutheran, Jewish, Reformed, and whatnot, it was necessary to give something of a unique identity to that strange hodgepodge by installing various safety valves, spiritual ventilation systems, and *nefanda* lists from pagan antiquity.[23]

Had the lawmakers limited themselves to what was absolutely necessary, it would not have been objectionable.

There is a small region in our country where the hamlets are too small to have more than one viable school, yet the population is mixed. In a few villages there are some individuals of different persuasions scattered among a population that is largely Roman Catholic, or nearly all Reformed. Finally, there are small towns which have lower-class populations with much religious variation, yet which are too small to permit separate schools.

The problem lies with those three cases. For about four hundred to five hundred schools in the land, the question arose as to how to maintain a decent school for this "mixed population," without compromising the quality of education; and no one would blame our legislators if they had drawn up guidelines to provide for this need in a practical manner, leaving much in the hands of the local governments.

But whoever thought that this was the intention of the legislators was mistaken. Apparently, their intention was not to minimize the problem but to expand it, and soon to generalize it.

---

22. M. D. van Otterloo, *Bijdrage ter toelichting der Schoolkwestie* (Amsterdam: Höveker & Zoon, 1874).

23. *Note by the author:* A list of unmentionables: names and words that should not be uttered.

Since they considered it beneath themselves to fend off the danger only where it was actually present, their arrogance brought them to locate the problem where it did not exist and to first create this thorny problem so that subsequently they might show their skills in dealing with such a threatening situation. They deliberately started a fire to show off the excellence of the extinguisher. Even where the walls were moist, the floor laid in stone, and the beams made of iron, the assumption still had to be that there was a fire, so as to render extinguishers indispensable. The danger of fire was declared to be permanent. *"Put out the fire of religious conflict!"* became the slogan of the masses.

All this served to label the mixed school as the "national" school, even in regions where there was no mixed population. One local policeman, of indifferent persuasion, with or without children, was a convenient figure for these municipalities. It saved the fiction of [needing] a mixed school for an unmixed population.

The result was adherence to an abstract theory and a deliberate ignoring of reality. Instead of asking, What is the actual condition of the population in the Netherlands? they convinced themselves and others that the national law should be ready to handle every eventuality. Who could guarantee that Veluwe dwellers[24] might not sell their property to people from Limburg?[25] Was it not possible that Frieslanders[26] might migrate to the Meyerei?[27] Was there a law of the Medes and the Persians that guaranteed the continuation of the current situation? If not, should not the law provide for all possible situations?

Thus the starting point became the (thoroughly untrue) assumption that in all municipalities without exception, a mixed population was the norm and that therefore the public school had to be cast in the mold of a mixed school. The mixed nature of the population was no longer a problem but became a welcome tool to promote liberal plans. Our liberalism would have been lost without a mixed population in our country. To discover a few Jews and a handful of Roman Catholics in a municipality of six thousand to seven thousand people was for the enlightened local governments a veritable stroke of luck. Had they not been there, our liberals would have

24. That is, orthodox Protestants.
25. Limburg was a predominantly Roman Catholic area.
26. A Protestant region in the far north.
27. A Catholic region in the far south.

gladly spent a fortune to get them there. They were the bridgeheads of the entire system.

Thus there was a great difference between the intended and the pretended purposes. They pretended to protect the conscience of the minority; they intended to force the consciences of both minority and majority into the doctrinal straitjacket of modern ideas.

After all, these modern ideas had the advantage that they had not yet been formulated in a creed or catechism. They were still in the public domain and not claimed by any particular church. From the viewpoint of the school-law advocates, the conscience clause eventually came down to this, that the creed of one church was kept in check by the creeds of the others. And since only modernist thought escaped this balancing act, its view was to set the tone for our public education.

The outcome proves it. At the so-called mixed school, which was to be accessible to all, nobody feels at home except the modern Christian, nobody feels at ease but the modern Jew. In actuality, the mixed, common, public school is inaccessible for the believing Christian, be he Reformed, Roman Catholic, or Mennonite.

Throughout the Veluwe the mixed school does not exist, or exists in name only. Brabant and Limburg simply ignore abstractions; their public education is essentially Roman Catholic. In the big cities, the free school keeps the state school at a respectful distance. Thus the law misses its mark for the larger part of our country. Its tyranny only succeeds in that smaller part, where either the majority has lost all positive faith, or the mixed nature of the population supports the school-law theory.

Thus the conscience clause of Article 23 of the School Law, which appears to protect the conscience, serves in reality to violate the conscience. Under the motto of freedom of conviction, the actual freedom of conscience is being undermined in our country.

Is it too much to ask, even from the viewpoint of our opponents, that an end be made to this ambivalence? Would anyone consider it unfair if we demand that a legal conscience clause (1) protects not an imaginary conscience, but the actual conscience of a Dutch citizen; (2) protects this conscience only when it is in danger; and (3) allows that conscience to decide for itself whether it feels threatened?

RESPECT FOR THE IDEAS OF OTHERS

Our school law prescribes that teachers "refrain from teaching, doing, or permitting anything that is inconsistent with the respect due to the religious ideas of those who think differently."

Did ever a less felicitous sentence flow from the pen of our legislator? Analyze that sentence and see where it leads you!

"Those who think differently":[28] that does not refer to any church denomination or religious association, but to the mass of the nation taken as individuals insofar as they think differently from the teacher or one of the pupils entrusted to his care.

One may not offend these "others." Excellent. Anything that might make it impossible for these "others" to attend the school must be removed and resisted. Could it be any better? The public school must be accessible to all. In that school, no child of our nation may be subjected to religious offense.

Does the law actually guard against this unbearable evil? On the contrary: the school is organized in such a way that a significant part of the population would declare: "The public school is inaccessible for my children. They are being offended in what is most sacred to them."

"That is a pretext!" the school board responds. "Impossible. There is nothing here that can offend you. Your complaint is imaginary!"

If it is true that "when one's conscience comes into play one must acquiesce in what the other approves," then this is an adequate response.[29] But if one rejects this tyrannical idea the response is meaningless. One cannot consult about the question whether one is offended. The question whether one's conscience is offended can only be decided by the complainant.

But what does Article 23 do? It requires, not that you respect the conviction with which others adhere to their beliefs, but that you respect the ideas in which they choose to formulate those beliefs. That is to say, not the ideas of a publicly recognized religion, but the ideas of those "who think differently," even if those ideas have never been proclaimed or heard and are therefore unknown to you.

For the Roman Catholic, it is a religious idea that marriage is a sacrament linked to monogamy. But in our country there are also Mormons whose religious ideas reject monogamy as immoral. And now the demand is made that the Catholic should respect the religious idea of the Mormon,

---

28. Originally *andersdenkenden*, also translated as "those of other minds."

29. See G. Groen van Prinsterer, *Nederlandsche Gedachten*, Sept. 9, 1869, p. 29.

who thinks differently; and conversely, that the Mormon is to respect the religious idea of the Roman Catholic.

It is a religious idea for the Roman Catholic that the prince-bishop of Rome is the vicar of Christ on earth. Conversely, it is a religious idea of the Protestant that it is a sin to acknowledge the pope as the vicar of Christ. Yet these parties who "think differently" are required to respect each other's religious ideas.

On a certain street lives a father who learned from his modernist pastor that to worship Jesus Christ as God revealed in the flesh and to revere his death as an atoning sacrifice for the sins of the world is blatant idolatry and inhumane and immoral, in league with the cult of Moloch. Directly across the street lives a father who "thinks differently," who learned the "religious idea" from Scripture that "in Jesus Christ the divine fullness dwells bodily, and that there is no redemption apart from his blood." Both of these citizens are now supposed to have respect for a "religious idea" that each detests.

This demand is patently absurd.

One may require of everybody not to suspect but to respect the sincerity, conviction, and seriousness with which others express their beliefs about God and spiritual matters. Human society demands that people not question or curtail anyone's right to think differently than you do. When opposing what I consider to be an error, I may use only words or means that leave untouched another's free determination of his conviction.

That, and that alone, is the duty of Christian forbearance. The right of a man to be master of his religious conviction may never be compromised; anything that would threaten this inalienable right, through force or financial pressure, through abuse of power, through mockery or ridicule, must be eradicated by every available means and permanently excluded.

But one cannot and may not demand respect for other people's *beliefs*. That would be a violation of the truth. That would be a fettering of the spirit. That would end in spiritual death.

And in point of fact, nobody harbors that respect. Those who "think differently" must, after all, be people who think; and how can someone who thinks not just tolerate what he thinks to be error but actually have respect for that error? The importance of truth makes such respect impossible. If our people and our country are to flourish, we must have an undiminished respect for the conviction with which someone professes his faith, but also an increase in the courage openly to combat what we consider error, without the slightest respect for it.

There is but one exception. When meeting with people for whom is sacred what I consider error I am forbidden to use the occasion to combat their error unless the intent of our meeting is the discussion of religious truth. And in case such an occasion should arise unintentionally, in such a way that prolonged silence on my part might create the impression that I support the error, I must confine myself to a polite and dignified expression of my own conviction.

Thus we must distinguish between two things that are confused in the school law.

First, it belongs to proper education to impress on every child respect for the right of every man to be master of his conviction. This is the virtue of Christian forbearance. It must be taught in every sphere of life, in every household, in every school, mixed or religious, state or free.

Second, it is the demand of love that I in the presence of others do not misuse the fact that they happen to be present by bringing up the points of conflict between their religious beliefs and mine; or, if my silence should send the wrong message, that I must leave unimpeded the respect I owe their personal presence and personal sentiments. This is especially important with children. Religious squabbles murder the sense of piety in a child's heart.

It follows that this respect cannot exist if no people are present who hold to different beliefs. Silence can therefore not be demanded in schools where all children are together in the same spirit. But this demand must be strictly enforced where others are present; misplaced zeal for one's religion (or antireligion) would deny the very nature of religion and damage a child's heart.

Article 23 of our School Law, confusing these two requirements, contradicts itself and is either unfeasible or immoral. Even from the perspective of our school-law advocates, it is our duty to remove this impropriety.

GETTING YOUR MONEY'S WORTH

People attribute to us the absurd idea that the nation should sacrifice millions of guilders for education without having any guarantee that it will receive high-quality education for that money.

This allegation is unfounded. To begin with, one must not gratuitously put absurdities on the lips of one's opponent. "Getting your money's worth" is a virtuous Dutch expression, and if you were to propose the opposite in our good Netherlands, you would not escape ridicule.

But in the second place, neither the attitude of the Antirevolutionary Party in general nor that of *The Standard* in particular[30] leaves any doubt that we attach great value to adequate, truly instructive, excellent education.

Anticipating a future revision of the Constitution and for now taking our stand on the existing law in relation to the principle involved, we place the duty and the right of the government over against each other and arrive at the following result:

The duty of the government is (1) to ensure that public education in our nation does not fall below the level in other nations, (2) to ensure that the pursuit of education does not become the privilege of the richer classes now that the costs of education have become higher relative to the financial ability of parents, and (3) to ensure that freedom of conscience is protected also in the field of education.

On the other hand, the government has the right to require a guarantee (1) that all have the opportunity to get an education, (2) that all instruction attains and maintains the necessary quality, (3) that school facilities do not jeopardize public health, and (4) that nobody's conscience is offended.

As for point 2, it is clear that the stipulations of the current law are too weak. Properly viewed, the government currently has no guarantee in this respect other than the teacher's certificate. That guarantee must be strengthened by extending to all primary schools the requirement that a certain minimum of subjects must be taught, and either that all of these are liable to inspection, or (in English style) that there is voluntary inspection in the place of subjecting the pupils to examinations. Note well: the financial issue is not in view here. Even if a school board were to refuse any restitution monies, it must still guarantee quality of instruction in its school.

Our schools have never been afraid of that requirement. We have always welcomed the visits of school inspectors. If you wish to interview our children to ascertain whether they are receiving a good education, your wish will only provide us with a welcome opportunity to display the viability of our schools. Indeed, let them come as often as they wish in order to convince themselves that in our schools the quality of reading, writing, and arithmetic, or the knowledge of science, geography, and history is at an adequate level. That would be fine with us. A poor school is best closed down. And if a poor school is flying a Christian flag we would be the first to wish its closure.

30. Kuyper's daily newspaper.

Only, school inspection must remain within its natural limits. In no way should it involve itself in the moral or religious training at the school, or in the spirit in which the instruction is given. It must limit itself to judging whether our schools produce results at least as good as the state school, minus its Kantian deism and its doctrine of moral autonomy.

That guarantee must be given to the nation by each and every school. Not in a system of subsidies, where the freedom and independence of the school are sold for a certain allowance, but as a requirement that must be met by any school in our country that wants to be accredited as a school. It matters not whether it rejects or accepts restitution monies. Monetary power may not extend a privilege of maintaining a school that is inferior and should not see the light of day.

And yet, that is the foundation of that system of subsidies that we reject. In that system, the needy school is forced to meet a certain standard, but the school that needs no money may be as inferior as it wants to be. That is demoralizing. It demoralizes the school that receives aid, since it is publicly humiliated. And it demoralizes the school that provides for itself, because it need not be concerned about compliance with any standard.

The system of restitution that we propose does not have a shred of this. It precludes any government involvement in the internal affairs of the school, its financial government, the hiring of teachers, the pedagogical tenor, and the spirit of the school. The school that receives restitution of the money it has advanced is not subjected to any humiliating condition that would not apply equally to all schools. There is no reason to brand a school as needy.

Meanwhile, the nation requires sufficient guarantee that its primary education is excellent; that all inferior schools will disappear; that the freedom of conscience of pupils and parents will be respected; and that we avoid, nay render impossible, that wretched arbitrariness by which meddlesome authorities so easily crush the free school under the thumb-screws of a system of subsidies.

WHAT IS AT STAKE?

The antirevolutionary movement has always opposed the state school because it is a school of the state,[31] and the state can neither educate (in

31. Kuyper's predecessor as leader of the antirevolutionary movement, Groen van Prinsterer, for the longest time actually favored a Christian public school, while allowing for a local option of separation into a school for Protestants and a school

the higher sense of the word) nor rear a child.[32] We have always allowed that if private initiative in starting and operating schools is insufficient or temporarily absent, the state must step in and take action,[33] and for that reason and to that extent the state school is welcome—albeit as a "necessary evil." We have candidly declared: the state school is necessary as a *supplement* to the private school.

In our view, a revision of the Constitution was not meant to incorporate in Article 194 any system that we favor, but solely to remove from it the untenable and fundamentally objectionable system of the party of 1857. We, too, took into account the need of that moment, and we certainly did not immediately want to render the state inactive.

Our concern was only with the principle. Our Constitution cannot truly be called Dutch as long as it contains as a principle the curtailing of education and the subordination of people's conscience to state interests. That protest continues. It will not be silenced unless the antirevolutionary movement dies out or flees the country.

Those who know the lay of our land cannot fail to see it: we will strive ceaselessly to remove the French system from our Constitution and replace it with Dutch principles. It is therefore foolish to try to convince the nation that Mr. Groen van Prinsterer should have abandoned this program. Rather, Groen, and we with him, maintain this firm demand without wavering, especially in the matter of education. "Any adequate guarantee of freedom of conscience in the matter of education"—we say today as we said in 1869—"must be preceded by a revision of Article 194 of the Constitution!"

But now note the second question: What will you do as long as you do not receive the guarantee of a constitutional revision?

In 1869 our movement responded: We must first ask for a change in Articles 23, 24, and 33.

---

for Catholics. Only when this proved politically unattainable did he switch to supporting the movement for free and independent Christian schools.

32. This was actually the argument of Groen's former friend turned political opponent, Minister Justinus van der Brugghen (1804–63), the sponsor of the School Act of 1857. To be sure, the education bill he tabled in Parliament did contain a clause that made private schools eligible for some funding from local governments; however, when a motion to remove this clause was tabled, Van der Brugghen did not defend it but acquiesced when the Chamber passed the motion.

33. This was the position of liberal leader Johan Rudolph Thorbecke, without, however, including a provision for equal funding of private and public schools.

In 1873 we responded: We shall do nothing of the kind. Nothing, because the opposition will not even grant us that minimum. Nothing, because the opposition will brush us off with an empty promise. Nothing, because the state school, however powerful, is still not powerful enough to force the breath out of our lungs. Our response therefore was instead: We must demand that constitutional revision immediately. Immediate revision of Article 194 must be our goal, without stopping halfway.

But not anymore, says Groen today. He abandoned that position and let go of that idea. Why? Because some of his followers had blunted the point by turning his cry of conscience into a political squabble.

And also because the situation has changed significantly since 1873, in three respects.

1. Under the leadership of Messrs. Moens and Kerdijk, the hold of the state school will be outfitted with a new engine of far greater horsepower, capable of ramming our school into the ground at the first attempt.

2. As a result of the expansion of tuition-free public schools and the dearth of teaching personnel for our private schools which has raised our operating costs, Christian schools now find themselves in a very precarious situation.

3. Today we may possibly achieve what is anything but a "minimum" or an "empty promise," and we may advance much further than our provisional demands ever did.

No one should therefore fancy that if our demand [to amend the school law] is honored, our battle against the un-Dutch element in our Constitution is over. That battle hardly plays a role here. Even if gold would flow to us like a river, that battle would continue undiminished—for the sake of our heritage; for the sake of our national identity; for the sake of performing what is our duty; for the sake of justice.

In the meantime the question is only this: How shall we fend off the fierce, rash attack by which Messrs. Moens and Kerdijk attempt to rob us of what little we still have? How are we to survive? That is not a political question but a cry for self-preservation.

Everyone has the right to raise that cry. Also the nonvoter, the disenfranchised.[34] The mother at least as much as the father. The humble peasant no less than the clever lawyer.

In a certain respect we are indifferent as to how any changes will be organized and implemented, so long as the improvement of education is not sacrificed to the interest of our schools, and our schools are not sacrificed to the improvement of education. Beyond this, we do not care about the form.

The liberal press has itself acknowledged that "any improvement of the state school will disadvantage the position of the private school." So liberals admit openly that it will worsen our situation. Nothing would please us more if they know a better remedy than what we have offered. We ask only one thing: let go of that harsh, uncompassionate attitude. Do not write, as *Het Vaderland* did: "Your situation will be worse, but that is inevitable!" One does not write about one's fellow citizens in that manner.

The monies that support the state school and those that support the private school eventually come from the same source, the national treasury. There lies the difficulty. For a nation naturally has only a limited number of millions available for education. Make that number as large as you like; even so, there is obviously a limit.

Thus far the state school has extracted such a disproportionate sum that only a very modest amount was left for the Christian school. Any change would therefore have to start by leaving more room for the less endowed school to spread its roots.

But now that this is impossible, now that the state school needs to exact more money than before if it is to hold its own, now even a child can understand that the free school is close to fading away—unless either the plans to improve the state school are shelved, or the sluice is opened whereby the water level would automatically rise on our side.

Can such a sluice be found in any other way than through restitution?

34. In 1875 only a little over 10 percent of males over twenty-three had the vote based on one's tax bracket. Universal suffrage was not introduced in the Netherlands until much later: in 1917 for men, in 1919 for women also.

SPEECHES AS A MEMBER OF PARLIAMENT

TEXT INTRODUCTION

As a member of the Second Chamber or Lower House in the Dutch Parliament, Kuyper spoke on a variety of subjects, but chief among them was always the school question. In his first term he pressed the issue hard. He had the moral support of a small number of members sympathetic to antirevolutionary principles, but on the whole Kuyper was a lone fighter. When first elected, Groen van Prinsterer (1801–76) had cautioned him to go easy on his fellow politicians,[1] but Kuyper could not help himself: too often he spoke like a pulpit orator. He studied deep into the night to master the details of legislative bills and did not hesitate to display his knowledge on the floor of the House. It didn't help that as a rookie parliamentarian he was roundly laughed at when he asked the government to draft a labor code to protect the working classes. His first term ended in complete nervous exhaustion and collapse.

By the time he returned to take a seat in Parliament in 1894, the situation had changed: he had helped organize the Antirevolutionary Party with a well-articulated program and had achieved a unified caucus and cooperation with the Catholic members. This enabled him to insist outright on

1. "You have always coupled your decisiveness with rare circumspection. *Qui va plano va sano* [slow and steady wins the race]. You know our nation. As long as you do not *effaroucher* [startle, shock, scare] it, it is quite capable of being galvanized for the highest interests of the land." Prinsterer to Kuyper, Feb. 5, 1874, in G. Groen van Prinsterer, *Briefwisseling* (The Hague: Nijhoff and Instituut voor Nederlands Geschiedenis, 1992), 6:506.

a complete revision of the national education system. Significant steps toward parity treatment of public and private schools were made during the Kuyper Ministry of 1901–5, and the eighty-year-long school struggle finally came to an end in the Pacification of 1917, taking effect in 1920.

Sources: Kuyper, Abraham. *Eenige Kameradviezen uit de jaren 1874 en 1875*. Amsterdam: Wormser, 1890. Kuyper, Abraham. *Parlementaire Redevoeringen. Deel I: Kameradviezen*. Amsterdam: Van Holkema & Warendorf, [1908]. Extracted, edited, and abridged by Harry Van Dyke.

SPEECHES AS A MEMBER OF PARLIAMENT

1874–1877; 1894–1901

MAY 14, 1875

The great founder of the liberal party in our country, Mr. Thorbecke,[2] was of the view that the state must never constitute itself the provider of education but act only where private initiative is wanting. Today's liberals have abandoned this position in favor of using millions upon millions from the public coffers to improve the public school by hiring more teachers and reducing class size, increasing salaries and expanding facilities, establishing new teachers' colleges, and so on and so forth—all to make the public

2. Johan Rudolph Thorbecke (1798–1872) was the primary drafter of the 1848 revision of the Dutch Constitution, which expanded civil liberties and the scope of authority of the States General.

school so strong as to make all competition from private schools impossible. When a member on this side of the Chamber pleaded for religion as part of the curriculum in the public schools of Java, the minister of the colonies replied: "In my opinion the best way, the only way, to combat error is enlightenment." Small wonder we are uneasy about the intentions of this government with respect to education.

The schools question is the greatest political question this country faces. As representatives of the people, we have a right to know where this government is taking us. What is its guiding idea? At a recent revival meeting in England I heard Mr. Sankey[3] sing:

Dare to be a straight-out man,
Dare to stand alone,
Dare to have a purpose firm,
Dare to make it known.

It summarizes my entire interpellation of this government. I stress the last line. Do not just have a strategy, but also *dare to make it known!* Do you intend to introduce a revision of the Primary Education Act that will enlarge the financial position of the public school to a considerable degree without at the same time offering us a *modus vivendi* of sorts in order that private schools will be able to survive: Yes or no?

Mr. Chairman, the minister has just now answered neither yes nor no. His Excellency says he wants to leave open the question whether, and if so how, the conscientious objections of private-school supporters can be met, but on the other hand he assures the Chamber that the basic concept of the public school will be maintained and that his government will not accept the system of restitution.

DECEMBER 13, 1875

A revision of the Primary Education Act, Mr. Chairman, must not be delayed any longer. Our nation lags behind other nations. The pedagogical element

3. Ira David Sankey (1840–1908) was a renowned American gospel singer. He made numerous trips to the United Kingdom with the evangelist D. L. Moody (1837–99), including one in 1874.

tends to be lost sight of. Nor has our nation made any moral progress since 1857, when the common school was mandated to teach "Christian and civic virtues": one need only look at the statistics of alcohol abuse, the swelling population of our penitentiaries, the proliferation of alehouses and asylums. The common school has not contributed to greater tolerance; it has instead inflamed party passions. History lessons at school have to be ever so circumspect: instead of presenting our nation's past as an epic about heroism, they feed our children a bland version that offends neither Protestant nor Catholic.

Every support in our contest with the public treasury, one after the other, has been taken away from us, and our freedom to act in the area of education has more and more been curtailed. The most elementary rights of our fellow countrymen are trodden underfoot. The suppression of conscientious scruples continues unabated, not so much of the well-to-do who have the means to have their children educated as they desire, but of the poor, the weak, the wretched, who under this law have no choice but to rely on charity to have private schools for their children.

I do not imply that primary education is a cure-all. By no means. Even if every child could read and write, the ills of our society would not disappear overnight. Studies have shown that the Chinese laborers in Virginia and the Chinese railroad workers in California can all read and write. But literacy alone is not enough; much more is needed. The slogan "Build schools and close the jails" has disappointed; criminality is only increasing. As English observers have noted: "That mere schooling can ever hope to abate the evil of juvenile crime is in our opinion a fallacy of the most dangerous nature" (Henry Mayhew). True education is delivered "not by the schoolmaster, but a Divine Spirit" (Frederick Maurice). And "reading and writing is no more knowledge than a knife and fork is a good dinner" (Cooke Taylor). Exactly! Education is an instrument with which one feeds oneself; it is not the food itself.

Nevertheless, antirevolutionaries will always have the interests of education at heart. After all, it was the Puritans, our spiritual ancestors, who were the first to contend for intellectual development also through schools. When the Reformation had come to Holland, the first concern of the synod of the Dutch Reformed Church was to establish good schools everywhere.

Mr. Chairman, nine of us in this Chamber have finally decided to use our right of initiative and before long submit a bill to revise the Act of 1857. We have never believed in the repeated claim that "the nation is attached to the common, religiously neutral school." Private schools, the more they were suppressed the more they grew. Attachment to the government schools, I dare say, is for a large part due to the financial advantage enjoyed by the parents who use it.

DECEMBER 8, 1896

Allow me to enumerate, Mr. Chairman, what we desire in the matter of private higher education.

1. That the automatic *effectus civilis*[4] of public university degrees be canceled and that henceforth the government itself examine candidates, from whatever university, to see whether they are fit for public office.
2. That private colleges and private gymnasia[5] have free use, besides libraries, of the laboratories.
3. That students of private schools be eligible for government bursaries.
4. That private gymnasia be given the right to confer accredited diplomas that give entry to the universities.
5. That private gymnasia receive public funding at a rate equal to that of the public gymnasia.

Our independent gymnasia have 1,746 pupils, the public ones 2,500. Only the latter receive public funding. If I place my son at a public gymnasium I benefit from 350 guilders in government subsidies, but if he attends a private gymnasium I fall financially outside the law and am left in the cold as far as equality before the law is concerned.

It must not remain the rule in our country that all those who wish to follow Christ also in education are discriminated against, in favor of those who do not follow him.

---

4. A degree with *effectus civilis* qualified its holders to become registered attorneys and justices or to serve as teachers of the classical languages in the public gymnasia. This access to public offices was denied for the longest times to graduates of Christian educational institutions.
5. *Gymnasia*: university prep schools.

DECEMBER 10, 1897

I concur completely with the opposition that primary education is not in the same category as higher education. In the latter, in fact, the wedge of principle *cuts even deeper*. The recent elections have shown that our nation consists of almost two equal halves, divided by two incompatible worldviews. Leading spokesmen of the liberals are correct when they say that we for our part believe in a *special revelation* and bow to it, whereas they, when it comes to things of this world—I am not talking about their personal relation to the Eternal One—do not accept this authority but on the contrary reject it and oppose it with *human reason*. To be sure, each camp harbors factions that disagree among each other on this or that point; but no sooner does an issue come to a head and touch on the fundamental principle, than the two sides of the nation stand as one man opposed to another. I believe the government must not take sides but allow these two forces to grapple in the bosom of the nation.

It is one of the achievements of our time that freedom of thought has become more and more dominant in country after country. My question to members opposite is: Will you not grant us the benefit of that freedom in the field of higher education?

Thus far we have not had that benefit. The opposition lives by the fiction that there is but one science and whoever disagrees with it is an obscurantist. But a fiction breaks up when it meets with the facts. The fact is that every branch of learning has different schools. Theologians are either orthodox or modernist. Criminology is divided over determinism or indeterminism. The historical accounts of Groen, Fruin, and Nuyens are anything but the same. The philosophy that Bolland teaches in Leiden differs not a little from that taught by Spruyt in Amsterdam. And in the natural sciences, Christian professors believe in God the Creator whereas other professors in the same department are evolutionists. How can people persist in the fiction that there is always only one science, established and absolute? Yet when we plead for a Christian university we are told, "You are out of touch with science." Is it right and is it fair, Mr. Chairman, that higher education in this country, which is paid for by both halves of the nation, exists only for the benefit of one?

MARCH 2, 1900

I fear I cannot cast my vote for compulsory school attendance. The idea dates from the Revolution, from a Danton who stated in France's National

Assembly: "We must reestablish the grand principle that children belong to the Republic before they belong to their parents."[6] "Reestablish," he said; he wanted to go back to the pre-Christian era! Of course good Hollanders do not easily descend to such extravagances, yet this is the seed which we imported in 1799 and has now germinated in the bill that is before us.[7] Just because primary education is *in the interest of the child* does not give the state the right to impose it by law. Child-rearing is first of all a parental task. Parents must stand for it. Their home is their castle. Theirs is the moral responsibility. To be sure, they may fail, and the result can be a wretched home life. But can the minister really do anything about that?

His Excellency has said that compulsory school attendance is also *in the interest of the state*. But if the state intervenes every time its interests are involved, then the citizen has no rights except by permission of the state. The enjoyment of his rights that inhere in his person and in the sphere of his home will depend each time on the government in power.

We will therefore vote against every article in this bill, Mr. Chairman, and support only such amendments that will reduce the evil to smaller proportions. If the government by means of this bill wants to combat absenteeism in primary education, it should put an end to the school struggle and enable all parents, of whatever beliefs, to send their children to a school of their choice without financial penalty.

MAY 2, 1901

The government promised this Chamber that it would compensate the private schools for the financial consequences of making attendance compulsory. ... Since then, Mr. Chairman, I have discovered that the minister's arithmetic is wanting. When I went over his figures for increasing salaries, hiring more teachers, enlarging school facilities or building new ones, I found that the costs of maintaining private schools have actually increased,

---

6. Stated by Georges Danton (1759–94) in the National Convention on December 12, 1793, during the debate about compulsory attendance of the public schools.
7. In 1795 a revolution ended the Dutch Republic and replaced the old regime with an administration modeled on the revolutionary government in France. After some years a new constitution installed a central government with departments headed by eight agents, one of which was the agent for national education. This agent was given supreme oversight throughout the land of all schools of higher and elementary education, all libraries, medical laboratories, and all institutions and societies for the promotion of the arts and science.

and increased significantly. After subsidies, our schools still depend for the greater part on private donations. We have few capitalists among us; donations come largely from the common people. ... However, we will not act like beggars in this Chamber. What we want is a revision of the entire regulation of primary education so that it may at last become healthy.

SPEECHES AS PRIME MINISTER IN PARLIAMENT

TEXT INTRODUCTION

By the time the sixty-four-year-old Kuyper entered Parliament as head of the Protestant-Catholic coalition government, he was a well-seasoned politician confirmed in his mastery of the thrust and parry on the floor of both Houses and supremely confident in his ability to steer his legislative program into law. Could he finally achieve the vaunted social legislation supported by the parties of the right?[1] Taking the department of Interior Affairs, he oversaw the preparation of a number of promising bills on a national pension scheme; national insurance programs for sickness, unemployment, and old age; maximum hours acts; collective bargaining regulations; and public health provisions, as well as a law promoting Sunday observance. However, these bills remained on the Order Paper when his administration suffered electoral defeat after four years in office as the result of a hard-fought campaign conducted by the parties of the left that focused chiefly on the person of the prime minister.[2]

Kuyper's signal achievement, however, apart from a Liquor Law and a Lottery Act, was in the area of education. Both a revised Elementary

1. Kuyper led a coalition of the right: thirty-three Calvinists and twenty-five Catholics, both conservatives and progressives, for a total of fifty-eight seats in the Second Chamber. The remaining forty-two seats were held by the political left: thirty-five Liberals, both old-school conservatives and secular progressives, and seven socialists.
2. The vitriolic nature of the 1905 campaign as conducted by the parties of the left is described colorfully but not unfairly in the popular biography by Frank Vanden Berg, *Abraham Kuyper* (Grand Rapids: Eerdmans, 1960), 255.

Education Act and an amended Higher Education Act garnered a majority vote and received royal assent. The law pertaining to primary schools created greater[3] financial equality between the two systems, public and private, and regulated teacher contracts. The law for universities finally gave *effectus civilis* to degrees from the Free University and also upgraded existing schools to create an Agricultural College in Wageningen, a School of Economics in Rotterdam, and a Technological University in Delft.

As he defended these bills, Kuyper was in full command of his intellectual powers and of the minutest legislative details. Many of his speeches cover half a dozen pages in the published proceedings. The nastiest opponents he at times addressed in a tone of righteous indignation or withering scorn. Yet he could also be conciliatory, acting the statesman who could strike notes of accommodation and good will, as the last extract below will show.

The selection includes the text of a few printed memoranda that are customarily exchanged between government and Parliament and which elucidate the government's intentions.

Source: Kuyper, Abraham. *Parlementaire Redevoeringen. Deel II–IV*. Amsterdam: Van Holkema & Warendorf, [1909–12]. Extracted, edited, and abridged by Harry Van Dyke.

3. Earlier, in 1889, Aeneas Mackay Jr. (1838–1909), leader of the first coalition cabinet of the Right, had sponsored an education act that made Christian schools eligible for a subsidy from the national government in an amount commensurate with the subsidy enjoyed by public schools; it also mandated public schools, which were mostly funded by local government, to charge tuition fees in order to remove an unfair advantage over private schools. The Act of 1889 marked a victory, at least in principle, for equality before the law of private schools alongside public schools. The Act of 1905 went further: it provided that the salaries and pensions for all teachers, in public and private schools, would be paid from the national treasury.

SPEECHES AS PRIME MINISTER IN PARLIAMENT

1901–1905

SPEECHES IN THE FIRST CHAMBER OR UPPER HOUSE

January 30, 1903

Mr. Chairman, the grave difficulties we face in the area of education also in our country stem chiefly from the fact that the nineteenth century began with a more-or-less-unified worldview so that all of education was organized in the same spirit. Understandably, when this unity began to erode, people tried to preserve it by reaffirming it or where necessary restoring it. In the meantime it has become clear that this unity of worldview is beyond recall. At every point it has fractured. We have to do with two basic worldviews that sharply oppose each other. That being so, the power of the state must not be used in favor of one of them. The contest between the worldviews must be decided in a free grappling of the spirits—provided the conditions of the tournament are equal—so that at last both sides clear the air and make it possible to reach a compromise, a certain modus vivendi that satisfies both sides. I believe we have begun to arrive at such a happy modus vivendi in the area of primary education and will eventually be able to complete it. The more we work in this direction the more we will attain peace in every area of our national life and the more we will promote the interest of education in all its branches.

February 1, 1905

The honorable senator from Friesland has the courage of his convictions. In an article with the title "The Right of the Majority," Mr. Van Houten[4] states, and I quote: "With the weapons of mind and spirit we are today engaged in a conflict over principles which is fiercer than at any other time in our history and which goes much deeper than that between Catholics and Protestants. It is not a conflict about certain dogmas but a clash between faith and unbelief. ... The illusion that this ferment can be kept out of politics is over."

Again, the late Professor Buys[5] wrote as early as 1869 that the school struggle is only a symbol of this conflict. Even if this symbol were somehow brought to an end, he wrote, "the struggle will continue, just as fiercely, and with new demands. And an extension of the franchise will not weaken the struggle but only increase its vehemence." The franchise was extended, and it completely vindicated Buys, except in one respect: in those days members like myself were subjected to bitter invectives, even personal insults, but today, though still diametrically opposed on the question, we treat each other with civility.

Meanwhile, Mr. Chairman, the honorable member tells us that we owe this civility not to Catholicism nor to Calvinism but to the Revolution. I beg to differ. As early as 1644 Goodwin, a true Calvinist, wrote: "We must have full liberty of conscience for all sects, even Turks, Jews and Papists."[6] Another author in that century wrote: "Religious persecution is spiritual

---

4. Samuel van Houten (1837–1930) was a member of the Liberal party who had served as minister of the interior from 1894–97 and later was in the Senate for Friesland from 1904–7.
5. J. T. Buys (1826–93) was a professor of law in the University of Leiden.
6. John Goodwin (1594–1665) was an English puritan preacher and a zealous advocate for expansive toleration.

murder, an assassination of the soul; it is raging against God himself, the most horrible of sins."[7] As for the French Revolution, the Christians were dealt with in the cruelest fashion during the September massacres. And when the Revolution came to our country and deployed its principles, not everything was sweet and light. One of our leading liberals has concluded that "the Christian parties on their standpoint have reason to complain about the tyranny of the liberal party which seeks to force upon them an education system that favors the sect of modernism under the deceptive slogan, 'with full respect for everyone's religious ideas.'"[8] And a modernist preacher stated recently: "Our education system has become untenable. We must have equality before the law. Not government supremacy, but government care. Even from a pedagogical standpoint we should not push the neutral school. How can a teacher nurture and form character and at the same time be neutral? In religious matters, too, neutrality is undesirable. If we want religion—God in us and we in God—then the education that is religiously neutral is a plague, a cancer."

February 1, 1905

Mr. Van Houten objects, Mr. Chairman, that our Higher Education Bill is "illegal" on the ground that the state cannot delegate its degree-granting control to a free university. But surely he knows that most universities, especially the great and prestigious ones, arose as free universities and were nevertheless given the right to grant degrees. He must know that there was once a London University that held no classes but was an association of examining scholars who as such had the right to confer degrees. Thus I think I am in good company, given that those authorities of the thirteenth and fourteenth century, too, were good legal scholars.

February 1, 1905

Mr. Van Houten and I appear to disagree very little on the meaning of *justice*, but not on what *freedom* means. His freedom leads only to state tyranny. He wants the government to operate schools that teach young people to

---

7. Kuyper refers here to an anonymously published treatise, *Liberty of conscience asserted. Or, persecution for religion condemned; by the lawes of God, nature, reason. Published by a Well-wisher to the kingdomes good* (London: Printed for R. A., 1649), 3.
8. Attributed to Allard Pierson (1831–96), a professor of art, aesthetics, and modern language at the University of Amsterdam.

practice critical thinking even if it goes against their faith. In other words, it is to be a school that satisfies Mr. Van Houten and his like-minded friends and with which all who think like him are content. That school, he says, must be financed from the public treasury, hence must receive favored treatment, because that is the only real school. Everybody else has full freedom to establish other schools, provided they do not ask for money from the public treasury. You are entirely free, but you will have to pay for it yourself. Thus the honorable member first takes [through taxes] from the purse of those who do not support public education the money needed for the government schools that he supports, and when the nonsupporters have spent all they could on education he says to them: "Now that I have pumped you dry you are welcome to establish schools with your own money."

That is not what I understand by freedom. As a minister of the Crown I refuse to endorse for one minute the view that one citizen can claim more rights than another. I do not wish in the least to abridge the rights of Mr. Van Houten and his adherents. I desire no special privilege for myself and my adherents. But what has to stop in this land is that there is a political party that says: we and our adherents are entitled to all the benefits of the public treasury, and those who do not agree with us will just have to wander about in the wilderness and live off wild honey and grasshoppers. That leads to dividing our people into two parts: one part that lives off the state, the lucky ones, and another part that is deprived, left out. There must be equality in the country, both for those who hold to the Christian and for those who hold to the modernist worldview.

February 2, 1905

Is it true what has been alleged here, that pastors and priests sometimes exert undue pressure in people's choice of school? That all depends. When a peasant sends his children to the public school in the village because he has been told by the headmaster that this is the best school and that it poses no danger to the children's faith, then that peasant is not always able to judge. And when the pastor pays him a visit and makes clear to him that he has been misled and that the instruction at the school does endanger the faith of his children, with the result that the man pulls his children from the public school, then no one should condemn this clergyman, for then he has done a good work, the same work that a liberal member performs when in the interest of raising their awareness he explains to less educated people what their interests are. Is this "undue pressure by clerics"? These men are only clarifying what look like unclear and muddy opinions to the people whom they are called to provide with information that is reliable.

February 2, 1905

Our Higher Education bill authorizes the government to declare graduates from a private university eligible for holding certain public offices. It could have stipulated more broadly: from whatever school. But then the natural effect would be that if persons applied for such posts while presenting a worthless degree from a nonaccredited institution, such applicants would be passed over. It is well known that several institutions in Chicago have learned this to their detriment. Does a sound and generous reading of Article 169 of the Constitution not require what we propose? That article states that no one may be excluded from any public office on grounds of his religious convictions. Now if the government were to continue to make eligibility depend on passing examinations in the public universities, and if several categories of people by reason of their religious convictions could not meet those demands, would that not amount to indirect pressure, would that not be a form of religious discrimination?

May 19, 1905

The honorable member has attacked one of my children by saying that appointments at the Free University are governed by nepotism. It is true, my son [Herman] was appointed there. But that does not give him the right to cast a slur on my son, as if he was not appointed for his scholarly qualities but because he was my son. The honorable member may insult me here as much as he wants, but he has to keep his hands off my children.

May 19, 1905

Our Higher Education bill seeks to provide liberty. It combats a monopoly that obtains in this country. That is the heart of the issue. As long as our population was happy with the way higher education was organized, there was no monopoly, because there was no competition. But as soon as a movement arose in the country that wished to establish other than public universities, the existing rules granting certain rights only to the public universities became an odious monopoly.

I believe I may safely assume that all members agree that higher education is *not* a natural task of the government. The liberal government leader Mr. Thorbecke said on November 24, 1852: "A country with only private schools might well thrive. Education is not a task of government. Government has to provide public education only because private persons usually fail in this task." In other words, private education should be the rule, public education the supplement. Is that so unthinkable? I point to the United States, where schools such as Harvard, Yale, Brown, Princeton, and so on represent a type of confessional school. James Bryce writes in his work *The American Commonwealth*: "Harvard retains a certain flavor of Unitarianism, ... Yale has always been Congregationalist, ... Princeton is still more specifically Presbyterian."[9] Granted, there are neutral schools as well, for example in Ann Arbor, Michigan, and in other states, especially in the West. But Bryce observes: "In all the older universities and in the vast majority of the more recent ones there is a chapel in which religious services are regularly held, short prayers on the five weekdays, ... and in most institutions every student, unless of course he has some conscientious objection, is expected to attend."[10] Moreover, Bryce notes that these different schools are not at all hostile toward one another; rather, there is good harmony among these universities and among their professors and students, despite the diverging beliefs.

That is what Calvinism has brought about in America. It did not fear liberty. There, private universities of the first order were erected independently from the state, to which nothing in our country can compare. There is a wide choice of universities. No one complains, and the narrowly defined nature of the schools is coupled with the greatest lenience and tolerance. I had the privilege of staying on the campus of Princeton for several weeks and was able to satisfy myself on the one hand that the Presbyterian character of the school was upheld and on the other that a broad conception of scholarship and warm relations obtained between professors and students of divergent views.

July 14, 1903

I have visited several academies in America, but I must say that the facilities and resources of our public universities cannot hold a candle to the facilities and resources such as observatories, laboratories, and so on of American universities that have not been established by the state. I do not

---

9. James Bryce, *The American Commonwealth* (London: Macmillan, 1888), 3:456.
10. Bryce, *American Commonwealth*, 3:457.

understand how anyone can maintain that higher education belongs to the sovereign rights of the state.

May 31, 1905

In 1875 Mr. Kappeyne[11] said in the Second Chamber that public education should be suffused with the modern worldview, and that if a minority in the land objected to the common public school "that minority will just have to be oppressed, for then it is the fly that spoils the ointment." Once minister, he sponsored the notorious Primary Education Act of 1878. I agree with the honorable member that Kappeyne was not a cruel man, eager to oppress the minority. He and I enjoyed a cordial relationship. But he held to a religion that is best described as the deification of the state. He believed sincerely that the power of the state should be used to lead the people according to the state's own principles. The state was for him the Moloch to which children could be sacrificed if need be. Thus with the best of intentions he became the father of the tyrannical law of 1878.

May 31, 1905

The honorable member points out that strictly speaking the Constitution does not grant the *right* to subsidies for private schools. In that he is correct. But when the question arises what is to count as *just and fair* among citizens of the same country, then it is only right that free citizens should not rule over the way of thinking of other citizens, and on that basis we may rightfully claim that if the state grants aid to one group of citizens it should compensate the other group as well.

May 31, 1905

The honorable member assumes that primary education is the responsibility of the government. We maintain that the first responsibility lies with the parents, not the government. Members opposite may not listen to me, but they likely will when I quote Thorbecke on the subject: "Other life-forces than that of the state must form and govern the church, education, science, and art. In these spheres the civil magistrate cannot give orders or compel. Education is not a task of government. The government has to provide public education only because private persons usually fail in this task."

---

11. Johannes Kappeyne van de Coppello (1822–95) was a liberal politician and prime minister of the Netherlands from 1877–79.

May 31, 1905

Mr. Van Houten honestly believes that the desire for private schools did not arise from any real need but was artificially stirred up. I have spent thirty years of my life in close contact with parents from the lower classes. I learned to appreciate the school in the village of my first charge as pastor, because its headmaster was a teacher to whom I personally owe a great deal. He was not only an uncompromising Christian, but he also worked very hard for any cause that promoted the kingdom of God. But he was one of the educators who began to see the dangers inherent in the spirit to which our primary education was exposed. Those dangers are hardly imaginary, and if I look back on the last twenty years I wonder whether members opposite still feel reassured about the spirit that has come to development in the public school. I believe I may say that not a few people (among whom are solid supporters of the public school) have not hesitated to declare that they are concerned about developments in public education. This too underscores the right of parents to desire a different school for their children.

One should not forget that many people are of the belief that when a child is raised apart from faith in Christ it suffers eternal harm. I do not ask whether all members of the Chamber think of it in this way, but it is the view of thousands upon thousands. To be forced to send one's child to a school where it will be nurtured in a spirit that is opposed to that of its parents is an evil that may no longer be perpetuated. The rich can afford to choose private schools, but the poor cannot. They too must have the opportunity to give their children an education that is in harmony with their basic convictions.

There is no neutral education that is not governed by a spirit of its own. And precisely that spirit of the religiously neutral school militates against every positive faith.

SPEECHES IN THE SECOND CHAMBER OR LOWER HOUSE

December 4, 1901

I wish to keep theology out of the debates in this Chamber. The history of Cromwell has given me such mortal fear of a bare-bones parliament, the "Parliament of Saints," that it will always be for me a shipwreck that serves as a beacon at sea. All the same, the red thread that has run through our discussions thus far is the question: Is there a connection between politics and religion? That all politics is indeed governed by faith or unbelief is the great truth, the great thought that has been expressed by Goethe in these words: "The single real and most profound theme of world history, to which all others are subordinated, is and remains the conflict between faith and unbelief." The honorable member for Emmen, Mr. Roessingh,[12] is correct when he thinks this conflict can be summarized in the antithesis between reason and revelation.

December 5, 1901

Members remind me that Gladstone[13] was an orthodox man but never mixed politics with religion. True enough, but that is precisely what I have always considered a big mistake in Gladstone, and the outcome has shown that when the Grand Old Man was gone his whole party went downhill and fell apart, with the result that the Liberal party in England finds itself in dire straits today.

We do not pretend to be a homogeneous cabinet. We are a broad coalition of the Christian parties, a cabinet on the basis of mutual accommodation. Whether we have a working majority and therefore make a viable government is not for us to say. That will be decided by this Chamber.

As for the secular parties opposite, there are three of them, two of which are divided over two factions. The liberals are divided over conservatives and progressives, the social democrats over the labor party and one independent socialist. Perhaps there are more; I don't know. Perhaps the gentlemen will undergo evolution—a concept they favor—and end up with dissolution.

As one learned observer has written: "The revision of the Constitution in 1887 brought about a broader electorate and broke the back of the liberal party. The Education Act of 1889 smashed its idol, the neutral government school, and took the first step toward the free school. This is a different freedom from what the liberals had set their sights on, a freedom of a higher order, one for which not they but the anti-revolutionaries fought a historic battle."

12. Petrus Hendrik Roessingh (1840–1916) was a pastor and liberal politician.
13. William Gladstone (1809–98) was a British liberal politician who served as prime minister for twelve years, from 1868–94.

What are our intentions with respect to a new Lord's Day Act? Mr. Tydeman,[14] the member for Tiel, need have no fear. Calvinists have never forbidden pleasures and amusements on Sunday that refresh mind and body and do not conflict with any divine commandment.

The first principles for the state are not taken from Holy Scripture but from those natural relations in life on which Scripture puts its stamp.

Ultimately, everything is concentrated in the question: Are the norms, the rules, the laws and ordinances of political, social, and domestic life governed by human will and approval or by a higher authority? I believe that in our legislative work the members on both sides of the Chamber will seek to apply the rule, "You shall love your neighbor as yourself" [Matt 22:39]. But the parties of the right will differentiate themselves from the parties of the left by the recognition that he who gave us this word first gave us the rule, "You shall love the Lord your God with all your mind and with all your strength. This is the *first* and the *great* commandment" [see Matt 22:37–38].

I much appreciate the loyal opposition promised by Mr. Borgesius,[15] the member for Zutphen and my predecessor in this office. But he will detect as little as possible of our Christian principles in the legislation we hope to introduce. Yet it will be there. It's just not our habit to serve up salt and potatoes separately; we boil them together, so that in the end one does not pick out the salt.

The member for Appingedam, Mr. Schaper,[16] has said that he and his fellow social democrats will *not* be a loyal opposition. But he mistakes loyal opposition for showing sympathy, rather than fighting with honest means only. ... Of course he meant the latter. But now he interrupts me and says: Our opposition will be *radical!* Good! That is exactly what I want: opposition that penetrates to the root of the question each time.

I have been asked, now that I have formed a government and bear the responsibility of governing, whether I have stowed away my democracy and put aside my love for social reform. I can only repeat what I said earlier. This Chamber has Christian democrats, liberal democrats, and social democrats, and I will always classify myself among the first group. But I will not

14. Meinard Tydeman Jr. (1854–1916) was a liberal politician who served in Parliament from 1891 until his death.

15. Hendrik Goeman Borgesius (1847–1917) was a liberal politician who served in the Second Chamber from 1877–1917.

16. Jan Schaper (1868–1934) was a journalist and socialist politician.

allow myself to be measured by what the gentlemen opposite understand by "democrat" and to be judged, if I do not measure up, not to be a democrat.

December 12, 1901

The honorable member for Goes, Mr. De Savornin Lohman,[17] has asked whether education must forever be linked to the government. Ideally, in the abstract, no. If the economic situation were such that all parents could afford to pay for the education of their children, then I do not see why citizens should have their freedom restricted any longer. But that is a long way off, perhaps a whole century. Meanwhile we have to reckon with reality. And therefore the provision of education rests with the government.

Mr. Tydeman has stated that subsidizing private *gymnasia* would be to go beyond what the law allows. I believe the law does not forbid it. There are seven such schools in the country, and I did consider putting them on our first budget, but I decided against it in order to give Parliament the opportunity to make a decision about it on the basis of principle. This cabinet wishes to observe the deference it owes to the Chamber, including the left.

December 13, 1901

The honorable member for Lochem, Mr. Helsdingen,[18] has asked whether I had received sufficient information about the incident in Arnhem, where the St. Vincent Society, a philanthropic organization, was prepared to give poor relief to a family on condition that the children of that family not attend the public school. My department has made inquiries and was cabled this morning that a letter was in the mail.

Mr. Ketelaar,[19] the member for Amsterdam District V, has drawn our attention to the recent Royal Decree stipulating requirements for private school buildings and has noted that they are less stringent than for public school facilities, while he thinks they should be the same. He should remember, however, that it is up to the parents or the boards of private schools, not the government, to provide hygienic facilities for the children. They don't measure up, he says, but that is easy for him to say: when the public school

---

17. Alexander Frederik de Savornin Lohman (1837–1924) was an antirevolutionary politician and member of Parliament from 1879–1921.
18. Willem Pieter Gerardus Helsdingen (1850–1921) was a socialist politician first elected to Parliament in 1901.
19. Theodore Matthieu Ketelaar (1864–1936) was a liberal politician and a fierce advocate of public education.

needs money it flows freely from the coffers of the municipal authorities or the central government. We, on the other hand, have to struggle to raise the money needed for our private schools. One should not conclude that we care less for the welfare of our children, but we are simply unable to do more.

December 6, 1902

The opposition evidently has a hard time understanding what a Christian government aims at. We aim to have laws enacted that are pervaded by the salt of the gospel. That would be a hopeless endeavor were it not for the fact that the old Christian traditions still exert a predominant influence in our political culture. The head of state still proclaims that she reigns by the grace of God. Every bill introduced in Parliament still begins with a prayer to the Almighty. The annual Speech from the Throne almost invariably speaks of our dependence on Providence. The state still honors the church of Christ in its various manifestations. The Christian holidays are still largely observed. Much of the Christian tradition lingers in the significance attached to marriage, parental authority, and public decency. Accordingly, the strength of Christianity in the bosom of the nation has proved so important that more than one cabinet, though leaning in an "anti-clerical" direction, in the end yielded on more than one point to the after-effect of the past. This fact helps explain why the much-feared antithesis[20] has not been so severe after all. This government is hopeful that it need not expect vehement opposition when already in this session it introduces proposals to increase the freedom of higher education.

As the honorable member for Amsterdam VII, Mr. Heemskerk,[21] has emphasized, what the parties of the right aim at is to terminate a situation in which one branch of education enjoys financial privileges as against a competing branch. Since the law [of 1889] accepts that public and private primary education in this country are equivalent, therefore it is only natural that a movement has arisen which will not come to a stop until the water levels in both polders are equal. This cabinet and the parties of the right are in complete agreement that the school struggle will not end until

20. Kuyper's emphasis for many years, in speech and in print, on the irreconcilable and nonnegotiable opposition or "antithesis" between the Christian and other worldviews had caused many to fear that once in government he would foster a spirit of division in the country.

21. Theo Heemskerk (1852–1932) was a leading antirevolutionary politician and later served as prime minister, from 1908–13.

it has attained its definitive resolution. That does not mean, however, that our wishes can be satisfied all at once. If the next election were to have a different result, a new government might feel justified in revoking all our legislative reforms. Such inconstancy would hardly contribute to the stability of our laws.[22]

DECEMBER 6, 1902

What is our aim? First, to ensure that the Christian part of our nation—I do not ask whether it is the majority or a minority—enjoys equal rights with the other parts; we wish to do this with respect to all three levels of education. Second, to check and if possible to break the demonic influences infecting our national life, such as alcohol abuse, gambling, public indecency, neo-Malthusianism,[23] pornography. Third, to shore up the Christian foundations that have historically existed in our country. And last, to prevent the workingman from being treated as an appendage of the machine and to counteract the enslavement of people to the power of money.

DECEMBER 9, 1902

The member for Appingedam, Mr. Schaper, spoke passionately yesterday about the class struggle that he and his party are determined to wage. Combine that with universal suffrage, and the social democrats are bound to try to gain the majority in both Chambers and then reform society in conformity with their ideal. Today he says not to worry, since wage earners will never form a majority, but allow me to make two comments. First, his party does not merely recruit among the working classes but also tries to win over teachers and other professionals. Secondly, Marxism has no other aim than to gain the majority for the proletariat and then have them do what they like with those who do not belong to the proletariat.

What is the Christian party to do in the face of this fact? Whoever confesses Christ and desires to help the oppressed and the wretched in the land is faced with this choice: Marx or Christ? This opposition is absolute, because Marx's historical materialism is an absolute, cosmological, all-encompassing system. Just as Christ governs the totality of things, so Marxism too seeks to control everything. It has made material things the main issue of human existence, and it regards all other relations in life as

22. From the memorandum of response, fall 1902.
23. That is, contraception.

arising from economic life. Its propagandists roam the country claiming that Christ is on their side, but both the Protestant and the Catholic labor movements[24] have resisted their advances, preferring if need be to forgo any economic betterment rather than abandon their confession. Should Mr. Schaper not acknowledge, Mr. Chairman, that this is a token of noble character and spiritual strength? They have not forgotten what Scripture says: "Therefore do not be anxious, saying, 'What shall we eat?' or 'What shall we drink?' … For the gentiles seek after all these things" [Matt 6:31–32]; and they cannot forget that the Lord has been very clear: "What does it profit a man to gain the whole world and forfeit his soul?" [Mark 8:36].

December 13, 1902

I have been criticized for saying that our high school curriculum is too intellectual to satisfy the needs of young women. I am told I should not generalize, and I concur. I fully agree that our high schools have boys who are far less talented intellectually than many a girl. Perhaps in the next generation some young women may well outshine many a man in intellectual achievement. But the question is to look at the average, for that is what a curriculum is geared to. If our secondary schools are too intellectual for our young men, they will probably not be helpful either in preparing our future women for gaining their rightful place in society.

December 16, 1902

It may have come as a surprise, Mr. Chairman, that Mr. Troelstra,[25] having won a by-election, has returned to this Chamber with a pledge to support equal treatment of private schools. To be sure, at the late congress of the Social-Democratic Labor Party a resolution was passed stating that social democracy should no longer "thwart the unity of the working classes in the face of believing and unbelieving capitalists for the sake of theological differences." I note, Mr. Chairman, that the interest of social democrats in parity treatment for private education does not stem from love of freedom

24. An organized Protestant labor movement began in 1876 and developed into a national Federation of Christian Unions in 1909; the dates for the Catholic labor movement are 1891 and 1906. Both arose out of protest against the spirit of the class struggle, even when it presented itself as bread-and-butter union activity. The labor movement among Christians stood for communal consultation and cooperation in the workplace between the employer and his employees.

25. Pieter Jelles Troelstra (1860–1930) was a journalist, lawyer, and socialist politician.

for private schools but from concern for the class struggle. It is nothing but a party tactic to lure support away from us. As Mr. Lohman has already reminded us, the supporters of Christian education will never sell their freedom for whatever subsidy the central government may proffer. If Mr. Troelstra's support is going to depend on terms and conditions unacceptable to us, we will decline his support.

Gentlemen opposite have on several occasions invoked the term *kleine luyden* [the little people]. So, am I pleased that the term seems to be catching on? Well, the term is not mine; it was coined by the Prince of Orange.[26] Did it refer to people who were poor and had to beg for money, people who had to be lured with promises of material benefits? No, the *kleine luyden* were people who did not ask for benefits but on the contrary enabled the prince through their monetary sacrifices to keep up the struggle for freedom.

Mr. Roessingh has remarked that despite the Compulsory School Attendance Act [of 1900] various municipalities have failed to provide decent school facilities. I agree that this is wrong, but we must not be unreasonable. Surely the honorable member has heard of transition stages? In the past year the number of school-going children has increased by 6.22 percent against a population increase of 1.62 percent. Obviously we are dealing with exceptional circumstances.

In that light, it will be important for fast-growing towns not to build too luxuriously. I also find that despite financial constraints some towns are planning many small schools. The government has advised them that fewer, larger schools may oblige the children to walk farther but will result in significant savings. The member's district is short 1,550 places to accommodate new pupils, but by building twelve wooden additions and several portables this shortage will almost have disappeared by 1903, aided further by plans for a private school in the district.

The member for Zierikzee, Mr. Pompe van Meerdervoort,[27] has pointed out that compulsory school attendance has resulted in a painful loss of

26. That is, William the Silent (1533–84), leader of the Dutch Revolt against their overlord, King Philip II of Spain. At one point the prince credited the lower middle classes with a major role in funding the hiring of mercenary troops to fight the occupying Spanish troops. These classes, Kuyper never failed to point out, were predominantly Calvinists who rebelled against the Inquisition and the 10 percent value-added tax imposed on the Low Countries by Spain.
27. Jozef Jan Pompe van Meerdervoort (1837–1918) was a judge and antirevolutionary politician.

income for low-income families. I agree that in those cases municipal poor relief is called for. I do not agree with Mr. Troelstra that the solution is to provide school meals and school clothing. It is the primary responsibility of parents to feed and clothe their offspring. The ancient philosopher Plato wanted to shift the education of children away from the parents to the state. Some people today want to put newborns in daycare centers, toddlers in kindergarten, and so on. This trend would end in putting the state in charge of all child-rearing and so destroy the family, a trend that will always be opposed by this cabinet.

Have we then no heart for the children from poor families, and do social democrats have a monopoly on concern for them? Allow me to inquire: Have they ever financed private schools to serve these children? Allow me to remind the member that it was one of ours, Mr. Feringa of Amsterdam,[28] who [in 1849] started the first poor school in our country.

December 12, 1903

The honorable member for Winschoten, Mr. Bos,[29] cautions the government not to spend too much all at once of the budget now approved for improving the vocational schools, because in the future this Chamber may turn stingy, as it often does when times turn lean. I could not agree more, but when he wants to tone down the big plans for the Polytechnical Institute in Delft I beg to differ. If we want to be competitive as a nation and support technical education at a level that will not be outdated a quarter-century hence, then thrift in this instance would not be wise. In addition to physics, chemistry, and other sciences we now need to move ahead and provide adequate facilities for a department of engineering. That our country lags behind economically can be blamed in part, I think, on our deficit in the technical field.

December 12, 1903

Members, after reporting that parents and also a teacher have complained about the bad books their children bring home from their secondary school library, now disapprove of my intervention, calling it a form of arbitrary

---

28. Nicolaas Mattheus Feringa (1820–86) was a teacher and a founder of the Society for Christian National School Education.
29. Dirk Bos (1862–1916) was a liberal politician and businessman, and served in the Second Chamber from 1901 until his death.

censorship. But what choice did I have? These schools fall under the supervision of the minister of internal affairs, and my choice was either to allow any books whatsoever or to impose some rules about acquiring books for these libraries. Is it not advisable, they ask, to keep the imagination alive among students who study mainly math and science? Indeed it is, but especially among this group the most one-sided imagination is being fed by the books they prefer but which we find unfit. They should be reading more history and the classics. Studies show that educated men of character are steeped not in bad literature, but in the great books of our civilization.

December 12, 1903

My opinion has been asked about a classroom size of fifty-five pupils. That is indeed cumbersome in one-room schools where six different grades have to be taught by one teacher. In other schools the size may still be too large, but given that there are eight hundred thousand school-age children and twenty-five thousand teachers and teacher trainees, the average class size is thirty-two (not counting the trainees it is forty-two). That needs to be lowered, to be sure; but those who wish to bring this number down to twenty-five should not forget that it would add eight million to the cost of primary education. To make some headway here, we need to follow a level-headed approach and not make impossible demands.

December 16, 1903

The differentiation in our national culture is a good thing. When we had a uniform public education system the spiritual temper of the nation was low. But struggle ensued and a rich life blossomed in the fight for schools where one's principles and beliefs are propagated. We are told that this has taken place at the price of national unity. I dispute that. Unity must not be sought in uniformity.

February 24–25, 1904

The aim of our Higher Education bill is the emancipation of higher education. It is in line with history, it is promoted by this bill in a fair way, and it is a demand of current developments in science and the academy.

It is in line with history. The bill proposes to amend the Higher Education Acts of 1876 and 1901. It has been my contention, expressed over many years, that since our country is composed of a mixed population of many different views and principles, the state is incompetent to make a choice from among them so that one dominates. The revised Constitution of 1848 declared education to be free. The Act of 1876 gave associations, foundations, and churches the right to erect schools for higher education, and it provided subsidies for our prep schools, the *gymnasia*. The Act of 1901 gave *gymnasia* the right to grant diplomas. The next step must to be to relieve free universities of their civil disabilities.

That step is taken in a fair way in the bill before you. At present the Free University [of Amsterdam] is authorized to grant degrees. However, its degrees are not equal to the degrees of the public universities: they do not have *effectus civilis*. Members opposite are content to let the students of the Free University first pass their exams at their own institution and then sit for the same exams at a public university. Is that fair? They call it quality control, which is nothing more than an insult to the serious academic work done at the Free University. It also practically doubles a student's task, for to be examined by a strange professor means that a student will also want to be familiar with that professor's instruction in research methods, source analysis, and so on.

The bill is a response to developments in the academy. A university is primarily a teaching institution, secondarily requiring its teachers to do research, while its students must find their way in existing knowledge and learn how to advance knowledge. What pedagogical system is best suited for this: that of indifference, or that of preference—inductive or deductive? The former starts with different parts of knowledge and builds up a worldview; the latter starts with a view of the whole of reality and from there demonstrates the *necessity* of its conclusions. The second system presupposes the organic coherence of the cosmos. The cosmos is the expression of God's thoughts, and science will not rest until human consciousness has comprehended these in their organic interconnection.

In many areas the designation "science" is now reserved for what can be observed, weighed, and measured. The Dutch term *wetenschap* is broader, yet it consigns all those other things to the area of *mystery*. This has become the antithesis: what the universities teach is science, what Christians hold dear and sacred is based on illusion and error. Modern developments have induced scientists to say to us: "We pursue genuine science, but you practice sectarian science." Fortunately, most professors will often say, "We do not know"; but what trickles down to people in the secondary schools, the press, and the general public is that what they once learned at the public university is the only genuine science.

The university world first attacked miracles, then stripped Scripture of its essence, then reduced Christ to the rabbi from Nazareth. In reaction, believers began to emphasize *the subject*. And once the subject reclaimed its rights, the consensus grew that all science and all certainty are ultimately based on [subjective] beliefs. Our country has two groups, acknowledged scholars who part ways when it comes to beliefs. Is the government now supposed to decide which group represents science, which does not? Is it supposed to say: I will grant benefits to the one, and consign the other to its own resources? We will not have fairness and equity until both groups receive equal treatment.

March 3, 1904

The honorable member is a teacher of law[30] and should therefore respect the rule that prosecutors should not play fast and loose with evidence. He has tried to amuse this Chamber by stating that academic standards at the Free University are maintained by dues-paying members of an association, people such as beer brewers and cobblers. I refuse to take the bait, except to say that the university in question has a board of curators. But first of all, this bill has not been introduced for the benefit of a specific institution but seeks to address an issue faced by all civilized countries, both in Europe and America.

The honorable member has asked me what I understand by Calvinistic chemistry. The question, put that way, makes me suspect that he has a different conception of science from me. Science is an organic whole and controlled in all its parts—in some perhaps more strongly than in others—by the specific life-principle that it presupposes. I will not weary the Chamber with a broad exposition of how every branch of science is ultimately controlled by Calvinist, Catholic, Lutheran, or rationalist principles.

What was it that caused so much dissatisfaction with the public universities? First, the things that went on during initiation week and in pub parties. Next, the deliberate exclusion from university chairs of foremost intellectual leaders such as Bilderdijk, Da Costa, and Groen van Prinsterer. Third, the confession of students who upon returning home stated that they had stopped praying and given up on the faith. Finally, the noticeable

30. Willem van der Vlugt (1853–1928) was a professor of law in the University of Leiden. He won a seat in a by-election after being nominated by the liberals for the express purpose of opposing the government's Higher Education bill.

influence of the same ideas in secondary schools, the press, literature, but there bathed in the cynical form of secondhand knowledge.

My own father would talk with me for hours on end, trying to undo the harmful influence I was undergoing at university. But he could not undo the attacks on Christianity couched in the theory of knowledge and the materialism taught there. And if he couldn't, can we expect mothers, widows, bank tellers to be able to? Next to the family, the church responded by providing more sophisticated catechism classes for university-bound students. And in the universities themselves, Christian students started their own clubs. These measures did throw up a barrier against the onslaught of unbelief. But what has been the result? That we have created a genre of "amphibians" who are believing Christians but who entertain views of science and their specific discipline that hail from a non-Christian worldview.

So long as unbelieving science could oppose Christian beliefs only piecemeal, with this specific theory or that special field of knowledge, it felt weak. But no sooner did the theory of evolution gain ground than the scholarly world, eager to have a unified theory, embraced Darwinism as the answer to everything. Since then, Christians have looked for a more general response and have struck out for a university of their own.

... I am informed here that the professors in Leiden have begun to realize that evolutionism is not the answer to everything and that they acknowledge the subjective side of research and scholarship. Yes, Professor Hendrik Lorentz investigates the qualified atoms of electricity, Professor Hugo de Vries looks at evolutionary leaps in the process of mutation, and Professor Rudolf Stammler argues for a higher law behind positive law—but all that has nothing to do with the subjective side of science. We shall not make any progress until scientists recognize that we have to do not just with cells and more minute principles but with the *directives* that are necessarily linked to them—that the ultimate explanation is not found in blind matter but in a Thinker who thought them up and called them into being—that is, in the Creator who made them.

Are we defending something antiscientific? The great philosopher Immanuel Kant did not think it irrational if scholars reckoned with revelation and were bound in their science by Scripture. I expect no support, however, from neo-Kantians, for they only widen the gap between phenomena and mystery and will never bring us to a comprehensive worldview.

The honorable member from Winschoten has compared the Free University to a cramming school where students are drilled in predigested knowledge, a feedlot where students have no choice in what they are fed. He wants students to have a choice. Well, it is at the public universities that they have no choice. There they are exposed to one worldview only; other worldviews are not considered, or dismissed as irrelevant. That is why this government has adopted the proposal[31] to allow for special chairs at the public universities where alternative approaches to science can be taught.[32]

Meanwhile, the honorable member for Leiden supports the humiliating demand that if the students from that "cramming school" want their degrees to have civil effect they have to be examined by professors from the public universities. At the same time he stated here earlier that a "trained parrot" from a private university, after his colleague in the law faculty "had a go at him," would likely not pass. Well, he should know how things are done at his department. Methinks he has given ample proof that I did not go too far when I said that double exams are a blight.

I can only conclude, Mr. Chairman, that a liberal attitude is not synonymous with the Liberal party. A true liberal, who contends for his principle but sees that his fellow countrymen do not share it, would be willing to make room for his opponents in the public arena.

March 8, 1904

I do not think it useful, Mr. Chairman, to debate all the amendments that have been introduced. We know that the opposition has determined in advance to vote against the Higher Education bill, no matter what. It all comes down to this. The parties on the left defend the modern worldview, which sets itself up as judge of divine revelation. The parties on the right, for all our differences of opinion, are convinced that the Christian worldview, which used to represent the thesis and today must defend the antithesis, cannot be stopped and will extend to every field of science. The only way to resolve the struggle between the two worldviews is to promote the untrammeled development of both. The opposition refuses this. They wish to restrict the science pursued by Christians and retain for their own

31. This was done via a friendly amendment by Alexander de Savornin Lohman, leader of the more conservative "free antirevolutionaries," who gave strong and eloquent support for Kuyper's education bills.

32. Privately endowed "special chairs" are found at most of Holland's thirteen universities. They offer courses which students can take for credit in a wide range of subjects, from Christian philosophy to humanism, theosophy, homeopathy, and conservation.

science the exclusive power which it enjoys at present and by extending this exclusivity to ensure themselves of triumph in the future.

March 3, 1905

What is the task of the government with respect to education? Government is to look after the well-being of the nation, for the present and the future, both materially and intellectually. It is to make sure that the nation's energies not decline but instead rise to the highest possible development, lest it fall behind other nations. If a government remains idle on this score in order to save money, it is a poor financier and a poor governor. At the same time government is to see to it that freedom of conscience not be oppressed. It is the family that gives rise to the state and provides strength for the future. Thus in this area parental influence must not suffer either.

April 5, 1905

In 1848 all parties agreed that exclusively public education did not satisfy the nation's needs, so freedom of education was enshrined in the Constitution. In 1889 consensus was reached that the free, independent, private school, being part of primary education, could not adequately fulfill its task unless it received some financial aid from the public treasury. The central government (though not local governments) would henceforth give financial aid "in equal measure" to both public and private schools. Our Primary Education bill merely seeks to correct any inequities that have since arisen, particularly in the area of teachers' pensions.

From the Memorandum of Explanation regarding the Primary Education Bill, Submitted to Parliament by Kuyper, Minister of Interior Affairs, and Harte van Tecklenburg, Minister of Finance, April 1905

In 1902, the central government and local governments combined spent some 18 million guilders on public education. Over the same period the private schools, if prorated on the basis of equality, would have received nearly 8 million. In reality they received 1.7 million in aid, thus saving the public treasury 6.3 million. If a similar calculation were made over the period of the past fifty years, it is evident that the very existence of private schools has saved the public treasury an enormous amount of money.

The partial aid through public funding, adjusted upward in 1890 and again in 1901, still did not abolish the shocking difference. For teachers' salaries and pension contributions alone, public schools received 24.40 guilders per pupil per year. Private schools received 7.55 guilders, thus less than one third; the rest of their operating costs are covered by tuition fees and for the greater part by voluntary contributions.

The supporters of private schools, after paying their taxes for public schools, have not been able to keep their monetary sacrifices in step with the rising costs of private schools, and the reason is obvious. While their contributions used to be shared by four hundred private schools, they now have to support over thirteen hundred schools.[33] Given that the Education Act of 1901, passed under the previous government, is based on the principle that public and private education are the two components of primary education in this country, the act should be amended accordingly.

At the same time, teachers in the private schools need to be protected against arbitrary treatment by the boards and associations that employ them. Hence the education bill now before you provides for letters of appointment that shall function as work contracts, stipulating the terms of employment such as duration and salary, and the possibility of appeal in case of earlier termination.

From the Memorandum of Response, Submitted by the Same Ministers, to the Provisional Report from the Chamber regarding the Nature and Intent of the Primary Education Bill, April 1905

Since the establishment in our country of the common public school in 1806, and its expansion by the Education Act of 1857, a growing difference in views about the deepest life principles which also govern education resulted in a situation where a species of neutrality had to be introduced in the schools that lacked all pedagogical pith and marrow or else gave priority to religious indifference. The unity that the neutral school had to represent did not square with reality. The children noticed it every Sunday or Saturday at church or synagogue, or even at school when pastor, priest, or rabbi separated them out for classes in religious instruction. The unity of the common neutral school was more an ideal abstraction than a tangible reality.

33. Namely, as a result of the Compulsory School Attendance Act passed under the previous administration.

I have been accused of fickleness because in 1875 I myself strongly opposed subsidies for private schools whereas today I defend them. But the reason for that, Mr. Chairman, was that at that time we fought for financial aid according to a system of "restitution" on grounds of justice and fairness, while a system of "subsidies" was then considered a form of charity. That was something the antirevolutionary faction could not allow to go unchallenged.

April 5, 1905

The organization of our primary schools, public and private, compares favorably with educational systems elsewhere. The school struggle is not about *organization*. It is about the *direction* of the schools. If members will allow me to speak not as a minister of the Crown but as a personal believer in Christ, then I think it is imperative that the education of my children be seasoned and colored by the implications of the principle I confess. There is much talk today of the "peaceful penetration of Morocco."[34] Well, I judge that a peaceful penetration of the Christian principle in education is absolutely necessary. I warmly support a school where I find that to be the case, be it a private or a public school.

For half a century we have fought over the direction of the public school: Should it be confessional or religiously neutral? Today a new element in education has entered the picture: an emphasis on *the interest of the child*. This shift has led some people to argue for still another reason why in the matter of religion the child should be taught with the strictest neutrality: it should be allowed to choose for itself later, when it is more mature. The stages of a child's development have to be taken into consideration.

But exactly here our ways part. As Jules Michelet wrote in his book *Nos Fils*: depending on whether or not one believes in original sin, the views of a child's needs will from the outset recede ever further apart in two totally opposite directions.[35] Michelet, like many members opposite, did not believe in original sin, but we for our part do believe that a child is conceived and born in sin. No sharper difference can be imagined. Now I ask, is this Chamber, which is a political body representing the people, is

---

34. France at this time claimed this North African country as its rightful "sphere of influence" in order to protect its economic interests in the unstable sultanate.
35. Jules Michelet, *Nos Fils* (Paris: Lacroix, 1870).

such a Chamber, I ask, competent to decide which view is right and which is wrong?

April 5, 1905

The fear has been expressed that more public funding will lead to more one-room schoolhouses. Would that be so bad? One must know that I attended one myself for six years.[36] My department has gathered some statistics from abroad. In Prussia, renowned for its education system, 21,500 schools out of 36,750 in 1901 had only one teacher. For Saxony the numbers are 905 out of 2,006, and for Switzerland 2,220 out of 4,391. How is it possible that those countries have not gone under? But perhaps the maximum enrollment at these small schools is twenty-five? It turns out that the number in Prussia is eighty (incidentally, the percentage of illiteracy in that country is 0.05; ours is 0.2). In Zurich the number is one hundred, with eighty as an option. Here in our country the maximum number entrusted to one teacher is forty. I do not necessarily conclude that small schools are better, but I do find these numbers rather reassuring.

April 5, 1905

I now come to the question of national unity. That unity is absolutely not promoted by a common school. Amsterdam from the beginning provided separate schools for Jewish children with Jewish teachers. One would have to conclude that Jew-baiting must have been rampant in that city. There is a lot of that in Russia, in Vienna, in Berlin, but I never noticed any of it in Amsterdam.

What has brought division in the nation is the common school. After it was installed, participants in the 1834 secession from the national church were persecuted; and in 1853 we even had no-popery riots! After the common school was reinforced in 1857, it did so little to foster toleration that the

36. A puzzling claim! The little boy Bram Kuyper was homeschooled according to all biographers, including his daughter Catherine M. E. Kuyper in her brief sketch, "Abraham Kuyper: His Early Life and Conversion," *The Calvin Forum* 16, no. 4 (November 1950): 64–67; republished in the *International Reformed Bulletin* (April 1960): 19–25, at 20.

liberal press never tired of fanning the fire of discord between Catholics and Protestants.[37]

So what remains of the claim that separate schools break the unity of the nation and that the common school unites us all? Nothing. It is an assertion that cannot pass the test.

April 11, 1905

What determines the range of action of public education? As Groen van Prinsterer already said: it is determined by private education. Private education extends its radius as far as it can; only where this ends does public education take over. Thus private schools should be the rule, and public schools the supplement.

April 12, 1905

The honorable member for Tiel, Mr. Tydeman, advises us not to look so much at other countries. But does he want to regard our country as an isolated case? Educational issues have a theoretical component and a practical component. The former requires taking our special circumstances into consideration. But when it comes to the practical implementation of one's educational ideas, it is wise to profit from the experience of other countries.

April 27, 1905

It has been suggested by members opposite that a private school should not only submit its curriculum to government inspectors, but also have it approved by them. I would not favor the latter, certainly not when religious instruction is part of the curriculum and inspectors are not necessarily of the same religious persuasion as the headmaster. And most certainly not when I hear the honorable member for Hoogezand, Mr. Ter Laan,[38] insist that some Bible stories are contradicted by the laws of nature and that these laws must in any case be respected. However, I do believe that the requirement to *submit* curricula to the inspectors is a powerful means to promote the interests of primary education and especially of that given

37. The two denominations disagreed on whether a teacher could ever use the Bible in class. There were Protestant voices that said: "Why not, if the inspector does not forbid it?" But Catholic clergy objected: "Never! Because a Protestant teacher will inevitably accompany Bible readings with biased comments."

38. Kornelis ter Laan (1871–1963) was a socialist politician who served in Parliament from 1901–37.

in the private schools. Although some private school curricula that I have seen are superior to the curricula of some good public schools, there are also many that are inferior, while some private schools do not even have a stated curriculum.

May 2, 1905

Members opposite propose to reimburse private schools for no more than two-thirds of their operating budgets, in order, they say, to allow at least one-third to be covered by "Christian charity." This sounds like the old interpretation of the words "the poor you will always have with you" as if it meant: "make sure you will always have poor people among you." Besides, instead of "charity" the term that applies more often is "mutual aid." Many cash-strapped private schools have not only been built but are kept in repair and cleaned with volunteer labor. Nor is that all. Many private school teachers could enjoy a salary of one thousand guilders in the public system but are content with a salary of six hundred guilders, saving the public system four hundred guilders a year. It seems to me that members have overlooked a wide variety of forms of "charity."

May 3, 1905

The fear has been expressed that the increase in subsidies from the central government to private schools will result in many public school teachers being laid off and having their income reduced to unemployment pay. The government believes that the number of layoffs will be minimal. However, since unemployment pay adds to its expenditures, it gladly adopts the honorable members' amendment to Article 39 that increases the rate at which municipal government will reimburse the central government for those payments.

May 4, 1905

The honorable member for Rotterdam District V, Mr. Van Raalte,[39] says that the government, from sheer rapacity, is "crossing the line of propriety" by railroading the Primary Education bill through parliament "by hook or by crook"—in other words, in defiance of laws human and divine. That puts this government on a par with the lowest sort of criminals. When a

39. Eduard Ellis Van Raalte (1841–1921) was a liberal politician and representative for Rotterdam V from 1897–1903.

man who normally uses choice expressions mingles his language with such poison, we know what bitterness must reign in his heart. He adds that this bill proposes the worst kind of "partisan measures." But, Mr. Chairman, is it a partisan act to propose the removal of restrictions to people's freedom of conscience with respect to the education of their children? Methinks the government deserves praise for defending this freedom against such heavy opposition.

April 5, 1905

National unity is in danger precisely when justice is denied, when liberty is abridged, when our citizens are hurt in their deepest convictions. That is what sows bitterness; that is what divides a nation. Let us rather join hands and resolve together to raise the education of our people to ever-higher levels. That cannot help but heighten people's sense of unity. The entire nation will benefit, and that is what this government expects from the passing of this bill.

PART FOUR

THE PEOPLE'S VOICE AND VICTORY

AN APPEAL TO THE NATION'S CONSCIENCE

TEXT INTRODUCTION

The event where this speech was held launched Kuyper onto the national stage. As a pastor in the Reformed church of Utrecht and a known advocate of Christian schools, he was asked to give the opening address at the general membership meeting of the Association for Christian National Primary Education, to be held in the city on the eve of the general elections for a new Second Chamber, where the national education system was likely to be once more a topic of debate.

The speech is one of Kuyper's earliest statements of what he saw as the ultimate goal in the school struggle: to find, instead of the *common school*, a *common ground* on which to base a national school system that all could agree to, a system of schools that would be separate but equal for all religious persuasions—Protestant, Catholic, Jewish, humanist, modernist, secularist.

The address called attention to the significance of the issue for the future of the country and noted that barely audible in the national debate was the voice of supporters of Christian schools, especially from the lower classes who did not have the vote. It argued that an "appeal to the national conscience" would reveal how widespread was the opposition to the common school as regulated by the Elementary Education Act of 1857. This act prescribed that the curriculum in all government schools include instruction in "Christian and civic virtues" while abstaining from anything that would be "in conflict with the respect owed to the religious ideas of those of other persuasions." Official interpretations of this wording explained that to avoid offending anyone, the act prohibited any reference to Bible or Christian doctrine.

Kuyper's address was followed by the adoption of a resolution calling for scrapping the word "Christian" from the act. The ensuing debate sealed the break with the irenical party in the land when Kuyper defended the resolution by saying that the word "Christian" in the circumstances was a "satanic" fraud perpetrated by a government that was more and more developing into a state hostile to Christianity. Whereupon his Utrecht colleague, the Rev. Dr. Nicolaas Beets, retorted that the proposal to scrap "something that in future might yet work for the good" had something "diabolical" about it. Kuyper blanched, but the chairman (Groen van Prinsterer) defended him by pointing out that the act was used in many towns and villages to delude parents into thinking that the common school was Christian, when in reality it did not stand for any substantive instruction in the historic Christian faith and was turning into a school for the modernist sect, favored by the ruling elite who used it to hoodwink Christian parents and dissuade them from starting separate Christian schools.

Source: Kuyper, Abraham. *"Het beroep op het volksgewetern": rede ter opening van de Algemeene vergadering der "vereeniging voor Christelijk Nationaal-Schoolonderwijs."* Amsterdam: B. H. Blankenberg, 1869. Translated by Nelson D. Kloosterman.

AN APPEAL TO THE NATION'S CONSCIENCE

... What then are we to ask of the nation's conscience? The sacred cause of education has brought us together, friends, so allow me to identify for you five features that constitute the demands of our movement with respect to education and which we hereby submit to the verdict of the nation's conscience.

In a country such as ours today, the state school must be mixed, and therefore must either purposely reject religion or else become the teacher of a religion that adopts the lowest common denominator of beliefs in the land. It must either be religionless[40] or else feature a Christianity that transcends differences of belief. That is the dilemma.

40. *Note by the author:* I continue to use this term even after the reprimand from Dr. Lamping. But I agree that "religionless" is no innocent epithet but a very serious accusation. The "religionless" common school is a sacrilege in our national life. But for that very reason I employ and defend that cutting qualification in order to make our people become aware of the abyss into which it is sliding with that (morally) impossible common school. [Lamping was the author of a brochure about "the state and public education in the Netherlands," *De Staat en het Volksonderwijs in Nederland*

With that fact in mind, then, we want to ask whether our nation, taken as a whole, as a moral entity, is prepared to deny its religious origin, such that it forfeits its right to be called a Christian nation. We wish the issue to be decided not by any philosophical system, even less by some political theory, but by the nation's conscience itself: Does its moral calling allow the surrender of religion for the sake of the common public school? Let it be decided before that tribunal whether the people of the Netherlands, which became a nation above all through the religious factor, has so fallen away from its origin that it can deny its past and acknowledge the religionless state as the headmaster of its youth, as the educator of its sons. And if, fearing that verdict, people choose the other horn of the dilemma and continue to speak in their law of "Christian virtues" and charter a "religion transcending differences of belief" as the religion of the state—again, not by philosophy or theory but by an awakened conscience, by a healthy sense of our national identity—then we must ask for a Dutch answer to the question whether that minimum of Christianity is really the Christianity of our forefathers, the Christianity that made our nation great and for which the blood of our people was shed.

Given our diverse population, the state school must either weaken or pass over in silence the chief factor of our national history, lest anyone be offended. Accordingly, the very serious question must be put to the same judge of the national conscience, whether mutilating our history does not violate our national life. If the state school is to bar whatever might offend a segment of the nation, we would like to place that unfree, fettered school before the free national conscience by asking the stinging question whether the nation is not offended at its deepest level when the most beautiful pages from its history are being torn out. Is it still our national history if teachers are allowed to mention dates and names, facts and events, but must carefully conceal the vital spirit that once animated that lifeless skeleton? We want the nation itself to decide whether it will passively tolerate this moral suicide whereby its glorious past, its history so full of sacred inspiration, atrophies into a patchwork of lifeless elements in which its vital pulse is no longer felt. Everyone will agree that not the analysis of facts but the physiology of a nation converts a dry chronicle into vital history. We want

(Leiden: S. C. Van Doesburgh, 1869), two opinion pieces published earlier in the prominent journal *De Gids* that gave voice to the resistance of the ruling liberals to Groen van Prinsterer's publicized proposals for amending the Act of 1857.]

to see the nation's conscience pronounce sentence on a public school that cannot infuse the veins of our history with the lifeblood of the nation.

If the flourishing of domestic life was always Holland's pride and honor, then Holland's people will have to decide whether it can condone the erosion of family life, and so the loss of family ties, indeed the breakup of family life altogether. Everyone senses that a school which brings everyone together does not reflect the diversity in families, preserves no harmony with them, let alone nourishes the sense of family. We want to see the national conscience pronounce sentence on a state school which for the larger part of the day summons our children from our homes yet increasingly erases every distinctive feature of families, eclipses the unique nature of domestic life and family lifestyles, provides uniform[41] guidance to every child, and so does not advance but hinders the formation of distinctive characters and so the establishment of distinctive families that possess more than nominal value.

Moreover, our nation has always prided itself on the freedom of its citizens. It has never tolerated external compulsion but has shed its blood for civil liberty. It has never allowed others to do for it what it could do for itself. To the conscience of that nation of free citizens we pose the question whether it may put up with the all-inclusive interference of the state that deadens its spirit. To the conscience of that free citizenry we submit the question whether it will allow a meddlesome state to take everything off its hands, including the right to its children—and whether it does not realize that the muscles of it civic strength can only weaken when liberty becomes unfamiliar once it chooses love of ease over devotion to duty, or at least does not demand back from the state its own sphere of action.

Finally, we wish to put the following solemn question to the conscience of Holland's people, who earlier than any other nation inscribed on its national banner the slogan of freedom of conscience: May freedom of conscience continue to be abridged in our country for the lower classes and the poor? True, the common man does not write a brochure, and the poor man is not given the floor at our campaign rallies. Yet a parent's heart has its values, and his conscience has its tender demands, the right of which must not be proportioned according to the daily needs they struggle with or the comforts that others enjoy. And so, to speak personally, I assess the grievance of others in terms of my own conviction. I too am a father, and

41. See also Abraham Kuyper, "Uniformity: The Curse of Modern Life," in *AKCR*, 19–44.

that is why I say that my parental heart would be pained and my conscience aggrieved if I were compelled to hand over the two sons God has given me to an education which I, by virtue of my personal right for which I am accountable to God alone, consider injurious and odious.[42] But then, I personally am not compelled. If I find no suitable school I will teach them myself. The rich are not compelled either; they have the money to provide the kind of education they prefer. And if that financial burden is too heavy for one individual, several can pool their resources and establish a private school. But the common man and the poor man ... these I defend, for these I speak. They are coerced, they are cut to the heart, their conscience is repressed. Or are we to believe that among the poor the life of parents is not as tightly bound up with that of their children? Should the conscience of the parents themselves not feel hurt at the injustice done to the souls of their children? And when that occurs, when the common man and the poor man are compelled (if the philanthropy of others brings no solution[43]) either to deprive his child of an education or to surrender it to a kind of education in which, on his view, the one thing needful is lacking, an education that can form the head but not the heart and therefore militates against his conscience—very well, when that occurs, we want the nation's conscience to render a verdict as to whether it will tolerate this abuse of the lower income groups, this breach of parental rights, this abridgment of freedom of conscience.

Piety, historical sense, flourishing family life, citizen's self-help, freedom of conscience: these are the five basic features which in our view are engraved too deeply on the face of our nation to be disregarded in the long run. Five demands which the state school cannot satisfy and which cannot

---

42. *Note by the author:* Personally, for my conviction as one who confesses the gospel, I am offended by what Dr. Lamping says on page 66 of his booklet about [our] fear of rationalism. His closing sentence—"Then close the school, that is safest of all; don't educate, then the education will not breed rationalists"—is inappropriate from the pen of a man who is discussing a vital issue within the hearing of the people. At this point in time I shall not enter into a discussion about it. But that education and pedagogy are two different things is a fact that the esteemed author knows full well—too well to be able to find an excuse for such partisan satire. For the sake of our country and in the interest of good journalism, may a better genius guide him in his new and extremely weighty task. [Mr. Lamping, a former minister in the national church, had just been appointed editor in chief of the liberal daily, the *Nieuwe Rotterdamsche Courant*.]

43. That is, by financing a local school for them.

come into their own until the fetters of the state school are loosed, the protection system is sent packing, and the complete and untrammeled freedom of education is recognized. Five vital questions that are indissolubly connected with our national character, not pursued from a partisan spirit but forced onto our lips by the nation's vital impulse from the heart, for the sake of and in the interest of the entire nation. Now then, to these questions we want the Dutch nation to give us an answer. Its own answer. Not an answer prompted by others but whispered by its conscience. Not an answer picked up in the turmoil of party passions but considered with calm sobriety in the heart. In other words, an answer of conscience, free of excitement, weighed before him to whom our nation, too, owes its origin, from whom our nation received its calling, and who as Judge of the nations will summon our nation to give an account of its moral endowment.

... The fact cannot be denied that our wishes are not shared by all. We can no longer close our eyes to the tangible truth that since 1795[44] our national life has undergone a very important metamorphosis. Next to Catholics and Protestants we now also have the revolutionaries vying to put their stamp on the newly developing Dutch nationality and to control the future of our nation. ... Now then, for each group we demand complete freedom, the unstinted right to work on the new shape of our nation. Each group must be in a position to contribute to constructing the new home in which the Dutch people shall live. ... And once we have established a common ground on which to base a national education system in which all groups and persuasions can express themselves freely and without hindrance, we shall then be ready to appeal once more to the national conscience by competing with the other groups for regaining, through moral power, that measure of influence on our national life which by virtue of history rightly belongs to us.

... Only when faith is your principle do you have a right to appeal to the nation's conscience. But then God himself shall plead for you in that national conscience.

I thank you.

44. Reference to the overthrow of the Dutch Republic and the founding of the Batavian Republic, inspired by the ideas of the French Revolution and achieved with the help of French revolutionary armies.

THE STRUGGLE

TEXT INTRODUCTION

This section with the heading "The Struggle" is the longest section of appendix O in *Ons Program*. In particular four of the twelve editorials reprinted there capture Kuyper's self-understanding of the high spiritual stakes in the school struggle.

On July 4, 1878, Kuyper responds to a series of allegations against the petitioners and a direct challenge that invoked Groen van Prinsterer's memory in opposition to the petition. On July 15, he outlines reasons for going directly to the king because Parliament has surrendered its moral authority. On July 19, he reminds the petitioners, lest any of them lose their own moral compass, not to become bitter but to pray for those who do violence to them: if there is to be victory, he writes, it must come by way of a humble spirit and not an arrogant one.

On July 22, finally, Kuyper does not shrink from openly framing the struggle as a conflict between the rich elites and poor ordinary Dutch folk.

The subsequent disappointment in the king's royal assent to the new school law is not included in *Ons Program*.

Source: Kuyper, Abraham. "De Worsteling." In *Ons Program* (Amsterdam: J. H. Kruyt, 1879), 720–37. Reprinted from *De Standaard*, July 15–August 2, 1878. Translated and abridged by John Bolt. Edited by Harry Van Dyke.

THE STRUGGLE

TO THE KING! NOT TO PARLIAMENT

From the outset, our rallying cry has been: *"To the King!"* We therefore resisted the whispering of some that suggested we first go to Parliament. Our refusal to do so was echoed by our people and is the exact reason that enthusiasm for what we are doing was not extinguished. Our Christian nation retains a love for the monarchy in its heart; this is less true of all that lecturing and sparring witnessed on the floor of Parliament. People are still willing to plead with the House of Orange but are too proud to beg from Parliament.

But doesn't this attitude toward Parliament indicate a lack of respect for the authorities ordained by God as his "servants"? Are we, who claim to be antirevolutionaries, not encouraging revolution among our people?

We reply: In a constitutional monarchy, such as ours, sovereignty lies with the king. Parliament represents the people; it is the nation "abridged," the nation at its core, and members of Parliament are charged with defending the people's rights over against the government.[1]

---

1. Kuyper's view of the role of Parliament is set forth in *OP*, 21–28, 104–7.

Parliament is there for us, not we for Parliament. As soon as its members are more interested in their own game than in the nation's interest, then *eo ipso* the nation is released from any obligations with respect to Parliament. Just as you fire a lawyer who was hired to serve your interest but now begins to side with your opponent, so here. This does not mean that the office of a lawyer is now dishonored or that one is released from one's lawful obligations; but from the moment that Parliament ceases to be the nation, one is entirely justified in withdrawing one's moral confidence from it and doing battle against it.

As a rule the people does not go to its king on its own initiative. This is not because it is lazy but because it has entrusted Parliament with being its advocate before civil authority. But when these tribunes of the people leave their post or forsake you and turn against you, then you must once again speak up for yourself. *Go to the king*, all you who have a complaint against Parliament.

One of our dailies suggested recently that Groen van Prinsterer,[2] if he were still alive, would undoubtedly have taken sides against us. After all, so we are assured, Groen was a statesman and therefore, with the keen eye of a statesman, he would have realized that eventually giving up the school struggle would be the only way to preserve the existing Christian schools from extinction.

Their argument boils down to this: It was Groen's agitation on behalf of the Christian schools that woke the sleeping liberal lions who otherwise would likely not have been inclined to revising the school law. But now, thanks to the uprising of believing Christians in the land, embittered liberals have themselves begun to mobilize against the Christian schools, and Parliament is in the process of "murdering" them. As a statesman Groen would have recognized the sour fruit of his titanic labors, and, bitterly remorseful, he would have acknowledged that his efforts were leading to the eventual demise of the Christian schools, not to their rescue.

So, liberals just can't help it; they are the fairest, most just, right-minded people in the world. If only we had kept quiet, they would not have raised a finger against us. But now that we have insisted on being heard, everyone understands that they cannot do otherwise than chastise us with scorpions instead of whips. There is an implied warning here that if we persist in

2. G. Groen van Prinsterer (1801–76) was Kuyper's political mentor and leader of the antirevolutionary movement.

our cause they will intensify efforts to destroy our schools. And it will be our own fault!

The paper can be self-satisfied because it tried to warn us before it was too late. Groen was a statesman, and if he were still living he would quietly surrender to the liberal position. With his departure thoughtful insight disappeared from the Antirevolutionary Party and was replaced by hotheaded agitation. It won't be long before this change in tactics will be paid for with a languishing, convulsing school that is dying away.

Let's consider this from another angle. We are, in effect, being told that we should be happy about the new school law because it would have been much worse were it not for the financial restraints placed on the national government by its enormous debt and inadequate resources, including the demands to deal with the insurrection in the Aceh region of Indonesia. Mr. Antony Moens, liberal member of Parliament for Sneek, proposed far greater resources, more demands, and additional administrative structure for all schools, a proposal that would "murder" the Christian schools. His proposals were defeated, not because of principle, but because the money was not there. But, be warned: the desire was there, and, once the money starts to flow again, then, o despised Nazarenes, your days are numbered at "playing school."

What shall we say to all this? For three things we give thanks:

First, we are grateful for the acknowledgment, generously and freely given, that the education bill now forged will practically make Christian schools impossible. We are also grateful for letting slip that further development of the intentions behind the law are likened to the "murder" of the Christian school. And, finally, we are grateful for the humiliating self-accusation that liberals intend to push this law through not because the schools require it but because our protest annoys them.

It is obvious what is going on here, in the highest form: *Habemus reum confitetentem.*[3]

Second, from the manner in which the paper in the same issue praises Mr. Moens it is obvious that the "murder" of the Christian school has already been decided, whether we are silent or not. If so, it is inexplicable to us why Groen is invoked as part of the opposition to our petition.

3. "We have something to confess."

And finally, they give us permission to recall that Groen's self-description—*Een Staatsman niet, een Evangeliebelijder!*[4]—also includes the possibility that the one who confesses the gospel, hoping against hope even in this perilous moment, would have remained true to the guiding principle of his life. We wish to enlighten the esteemed author of this article by adding that Groen's best and truest friends are certain that it would have been the crowning glory of his old age if God had granted him the opportunity to see with his own eyes this people's protest that is "not of statesmen but of confessors of the gospel."

THE SCHOOL LAW IS FATAL FOR THE POOR

The whole school question is a matter of rich and poor.[5]

If you are very rich, even if you are blessed with twelve children, for you personally there is no "school question." This is true at all levels: elementary schools, secondary schools, and higher education. If in your child's early years of education you are unable to find a Christian school, you can afford to hire a Christian man as a governor or a Christian woman as a governess. And if there is no Christian secondary school or Christian gymnasium available where you live, you can send your son to a boarding school, or if need be to Eton. Furthermore, if you don't trust the universities of your country you are still free to send your young people to Lausanne or Edinburgh. If you are rich, really rich, and can dedicate hundreds and hundreds to each child, then of course there is no school burden for you. You are free and can do as you wish.

But ... woe to you if you don't have that much money. You are forced to send your children to non-Christian schools, starting with elementary education. Either you receive help from friends to send your children to a Christian school or you are forced to send them to a school without the Bible. If there is no help available, Christian parents must choose: "My child will not attend school,[6] *or* my child will have to go to a public school." This ultimately comes down to: "Either I send my child to the public school, or

4. "Not a statesman, but a confessor of the gospel!" In its original context, Groen's cryptic statement meant "It is not as a professional politician that I ask to be reelected, but simply as a witness to the Christian gospel as applied to the issues."
5. The revised Elementary Education Act of 1878 mandated reducing class size and upgrading school facilities for all schools, public and private, while providing financial aid for public schools but excluding private schools from the same.
6. A real option, since compulsory attendance was not introduced until 1900.

I let my child run wild." We are therefore at the point in the Netherlands where, *except for the rich,* it is no longer possible for all parents who so desire to send their children to a school with the Bible.

That is why this law is so fatal for the poor. That is why the injustice done to us is so offensive. This is the ignoble reality that the liberals are creating, and about which we have not minced words. And we are happy to add: "That is also the keynote of our message to the king!" The rich are free; the poor are coerced. That is what is so galling about this fateful law against which we ask our sovereign for redress.

KEEPING A PROPER SPIRIT

To our regret it cannot be denied that some of our spiritual compatriots have become embittered against those who are pushing the new school law. This is disturbing but understandable. Our nation is being plundered by a small coterie of elites who have managed to create an "all-determining majority in the *pays légal*" even though they are a decided minority in the "*pays réel.*"[7] Having created a large sociocultural, legal, political, academic, educational bureaucratic structure to further the liberal agenda, they see the school struggle as a challenge to their hegemony. They regard the nation as properly under their control and consider dissent as an affront to the new aristocracy, which has been labeled as a "nobility of civility" but is more properly termed a "nobility of unbelief."

After all the assaults against orthodox Christians in church and school, which have made life so difficult for us during the last twenty-five years, it is understandable that some of us are brought to the boiling point by the mockery and taunts that greet us now that we finally gather our voice and appeal to our king's heart. Given this abuse, it is not surprising that the longing to vindicate ourselves has led some to feeling deep resentment. In the face of the false accusations brought against us we understand the temptation that leads to hot blood and sharp tongues.

However, it is precisely for that reason that we are required, now that the petition drive is at hand, to remind our brothers in every corner of the land about the sacred cause for which we stepped into the breach—namely, the name of our Lord Jesus Christ, who "when he was reviled, did not revile in

7. That is, the few who have the vote (*pays légal*) dictate the policy for the entire nation (*pays réel*).

return; when he suffered, he did not threaten" [1 Pet 2:23], I earnestly plead with you: be on guard "that no 'root of bitterness' springs up" [Heb 12:15].

Justice will come to us. I do not say this as a prophecy based on human reckoning but because I know that the powerful and cunning coterie arrayed against us is nothing compared to the might of our God if he were to rise up and come to our aid. But never forget that we will only be able to live by faith in the heat of this battle if we follow the command not to allow our faith for even one moment to deteriorate into bitterness. The reason is plain: our faith can never set bitterness over against bitterness but requires that we should "pray for those who despitefully use you, and persecute you" [see Matt 5:44].

The final installment in the series of editorials incorporated into appendix O is dated August 2, 1878, one day before the petition was presented to King William III. Its tone is remarkably celebrative: God has done great things for us! Kuyper points to the short time in which the three hundred thousand signatures were collected in the face of strong opposition and lack of adequate organization. The result was beyond all expectation; no one had believed this could really happen. A national spirit, he summarizes, has come to expression that is opposed to the ruling classes who are leading the nation astray. Kuyper concludes with a plea to his followers to walk in humility, to continue to love the truth, to be fervent and persevere in prayer, and to expect nothing from men but everything from God.

THE PEOPLE'S PETITION

TEXT INTRODUCTION

A decade of intense involvement in the major ecclesiastical and educational conflicts of Dutch life eventually took its toll on Kuyper. In 1876 he experienced his second major breakdown and took a fifteen-month leave—from February 1876 to April 1877—from all his responsibilities, including editing *The Standard*. When he returned from his convalescence abroad he resigned his seat in Parliament. His mentor and friend Groen van Prinsterer (1801–76) had died during his absence. Kuyper now resolved to dedicate himself to constructing a unified, national antirevolutionary movement.

The efforts by liberals to secularize Dutch primary education intensified after the defeat of the conservative coalition in July 1877. The new liberal government, led by Johannes Kappeyne van de Coppello (1822–95), introduced an education "improvement" bill on March 11, 1878, that placed additional burdens on private schools and threatened their future. After the bill had passed both chambers of Parliament, awaiting only the king's signature to become law, Kuyper became one of the leaders of a "people's petition" that pleaded with the king not to sign the bill. In less than a week's time—July 22–26, 1878—just over 305,000 Dutch citizens had signed the petition. This petition, along with a Roman Catholic one containing 164,000 signatures, was presented to King William III on August 3, 1878. The king received the petitioners politely but on August 17 signed the bill.

Though this particular battle was lost, the petition campaign served Kuyper's culture-war ambitions well, as it facilitated peace with the Roman Catholics and catalyzed growth of the antirevolutionary movement. If the forces opposed to Christian schools hoped that the new law would bankrupt them and eventually eliminate them, they badly miscalculated. In spite of the legislative defeat, the remarkable success of the petition drive called attention to the strong support for Christian schools among the Dutch people and gave a preview of the potential reservoir of voters only waiting to be mobilized. In fact, the next year saw two significant events that shaped Kuyper's subsequent career. On January 24, 1879, Christian school supporters organized into a national educational alliance called "The School with the Bible," and on April 3, 1879, the Antirevolutionary Party met in its first national convention, adopted the party platform written by Kuyper, and elected him as chairman of its national committee, in effect the titular head of the party.

The material here excerpted from these editorials shows that Kuyper had lost none of his passionate zeal or rhetorical fire after his breakdown. For those inclined to wonder whether his fierce antithetical call to Christians to stand up for the Bible and their faith might be a touch overwrought, it is worth recalling Kappeyne's response in Parliament to Kuyper in an earlier debate about the schools. On December 8, 1874, here is what Kappeyne said about supporters of private Christian education: "Our ideal as progressive liberals is: tuition-free primary education in religiously neutral government schools for the entire population. If I were told that if this is your wish you will oppress the minority, I am almost inclined to say: 'Well, let the minority be oppressed, because then that is the proverbial fly in the ointment and has no right to exist in our society.'"

The unabridged first edition of *Ons Program* includes numerous appendixes (*Bijlagen*), each consisting of articles originally published as editorials in *The Standard* in which Kuyper commented on topics that would soon form part of the Antirevolutionary Party platform. The thirteenth chapter of *Ons Program* ("Concerning the Schools," pp. 465–737) is the longest in the book, and Bijlage O (pp. 438–737) is also by far the longest appendix. It consists of fourteen sections, and the material here excerpted comes under section 14.II, (d) and (e). The entire section 14.II is dedicated to the new school law passed through parliament by the Kappeyne government in March 1878.

Source: Kuyper, Abraham. "Het Volkspetitionnement." In *Ons Program* (Amsterdam: J. H. Kruyt, 1879), 714–20. Translated, abridged, and annotated by John Bolt. Edited by Harry Van Dyke.

THE PEOPLE'S PETITION

A SCHOOL WITH THE BIBLE

It is now time for all who refuse to be cut off from their Bible to go to the king and then, as faithful parents, protest a law which will also cut off our children from the Bible in school. A school with the Bible! That says it all! Everyone can understand our slogan; it speaks to every conscience.

A school with the Bible, not a school where the Bible is hidden away in a corner or a desk drawer. Instead, as the Bible's own regal self-understanding demands, a school where it receives a place of honor and love.

A school with the Bible, not in spite of the law, nor snuck in as contraband by a smuggler when the watchful eye of the authorities is momentarily diverted. Instead, by way of a lawful liberation, the Bible, not tolerated as a special privilege but for the sake of justice.

A school with the Bible, one where the head of the school is a man of the Bible, a teacher who therefore can nurture children in accordance with their needs because he himself is a man fed by the Bible, has learned from the Bible, and who in a life of piety is like "a child among children."

With unerring instinct and sure grasp, our people realized without hesitation that the school struggle came down to one thing: "the Bible or not the Bible."

In this struggle our nation, our people, have only one overwhelming, preponderant, all-embracing concern, and that concern is: the Bible! Their instinct tells them this because our nation remains in bone and marrow a Protestant nation. It senses that its glory will depart with the departure of the Bible.

"The Bible or not the Bible" is in the first place not a schools issue but a matter of life and death for our nation. All that drivel about the Bible still being available in the church and the home misses the point and fools no one anymore. Everyone, whether he hates or loves the Bible, knows full well that the role of the Bible in the school is the only way that the next generation will keep the Bible also in church and home.

And that is why those in power need to think twice before they use this wretched law to cut our children off from the Bible and strike a blow at the very root of our national life from which it may never recover.

The preceding consists of excerpts from Kuyper's first two editorials. The next one (June 22) is an explanation why Kuyper felt it was necessary to prepare a distinct, Protestant petition when the Roman Catholic process was already well under way and much cost and energy could have been saved by simply riding piggyback on it. Kuyper argues that "freedom for the Bible" by the people and for the nation was at stake. Appealing to the example of the "three great Protestant states of England, Prussia, and the United States, as well as the three smaller ones of Sweden, Norway, and Denmark," where such "schools with the Bible" are a reality, he points out that it is the "neutralists" or secularists who stand alone in "the entire civilized Protestant world." While he expresses his admiration for the remarkable and almost perfect organization and execution of the Roman Catholic petition drive—which can be attributed to the strong hierarchical structure of the Roman church—he exalts in the efforts of the admittedly less organized and more hurried effort of our Protestants[1] *"in order that the impulse for spiritual freedom can continue to pulse through the blood of our souls." In his next editorial Kuyper goes after the illiberality of the liberal Dutch press.*

THE SPIRIT OF THE PETITION DRIVE

Among the higher and lower circles of our like-minded supporters there exists a general and deeply felt outrage and offense at the shameful way

1. Local chapters of the Anti-School Law League (founded in 1872 to campaign against the Act of 1857) helped collect signatures from all concerned individuals. The Catholic petition was signed by heads of households.

the liberal press slanders and characterizes our decision to go to the king. Its stories about our petition should never have seen the light of day. If we initially dared hope that the denigration of our petition, once challenged and unmasked as false, would be retracted—alas! That hope in the integrity of our opponents was dashed the more the tide turned in our favor. Shown by unassailable facts that they were wrong, the next day they brazenly continued to repeat the same falsehoods.

They have no appreciation of our distress. There is not even the slightest indication of any willingness on their part at least to grant a defeated opponent the respect of a parting salute. The simple fact that we want to go to the king to petition that our children might have the opportunity to attend a school with the Bible elicits from these "liberal," "tolerant," "humane" gentlemen such furious passion that they forget that they are "polite," "developed," "civilized" people and are able to justify to themselves that which can only be injurious to us.

We see little benefit in pursuing further challenges to such conscious and deliberate misrepresentation. Brothers, in this perilous moment let us be true to each other and to our God. And let us honor to the end the sacred task to which we are committed, also through our dedication and the integrity of our word.

If there was ever a movement that owes its existence to the remnant of believing Protestantism in the Netherlands, it is our people's protest against liberal coercion in the area of education. From whatever angle one observes this development, one can only rejoice in seeing the evidence that all is exceptionally well; in a threefold sense:

Exceptionally well in unity of heart and mind, because in spite of the opposition of a powerful and apparently irresistible force against our weak group with its differences of opinion, we have not been prevented from uniting as one man against everything that offended our hearts.

Exceptionally well in the spontaneous response from all sides and all places, without the least stress and effort, revealing the most heartfelt interest, warmest zeal, and noblest dedication.

Above all, however, this excellence is revealed in the quiet dedication and calm resoluteness that kept its birth free of excess and extinguished the flame of false fire before it could be placed on the altar.

Kuyper continues by comparing the "calm and dignity of our movement" with previous public expressions of opposition to government policy that were less noble, and he expresses gratitude for the character and tone of the "people's petition" efforts. He concludes with significant comments about the need for fervent, confident prayer.

We will be the first to acknowledge that our dedication does not yet measure up to the seriousness of the issue and that our faith, even in our inner circle, remains far below the weight of our task. At the same time, not praising human beings but our God who works in people, we gratefully acknowledge the brotherly unity, the natural course of events, and the peaceful manner that characterizes this expression of the national conscience. All this has lent such a rare degree of beauty to what is happening that our hope for the future has sprung to life in a surprising way.

We must not leave our hope there but seriously work on it. Let us not doubt, even if the king disappoints us. We must not murmur but reverently acknowledge that this too is in God's purpose for us, whether it be as a result of our unfaithfulness or for the glory of his name. This possibility of disappointment must not weaken our conviction or temper our prayers. Whoever does not believe that what he prays for can come to pass and does not hope that it will come to pass should cease praying. At the very least, such prayer is forced, a formality, praying without truth and power. We must not waver in our hope that the king will refuse to sign the law. Only if we dare to abide in this hope will the courage, the passion, and calm spirit continue to rule our members. No, no! We are not involved in a sham fight but are fully engaged in a battle to liberate, with God's help, the oppressed people of our nation. That is why we continue to call on God, to plead with the One who can powerfully turn the heart of the king. That is why we continue in our hearts and homes to make straight a highway for our God so that there be no curse on our people when he comes to deliver us. Indeed, that is why we go forth, in wider and wider circles, to spread our message, to enroll all who have bottled up the multitude of offenses against us and wish to join us in going to the king to ask for justice for our children.

The editorial of June 25, 1878, "Habemus reum confitetentem" ("We are forced to admit"), turns the tables on liberal claims that they represent the "majority" of the Dutch people.

A WELCOME ADMISSION

The liberals, once in power and supported by a liberal press, take as self-evident their own superiority as the voice of reason and progress and simply assume that they represent not only what is best for the whole nation but also that their views are held by an overwhelming majority of Dutch citizens. They regard resistance to the direction of the state schools as nothing more than the outdated grumbling of a negligible minority. Nonetheless, the opposition refuses to lay down its arms. Recently, a liberal member of Parliament in desperation carelessly threw down the gauntlet: "Let the nation vote on this in a referendum, and you will see what the opposition amounts to." No sooner had the member of Parliament said this than his liberal cohorts began to backtrack. A liberal newspaper suggests that a plebiscite is a bad idea because the results might not be so favorable to the liberal viewpoint. It arrogantly divides the nation into two groups: "Those who are competent to judge the School Law and those who are not; the latter are in the majority." Then follows this remarkable and revealing statement: "If we grant that those in the first group all support the School Law (we know this is not true but let us take what is the most generous number for our side), we would still be outvoted by the vast majority."

The newspaper in question has not admitted this willingly but has been forced to do so by the people's petition. It has taken less than four weeks for the truth to be revealed and for liberals to admit they were wrong. This admission is worth its weight in gold, because their vision for primary state schools is now exposed in all of its coercive character. According to their own testimony, liberals intend tooth and nail to resist the nation's majority.

AS SHEEP AMONG WOLVES

TEXT INTRODUCTION

During his lifetime Kuyper penned more than thirteen hundred devotionals or meditations on a theme taken from Scripture. Until 1877 they were published in the Sunday supplement of the daily *De Standaard*; after that date, until 1920, the last year of his life, these meditations appeared in the weekly *De Heraut*. The one titled "As Sheep among Wolves" was written in the mid-1890s during a relatively tranquil period in the school struggle. Kuyper reminds his readers that a Christian school is not an evangelistic instrument but a training center for future warriors in God's kingdom. At the same time he faults parents who risk sending their children to a secular school. He also manages to insert a warning against letting the prevailing social stratification determine what friends their children may choose to associate with.

Source: Kuyper, Abraham. *Als gij in uw huis zit. Meditatiën voor het huislijk saamleven*. Amsterdam: Höveker & Wormser, 1899, chap. xxv, pp. 105–9. Translated by Harry Van Dyke. An earlier translation by John Hendrik De Vries appeared in *When Thou Sittest in Thine House: Meditations on Home Life* (Grand Rapids: Eerdmans, 1929), 171–76. It was reprinted (Wipf and Stock: Eugene, OR, 2009).

AS SHEEP AMONG WOLVES

When it comes to educating their children, some Christian parents put themselves above the Lord Jesus.

Christ clearly stated that the difference between his followers and the world is like the difference between sheep and wolves. Some parents apparently know better. They think their children and the children of the world are all the same. So they don't see any danger when their baptized children, dedicated to Christ, make friends—even bosom friends—with children their own age from families that do not follow Christ. And when it comes down to a choice between children of a lower class but from Christian homes, and children of higher social standing but from non-Christian homes, they all too often prefer that their offspring associate with children of the "more respectable" class.

It gets worse. When these parents have to choose a school for their children they again are wiser than Jesus and refuse to believe that here too the difference between sheep and wolves applies. In general, of course, they are in favor of Christian education as the best option. All things being equal, they would prefer to enroll their children in a Christian elementary and a Christian secondary school.

But things are not always equal. If the Christian school is more expensive, or has fewer resources, or is located in a working-class neighborhood, the choice for a Christian school has to take a back seat, and the child is sent, as Jesus would say, among wolves—though they like to improve on Jesus by saying: among more respectable people.

But, you will say, Jesus did the same thing. He did not keep his disciples isolated. He said himself: "Behold, I am sending you out as sheep in the midst of wolves" (Matt 10:16).

And so he did. With this difference, however. Jesus sent them among wolves *when they were ready*. Nowhere in Scripture do you read that when he chose Peter and Andrew, James and John and the others to be his followers the Lord first sent them to the schools of the scribes or to the academy in Jerusalem. These men had first gone to the school of John the Baptist. Not exactly a "respectable" school, but one located in the wilderness, headed by a man dressed in an animal skin, with all sorts of sinners and publicans as pupils—definitely a "separate school." But then Jesus had started his own separate school and taught his pupils at two levels: first the twelve, then the seventy. And he was so concerned that his disciples might come under the wrong influence that when they met up with teachers of the other schools it was almost always Jesus who carried on the conversation, shielding his disciples.

Thus Jesus, who evidently thought quite differently about education from the parents I mentioned, educated his disciples in isolation from any influence of the official schools. Only when they were sufficiently educated and prepared did he charge them to begin their official ministry, sending them out into the world with those words: "Behold, I am sending you out as sheep in the midst of wolves."

Of course there comes a day when this has to be done. Once our children are mature they have to go out into the world. Then withdrawal into isolation is out of place. Jesus himself prayed: "I do not ask that you take them out of the world, but that you keep them from the evil one" (John 17:15).

Our children too are called to battle in their lifetime for Christ and against the world. Only then will they receive a crown one day. And you cannot do battle against the world if you keep yourself in isolation. You have to step out into the world, and as a sheep of the fold take the risks of being in the world, among the wolves.

That is what you have to do. And your children eventually have to do the same. But not until they are prepared, until they are mature, until they are well armed and properly equipped.

But some parents do not mean it that way at all. They do not tell you: "My son, my daughter is already so mature, is burning with such zeal for the Lord Jesus, that they can't wait to go out among the wolves to do battle for the Lord."

No, nothing of the sort. If these parents had fostered such zeal for the Lord in their children, they would be the first to enroll their children in a school where Christ is held in honor.

But they have not fostered any such zeal. No such zeal is kindled in the hearts of their children. That is why these children find the wolves so attractive and pleasant, and why they say: "Father, Mother, we'd rather go out among the wolves. Won't you let us go and be with those strong, robust animals? It's so stuffy among the sheep."

And those parents will reply: "Well, son, daughter, we don't want to force you. If it can make life more fun for you, go and be with the wolves. But don't let them bite you. Do be careful."

That is the situation. It arises only when people rank their own insight higher than Jesus' pronouncement, when they do not really believe what he said, when they believe in Jesus in the abstract but do not surrender to his word.

These parents will say, "Sure there is a grain of truth in the warning. Some people are indeed wolves. But to begin with, not all of them are. Also, there are wolves and wolves. Some people at least are not savage, greedy wolves. Some wolves among them are even lovable."

After having weakened their position by all sorts of shallow arguments, they go on to reason further in the following vein: "Our children have always been present when the Bible was read at family devotions. We have always given them a good example. They're not at all hostile to the faith. Besides, so long as they have not accepted Jesus as their personal Savior it makes no difference whether we send them to a Christian school or not. If they are truly children of God, the Savior will protect them even among wolves."

Oh, the heart is "deceitful above all things, and desperately sick; who can understand it?" [Jer 17:9].

And they call this "loving our children"! These are parents who have made a solemn vow at the baptism of their infants.[1] And every evening finds these parents on their knees, praying that God will protect their child. But they haven't the faintest notion what it is *to tempt God*. We need to ask them:

1. The vow that Reformed parents make at the baptism of infants reads: "Do you acknowledge the doctrine taught in this Christian church to be the true and complete doctrine of salvation ... and promise to instruct this child in the aforesaid doctrine *and cause it to be instructed therein* to the utmost of your power?" (emphasis added).

After showing such feeble love for your children, do you really think you can pray that prayer based on a prompting by the Holy Spirit?

Think of the implications when Jesus draws such a sharp contrast between sheep and wolves. Does he mean to say that his followers are all gentle and loving and the people of the world are all as evil as wild animals?

Not at all. Jesus' words have nothing to do with that kind of self-flattery and condescension toward people of the world. Just take a look once at sheep in the meadow: how violently they can butt; at times they can be anything but lovable.

The point is this: just as a watchdog is strong in its own yard, so the people of the world are so much stronger in the world than you are. You are no match for them. Your children too will be defenseless against them; once they enter their company they are lost.

That first of all. And in the second place, the people of the world are fanatical in their zeal for the world, and they are bent on saturating your children with the spirit of the world, even as your children at first offer resistance. They will not rest until your children too are completely wrapped up in the world. That is why Jesus calls them wolves. They want your children to become as they are; they want to absorb them, to spiritually devour them.

In the face of them we and our children are like defenseless sheep—but as lambs of the flock of Christ. Not as a deer or an ox, which too are assailed by wolves; but as lambs. How so? Because when the wolves attack, a deer will defend itself with its antlers until it drops, but a sheep *flees to its shepherd*.

So this is the secret of Christian education. Keep your children in the company of Jesus and educate them under the shadow of his wings until they are ready. And when they are ready, send them out into the world, among the wolves, but as sheep—as young people whose shield is the Lord.

SPEECH MARKING THE FIFTIETH ANNIVERSARY OF THE CHRISTIAN TEACHERS ASSOCIATION

TEXT INTRODUCTION

The school struggle in the Netherlands dates from the first half of the nineteenth century. The Education Act of 1806 organized elementary education by establishing a system of common schools for the country, to be funded from the public treasury. Initiatives to establish schools other than public schools required authorization from municipal or provincial authorities.

Separate schools with a positive Christian stamp were first organized by members of the secession churches following their break with the national church in 1834. They objected to the watered-down Christianity of the public school. However, their separate little schoolhouses, when discovered, were denied authorization and forced to close down. (It was one of the factors that induced them to emigrate to Michigan and Iowa.) When friends of the *Réveil* in The Hague tried to organize a school they too were blocked. A royal decree of 1842 was meant to alleviate this bureaucratic obstruction, but in practice applications for authorization were often still denied. Freedom of education was not guaranteed until the liberal Constitution of 1848, although it contained no provisions for the funding of separate schools. Nevertheless, often despite financial hardship, the Christian school movement grew slowly but steadily. By 1854, the number of teachers in Christian schools made it possible to establish a professional organization, the Association of Christian Teachers [men and women] in the Netherlands and Its Overseas Possessions.

And so it was that in 1904 the association celebrated its fiftieth anniversary. It did so during a three-day event in Amsterdam's Concertgebouw, with twelve hundred teachers in attendance. Some special features: a cantata of praise, composed by school principal and music teacher J. C. de Puy (1835–1924); a cruise on the river IJ; and a congratulatory address by the prime minister.

In his address Kuyper praised the important work accomplished by members of the association, at times at great personal hardship and financial sacrifice. He also challenged them, now that parity treatment with the public system was imminent, to put their shoulders to the wheel as they entered the next phase of developing the Christian school movement.

Some comments toward the end of the address remind us of the class nature of the school struggle: the battle for Christian elementary education thus far had been especially a battle on behalf of the lower classes; the next phase would have to concentrate on post-elementary Christian schools for the "higher" classes. That too was part of the mandate of the Kuyper ministry, and the support of educators would help prepare this endeavor for success.

Source: Anniversary address at the annual general meeting of the *Vereeniging van Christelijke Onderwijzers en Onderwijzeressen in Nederland en de Overzeesche Bezittingen*, held in Amsterdam on May 24–26, 1904. Stenographic report in *De Standaard*, July 18, 1904; extracts in F. Kalsbeek et al., eds., *Van Strijd en Zegen. Gedenkboek van het christelijk onderwijs, 1854–1904* (Leiden: Eduard IJdo, 1904); extracts reproduced in J. C. Rullman, *Kuyper-Bibliographie* (Kampen: Kok, 1940), 3:270–76. Translated, edited, and abridged by Harry Van Dyke.

SPEECH MARKING THE FIFTIETH ANNIVERSARY OF THE CHRISTIAN TEACHERS ASSOCIATION

Brothers and sisters,

I stand here on this occasion not as a minister of the Crown but as a fellow believer and, since I am still a professor, as your fellow teacher. I have been asked to serve as your honorary chairman, with the thought that my high office might add some honor to this assembly. For my part, however, I would like to declare that for me to be allowed to stand here and address you is an honor that surpasses many other honors which the Lord in his grace has given me.

I have come to your golden jubilee, first of all, to bring you a word of thanks on behalf of the Christian people in our country.

You began your festive gathering just now in the right spirit: to God alone be the glory.[1] But that should not prevent us, as we participate in your celebration, from extending to you a word of heartfelt gratitude for what you have done for our country in the past fifty years.

I think back on the time when the school struggle, now coming to a close, was still being waged with great vehemence and bitterness. Those who had the courage to be a Christian schoolteacher were slighted and insulted every day. Not that I pity you; a cup of scorn every day is the most healthful of drinks. It heightens your energy to fight, it increases your strength to resist, and at the end of every day and the start of every new day it causes you to look up to him who alone can give you strength and energy and fill you with holy inspiration. I speak from experience.

I bring you this vote of gratitude for the sacrifices you made for the benefit of the nation especially in the first years of the struggle. For many years you put up with a lower position in society than was enjoyed by your colleagues in the public system. You got by in often inferior facilities, you made do with insufficient resources, and you accepted lower salaries in order to serve the cause that was sacred and dear to you. You bore that scorn and that opposition, and you made those sacrifices without regard to the future. You did not know what the outcome would be. It might well have been that your prayers were not heard and that God did not crown your labors, and that the rich reward was not to be yours here on earth but only hereafter. But, praise God, that did not happen. Rich was the fruit, great the outcome, and surprising the end result of your exertions for the good of our country and our people.

Your association has made history! You have turned our history around and put our country on a different course. Think of what our situation would be today but for your action! You have loved the child, and you would not be called teachers if love for the child did not always come first among you. Is it little that in the battle of the spirits, all these fifty years, thousands, ten thousands, nay hundreds of thousands of children have been drawn to God's word, to Jesus' love, to the sacred traditions of past generations? And not only has your salutary influence extended to those children, but each of you, in the town or village where you live and work, in order to

1. The meeting had just sung No. 96 of the *Evangelische Gezangen*, "Halleluja, eeuwig dank en eere," a hymn expressing eternal gratitude and glory to God and ending in a prayer for love, grace, and communion of the Triune God.

get those children to attend your schools you have visited the parents and moved them to do their part and make a sacrifice by paying a much higher tuition than what it would cost them to obtain an education for their children elsewhere. And precisely those sacrifices brought a blessing as well, for they continually feed and foster love for Christian education.

Through the children your school's impact touched the families and the communities where you live. Through your tireless efforts and unremitting exertions the parents gradually embraced the Christian principle of honoring God and slowly began to break with everything that degrades life. In fact, some among you, if I may put it this way, have been little Groen van Prinsterers, men who personally took up and reflected on the great thoughts of Groen and then translated them for the general public. You converted the large banknotes of Groen into small change and adapted them to the environment in which you lived.

In this way you have been used, by the grace of God, to throw up more and more bulwarks against the unholy forces that had already made great progress in taking possession of our people and seizing the heart of the nation. Thanks to your labors, thanks to your exertions, thanks to your sacrifice and suffering, religion has once again been put at the center of life, even as a certain current that was present also in our country wished to push religion into a quiet corner so that its rays could no longer illumine public life. Through your instruction, your dedication, your influence on the children as well as on the homes, you have firmly planted in thousands upon thousands of families within our borders the moral principles that were being unraveled. You have reinforced the consciences that were being watered down and poured steel into them, so that ever broader circles of your pupils have come to realize: we are not free to do just anything, because God does not want us to; and what God does not want, we may not do, no matter how strong the temptation.

The speech continued by relating how the effect of the wildcat railway strikes earlier in the year had been mitigated by the wholesome influence of people who had attended a Christian school. It also credited Christian education for a turn for the better in the creation of Dutch literature. The speech continued:

Nevertheless, you will be facing new challenges. In the days of struggle and opposition you were inspired and united by a flame of holy enthusiasm. That flame blazed forth in the great people's petition of 1878. That enthusiasm brought about a turn in the course of events, until the school struggle was brought to an end by Lohman's fearlessness in fighting for our cause and Mackay's skill in drafting and defending his education bill [of 1889].[2] The opposition, worn down by the struggle, finally admitted defeat. Since that moment, the law has recognized that Christian schools constitute an equal—in fact an indispensable—component of elementary education in our country.

That outcome, however, not only concluded the school struggle in principle, but it ushered in a wholly new phase in the development of Christian education. You now face the question whether you have enough inner strength to meet the challenges of this new period. This second phase is characterized more by the trowel than the sword, and the wholesome influence on you of former scorn and opposition is no longer at work. Many of you are now better off, the range of your activities has broadened considerably, and it may even be said that compared to the past you have come to enjoy honor and a measure of affluence. A number of your members serve with distinction as government school inspectors. Before long a bill will be tabled in Parliament designed to improve your financial position, enhance your legal security, and increase your control over teacher education.[3]

Compared to former days, the present situation is like an oasis in the desert. You now find yourself in the oasis, but it also means that you continually face new difficulties. You are asked: How does the school relate to the church? And how to its founders and those who maintain it? What should be the relation between the headmaster and the other teachers? What are the pedagogical guidelines that derive from your Christian principles?

On all sides the issue is to convert the situation of living in huts to a situation of living in a well-appointed house. And of course you would not be Dutchmen if you did not strongly disagree among yourselves on these issues. ... Yet the history of our country also shows that in the end a basis

---

2. Both Alexander Frederik de Savornin Lohman, Esq. (1837–1924) and Aeneas Mackay Jr. (1838–1909), well-known champions of Christian education in and out of Parliament, were seated on the platform behind the speaker.
3. Kuyper is here telegraphing the coming of the Primary Education Bill sponsored by the Kuyper ministry and adopted by both houses of Parliament in May 1905.

of unity was always found. So speak your minds, also where your personal interests are at stake. That may sound egoistic, but to defend your interests is your right. Only, redouble your prayers that the Lord may set a watch before your mouth and keep the door of your lips [see Ps 141:3 KJV]. Take care that the heroism which for a long time flared up so brilliantly among you, even though it cannot dominate your activities at the moment, continues to glimmer as a spark in your heart, so that if ever the need should arise the old flame can burst forth with the same heroism that once moved those who came before you.

We shall never allow the Christ of God to be robbed of his honor as our King. Unlike many others, we not only honor him as Teacher and Example, but we kneel before him as our Lord and our God.

One more thing, brothers! Do not rest on your laurels, but with unremitting courage and devotion—and increased strength and energy as your numbers grow—carry on the hard work to complete the great task you have undertaken. Never think: we have reached our limit now that a full one-third of the nation's children attend schools where the name of Jesus Christ is mentioned. Make no mistake: you may not limit your ideal to that one-third; you must strive to reach two-thirds; and our entire nation should be so dear to you in the depth of your soul that ultimately you want to claim *three-thirds* of our population for the honor and the name of Christ!

You also need to broaden how you see your task. Too few young men are ready to serve their country, and too many are content to stay aloof from public life. You must do your part in equipping youth to stand for public office and so come to the aid of their country.

There is still more. While the chief aim in the school struggle thus far has been to motivate the lower classes, in this second phase of the struggle we are to work on the middle classes. Preoccupied with commerce and industry, they are little exposed to the salutary influence of Christianity, and hence run the danger of being taken up in the broad current that leads away from Christ and ends up corrupting the life of individuals and the life of society. Let no one say: those people have strayed too far; they are beyond hope. On the contrary, you who have compassion for the lower classes should have no less compassion for the higher classes. It is your calling not to rest until the beneficial effects of Christian education start to work in those circles as well.

Brothers and sisters, our struggle for the principle of Christian education has come to an end, and God grant that it never return. But that does not mean that the struggle of the spirits is over. On the contrary, the contest between the two forces that contend for the soul of the nation has only intensified. The waves of unbelief are pounding our shores with increasing force and threaten to flood the entire nation. We wrestle not against flesh and blood, nor against specific people. We face a struggle, rather, that arises from the spiritual world and penetrates life in the very heart of the nation. It is a struggle that no longer allows people to be satisfied, as in former times, with a "moderate Christianity" and with "Christian and civic virtues" and with Christian trappings during weddings and christenings. It is a struggle that increasingly attempts to repel the Christ himself—his name, his word, his work—a struggle that will not rest until it has created a situation in our country where nothing in public life reminds one of Christ. It is the struggle of a mighty spirit that deliberately breaks with the past because it fancies it is powerful enough to create a new life on its own. When the principles of justice are being uprooted and the most basic rules of public morality are slipping away, the cardinal question has become: What spirit will control the heart of our nation: the Spirit poured out on Pentecost, or the spirit from the abyss?

I call on you, brothers, to participate mightily in this struggle—provided that even if you were to triumph you would never want to injure the rights of your opponents. Always remember that your opponents are your neighbors whom you are to love and fellow citizens who share our country. Never act in order to dominate; your only task is to establish a strong presence in the country so that when others try to dominate you your resistance is powerful enough to prevent the Christian part of our people from being oppressed again. Your struggle is for the nation, not for a sect or a coterie. In the midst of the struggle your love should go out to all people and your prayer should be: "O God, save our poor country!"

And now, brothers and sisters, in view of my age I do not expect to have the honor to address you another time, so allow me to summarize my address in one word:

With the child in your arms you have taken your stand at the foot of the cross.

Don't ever let go of that child, and don't ever let go of that cross!

And God, the God of our baptism, he will prosper you.

I thank you.

AFTERWORD

FAITH, FINANCES, AND FREEDOM

Abraham Kuyper repeatedly summarized the Antirevolutionary educational program with the motto: *Free schools the norm, state schools a supplement*. He believed that a national system of free schools was not only the best way to serve Christian parents, but also the best way to serve all parents. It was best for all children to experience a unity of worldview and values between school and home. It was best for all parents to build schools which they could fully trust and support. It was best for teachers to be released from the sterile teaching of mere "facts" and be able to teach meaning behind those facts. It was best for pedagogy to come out from its subservience to either church or state and blossom from its own roots. Lastly, it was crucial for the nation that its citizens, most of whom were parents, develop the voluntary initiative and resilience which was so indispensable to a free nation.

Accordingly, Kuyper urged all adult citizens[1] to consider the depths of their primary experience, the foundation of their beliefs, values and

1. Kuyper appealed to all citizens to lend financial support to the schools they believed in. It was his original hope that all schools would be funded through tuition and philanthropy, and only when this was insufficient would the government offer a limited level of aid to parents to enable them to fulfill their parental duty of maintaining schools.

conceptions, and establish schools in which children could live and learn in a manner that reinforced that fundamental way of being and of knowing. If they were atheists they should establish free atheist schools. If they embraced a rationalist and/or moralistic approach to life and learning, then they should establish Modernist[2] schools; and, of course, likewise for parents who treasured the Calvinist and Roman Catholic faiths. In retrospect, this was clearly as far removed from a theocracy as one could get; people of all religious (and educational) perspectives would be free to find other likeminded people and establish self-governing schools for their children with an equal (per child) claim to the state's resources.[3] What would not be allowed was any attempt to impose a worldview upon children against the knowledge and wishes of the parents.

But Kuyper faced enormous opposition to such a plan, as the writings in this volume demonstrate. For the first half of the nineteenth century, while the Dutch educational system was centrally organized along the French model, constitutional law actually forbade any school to operate independently of the Dutch government (and the Dutch Reformed Church), even if it was privately funded. Not only was the nation accustomed to one state church, charged with teaching all Dutch children, but the new school leaders also found themselves unable to embrace the laudable Dutch history of religious tolerance.[4] It was greatly feared that allowing other denominations to educate children would inevitably open the doors to

---

2. See the introduction to this volume for a brief exploration of what this term meant in the nineteenth-century Netherlands.
3. See also the introduction for an important clarification of the principle of educational liberty. In the Netherlands, worldviews which qualify for the privilege of separate schools do not include any that openly espouse violence, nor those which base their faith, values, and convictions on race, gender, or economic status. There are no schools, for instance, which serve only girls, or which are geared to the upper class, or which teach only those of Dutch (or Middle-Eastern) descent. There are no schools which advocate white supremacy or jihad. All schools are required to teach in the Dutch language and to teach about other religions from the standpoint of mutual tolerance.
4. Kuyper argued that the rise of religious tolerance had been the fruit of the Protestant Reformation, and in particular of the Calvinist belief in the sovereignty of God regarding salvation. For if salvation was no longer considered a work of man (either as an individual or through a human institution), but entirely the work of God alone, by grace alone, then it was useless and even dangerous for the state to have as its goal the promotion of one particular religious confession. Such attempts eventually devolved into tyranny. If God, in his common grace, "caused his sun to shine

sectarian extremism and chaos. The first free schools in the Kingdom of the Netherlands were operated illegally in the 1840s by Protestant Dissenters who suffered greatly for having seceded from the state church. Stories abound of having to hide their schools in barns, quickly to be disassembled if a state official appeared. The new Constitution of 1848 provided legal recognition of privately funded free schools, but because the Netherlands suffered a prolonged economic depression during the later decades of the nineteenth century, many parents found this to be a liberty in name only. And while that constitution required that state schools teach "all Christian and civic virtues," this was no comfort to parents who knew their local schools to be infused with the deistic Christianity that replaced sin with ignorance and Christ the Savior with Christ the good example. The more Kuyper carefully exposed the education that was being offered in the state schools the more Calvinist and Roman Catholic parents realized that they had no choice but to remove their children from such institutions and establish free schools at enormous sacrifice.

The government continued to grant substantial subsidy to state schools and to deny free schools any support. Parliamentary leaders saw no reason to provide for free schools, when "educationally adequate" schools were offered free of charge to all children. Old Liberals[5] hung on to the dream of a state church governing state schools in the one true religion. And the New Liberals[6] espoused the dream of state schools educating the population out of orthodox Christianity and into a deistic and moralistic Christianity. In the 1870s it was only the Antirevolutionary Party which argued that no one type of school could possibly be appropriate for all Dutch children, given the variation and intensity of religious conviction among the population.

If, at this point, the state subsidies for state schools had been withdrawn, so that all schools had relied exclusively on tuition and philanthropy, the free schools would have been much less disadvantaged. Alternatively, had the state not required that free school advocates (roughly two-thirds of the population) be taxed at the same rate as those who favored the state schools, the free schools might have survived without a revision of the Constitution.

---

and his rain to fall upon both the just and the unjust" (Matt 5:45), then should not men do likewise? See Abraham Kuyper, "Calvinism: Source and Stronghold of our Constitutional Liberties," in *AKCR*, 279–317, at 305.

5. That is, the Conservatives.
6. That is, the Radicals who had embraced the political theory of the French Revolution.

But the political philosophy which prevailed among the elite class did not allow of either arrangement. Inequality between state and free schools was acceptable in the light of the conviction that deistic moralism (sometimes as a segue into secularism) was self-evidently neutral.

In Kuyper's first comments about the financing of free schools, therefore, he argued that a system which financed only state schools against the conscience of two-thirds of the population was fundamentally unjust, especially when it relied on taxation drawn from the entire nation in order to do so. Such a system granted to one segment of the population a financial privilege at the direct expense of all other segments. It enabled a relatively new belief system to be imposed upon the children of the poor. And since the same inequity obtained for higher education, the "modernist" leadership over every aspect of Dutch society (in politics, medicine, business, journalism, art, schools, and university) which had arisen during the first part of the nineteenth century, was confirmed and strengthened in the second part of that century.

Kuyper pointed out that in contrast to the stated reason for removing doctrinal religion from public schools (to achieve national unity), the policy had actually resulted in increased polarization and distrust between different segments of the nation, and, Kuyper argued, it could not be otherwise. Substantial differences of belief were irreducible, non-negotiable, and at their core, impervious to fusion with each other; they simply could not be eradicated. The attempt to teach a religion "acceptable to all" had the effect of promoting religious skepticism and was, in reality, an attempt to change the religious belief of their citizens from the top down. While Kuyper initially was unsuccessful in convincing many members of Parliament, he was able to open the eyes of many Calvinist and Roman Catholic parents, who knew a false gospel when they heard it, and were ready to endure incredible injustice to protect their children from such teaching. As they realized what was now being taught in the state schools, they felt bound by their conscience to remove their children from such teaching. Not having any say in what was taught in state schools, the only recourse they had was to exit them and establish free schools at their own expense, which they did in increasing numbers during the 1870s and 1880s.

Between 1869 and 1920 Kuyper's practical and political advocacy for school funding went through three distinct phases. At the same time, with each new proposal he consistently referred back to three foundational Christian principles which guided the Antirevolutionary Party in the issue of school funding: freedom of conscience, equal treatment of religion under the law, and the place of schools within civil society. The rest of this essay consists of two parts. In Part 1, I explore Kuyper's thinking in regard to each of the above-named Antirevolutionary principles, and the corresponding financial arrangement for schools which he considered his ideal throughout his career. In the second part, I discuss the three kinds of compromise which Kuyper was willing to accept until such time as their ideal might be realized: restitution, partial funding, and complete funding. Included by way of a conclusion are a few thoughts on the implications of Kuyper's thinking for North America in the twenty-first century: namely, a voucher system that would give all parents substantial school choice without financial penalty.

I. THREE GUIDING PRINCIPLES REGARDING FINANCES

The first principle which guided Kuyper and the Antirevolutionary Party in regard to the funding of all schools was the belief that the Dutch constitutional principle of *freedom of conscience and religion,* when consistently applied to education, required that all parents have the right as well as the opportunity to send their children to a school which shared their deepest convictions and experience. Obviously this would require some form of financial assistance for parents who were unable to provide the full tuition for such schools. Kuyper argued that it was fundamentally unjust that any Dutch parent be forced, by reason of their poverty, to submit their children to teaching which either directly or implicitly violated their conscience. It is interesting that although the Netherlands had historically experienced severe tensions between Roman Catholics and Protestants, Kuyper found common ground with Catholics in their mutual desire for distinctly religious schooling for their children.

According to this principle of liberty of conscience, he also insisted on the principle of *liberty from unwarranted state intrusion into the operation of the schools*.

Kuyper did not shrink from state requirements of minimum standards that must be met by all schools. He believed that the state had a responsibility to ensure that the formation of the nation's youth not fall below that of surrounding nations.

> If men want to examine our children, in order to judge if they are receiving a solid education, we would welcome the opportunity to show the capability of our schools.[7]
>
> Only, [we must recognize that] inspection has its natural limits. It may not concern itself in any way with the moral or religious education, nor with the spirit in which the education is given. It must limit itself to seeing whether our schools reach at least the same standards as the state schools apart from their Kantian deism or teaching of moral autonomy.[8] ... All interference of the government with the inner affairs of the school, its financial administration, the hiring of teachers, the academic tenor, and the spirit of the school is entirely prohibited.[9]

He supported laws which stipulated that certain subjects be taught in all elementary schools; that a minimum of hours were given to those subjects per week; that minimum academic, health, and building standards were met; and that teachers were properly qualified.[10] He insisted that free schools never become an excuse for shoddy teaching. There "was as little excuse for a bad free school as for a bad state school." At the same time, he insisted that all supervisors understand and abide by the limits to their regulatory authority. They must never intrude upon the fundamental culture and worldview upon which all subjects were taught. One of state's most holy responsibilities was to *protect the effect of belief* upon how one interprets history, appreciates science, disciplines students, and organizes the school day by avoiding all government regulation of those matters. Any regulation which touched on matters of religion, anthropology, sociology, and philosophy of education should be strictly forbidden. Because the state was incompetent to evaluate the pedagogical program of schools to

7. Abraham Kuyper, *De Schoolkwestie IV* (Amsterdam: J.H. Kruyt, 1875), 20–21.
8. Some Conservatives and Liberals wondered how the teaching of (traditional) morality could possibly offend Christian sensibilities. Their offence is explained by what Kuyper refers to as "the teaching of moral autonomy." It was the teaching that man is autonomous, free to choose (and change) his morals as he deemed fit, that was offensive. In an orthodox Christian view, morals are revealed by God and it is man's obligation to explore these, and to learn how to apply and obey them.
9. Kuyper, *De Schoolkwestie IV*, 20–21.
10. Abraham Kuyper, *Parlementaire Redevoeringen*, 4 vols. (Amsterdam: Van Holkema en Wahrendorf, 1908–1912), 3:391–394 and 4:464–478.

any great depth, it should restrict its oversight to that of guaranteeing the achievement of *minimum* academic standards.[11]

Accordingly, during his term as prime mimister, Kuyper defended the idea that all schools be required to write and submit to the inspector general an extensive "curriculum plan" which clearly stated their worldview and mapped out their goals and methods for every subject in light of that worldview. But he also insisted that these plans should never require the *approval* of a state inspector, for that would assume that inspectors could step outside of their own worldview in order to objectively evaluate the program of other worldviews, an assumption he believed was false.[12] The attempt to do so would inevitably result in a serious infringement on the distinct identity of free schools. He wanted the state to require that parents, duly elected leaders, and teachers in all schools clarify *for themselves* how their values and faith would affect the education they provided. For Kuyper and the Antirevolutionary Party (ARP) it was thus imperative that any system of funding free schools not become a means by which the state gradually gained control over those schools.

Secondly, Kuyper consistently articulated the principle of *equal treatment of religion under the law* especially in regard to the financial support of free schools. It was fundamentally unjust, he argued, that parents of one worldview be able to educate their children with tax money raised from all citizens, while two-thirds of the population were unable, on grounds of conscience, to send their children to those schools. It amounted to a state-sanctioned monopoly of state funding by one particular worldview which defied not only the Dutch constitution, but also their long history of religious tolerance. Because the state was neither called nor equipped to discern which religious and educational perspective was objectively true, it must remain neutral by supporting free schools and state schools on a parity basis. Justice demanded nothing less.

---

11. The distinction between what could and could not be regulated would become tricky, of course, just as the distinction between facts and values has been challenged. Kuyper's answer to this was to insist on a minimum of regulation for those agreed-upon values which yielded themselves to measurement. In the Netherlands today, there are umbrella organizations which enable schools to regulate themselves via intermediary bodies.
12. Kuyper, *Parlementaire Redevoeringen*, 4:464–478.

On the ninth of April, 1877, Kuyper wrote an article in *De Standaard* in which he clarified this principle. Referring to the few Antirevolutionary men who had been elected to Parliament at that time, he wrote:

> Standing their ground, they will soon clarify the decisive principle: GOVERNMENT EQUALITY FOR NEUTRALISTS AND NON-NEUTRALISTS. Over this foundational principle, there was no disagreement among us. ... To both the same amount, whether much or little!—See, that is our self-authenticated formula. The formula whereby we do not beg for alms, but insist on our rights.[13]

The third principle that guided Kuyper and the ARP on the issue of school funding was the belief that *educational institutions should arise out of civil society*, from the ground up, through the free initiative, dedication, and sacrifice of parents, teachers, and community members. This was important not only because pedagogy needed to be freed from its former subservience to church and state, but also because parents needed this responsibility in order to develop habits of initiative, self-help, and resilience, characteristics that were essential to the healthy functioning of a free society. Kuyper was convinced that an education system in which parents were responsible for establishing, governing, and funding their children's school provided vital experience necessary to their taking initiative in other areas of society. Only when parents failed to initiate schools themselves should the state organize temporary schools which would be transferred to parent government as soon as possible.

Thus the following three principles guided the ARP regarding the educational laws they espoused, supported, or opposed:

- *Freedom of conscience* for all parents to provide for their children an education in harmony with the faith, values, and experience in their homes. Accordingly, schools must be free from all state intrusion into the distinct identity of the schools.

---

13. Abraham Kuyper, *"Ons Program" (Met Bijlagen)* (Amsterdam: J. H. Kruyt, 1879), 673. Note: This 1,300-page volume should not be confused with *Our Program* (Bellingham, WA: Lexham Press, 2015), which is a translation of the 1880 abridged edition of the work, which lacks the "Bijlagen" (Appendices).

- *Equal treatment under the law, for both free and state schooling,* especially as regards financial support.
- *The rightful place of schools in modern society,* established from the ground up, by the free initiative, private funding, and self-governance of the people.

Kuyper considered these three principles—liberty, equality, and free initiative—to be so intertwined that each required the others for its own success. Freedom of conscience was meaningless unless the state guaranteed that right by ensuring that all parents could choose their children's school. At the same time, equal access to financial aid must so operate that it did not undermine either the free initiative of parents or the school's ability to pursue their educational program within their particular worldview. Lastly, the free initiative of parents would not last long if the state were allowed to interfere in the heart of the curriculum. Schools must be independent in order to be free. Schools must be free in order to guarantee liberty of conscience. And schools must be treated equally if either liberty or independence was to be possible.

Subvention

In accordance with these three antirevolutionary principles, Kuyper's abiding ideal was for a national educational system of free schools, the funding of which in some respects resembled a voucher system. He called this arrangement *subvention.* In its basic form it required that all elementary schools be funded first and foremost by a combination of parental tuition and private charity. Tax levies would decrease by the amount of subsidies currently going to state schools, thereby freeing up the means for all interested parties to fund and maintain their schools. Schools would be free to educate according to their (properly defined) religious or educational perspective. And, as a safety net for situations when parents could not afford tuition and when private charity proved insufficient, the state would grant financial aid *directly to parents according to their need and independent of which school they chose for their children.* This safety net was to fall under the welfare laws, not the educational laws. Its purpose was to enable parents to fulfill their parental duty in times of hardship, and its duration was to be temporary.

> Such a subvention could decrease gradually and according to set rules and eventually be terminated so that it would

> contribute to strengthening and stimulating citizens' resilience, and so that the voluntary principle could send out deep roots into the entire nation.[14]

Kuyper insisted that state funding go directly to parents, on the basis of actual need. He was convinced that giving state support to parents who did not need it would undermine their moral strength and resilience. For the principle of voluntary self-government to triumph, not one penny of state aid should be given either to the schools or to any parent beyond their inability to provide for their children's education.

> The [revolutionary] principle leads to a school that is completely paid for by the state and is open to everyone. They do not want to hear about direct state aid to parents—only of aid that goes to the schools. This destroys the sense of freedom, the sense of right, and the sense of shame among our citizens, and delivers to the ruling elite a passive population that men can direct at will. ... The difference between the revolutionary and the antirevolutionary principle in this matter can, therefore, be summarized as follows: The antirevolutionaries disapprove of every state aid for schooling and demand that if it cannot be avoided, such aid be provided according to Article 196 of our Constitution [regarding poor relief], and never on the basis of Article 195 of the Constitution [regarding education].[15]

Not all Christians agreed with Kuyper on the matter of school funding. In 1885, a Calvinist pastor by the name of Tinholt wrote a series of articles in *De Banier*[16] in which he proposed that all elementary schools be funded by the state and governed by parent boards.[17] Teachers would openly declare their religious principles and parent boards would choose teachers according to the demands of the parents sending children to that school. If all parents in a neighborhood wanted a Christian education, entire schools

---

14. Kuyper, *"Ons Program" (Met Bijlagen)*, 471–476, a reprint of an article entitled "The Money Question," which appeared in *De Standaard* of 20 Dec. 1878. The quotation is from page 475.
15. Kuyper, *"Ons Program" (Met Bijlagen)*, 476.
16. *De Banier* was a journal established by the Calvinist dissenters who had seceded from the Dutch Reformed Church in 1834.
17. Reprinted as *Een Twistappel en zijne wegruiming: een voorslag tot oplossing der onderwijs-kwestie, tegen bestrijding verdedigd* (Utrecht: Breijer, 1885), 3–32.

could be Protestant or Catholic. If the demand was mixed, there would be teachers from each denomination. Parents could freely choose the kind of teaching they preferred; teachers would be released from the requirement to teach facts separate from meaning (or worse yet, teach according to a worldview which they hid); and the state would make sure that there were quality schools for all. While Kuyper agreed with Tinholt's goals, he vehemently disagreed with his proposed methods—so much so that he responded immediately with the following asterism in *De Standaard*:

> For thirty years our Christian people, led by its best leaders, have worked for the *free Christian school*. That effort has not been put to shame. The school has become a force in the land. Yet no sooner does the hope arise on the horizon that before long free schooling shall be the rule, then there begins to awaken among our friends again the appetite for the state trough. Pay attention to this phenomenon! The kernel is still small—but in it lies the inexorable death of all your free schools. *Sat sapienti*: A word to the wise ...[18]

He then published three articles in *De Standaard* outlining his principled objections to Tinholt's proposal.[19] Kuyper clearly opposed an arrangement whereby Christian education would be subsidized by the state and he predicted that within three years all free schools would have relinquished their independence and become state schools. They would thereby lose not only their freedom of operation, but also any hope they had for substantive and distinct Christian influence in society (because parents would not have developed habits of voluntarism). Such a system, Kuyper insisted, represented a kneeling before the false god of Mammon.[20] In an article entitled "The Ambush" Kuyper continued:

---

18. This brief editorial appeared in *De Standaard* of 18 March 1885 and was reprinted in Abraham Kuyper, *Starren-Flonkering; een bundel drie-starren* (Amsterdam: Drukkerij De Standaard, 1932), 182–183. The phrase "hope on the horizon" may have been inspired by the inevitable extension of the franchise which would put the Christian parties at the helm of government. If so, history proved Kuyper right when the Mackay ministry took office in 1889 and sponsored a revised Education Act that recognized free schools as a legitimate part of the nation's education system and provided them with some financial relief.
19. See the chapter, "Government Funding or Citizen Initiative?" in this volume.
20. Abraham Kuyper, "De Ondergang der Vrije Christelijke school," *De Standaard*, 23 March 1885.

> Here is a crossroads. One cannot walk right and left at the same time. State interference, or citizen initiative! That is the choice. And in this choice, we, together with the entire Antirevolutionary Party, according to its platform, have chosen for citizen initiative and against state interference, especially in matters of church and schools. ... [We have insisted upon] the voluntary principle that seeks strength in the spontaneous initiative of the citizenry. ...
>
> Precisely the fact, men and brothers, that you have been forced to erect and support your own schools, to train teachers and sacrifice money for them, that is precisely what has built up your strength—while the liberals, who didn't need to do anything, who could eat from the state's trough, have lost strength. The practical school struggle, if nothing else, spurred on your national strength and made you what you are![21]

In another article entitled "The Fatal Proposal," he acknowledged the fact that distinctly Christian teaching would be allowed under Tinholt's proposal but insisted that the state subsidy and control would quickly undermine that independence and distinction.

> What *De Banier* has to answer for is just one point: will the school of its proposal be under the authority of the state, yes or no? ... Who ultimately will be in charge? ... Whose prerogative will it be to say: This is how things will have to be done!
>
> For realize this well: implicit in this fatal proposal is a public policy, a political direction, and a political principle. What do you want, men and brothers? A government as in France, one that does everything for you, decides everything for you, and paralyzes your spontaneity, one that snuffs out your spirit of liberty?[22]

It is interesting to note that at this point in time Kuyper considered only those schools to be free which met the three conditions mentioned above. They needed to be initiated, organized, and maintained voluntarily by free associations. They needed to be financed by parents and philanthropy (with state assistance going directly to parents only, according to need). And state

---

21. Abraham Kuyper, "De Hinderlaag," *De Standaard*, 27 March 1885.
22. Abraham Kuyper, "De fatale Voorslag," *De Standaard*, 13 April 1885.

regulation needed to be limited to matters of universally approved measureable standards, and even then restricted to minimum standards so as not to even unintentionally impinge on the underlying worldview and culture of the curriculum. Legal, financial, and pedagogical independence: these three were absolutely essential if a school was to rightfully call itself "free" from state control:

> In our free Christian schools we ourselves are sovereign. No one can tell us what to do. We are lord and master in that house. And if the government should ever try to break and enter, it will be an injustice and we will challenge it in the courts.[23]

Kuyper was successful in convincing the majority of the orthodox Calvinists that Tinholt's proposal was dangerous, and the controversy soon dissolved.

II. THREE PRAGMATIC COMPROMISES

As the school struggle progressed, and the educational principles of the ARP were clarified and communicated, Kuyper realized that the Antirevolutionaries needed to address the needs of the moment by taking small steps, designed to keep the free schools alive while they simultaneously sought to persuade those in power of the rightness of their cause.[24] He acknowledged that each proposal he set forth in this manner was incomplete, sometimes even appearing to directly contradict one or more of his educational principles. But given the powerful opposition to the ARP educational program in Parliament, progress, he knew, would be slow, and in the interim free schools needed to be kept alive. If there had been a more democratic system of suffrage, independent of any property qualification, Parliament would have represented the people far more accurately and a system of subvention would have met with success far earlier. But the Netherlands was only slowly emerging from a class-based society with

23. Kuyper, "De fatale Voorslag."
24. One of Kuyper's greatest achievements was to convince not only the Catholics, but also the Old Liberals of the rightness of their cause. By appealing to principles such as liberty and equality which were imbedded in the Dutch heritage, he was eventually able to convince them that all religious and educational groups of citizens deserved equal treatment under the law, especially when it touched upon the tender interests of their children. The new liberals, like Kappeyne, were much more radical and revolutionary. They formed the bulk of resistance to free schools.

its census democracy, and the ARP had to be patient and accept steps of progress which, when considered out of context, could appear inconsistent. From the beginning, Kuyper proposed short-term measures, stop-gap solutions which would enable free schools to survive until such time as either the suffrage laws were changed or they were able to appeal to their opponents' sense of justice and fair play, or both. Thus, from 1869 until 1889, Kuyper proposed a system of *Restitution*; from 1869 until 1910, he argued for *Partial Subsidy*; and from 1911 until 1920, he put his weight behind a program of *Full Subsidy* for all schools.

Phase I: Subvention his Ideal, Restitution his Compromise, 1869–1889

During the first period of Kuyper's leadership in the school struggle, he appealed to the Dutch people to recognize the fundamental right of all parents to educate their children according to their conscience.[25] Until that right was recognized by the people and by Parliament, there could be no possibility of subvention. If it was eventually recognized, then a system of free schools would follow logically. He posed several questions to the nation. Was the Netherlands to be the only nation in Europe where an orthodox Christian education was only available to the wealthy? Did the cherished principle of freedom of conscience, ensconced in the Dutch constitution, not also apply to the education parents were allowed to provide for their children? Was education to be directed by a centralized committee in The Hague, or was it to be directed locally by parents? These questions had the effect of awakening many citizens to what they had lost over the decades since they had accepted the French model of education. But he also understood that those who considered the autonomy of man to be self-evident would not see things the same way. The radicals considered free schools to be entirely unnecessary because they considered their own worldview to be neutral in regard to religion. From their point of view, so long as neutral and adequate education was available at no cost, free schools could not be considered anyone's right. In addition, the state schools were thoroughly accustomed to the privilege of direct state subsidy and would not give that up without a fight. Also the state did not at that time have access to reliable information about the financial means of citizens relative to the cost of living in different areas of the country. Thus, not only did the state see no

25. See especially, "An Appeal to the People's Conscience" in this volume.

need to offer financial help directly to parents, but it also lacked the ability to do that fairly.

Kuyper therefore advocated for a temporary system of Restitution, in which the state would return to free schools the money they saved the state. Of course, there were situations in which the free schools saved the state very little because they were small and state schools were large enough to accept all of their students anyway. Moreover, state schools sometimes competed aggressively for Christian families by bending the law and providing orthodox teachers and curriculum in areas that were strongly Calvinist or Catholic. But there were enough situations in which free schools were sufficiently large that they did save the state a lot of money, and it was this money that Kuyper argued should be given back to the free schools. He repeatedly stated that the Restitution system was not a principled solution to the school struggle, its primary merit being that it lessened the injustice of an inherently unjust system. He saw it as a way to help free schools survive until constitutional revision could implement a system of subvention. And yet, it was still unacceptable to leaders in Parliament, and never became law.

Phase II: Subvention his Ideal, Partial Funding his Interim Solution, 1889–1910

In 1888, as a result of an expansion of the suffrage, the religious parties gained a majority in Parliament and a prime minister was appointed from the ARP. One year later, Prime Minister Mackay submitted an education bill which recognized free schools as an integral part of the national school system. It granted a small subsidy to free schools and required all schools to charge tuition. Kuyper surprised many by supporting it. Although he had openly opposed such a financial system (preferring that state aid go directly to parents), he understood that it nevertheless contained the kernel of recognition that education was not neutral in relation to worldview. Although the subsidy granted to free schools was inadequate, it was nevertheless the first time that financial aid had ever been given to free schools on the basis of right and not as a temporary grant. As Kuyper later explained, although the subsidies in Mackay's act were far below what state schools received, at least they were not arbitrary or temporary, but guaranteed and regulated by law.[26] Of course, he would have much preferred that state money went

26. Kuyper, *Parlementaire Redevoeringen*, 4:384.

directly to parents and only to those who could demonstrate their inability to pay tuition themselves. His ideal remained that no schools receive direct state aid: that equal treatment under the law be achieved by the state granting no subsidy to either state or free schools. But he welcomed this bill for what it did recognize, in the hope that the financial arrangement could eventually be changed to one of subvention.

> Our general principle is *equality for all citizens!* And our concrete principle is *limited state interference*, especially in matters of education.
>
> If we divide our citizens, according to the requirement of the moment, into neutralists and non-neutralists, then *it remains our ambition to work for a future in which the state purse offers financial support to neither the one nor the other group*. And yet, for that to happen we need a revision of our Constitution. But, as long, therefore, as our concrete principle cannot yet be realized[27] we will nevertheless work for the triumph of our general principle and rest not until at least legal equality is reached by the abolishing of privilege. ... To both the same amount, whether much or little!—See, that is our self-authenticated formula. The formula whereby we do not beg for alms, but insist on our rights.[28]

In his newspaper he clarified his thoughts:

> Not as if this bill meets all of our wishes. That is impossible under our current Constitution. But this bill brings us forward a big step, because it honors legal equality between principles; because it puts into the foreground the duty of parents to care for the education of their children; because it recognizes the freedom of the government to support good schools, even if they are religious; because it prepares and promotes the development of the free school. If this bill is approved our nation will learn to appreciate the advantages of the free schools. ... For this happy opportunity we thank God first of all, and in

27. This is a slightly confusing passage, but appears to imply that the limitation of state interference cannot be achieved as long as the state insists on granting subsidies to schools. He later changed his mind on this issue.
28. Kuyper, *"Ons Program" (Met Bijlagen)*, 673 (emph. added).

> the second place Minister Mackay. May this bill be the beginning of the end, not of his administration, but of the school struggle.[29]

Characteristically Kuyper was ready to work within an imperfect system if it would lay the groundwork for a more principled solution in the future. Waterink, a professor of pedagogy in the Free University, notes that three years later Kuyper pointed out that the granting of state aid directly to schools failed to guarantee every parent the right to a school in harmony with their conscience, so that Kuyper could not yet support compulsory schooling laws. He wrote that his objection "would for a large part fall away if the matter had been arranged the way that we continually pressed for, namely that government aid would come to the child, not to the school or the teacher."[30] He had been disappointed but he understood that this bill was a step forward in the right direction which he would not hinder by complaining that it was not yet perfect. As Waterink put it, "Kuyper was far too great a tactician to make difficulties, in days of such fundamental decisions, about the *methods* of resolving the issues."[31]

Not all Dutch Calvinists greeted the Mackay bill with enthusiasm. On the 13th of August, 1889, the board of directors and head teachers of the Christian schools in four adjoining villages sent an open letter to Prime Minister Mackay and to many newspapers around the country, stating their concern that state subsidies to free schools would stifle the free initiative of the people. They insisted that state subsidy should only be given after private charity had been appealed to. And they insisted that state subsidy should only ever be considered a temporary solution. Kuyper was certainly sympathetic as he later recalled in June of 1903, in an article published in *De Heraut*.[32]

But while Kuyper shared these concerns, he took a stand against some of the more extreme opposition to Mackay's bill. The Rev. Dr. Willem van den Bergh, for instance, believed that legal equality between state and free schools would *inexorably* lead to the dissolution of the free schools' distinct identity. Kuyper responded by arguing that as long as subsidy was *partial*

---

29. Quoted from *De Standaard* of 17 April 1889 by J. Waterink, "Dr Kuyper en het onderwijs," in *Dr. A. Kuyper, Gedenkboek, 1837–1937* (Kampen: Kok, 1937), 177–78.
30. Quoted from *De Standaard* of 13 June 1892, in *Dr. A. Kuyper, Gedenkboek, 1837–1937,* 178.
31. *Dr. A. Kuyper, Gedenkboek, 1837–1937,* 177.
32. Abraham Kuyper, "De Wet op het Hooger Onderwijs," *De Heraut*, 14 June 1903.

and equal it might decrease the level of free initiative among parents but not completely destroy it. Van den Bergh considered any acceptance of state subsidy a sign of a lack of trust in God's faithfulness and a sure step in the direction of socialism. He even went so far as to say that any state subsidy to free schools was unjust toward the opponents of Christian education because their taxes would be used to promote Christian schools. Kuyper could only shake his head at such scruples. He did not waver in arguing that liberty for free schools was not incompatible with state subsidy ... *as long as that aid remained partial* so that parents were required to pay a significant portion of the cost of their child's education.

Five years later, in 1894, The Union "A School with the Bible"[33] formed a committee to study the educational issue afresh with the aim of defining unified guidelines along which the various Christian parties would work. At the time of these important committee meetings, Kuyper was out of the country for health reasons. Prominent Protestant leaders Mackay and Savornin Lohman steered the committee in a direction very different from that of the ARP. It was their conviction that Christians should work toward full state subsidy of all elementary schools, both public and private, to be financed through a "school tax," hence from government revenue to which all taxpayers contributed. Lohman, particularly, was convinced that unless there was complete state support of all schools, free schools would never become the norm:

> If the school is to remain free in relation to the state and if the parents, including the less fortunate, are to truly have free choice, then the arrangement of money must be as simple as possible, and then the existence of the schools must not depend

33. The organization called *De Unie: "Een School met den Bijbel"* was a national fund-raising federation of the local committees that helped organize the People's Petition of 1878 against Kappeyne's education bill. It was formally constituted on January 23, 1879, the 300th anniversary to the day, of a signal event in the sixteenth-century Dutch Revolt: the creation of the *Union* of Utrecht, a defensive league of the seven northern provinces of the Low Countries in opposition to Spanish rule. One of the school Union's first projects was to organize an annual national door-to-door collection in support of Christian schools, which, in its first 18 years, had yielded one and a half million guilders. When one considers that yearly tuition for schools in some locations amounted to only five guilders, one can better appreciate the enormity of that voluntary effort. See A. Kuyper, "Een twistappel," *De Standaard*, 26 Oct. 1896.

> upon any private contributions. Preferably the state would allow the users [parents] to pay, but this is a question of sharing the burdens [via taxation]. We are of the opinion that this solution is in harmony with our principles.[34]

In Kuyper's absence, his colleague at the Kampen Seminary, Herman Bavinck, expressed his principled opposition to a system of complete state funding of all schools.

> The question of whether parents must pay tuition continues to be answered [by the ARP] in the affirmative. The state does have a calling in regard to the school. It must be supportive and helpful, but not until after the churches' deacons have done what they can. The system of Mr. Lohman is really not a "contribution system" because *everything* comes from the state. That has never been the Antirevolutionary principle. The earlier idea [in 1857] was separate *State Confessional schools*. When this proved unfeasible, Dr. Tinholt proposed in *De Banier* the same idea that Mr. Lohman now proposes, with slight alterations. The Antirevolutionary Party at that time vigorously and unanimously resisted that plan. ... Mr. Lohman acknowledges that raising funds from parents and private donors is *useful* to schools, but I think it is *absolutely necessary*. For, if all financial bonds between the parents and the teachers are let go, the consequence will be that gradually you will not be able to speak about a spiritual and moral bond. Then the Christian school is gone.[35]

The Christian teachers understandably liked the initial Union Report. After years of sacrifice on their part, the thought of receiving salaries, pensions, and school materials commensurate with their public school associates and with no infringement of their liberty to teach a religious worldview sounded wonderful. After much discussion and against the advice of the ARP the report was approved.

---

34. A.F. de Savornin Lohman, quoted in J. P. Kuiper, *Geschiedenis van het Christelijk Lager Onderwijs in Nederland,* 2nd rev. ed. (Amsterdam: Bottenburg, 1904), 334.
35. Herman Bavinck, quoted in *Geschiedenis van het Christelijk Lager Onderwijs in Nederland,* 335–36.

It soon became evident, however, that the lack of support from the ARP, and in particular from Kuyper, was a major obstacle to unified action among the Christian parties. Upon his return to the country in the spring of 1896, Kuyper and fourteen other men voiced their concerns. They argued that the Report worked contrary to the antirevolutionary principle that every parent should pay a substantial portion of the cost of their child's schooling. They further argued that the system proposed by the Report was built upon socialist first principles and would have the effect of stifling the moral initiative and liberty of the people. Lastly, they argued that centralization of funding would cause the cost of education to rise precipitously and unnecessarily.[36]

Kuyper set to work to communicate the rationale behind their objection to the Union Report. He contributed a series of *Standaard* editorials between 26 October and 31 December 1896, which once more set forth his principled opposition to a system of complete state subsidy for all schools. He laid out the argument that the difference between partial state funding and complete state funding was a difference in *kind*, not simply in *degree*. Thus, the issue was a matter of first principle, not just of strategy.

Kuyper's first argument was that the moral resistance and free initiative required by citizens to establish and maintain free schools would be weakened and eventually destroyed by complete subsidy:

> Our great strength in the school struggle thus far has been that we had so much need. It sent us to our knees and prayer united us. That devotion and commitment made us willing to make great sacrifices. As long as that strength held, we stood strong, no matter what happened. And the Mackay Act did not in any way break that formidable strength because the subsidy received at that time did not so much lessen the financial burden as it enabled us, and in part forced us, to improve our schools.
>
> Every action in the school struggle contributed to the endurance, nurture, and reinforcement of our moral resilience. That made us into a power in the land. And whereas public funding

36. Cf. P. de Zeeuw, J. Gzn, *De Worsteling om het kind: de strijd voor een vrije school historisch geschetst* (Amsterdam: Kirchner, 1925), 353–54.

of the liberals was the cause of their debilitation and decline, the funds given out of love worked to steel and to strengthen us.

If you would now reverse this, and fund our schools along with the state schools completely from the state or with a very low school tuition or a school tax ... not only would the parental sense of duty weaken, but before we are ten years further, you will have broken, once and for all, the entire powerful factor of your moral resistance.

Then your strength in the country will diminish, your weapons will rust, and before you know it, the opponent will punish your lack of carefulness by passing a new law that puts all elementary schools under the state and destroys the institution of free schooling.[37]

Kuyper again warned that cost-free education would inevitably lead either to state interference or to socialism:

> ... The main point is that the Mackay law embodied a completely just principle, which when it stays within its natural borders is life-giving, but which, when it goes beyond those borders, works death. Petroleum provides you with light and warmth only when it is limited to a certain amount, but when it exceeds that amount the oil bursts into flames and threatens your life. Welfare is certainly needed for whomever cannot afford the standard that the state has set. *Whatever goes beyond that and subsidizes all equally goes directly against our principle.*[38]

Kuyper was clear: the difference between partial subsidy and complete subsidy was one of principle. When subsidy was partial and stayed within its limits it was life-giving. When it exceeded those limits, it threatened life. A week later, Kuyper explained why the ARP was open to any subsidy at all given their expressed ideal of subvention:

> The Free schools would not ask for one penny if the costs of the *public* schools came from a separate tax which was laid only upon those who support the public school. But as long as men take money for the public school from us, the

37. Abraham Kuyper, "Een twistappel" [A Bone of Contention], *De Standaard*, 26 Oct. 1896 (emph. added).
38. Kuyper, "Een twistappel."

> Antirevolutionaries, money that we could otherwise use for our own free schools, it is only a matter of justice that men would give us back a sufficient amount of that money for our own schools. The supporters of the free schools pay at the least five million to the public schools and receive one million back. This is not fair and not just.[39]

In an editorial on November 9, 1896, Kuyper argued that if the first Union Report were ever successfully implemented, it would in effect take their schools out of civil society and place them under the state. Parents would become indifferent and thereby incapable of the level of commitment which starting and maintaining a school required:

> The best lesson is the best example. Only through the example of the free school, the school of the parents and paid for by the parents, do we believe that the nation, insofar as it has not already reached this point, will be won for the higher standpoint of freedom of education.[40]

Many teachers, members of the Union, had initially voted for the first report but began to change their minds. Kuyper empathized with them, stating that if it were indeed possible to receive full funding from the state without risking infringement of their liberty, he would support it wholeheartedly. But the risk was too great.

When another newspaper questioned the wisdom of Christian schools accepting any state subsidy at all, in an argument similar to Van den Bergh's of a few years previous, Kuyper again took the opportunity to draw an important distinction between partial and complete subsidy:

> First, the concept of subsidy not only does not require complete subsidy but completely closes the door to that option. You support someone who is still walking; someone who can no longer walk on their own you do not support but you carry. The very concept of subsidy contains within it the idea that it not be anything other than a contribution to the total amount, and therefore never exceed certain limits.[41]

---

39. Abraham Kuyper, "Oriënteering," *De Standaard*, 6 Nov. 1896.
40. Abraham Kuyper, "Uit de Pers. Het Unie-Rapport," *De Standaard: Bijvoegsel*, 9 Nov. 1896.
41. Abraham Kuyper, "Misverstand," *De Standaard*, 14 Nov. 1896.

In a series of five *Standaard* articles entitled "The Principled Objections to the Union Report," which began on Friday, November 13, 1896, he reiterated that state funding of free schools could only be compatible with liberty if it was limited (that is, partial) and if it was combined with mandatory parent tuition. To accept full funding for free schools would be to abandon their Antirevolutionary principles:

> The Union Report [as it now stands], which consistently seeks equality, does so by exchanging the antirevolutionary principles for those of the Liberals. The motto of the Liberals was always: Education is a responsibility of the state; parents should pay as little as possible, preferably nothing; charitable help has no place in education. The motto of the Antirevolutionaries, by contrast, was and remains: Child-rearing and education is the responsibility of the parents; the parents should therefore pay as much as possible themselves. When this is not possible, then Christian love [that is, private charity] for our Christian school should form the primary source of income. Thus, the convictions of Liberals and Antirevolutionaries about this subject are diametrically opposed to one another. ...
>
> Legal equality can be acquired in two ways: (1) by requiring that state schools, too, should be supported primarily by parents and charitable donations, and only partially by the state; or (2) by our accepting the system of the Liberals in which the parents are not allowed to pay anything for their children's education, ... Either way achieves legal equality; but in the first instance by upholding, and in the second instance by abandoning the antirevolutionary principle. The Report opts for the latter and buys the legal equality at the expense of our spiritual principle.[42]

On November 27, 1896, Kuyper explained that, contrary to Liberal political theory, Antirevolutionaries insisted that school taxes and school tuition were very different methods of school funding based upon two opposing political principles. Antirevolutionaries could accept a system in which the costs of education were shared by taxes and parental tuition, but they had

42. Abraham Kuyper, "De principieele bezwaren tegen het Unie-Rapport, III," *De Standaard*, 18 Nov. 1896.

to utterly oppose a system whereby the entire cost of education was paid for by taxes alone. Such a system rested upon the concept that education was a fundamental task and responsibility of the state: "But Anti-revolutionaries, of course, neither can nor may adopt this fiction."[43]

Kuyper then declared that the time to work for the subvention system had come. Unlike in 1889, the government now had official information by which to ascertain the financial ability of citizens in relation to the standard of living in their particular locality. There was therefore no longer any reason to wait: the subvention system was feasible.[44] State aid going directly to free schools must now be aggressively opposed:

> Making direct payment to the school has the very serious and negative consequence that the teachers and school boards, who receive furniture, lighting, heat and so on, and in addition pensions from the state, whether they want to or not, will inevitably lean upon the state, incline themselves toward the official nature of the state, and hereby gradually come under a spirit which kills the free life of the citizen.[45]

The board of the Union took these concerns seriously and installed a new committee to investigate the many objections to the Report. After almost three years this committee came up with a proposed "Revised Union Report" which contained two major changes to the original Report. First, all schools would be required to charge tuition: cost-free education would no longer be supported by any of the Christian parties. Secondly, all schools would be granted a subsidy from the national government sufficient to operate a bare-bones school; the rest of their budget would have to come from parents and charity.[46] The revised Union Report was voted upon and unanimously adopted in the association's annual membership meeting of April 17, 1900.

By May of the following year, Kuyper's position concerning the possibility of subvention had significantly changed. While he still insisted that complete state funding was rooted in revolutionary principles and would, if implemented, result in the demise of truly free schools, he nevertheless

43. Abraham Kuyper, "De principieele bezwaren tegen het Unie-Rapport, V," *De Standaard*, 27 Nov. 1896.

44. Kuyper, "De principieele bezwaren tegen het Unie-Rapport, V."

45. Abraham Kuyper, "De principieele bezwaren tegen het Unie-Rapport, VI (Slot)," *De Standaard*, 30 Nov. 1896.

46. P. de Zeeuw, J. Gzn, *De Worstelling om het kind*, 353–354.

began to accept that *subvention*, a system of support directly to parents, was no longer possible. On May 31, 1901, he wrote in *De Heraut* that while subvention was still their ideal, because of the drastic increase in the cost of schooling, and because of the refusal of Parliament to require that state schools give up their subsidies, there was very little hope that subvention could ever become a reality in the Netherlands. The cost of schooling had risen to approximately twenty-five guilders per child, a sum which the free school communities were simply unable to pay for themselves.[47] "Men can require it, but it is an unreasonable requirement, a requirement that comes up against the limits of our financial ability."[48]

Some state funding had become indispensable, and the Antirevolutionaries needed to adjust their expectations to this new reality. The system of partial subsidies was now no longer their interim strategy, but their primary strategy, in order to stave off a revolutionary system of complete school funding through taxation. The job of the ARP was now to work for equality, liberty, and voluntarism by insisting that state schools charge at least *some* tuition and by increasing the amount of subsidy to free schools:

> Attention has recently and with good reason been paid to the danger that hides in the steady increase of subsidies that are offered to our free schools. There is no question that, if we could choose, every Christian among us would declare himself to be against all subsidy and by far prefer a situation in which all costs of elementary, secondary, and tertiary education would be completely and exclusively paid for by those who either make use of that education or have an interest in it. The parents are and remain the first called, and if the parents fail in their financial strength, then it is best if Christian love is sufficiently available to help them in this need.
>
> So we understand it completely when there are still those among us who do not see the subsidy system winning the day without aversion, and who do not receive the gifts from the federal budget without protest. There are even a few schools that refuse all subsidy outright and who manage from their

47. Abraham Kuyper, "Subsidiën," *De Heraut*, 31 May 1901.
48. Kuyper, "Subsidiën."

> own means. And still, however beautiful this is, it appears to us that this high ideal has become once and for all unfeasible. ...[49]

In the same year (1901), after another expansion of the suffrage, the Christian parties again gained a majority in parliament and the queen appointed Kuyper as prime minister. He set about working to equalize the subsidies given to free and state schools. At last, in 1905, a revision of the Elementary Education Act significantly increased the subsidy for all elementary schools, raised the salaries of both free and state school teachers equally, and stipulated that all teachers' pensions would no longer be paid by the municipality but by the national government.[50] The public school teachers especially appreciated this last addition since their continued employment was not as secure as it had been in the past now that the demand for free schools was growing exponentially. A similar revision of subsidy for secondary schools was also enacted. And Kuyper's law for Higher Education finally granted private universities the right to grant diplomas "*cum effectu civili*"—that is, with the same legal status as diplomas from the state universities.[51]

Although Kuyper worked hard as prime minister to increase the subsidies for all schools, several speeches given during this time reveal that he still firmly intended for state subsidy to be a *supplement* to parental tuition and private charity at all schools:

> I have always been convinced that cost-free education when it is the rule, or is provided too easily, brings harm to the moral resilience of our people. At schools where I myself was a board member for many years and which drew almost all their children from the small working-class, no school tuition was charged, but it was explained to everyone that families who were able to give would have an opportunity every week to give something extra toward the costs [of operating the school].[52] Now then, merely by appealing to their sense of

49. Kuyper, "Subsidiën."
50. P. A. Diepenhorst, *Onze Strijd in de Staten-Generaal*, 2 vols. (Amsterdam: Uitgeverij De Standaard, 1927–1929), 1:461.
51. W. F. A. Winckel, *Leven en arbeid van Dr. A. Kuyper* (Amsterdam: Ten Have, 1919), 138–44.
52. It was the custom in many Christian schools for teachers to collect tuition fees from the children every Monday morning.

> honor, parents' awareness [of the need] grew so strong that they collectively contributed an average of five guilders per family per year. I believe that this method contributed more to the moral uplifting of this class than if people had simply been given that education for free.[53]

In another parliamentary speech Kuyper reiterated his concern that partial subsidy not be construed as justifying unwarranted state regulation over elementary schools. Because of the inextricable intertwining between common-grace learning and that which was founded upon a particular worldview, it was not an easy task to regulate the former and exempt the latter. The lines of demarcation between science and worldview were not so easily drawn even by professional philosophers, much less by local school inspectors:

> There can be no thought of setting guarantees for the quality of education unless two things are demonstrated; first, that such a guarantee can reach its goal; and secondly, that such a guarantee will not touch the unique character of free education in its various formations. And it appears that an undertaking which aims to meet both of these requirements is quite a risky business. ... There is reason to doubt that the members [sitting] opposite to me have given sufficient thought to the difficulties that this problem poses. The difference between [so-called] neutral education and positive-Christian free education is not simply the inclusion or exclusion of religious learning materials, but on the contrary is a matter that governs the entire nature of the school. From two very divergent foundational principles, completely different conclusions will be drawn about the pedagogical rules that must find expression in schools. Their different views of the child result in disagreements about the psychological factors which must be reckoned with, about the goal of education during the younger years, about the methods that must be used and about the meaning of the application of those methods, for example, in rewards and punishment.[54]

53. Kuyper, *Parlementaire Redevoeringen*, 2:657.
54. Kuyper, *Parlementaire Redevoeringen*, 4:348.

> Equality of [academic] level between two directions that differ in their starting points and in their methods cannot be accurately measured with a common formula. And if one tries to guarantee quality through inspection, there will be the same problem as we have already seen: every inspector will judge the quality of education according to his own pedagogical concepts, without being able at all to justly and accurately judge the level of an education which is built upon totally different pedagogical principles.[55]

That not all of parliament understood this, is evident from Kuyper's rejection of a proposal that free schools would be required to submit their curriculum plans for approval to state-school inspection committees. Kuyper explained that he would heartily support such a law provided that the free schools had a separate inspection for their own schools.[56]

As subsidy to free schools increased, Kuyper was busier than ever clarifying that this partial subsidy gave the state no power over the actual educational program within free schools. When one of his colleagues in parliament described free schools as having a mixed private/public character, Kuyper set him straight.

> Mixed schools are those schools that are organized or governed jointly by local government and a church or a private association or person. ... If, in establishing free schools and setting up its rules, bylaws and board, a partnership or input in the matter was given to the government—then the comparison would make sense. ... But my Government's proposal gives absolutely no say at all to the municipal, provincial, or national governments. ... No, the care for education is primordially the task of the parents, not of the government. The parents need to take care of that. ... The care for education does not flow directly from the nature of government.[57]
>
> Whenever private initiative does what government would only have to do in cases of neglect [that is, educate children], private initiative is fulfilling a national task which the nation

55. Kuyper, *Parlementaire Redevoeringen*, 4:349.
56. Kuyper, *Parlementaire Redevoeringen*, 4:396.
57. Kuyper, *Parlementaire Redevoeringen*, 4:981–983.

> has not received from the government and which the government has not laid upon it, but one which the nation takes upon itself of its own initiative, a task which originates in the family and which, while it does indeed lighten the task of the government, should never, under any circumstances, be called a public service.[58]

On 14 June 1903, in an article in *De Heraut*, Kuyper again defended his acceptance of increasingly higher subsidies to his orthodox Calvinist constituency. He reiterated that although a system of subvention was still their ideal, it had become once and for all unfeasible and must be given up, not as a compromise of their principles, but in order to find another way to meet their principles:

> The subsidy system has our sympathy only in a very limited way. Subsidy from the state is and remains a silver cord. The serious objections against subsidies which were brought earlier by Dr. van den Bergh, and now again by many brothers, we do not count lightly. Every connection that makes our free schools dependent upon the state can eventually oppress. The ideal standpoint that both our elementary and our higher Christian schools would live exclusively from the voluntary gifts of our Christian people is what we would most like to have. ... But, however high this ideal standpoint is, practice has taught us that our Christian education could not maintain its struggle with the state schools without subsidy.[59]

He reminded them that the costs of maintaining their own churches and taking care of their poor were so high[60] that it was literally impossible to think about paying, on top of that, the total costs of free schools. Neither the parents nor private charities could manage this. He warned against the "solution" of paying their ministers and teachers much lower salaries. "He who curtails the wages of the worker has only himself to blame when the

---

58. Kuyper, *Parlementaire Redevoeringen*, 4:226.
59. Kuyper, "De Wet op het Hooger Onderwijs," *De Heraut*, 14 June 1903, quoted in J. C. Wirtz Czn, *Bijdrage tot de geschiedenis van den schoolstrijd* (Amsterdam: Spruyt, 1926), 191.
60. The free churches founded in the wake of the *Afscheiding* of 1834 and the *Doleantie* of 1886 lacked the endowments of the national church.

work itself thereby suffers harm."[61] He added, however, that financial hardship was not a sufficient and principled reason for accepting state subsidy:

> Need alone does not create legal grounds. But the legal grounds lie here: the state may not prefer one religious group over another. When the government gives tons of gold every year to the [so-called] neutral school, then the competition between the state school and the free school is unfair unless the free school also receives state support. The state may not choose sides: it may not build beautiful school palaces and give rich salaries to those who want a religionless education, while the supporters of Christian education receive not one cent. And that is all the more true because the state does not possess anything of its own; it gets all its money from the pocketbooks of the citizens. ...[62]

Kuyper's tenure as prime minister was confined to one term but he continued to work in other venues for liberty of education on the basis of legal equality, partial subsidy, and religious and pedagogical independence. And yet, sometime between the years 1905 and 1910, Kuyper changed course one last time and finally decided to support a constitutional amendment which would require all free schools to accept full state subsidy.

Phase III: Subvention his Ideal, Complete Subsidy his Compromise, 1912–1920

In 1910 by a Royal Decree, a committee was established to consider constitutional reform, including amending Article 194, the Education Article. This committee was chaired by Prime Minister Theodore Heemskerk, and composed of nineteen members, of whom eleven were regarded as belonging to the religious "right," including Kuyper and Lohman. Two years later, in 1912, this committee submitted their proposal. All primary education would be financed from the public treasury[63] and free schools would be guaranteed independence regarding their choice of educational materials

61. Kuyper, "De Wet op het Hooger Onderwijs."
62. Kuyper, "De Wet op het Hooger Onderwijs."
63. Diepenhorst, *Onze Strijd in de Staten-Generaal*, 1:463. Schools were still allowed to charge a nominal fee of the parents, but such was no longer absolutely necessary in order to operate a decent school.

and appointment of teachers.[64] Although Kuyper had repeatedly insisted that a system of full state funding would destroy free schools, he now spoke and wrote in firm support of this proposal, calling it a triumph of the ARP principle, which if it did not come in 1913, would surely come in 1917, when the committee's proposal would be included in negotiations preparing for a revision of the Constitution:

> And now, finally, we literally find in a proposed law that has come from the Crown to Parliament that which has consistently been the prayer of our hearts and the hope for which we worked: *Free schools the norm in the Constitution and state schools introduced only where free schools are lacking.* No wonder there was cause for rejoicing and thanksgiving! At long last, Groen's dearest prayer and the supplication of all of God's people are nearing their fulfillment. The end is in sight! ... After an oppression of eighty Spanish years a second monument to our citizens' freedom will be established in our good Netherlands!
>
> Now that we have entered this third act,[65] we go from success to success; our schools have multiplied to over a thousand, and millions flow to us from the state treasury. ... Surely it will come to pass, when this proposal presently becomes law, that every Christian church will feel called to assemble all God's people in services of humble thanksgiving, in order to give thanks for such unmerited grace.[66]

This 1912 proposal was strongly opposed by public school advocates who, in addition to opposing any state funding of religious schools, were also concerned that without the competition with public schools, free schools

---

64. J. L. van Essen, "The Struggle for Freedom of Education in the Netherlands in the Nineteenth Century," in idem, *Guillaume Groen van Prinsterer: Selected Studies* (Jordan Station, ON: Wedge, 1990), 70.
65. Kuyper, now 75 years old and looking back, summarizes the drama of the school struggle in three acts: Act One: decades of Liberal tyranny, a hopeless "to be or not to be" struggle; Act Two: the days of fighting man-to-man, the People's Petition, the widening of the franchise, election victories, and the proliferation of Christian schools; Act Three: time when things started to go our way, the opposition shrank back, we pressed on and finally achieved principled equality before the law. See Abraham Kuyper, *De Meiboom in de kap* (Kampen: Kok, 1913), 7–10.
66. Kuyper, *De Meiboom in de kap*, loc. cit.

would fail to maintain academic standards.[67] The proposal did not pass but one very similar to it did in 1917 when the revision of the Constitution gained parliamentary approval. Then, in Kuyper's waning year, the Visser Act of 1920 worked out that constitutional reform into concrete educational policy. The objections of public school advocates were somewhat pacified by the guarantee that free schools would no longer be allowed to receive any private donations or retain ownership of their school buildings.[68]

Kuyper's enthusiastic support of the constitutional reform of 1917 is somewhat difficult to understand, in light of his repeated and principled opposition to earlier versions of such a proposal. Of course Kuyper understood the need to compromise, but for him to call this the answer to their prayers is puzzling. While Kuyper had consistently worked for legal equality, he had also consistently opposed complete funding for free schools on the grounds that it would undermine the free initiative of the parents and the pedagogical independence of the school. His support of this bill can therefore be described as a substantial change in his thinking about how best to pursue his ideal of "Free schools the norm and state schools a supplement." Unlike his adjustment to the idea of subsidy in 1889, which he explained as a change in tactical strategy, this change represented the acceptance of a system which Kuyper had clearly and repeatedly warned would seriously endanger the continued freedom and existence of Christian schools.

Kuyper's explanation was primarily one of practicality: it simply wasn't possible. The costs of schooling had risen enormously. His constituency could not afford to pay for free schools as well as for free churches. The state schools refused to give up their complete subsidy and without that same level of subsidy, the free schools were in danger of becoming second-class schools. Surely that was a situation that had to be avoided at all costs. In 1917, in his book *Antirevolutionary Statecraft*, Kuyper addressed the issue of why after working so hard for the revision of the Union Report, the ARP had so quickly abandoned the Revised Report as a practical guideline. Extensive quotations from this memoir may be helpful:

> These circumstances finally made it necessary that we let go of our earlier position regarding school costs, and take the almost opposite position in which ... the government would pay

67. Diepenhorst, *Onze Strijd in de Staten-Generaal*, 1:465.

68. Each private Christian school facility was "sold" to the national government for one guilder.

for virtually all the costs of education that were not covered by school fees. ... The almost unbelievable rise in the costs of education that gradually could no longer be ignored made the maintenance of our first standpoint literally impossible. The numbers spoke volumes. ...

[At this point Kuyper provides some figures. Since 1860 the Dutch population had risen from roughly 3 million to 6 million inhabitants, whereas in the same period education costs had multiplied by a factor of fifteen. His figures showed that since 1880, attendance at state schools had risen by 38% and at free schools by 300%, for a national total of school-age children from a little over half a million to just under one million pupils.]

In view of this completely altered situation, the ideal of providing for the needs of our Christian schools was no longer practical. *The ideal was and remains that every married couple provides for the schooling of their offspring and where limited income prevents this, Christian love for the needy would come into play.* But Christian philanthropy also has her limits and these were continually surpassed by the needs of the school. ...[69]

We came up against a clear impossibility. Our group, comprised primarily of the "little people," would have succumbed under continually rising demands. School after school would have gone bankrupt. ... That is why we had to abandon our earlier ideal and had to work from now on for equal government provision for both sorts of schools.[70]

Ever since 1869 our first principle and starting point had been that the free school should be the rule and the state school only a supplement. So we could not even think of making the state schools which should be merely a supplement into the favorite child of the national and local governments. *It should have been the case that both public and private schools were financed by their own supporters. But the public school supporters did not dream of any such thing*, and continued to give themselves more

69. Abraham Kuyper, *Antirevolutionaire Staatkunde*, 2 vols. (Kampen: Kok, 1916–1917), 2:461–63 (emph. added).
70. Kuyper, *Antirevolutionaire Staatkunde*, 2:464.

> and more funds from the public treasury. This made the system of voluntary funding impossible.[71]

Kuyper here described the acceptance of complete subsidy as a necessary and unfortunate compromise, but he did not go so far as to admit of a principled defeat. Surely, it met their principle of equal treatment under the law. In several of his speeches and writing at this time, he referred to the new constitutional amendment as a principled victory for the ARP: "… and in this issue of justice, our principle did not suffer in the least, but strengthened by the triumph we reached, will soon be operating all the stronger in our entire public life."[72] But whether the new constitutional amendment would sufficiently accommodate their other two principles, that of liberty from state intrusion and of sustaining parental free initiative (when their financial sacrifice was no longer required) remained a question that Kuyper does not appear to have directly addressed.

There are indications in some of his later writing that he was entertaining quite a different view of the nature and role of the state than that which he described in the Stone Lectures of 1898. In an important speech to the assembled ARP delegates given in 1918 under the title "What Next?" he expressed his sincere appreciation for how the state had been able to significantly raise the "common grace consciousness" of the lower classes. They were learning to reflect in a deeper way; they were learning to organize and to pursue their interests by lawful and effective means—and Kuyper did not describe this as an accomplishment of the free schools, but rather as an accomplishment of the state:

> It was the government of the land that enabled him [the wage-earner] to climb to a higher level through improved schools. Compared to half a century ago, the wage-earner stands at a much higher level today. His thought-world is enriched, his insight into life is clarified; his fortitude has doubled. That has led, rather quickly in fact, to his realization of the power of cooperation. And so now in all developed countries we see workers facing life's challenges not as individuals, but in a spirit of collaboration and cooperation. This has tripled the importance of the worker in society. The wage-earner has

71. Kuyper, *Antirevolutionaire Staatkunde*, 2:464–465 (emph. added).

72. Kuyper, *Antirevolutionaire Staatkunde*, 1:531.

> become more informed; he has become a person of greater insight and knowledge. He has mastered the intricacies of life on a much broader scale than before.[73]

Interestingly, Kuyper also described the state as the "backbone of society" which enabled the blossoming of the social spheres. In sharp contrast to Kuyper's views expressed in the Stone Lectures that the state was a mechanical instrument, he now declared:

> Our watchword must remain that all social action shall retain its free and independent character. But we must start by relying on the state to provide the structures for our social life. The old idea that government and legislation must stay out of the life of society has had its day and is no longer tenable. Circumstances increasingly oblige government to protect the freedom of social life precisely by binding it to the regulations of the law. We may even have to go so far as to say that the government must take over a part of the social task. Think of the post office and the telegraph. ... The state saw itself as self-evidently called to furnish new provisions and it did so not out of arbitrariness or the will to dominate but because the need drove government to it.[74]

He spoke approvingly of a number of social functions which in recent times had come under the control and management of the state, such as the construction and maintenance of roads, the fire department, and the police. He spoke also of the increasingly larger scale of life in which massive amounts of materials and great power over nature (steam, electricity) could no longer be handled by a single employer.[75]

> In continually broader and ever expanding spheres the state spread out its custodial care. And it did so, not in order to replace the forces in society with state enterprise, but in a very different and definite manner; namely, to enable a much richer blossoming of the social life of private citizens through its care and oversight. No one complains about this state interference;

73. Abraham Kuyper, *Wat Nu? Rede ter opening van de deputatenvergadering, 2 May 1918* (Kampen: Kok, 1918), 19–20.
74. Kuyper, *Wat Nu?*, 16–17.
75. Kuyper, *Wat Nu?*, 17–18.

> rather, people on all sides enlist it. So much so that in an ever more defined sense, the Government has had to act in order to replace the task of the citizen.[76]

In these passages, Kuyper appears almost surprised at what he had witnessed of the growing power of government to accomplish social good by supporting and even structuring the action of the social spheres (business, arts, medicine, the family, and so on). It is possible that the reversal of his thinking about the financing of free schools (from avoiding complete subsidy at all costs so as to prevent state intrusion into free schools and prevent the decline in parental free initiative) was, in his mind, not only an unfortunate compromise required by the skyrocketing costs of education. It may also have been his "instinctive" cooperation with a reality which he had only just begun to understand, that of the state as being of benefit to society, not merely by curtailing sin, but also by providing a necessary "backbone" to the social spheres, especially in an era of huge undertakings and expensive tasks.

It could very well be that the culmination of the school struggle in the Constitutional Revision of 1917 was the catalyst which forced him to grapple with this new understanding of the nature and calling of the state. Just exactly how this new way of thinking fit together with his central social concept of the antithesis, and more particularly with his concern that the state not infringe upon the independence of free schools and not destroy the voluntary free initiative of parents, is not clear. Perhaps Kuyper simply did not have time to develop his social theory any further, and left it to others who came after him.

CONCLUSION

The history and cultural context of the development of the Dutch educational system is obviously very different from that of the United States and Canada. If during the nineteenth century, for example, the United States had been faced with the outlawing of all private schools, with the sudden imposition of a centralized school system in which the majority of parents had no voice in their children's education, with a prolonged economic depression, and with public schools which taught a form of religion gravely at odds with the prevalent Protestant Christianity, it is entirely possible that a school struggle such as Kuyper led would have developed here as

---

76. Kuyper, *Wat Nu?*, 18.

well. But that was not the case. America offered economic opportunity far beyond that of the Netherlands. Most public schools at that time taught the basic tenets of traditional Protestantism, which reflected the preference of the majority of citizens. The United States had a decentralized educational system that offered parents significant input and voice into the running of their children's local schools. And, if there was opposition to the public schools on the basis of religion (as there was, for instance, by some Catholics), there was not only complete freedom to start separate schools, but a greater ability to fund those on their own.

It was not until the U.S. Supreme Court decisions in 1963 and 1965 outlawed the inclusion of prayer and the teaching of the Bible as revealed truth in the public schools that resistance began to develop against a system which imposed the *de facto* teaching of secularism in the name of neutrality. Fifteen years later saw the rise of home-schooling and eventually there was a significant exodus of evangelical and traditional Catholic families from the United States public schools. This exodus has increased in recent years with the dissatisfaction of parents with the sexual mores taught in many public schools. Similar developments in the provinces of Canada in recent decades have led to the proliferation of private religious schools.

Currently we find our nation deeply divided and polarized along lines that are not completely independent of religion. Different groups talk past each other in an ever more urgent struggle to dominate the public square. In times such as these, people with competing narratives who care deeply about the social fabric of our nation will either seek to control the public school system, accept the necessity of starting private schools with an unjust financial burden, or work for a system which recognizes the right of parents from multiple worldviews to establish their own schools with equal claim to public support. Not only would the latter approach help to defuse tensions by ending the "winner takes all" competition for control of our public schools, but it would also relieve the grievous violation of conscience suffered by thousands and thousands of parents who take offense at the "indoctrination" in the public schools, but have no viable alternative, due to poverty.

Some middle-class parents hesitate to accept any state aid for their religious schools, out of concern that it will inevitably bring unwelcome intrusion into the distinct identity of their schools. They are willing to suffer inequality and injustice in order to preserve their liberty, and that is understandable. But for Christian single mothers in the inner city who know the grievous harm that will come to their children in the local public schools,[77] some kind of outside assistance is necessary for them to even dream of the "luxury" of providing their children with a Christian education. Christian charity has provided a lot, but for a myriad of reasons, that charity has not been sufficient to meet the enormous demand for religious education among the poor. The adoption of some form of principled pluralism in the structure of our educational system must, therefore, be viewed as a matter of *justice for the poor*, as well as for religious parents.

Recent Supreme Court decisions have recognized that in certain circumstances, the state may not discriminate against religious schools. If it offers to improve the playgrounds of public schools, then religious schools may also expect such help. The first amendment, which for many decades was interpreted as providing protection *against* the intrusion of religion in the public sphere, is now being interpreted as providing protection *for* religious expression in the public sphere. The issue is by no means settled but it is a start. The next step might be to make education vouchers available to all parents who desire to send their children to private schools, a simple but equitable means to enable parents to choose (or establish) a school for their children without undue financial penalty. Of course, the Enlightenment myth that removing any reference to God is somehow religiously neutral would need to be directly challenged. A public re-examination of the principles of liberty of conscience, equality under the law, and free initiative would be vital. But such an exercise may well be essential if the United States is to overcome our current polarization and embrace afresh the *E pluribus unum* of our founding vision. Healthy nations acknowledge differences and yet find common ground in the shared value of mutual tolerance.

Wendy Naylor

---

77. In addition to the violation of conscience that public schools represent for Christian parents, recruitment for gang membership happens at a very young age in inner city schools.

APPENDIX

LEMKES' WISH

TEXT INTRODUCTION

When the Christian school movement in the Netherlands won its eighty-year struggle for parity treatment with the public system, voices were raised that said: Now our second struggle needs our full attention—developing a distinctive Christian approach to pedagogy and educational philosophy. Initial ventures into those fields were already underway, but after several provisional articulations they never quite reached definitive form in Kuyper's lifetime.

The letter reproduced on the following page contains a cry for help from an in-service teacher who sensed that the prevailing psychology, pedagogy, and anthropology that he and his fellow teachers were "plodding along with" were of suspect origin and needed to be replaced by ones of their own. Hence he turns to the man whom he believes can provide them.

Source: Historisch Documentatiecentrum, Free University Amsterdam, Kuyper-archief, letters ## 5282 and 5288a.

APPENDIX

LEMKES' WISH

CAN DR. KUYPER NOT GIVE US AN ANTHROPOLOGY?

Alphen aan den Rijn
27 May 1893

Dear Sir and Brother,
Although I know that you are overwhelmed with important work, still I venture to ask you to consider something that may already have occurred to you yourself: to present us in due time with a *psychology*.

Since the year 1854, when we publicly voiced this desire at our very first meeting of the Association of Christian Teachers in the Netherlands, that wish, after all that has already been published, has not only stayed with me but has become stronger. I have yet to come across something that made me exclaim, "Eureka! I found it!"

In your writings I repeatedly catch hints, mere casual remarks that have instilled in me the wish that God might grant you the time and strength for providing us with "a description of man." If it cannot be in detail, then only in outline. But do rid us, if possible, of the notion, mostly blown over from Germany and in *Christian garb*, of man as body, soul, and spirit, an image with which we have plodded along until now.

You who have pondered everything of importance, surely you have an anthropology in your head and heart which I urge you to share with us. It is my conviction that there is a *demand* for it in our time, and that you will not take it ill of me that I have taken the liberty to write you this.

Respectfully yours,
H. J. Lemkes, Sr.[1]

Kuyper's reply, on a typewritten postcard, dated 3 June 1893, reads:

A Christian psychology is certainly needed, but it cannot be had just like that. I will not get to it until my dogmatic theology is published. But I will talk about it some time with Professor Woltjer.[2] Dr. A. K.

---

1. Hubertus Johannes Lemkes (1828–97) started out as a teacher's aide at the age of 16, and at age 24 was asked to head up a new Christian school in the town of Alphen aan den Rijn. He accepted the challenge despite the very low salary, "because if I don't go, no one will on those conditions, and parents will keep their children at home rather than send them to the public school."
   Lemkes was co-founder of the Association of Christian Teachers in the Netherlands and the Overseas Possessions and served for many years as its secretary. As a headmaster, he was often harassed by local supporters of the public school. He stubbornly resisted smallpox vaccination for the children who attended his school because at this time Jenner's cowpox serum was risky (one of his own children had become handicapped as a result of inoculation). But Lemkes had still another reason for resisting vaccination: "If the authorities in the interest of public health bring vaccination into the schools that we started and still pay for, what will prevent them tomorrow from taking the Bible from our schools in the interest of public order?" Arraigned before the courts, he was convicted of flouting the law; he appealed, lost, and resigned as principal, at age 45. Lemkes spent the rest of his life as an evangelist of the Darbyite Brethren. See F. Kalsbeek et al., *Van Strijd en Zegen, 1854–1904. Gedenkboek van het Christelijk Onderwijs* (Leiden, 1904), pp. 553–560.
2. Lemkes did not live to see his wish fulfilled. Kuyper never got around to publishing his systematic theology, even though the five-volume *Dictaten Dogmatiek* (1891–1900) contain students' class notes of his lectures in the field, and his three-volume *Encyclopedie van de Heilige Godgeleerdheid* (1894) constitutes his "Introduction" to the discipline of theology as a whole. As for Kuyper's colleague, Professor Jan Woltjer (1849–1917): he started teaching a course in pedagogy in that same year, 1893, which he continued for twelve years, but its contents were never published except for the occasional address to educators; see H. van der Laan, *Jan Woltjer, Filosoof, Classicus, Pedagoog* (Amsterdam: VU Uitgeverij, 2000), 169–93, 218–25. And Kuyper's younger colleague, Professor Herman Bavinck, did not begin publishing his studies of psychology until 1897 and pedagogy until 1904. Cf. C. Jaarsma, *The Educational Philosophy of Herman Bavinck* (Grand Rapids: Eerdmans, 1935).

BIBLIOGRAPHY

Akkermans, P. W. C. *Onderwijs als constitutioneel probleem*. Alphen aan den Rijn: Samson, 1980.
Alsted, Johann Heinrich. *Scientiarum Omnium Encyclopaediae*. 4 vols. Leiden: Huguetan and Rauaud, 1649.
Van Belle, Harry A. "Vision and Revision: Neo-Calvinism in The Netherlands and Canada." In *Rethinking Secularization: Reformed Reactions to Modernity*. Edited by Gerard Dekker, Donald A. Luidens, and Rodger R. Rice. Lanham, MD: University Press of America, 1997.
Vanden Berg, Frank. *Abraham Kuyper*. Grand Rapids: Eerdmans, 1960.
Bilderdijk, Willem. *De Ziekte der geleerden*. Amsterdam and The Hague: Allart, 1807.
Bratt, James D. *Abraham Kuyper: Modern Calvinist, Christian Democrat*. Grand Rapids: Eerdmans, 2013.
Bryce, James. *The American Commonwealth*. Vol. 3. London: Macmillan, 1888.
Bryk, Anthony S., and Barbara Schneider. *Trust in Schools: A Core Resource for Improvement*. New York: Russell Sage Foundation, 2002.
Chaplin, Jonathan. *Herman Dooyeweerd: Christian Philosopher of State and Civil Society*. Notre Dame, IN: University of Notre Dame Press, 2011.
Clarence, Leo. *Le Monde moderne*, no. 68 (August 1900).
Czn, J. C. Wirtz. *Bijdrage tot de geschiedenis van den schoolstrijd*. Amsterdam: Spruyt, 1926.
Diepenhorst, P. A. *Onze Strijd in de Staten-Generaal*. 2 vols. Amsterdam: Uitgeverij De Standaard, 1927–1929.
van Doorn, J. A. A. "Meer weerstand dan waardering: De Revolutie-ideeën en de Nederlandse politieke traditie." In *Van Bastille tot Binnenhof: De Franse Revolutie en haar invloed op de Nederlandse politieke partijen*. Edited by R. A. Koole. Houten: Fibula, 1989.

Dr. A. Kuyper, Gedenkboek, 1837–1937. Kampen: Kok, 1937.

Dreher, Rod. *The Benedict Option: A Strategy for Christians in a Post-Christian World*. New York: Sentinel/Random House, 2017.

Dwyer, James G. *Religious Schools v. Children's Rights*. Ithaca, NY: Cornell University Press, 1998.

Van Dyke, Harry. "Abraham Kuyper between Parsonage and Parliament." In *Calvinism and Democracy*. Edited by John Bowlin, The Kuyper Center Review, 4:184–85. Grand Rapids: Eerdmans, 2014.

Eberstadt, Mary. *It's Dangerous to Believe: Religious Freedom and Its Enemies*. New York: Harper, 2016.

van Essen, J. L. "Groen van Prinsterer's Tactics in his Campaign for Freedom of Education." In *Guillaume Groen van Prinsterer: Selected Studies*, 79–88. Jordan Station, ON: Wedge, 1990.

———. "The Struggle for Freedom of Education in the Netherlands in the Nineteenth Century." In *Guillaume Groen van Prinsterer: Selected Studies*. Jordan Station, ON: Wedge, 1990.

Fertig, Ludwig. *Zeitgeist und Erziehungskunst: Eine Einführung in die Kulturgeschichte der Erziehung in Deutschland von 1600 bis 1900*. Darmstadt: Wissenschaftliche Buchgesellschaft, 1984.

Fukuyama, Francis. "Trust: The Social Virtues and the Creation of Prosperity." In *The Essential Civil Society Reader: The Classic Essays*, edited by Don E. Eberly, 257–66. Lanham, MD: Rowman & Littlefield, 2000.

Galston, William A. *Liberal Purposes: Goods, Virtues, and Diversity in the Liberal State*. Cambridge: Cambridge University Press, 1991.

———. *Liberal Pluralism: The Implications of Value Pluralism for Political Theory and Practice*. Cambridge: Cambridge University Press, 2002.

Garnett, Richard W. "Things Not Caesar's." *First Things*, March 2012.

Gilhuis, T. M. *Memorietafel van het Christelijk Onderwijs: De Geschiedenis van de Schoolstrijd*. Kampen: Kok, 1974.

———. *Memorietafel van het Christelijk Onderwijs: De Geschiedenis van de Schoolstrijd*. 2nd ed. Kampen: Kok, 1975.

Glenn, Charles L. *The Myth of the Common School*. Amherst: University of Massachusetts Press, 1988.

———. *Contrasting Models of State and School*. New York: Continuum, 2011.

Glenn, Charles L., and Jan De Groof, eds. *Balancing Freedom, Autonomy, and Accountability in Education*. 4 vols. Nijmegen: Wolf Legal Publishing, 2012.

Goodhart, David. *The Road to Somewhere: The Populist Revolt and the Future of Politics*. London: Hurst, 2017.

Greenfield, Liah. *Nationalism: Five Roads to Modernity*. Cambridge, MA: Harvard University Press, 1992.

Hansard's Parliamentary Debates, vol. 199. London: Buck, 1870.

Hansen, Erik. "Marxism, Socialism, and the Dutch Primary Schools." *History of Education Quarterly* 13, no. 4 (Winter 1973): 367–91.

Henderson, R. D. "How Abraham Kuyper Became a Kuyperian." *Christian Scholar's Review* 22, no. 1 (1992): 22–35.

Heslam, Peter S. *Creating a Christian Worldview: Abraham Kuyper's Lectures on Calvinism*. Grand Rapids: Eerdmans, 1998.

Hill, Paul. "The Supply-Side of School Choice." In *School Choice and Social Controversy*, edited by Stephen D. Sugarman and Frank E. Kemerer. Washington, DC: Brookings Institution, 1999.

Hollinger, David A. *After Cloven Tongues of Fire: Protestant Liberalism in Modern American History*. Princeton, NJ: Princeton University Press, 2013.

Hulsman, G. *Moderne wetenschap of bijbelse traditie*. Utrecht: Kemink, 1897.

Janet, Paul. *Philosophie de la révolution française*. Paris: Germer Baillière, 1875.

Kossmann, E. H. *De lage landen 1780–1980: Deel 1 1780–1914*. Amsterdam: Olympus, 2001.

Kruijt, J. P. and Walter Goddijn. "Verzuiling en Ontzuiling als sociologisch process." In *Drift en Koers: Een halve eeuw sociale verandering in Nerderland*, edited by A. N. J. Hollander et al. Assen: Van Gorcum, 1962.

Kuiper, J. P. *Geschiedenis van het Christelijk Lager Onderwijs in Nederland*. 2nd rev. ed. Amsterdam: Bottenburg, 1904.

Kuyper, Abraham. *"Het beroep op het volksgewetern": rede ter opening van de Algemeene vergadering der "vereeniging voor Christelijk Nationaal-Schoolonderwijs."* Amsterdam: B. H. Blankenberg, 1869.

———. "Memorandum," dated Feb. 4, 1874. In *Groen van Prinsterer. Schriftelijke Nalatenschap: Briefwisseling*, 6:735–38. The Hague: Instituut voor Nederlandse Geschiedenis, 1992.

———. *De Schoolkwestie I. Naar Aanleiding Van Het Onderwijs-Debat in De Kamer*. Amsterdam: J. H. Kruyt, 1875.

———. *"Ons Program" (Met Bijlagen)*. Amsterdam: J. H. Kruyt, 1879.

———. "De Ondergang der Vrije Christelijke school." *De Standaard*, 23 March 1885.

———. "De Hinderlaag." *De Standaard*, 27 March 1885.

———. "De fatale Voorslag." *De Standaard*, 13 April 1885.

———. *Niet de Vrijheidsboom maar het kruis*. Amsterdam: J. A. Wormser, 1889.

———. *Eenige kameradviezen uit de jaren 1874 en 1875*. Amsterdam: J. A. Wormser, 1890.

———. *Encyclopaedie der heilige Godgeleerdheid*. 3 vols. Amsterdam: Wormser, 1893–94.

———. "Een twistappel." *De Standaard*, 26 Oct. 1896.

———. "Oriënteering." *De Standaard*, 6 Nov. 1896.

———. "Uit de Pers. Het Unie-Rapport." *De Standaard: Bijvoegsel*, 9 Nov. 1896.

———. "Misverstand." *De Standaard*, 14 Nov. 1896.

———. “De principieele bezwaren tegen het Unie-Rapport, III.” *De Standaard,* 18 Nov. 1896.

———. “De principieele bezwaren tegen het Unie-Rapport, V.” *De Standaard,* 27 Nov. 1896.

———. “De principieele bezwaren tegen het Unie-Rapport, VI (Slot).” *De Standaard,* 30 Nov. 1896.

———. *An Encyclopedia of Sacred Theology: Its Principles.* Translated by J. H. De Vries. New York: Charles Scribner’s Sons, 1898.

———. *Lectures on Calvinism.* Grand Rapids: Eerdmans, 1994 [1898].

———. “Subsidiën.” *De Heraut,* 31 May 1901.

———. “De Wet op het Hooger Onderwijs.” *De Heraut,* 14 June 1903.

———. *De Gemeene Gratie.* Vol. 3. Amsterdam: Höveker & Wormser, 1904.

———. *Parlementaire Redevoeringen.* 4 vols. Amsterdam: Van Holkema & Warendorf, 1908–12.

———. *Voor Den Slag.* Utrecht: G. J. A. Ruys, 1909.

———. *De Meiboom in De Kap.* Kampen: Kok, 1913.

———. *Heilige Orde: Rede in Den Bond Van Antirevolutionaire Kiesvereenigingen Te Amsterdam Gehouden Op 30 Mei 1913.* Kampen: Kok, 1913.

———. *Antirevolutionaire Staatkunde.* 2 vols. Kampen: Kok, 1916–1917.

———. *Wat Nu? Rede ter opening van de deputatenvergadering, 2 May 1918.* Kampen: Kok, 1918.

———. *Starren-Flonkering; een bundel drie-starren.* Amsterdam: Drukkerij De Standaard, 1932.

Kuyper, Catherine M. E. “Abraham Kuyper: His Early Life and Conversion.” *The Calvin Forum* 16, no. 4 (November 1950): 64–67; republished in the *International Reformed Bulletin* (April 1960): 19–25.

Lamping, J. A. *Kerk en School. Een woord aan het volk van Nederland.* Rotterdam: H. Nijgh, 1869.

———. *De Staat en het Volksonderwijs in Nederland.* Leiden: S. C. Van Doesburgh, 1869.

Langedijk, D. *De Schoolstrijd.* The Hague: Van Haeringen, 1935.

Lessing, G. E. “Anti-Goetze” (1778). In *Werke,* edited by H. Göpfert. Vol. 8. Munich: Carl Hanser Verlag, 1979.

Levin, Yuval. *The Fractured Republic: Renewing America’s Social Contract in the Age of Individualism.* New York: Basic Books, 2016.

Liberty of conscience asserted. Or, persecution for religion condemned; by the lawes of God, nature, reason. Published by a Well-wisher to the kingdomes good. London: Printed for R. A., 1649.

Marsden, George M. *The Twilight of the American Enlightenment: The Crisis of Liberal Belief.* New York: Basic Books, 2014.

Mensch, Elizabeth, and Alan Freeman. *The Politics of Virtue.* Durham, NC: Duke University Press, 1993.

Michelet, Jules. *Nos Fils.* Paris: Lacroix, 1870.

Monsma, Stephen V., and Stanley W. Carlson-Thies. *Free to Serve: Protecting the Religious Freedom of Faith-Based Organizations*. Grand Rapids: Brazos Press, 2015.

Naylor, Wendy. "Religious Liberty and Educational Pluralism: Abraham Kuyper's Principled Advocacy of School Choice." In *The Wiley Handbook of Christianity and Education*, edited by William Jeynes, 325–53. Hoboken, NJ: Wiley-Blackwell, 2018.

Neuhaus, Richard John. *America against Itself: Moral Vision and the Public Order*. Notre Dame, IN: University of Notre Dame Press, 1992.

Nisbet, Robert. *History of the Idea of Progress*. New York: Basic Books, 1980.

Onderwijsraad, Artikel 23 Grondwet in maatschappelijk perspectief. Nieuwe richtingen aan de vrijheid van onderwijs. Den Haag, 2012.

van Otterloo, M. D. *Bijdrage ter toelichting der Schoolkwestie*. Amsterdam: Höveker & Zoon, 1874.

Ozouf, Mona. *L'école de la France: Essais sur la Révolution, l'utopie et l'enseignement*. Paris: Gallimard, 1984.

Penjon, A. "L'Autorité." *Revue Philosophique de la France et de l'Étranger* 74 (1912): 458.

Poulin, Paulin. *Religion et Socialisme*. Paris: Librarie Internationale, 1867.

Powell, Arthur G., Eleanor Farrar, and David K. Cohen. *The Shopping Mall High School*. Boston: Houghton Mifflin, 1985.

van Prinsterer, G. Groen. *Briefwisseling*. Vol. 6. The Hague: Nijhoff and Instituut voor Nederlands Geschiedenis, 1992.

Publicatie van den Senaat der Vrije Universiteit in zake het onderzoek ter bepaling van den weg, die tot de kennis der gereformeerde beginselen leidt. Amsterdam: J. A. Wormser, 1895.

Ratzsch, Del. "Abraham Kuyper's Philosophy of Science." *Calvin Theological Journal* 27, no. 2 (1992): 277–303.

Renan, Ernest. *Questions contemporaines*. Paris: Michel Lévy Frères, 1868.

Reno, R. R. "The Public Square." *First Things*, April 2014.

van Riel, Harm. *Geschiedenis van het Nederlandse Liberalisme in de 19e Eeuw*. Assen: Van Gorcum, 1982.

Rigg, James Harrison. *The Natural Development of National Education in England*. London: Training College, Westminster, 1875.

Rijnsdorp, C. "'Met vreugd naar school' (Herinnering en tijdbeeld)." In *In het honderdste jaar: Gedenkboek Stichting Unie 'School en Evangelie' 1879–1979*. Kampen: Kok, 1979.

Sieyès, Emmanuel Joseph. *Qu'est-ce que le Tiers Etat?* 1789.

Thiessen, Elmer John. *Teaching for Commitment: Liberal Education, Indoctrination, and Christian Nurture*. Montreal: McGill-Queen's University Press, 1993.

———. *In Defense of Religious Schools and* Colleges. Montreal: McGill-Queen's University Press, 2001.

Thorbecke, J. R. *Brief aan een lid der Staten van Gelderland over de magt der Provinciale Staten uit Art. 220 der Grondwet*. Leiden: P. H. van den Heuvell, 1843.

Tinholt, Lambert. *Een Twistappel en zijne wegruiming; een voorslag tot oplossing der onderwijs-kwestie, tegen bestrijding verdedigd*. Utrecht: C. H. E. Breijer, 1885.

Een Twistappel en zijne wegruiming: een voorslag tot oplossing der onderwijs-kwestie, tegen bestrijding verdedigd. Utrecht: Breijer, 1885.

Weber, Eugen. *Peasants into Frenchmen*. Stanford, CA: Stanford University Press, 1976.

Winckel, W. F. A. *Leven en arbeid van Dr. A. Kuyper*. Amsterdam: Ten Have, 1919.

Wolterstorff, Nicholas. "The Role of Religion in Decision and Discussion of Political Issues." In *Religion in the Public Square: The Place of Religious Convictions in Political Debate*, edited by Robert Audi and Nicholas Wolterstorff. Lanham, MD: Rowman & Littlefield, 1997.

Yancey, George, and David A. Williamson. *So Many Christians, So Few Lions: Is There Christianophobia in the United States?* Lanham, MD: Rowman & Littlefield, 2015.

de Zeeuw, P., and J. Gzn. *De Worsteling om het kind: de strijd voor een vrije school historisch geschetst*. Amsterdam: Kirchner, 1925.

Zoontjens, Paul J. J., and Charles L. Glenn. "The Netherlands." In *Balancing Freedom, Autonomy, and Accountability in Education*, vol. 2. Nijmegen: Wolf Legal Publishing, 2012.

ABOUT ABRAHAM KUYPER (1837–1920)

Abraham Kuyper's life began in the small Dutch village of Maassluis on October 29, 1837. During his first pastorate, he developed a deep devotion to Jesus Christ and a strong commitment to Reformed theology that profoundly influenced his later careers. He labored tirelessly, publishing two newspapers, leading a reform movement out of the state church, founding the Free University of Amsterdam, and serving as prime minister of the Netherlands. He died on November 8, 1920, after relentlessly endeavoring to integrate his faith and life. Kuyper's emphasis on worldview formation has had a transforming influence upon evangelicalism, both through the diaspora of the Dutch Reformed churches, and those they have inspired.

In the mid-nineteenth-century Dutch political arena, the increasing sympathy for the "No God, no master!" dictum of the French Revolution greatly concerned Kuyper. To desire freedom from an oppressive government or heretical religion was one thing, but to eradicate religion from politics as spheres of mutual influence was, for Kuyper, unthinkable. Because man is sinful, he reasoned, a state that derives its power from men cannot avoid the vices of fallen human impulses. True limited government flourishes best when people recognize their sinful condition and acknowledge God's divine authority. In Kuyper's words, "The sovereignty of the state as the power that protects the individual and that defines the mutual relationships among the visible spheres, rises high above them by its right to command and compel. But within these spheres ... another authority rules, an authority that descends directly from God apart from the state. This authority the state does not confer but acknowledges."

ABOUT THE CONTRIBUTORS

Charles L. Glenn (Ed.D., Harvard University; Ph.D., Boston University) is professor emeritus of educational leadership and policy studies at Boston University. His more than a dozen books deal with comparative (North America and Europe) history and policy concerning educational freedom and the rights of ethnic and religious minorities. For two decades (1970–1991) he was the Massachusetts state official responsible for educational equity.

Wendy Naylor (Ph.D., University of Chicago) worked in the Netherlands for over ten years, helping to establish two Christian schools in Amsterdam. She has also traveled extensively to assist teacher training projects, primarily in Europe and South America. Her dissertation was on the educational thought and work of Abraham Kuyper. Since moving back to Chicago, she has also worked on the board of a new Christian school, and served there as acting principal.

Harry Van Dyke (D.Litt., Free University of Amsterdam) is a professor emeritus of history at Redeemer University College, Ancaster, Ontario, and a fellow of the Dooyeweerd Centre for Christian Philosophy.

SUBJECT INDEX